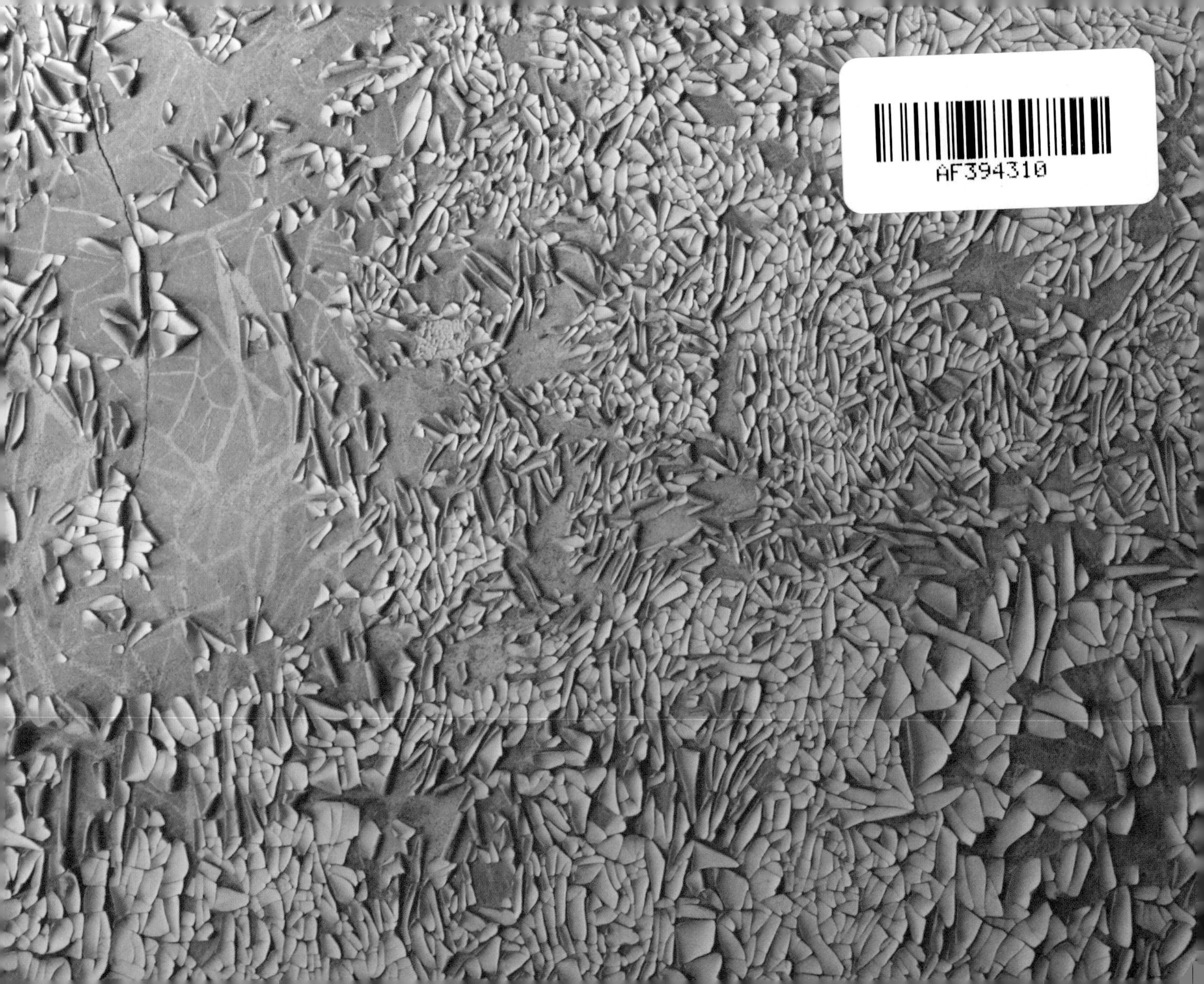
AF394310

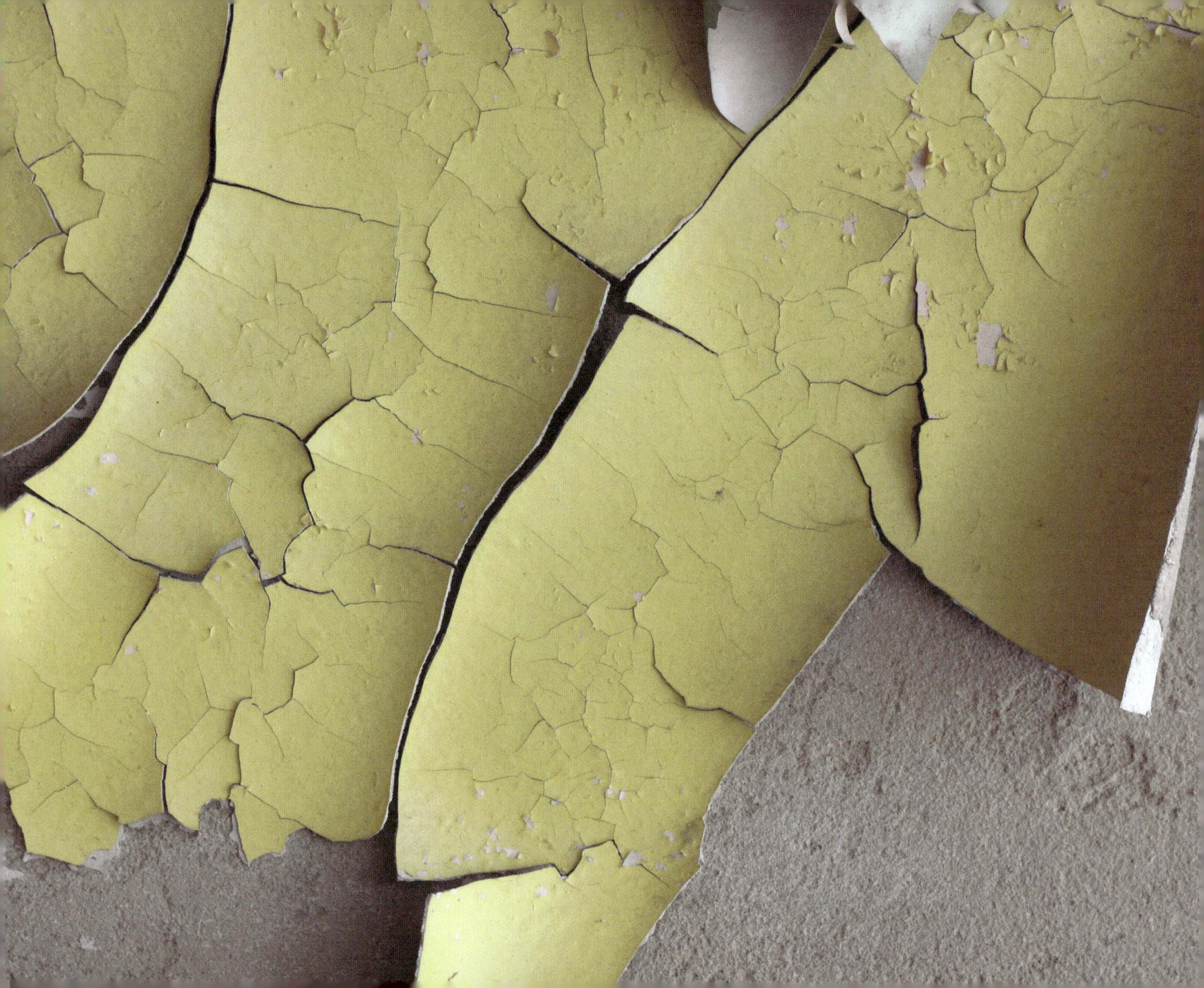

'Wild, dark times are rumbling toward us, and the prophet who wishes to write a new apocalypse will have to invent entirely new beasts...'
Heinrich Heine, *Lutetia*

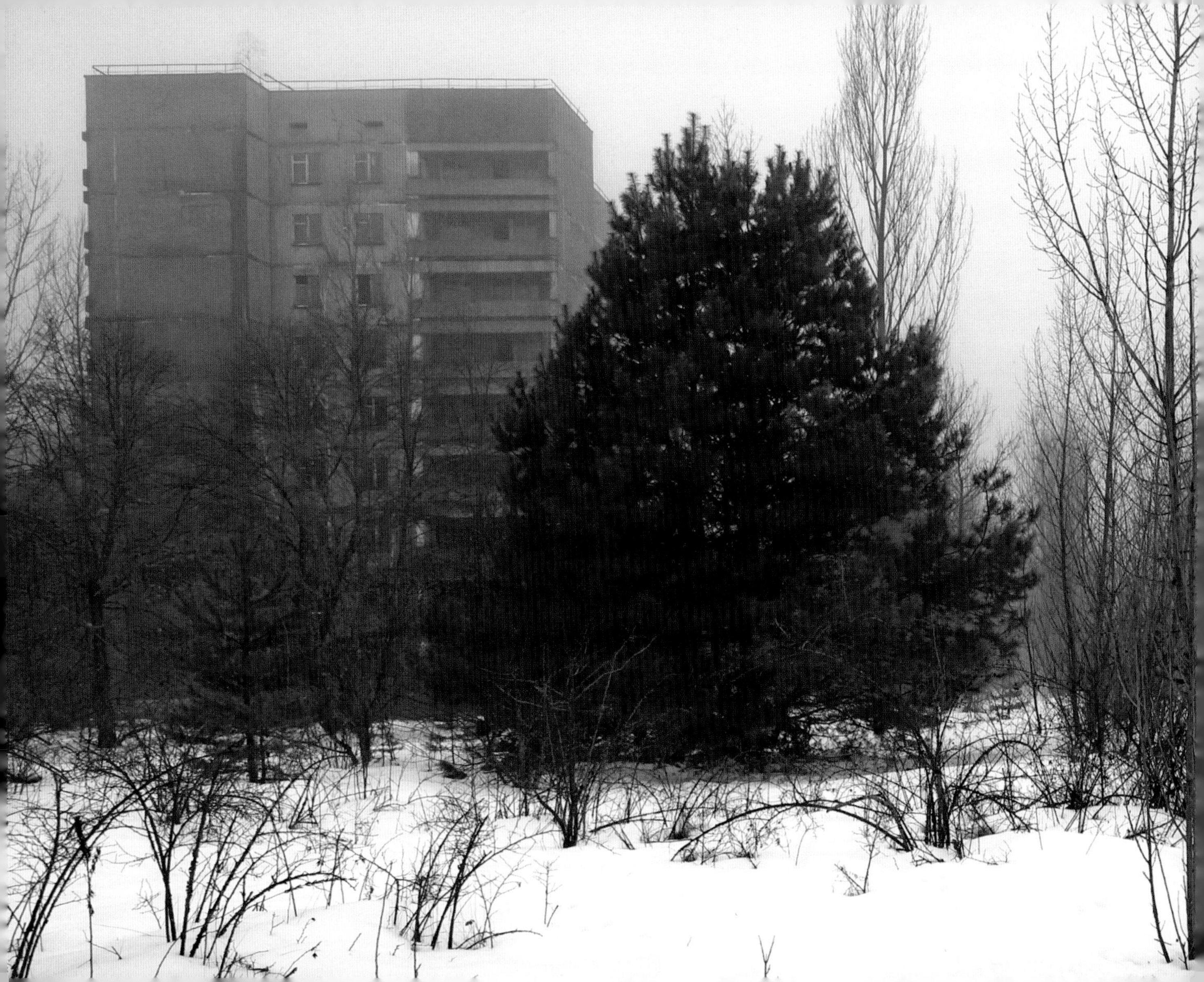

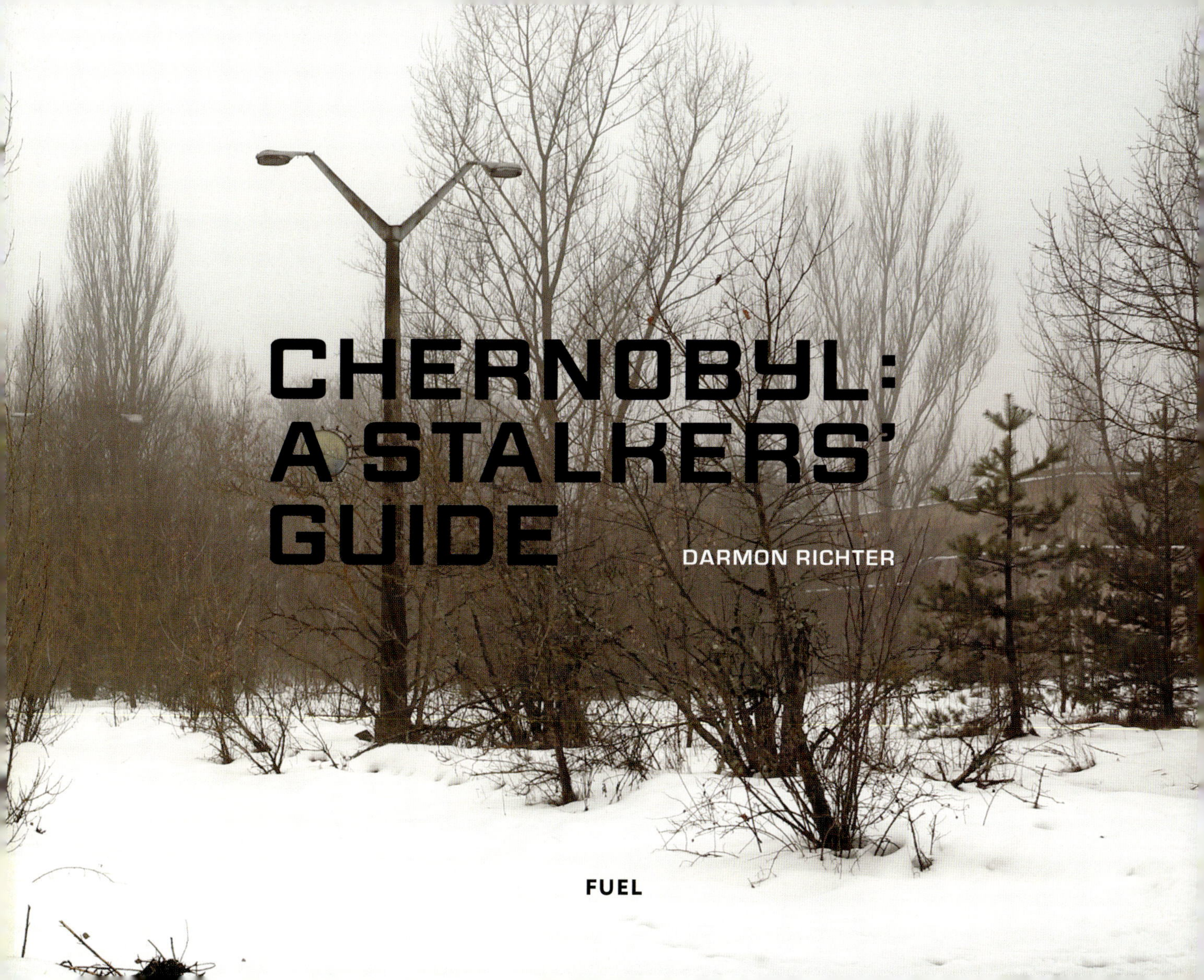

CHERNOBYL:
A STALKERS'
GUIDE

DARMON RICHTER

FUEL

previous page: Kurchatov Street, Pripyat.

page 10: Pripyat city sign, Microdistrict 4. Vandals have painted the sign in the colours of the Ukrainian flag. Graffiti underneath reads 'We make money from tragedy', a criticism aimed at the Chernobyl tourism industry.

page 11: A tame fox poses in front of the sign pointing the way to Pripyat from the Chernobyl Nuclear Power Plant.

PROLOGUE: THE DEAD CITY 12

1. NIGHTMARES AND PREMONITIONS 18

2. ATOMGRAD 36

3. WORMWOOD STAR 62

4. NUCLEAR TOURISM 84

5. JOURNEY TO THE CENTRE OF THE ZONE 110

6. MONUMENTEERING 142

7. BELARUS 164

8. THE ROOM 186

9. HALF-LIFE 216

EPILOGUE: THE CHERNOBYL RAVE SCENE 234

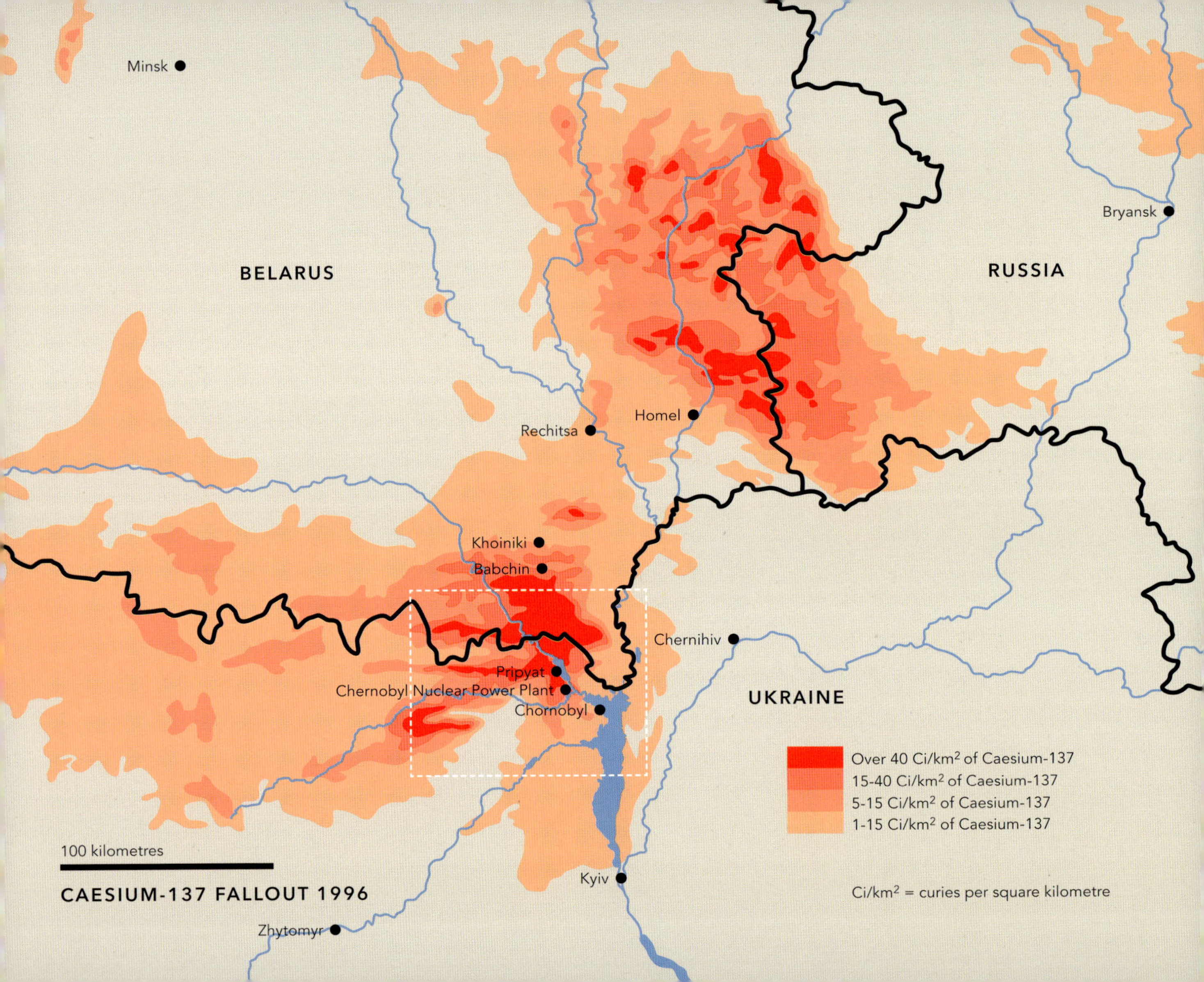

Minsk
BELARUS
RUSSIA
Bryansk
Rechitsa
Homel
Khoiniki
Babchin
Chernihiv
Pripyat
Chernobyl Nuclear Power Plant
UKRAINE
Chornobyl
Over 40 Ci/km² of Caesium-137
15-40 Ci/km² of Caesium-137
5-15 Ci/km² of Caesium-137
1-15 Ci/km² of Caesium-137
100 kilometres
Kyiv
CAESIUM-137 FALLOUT 1996
Ci/km² = curies per square kilometre
Zhytomyr

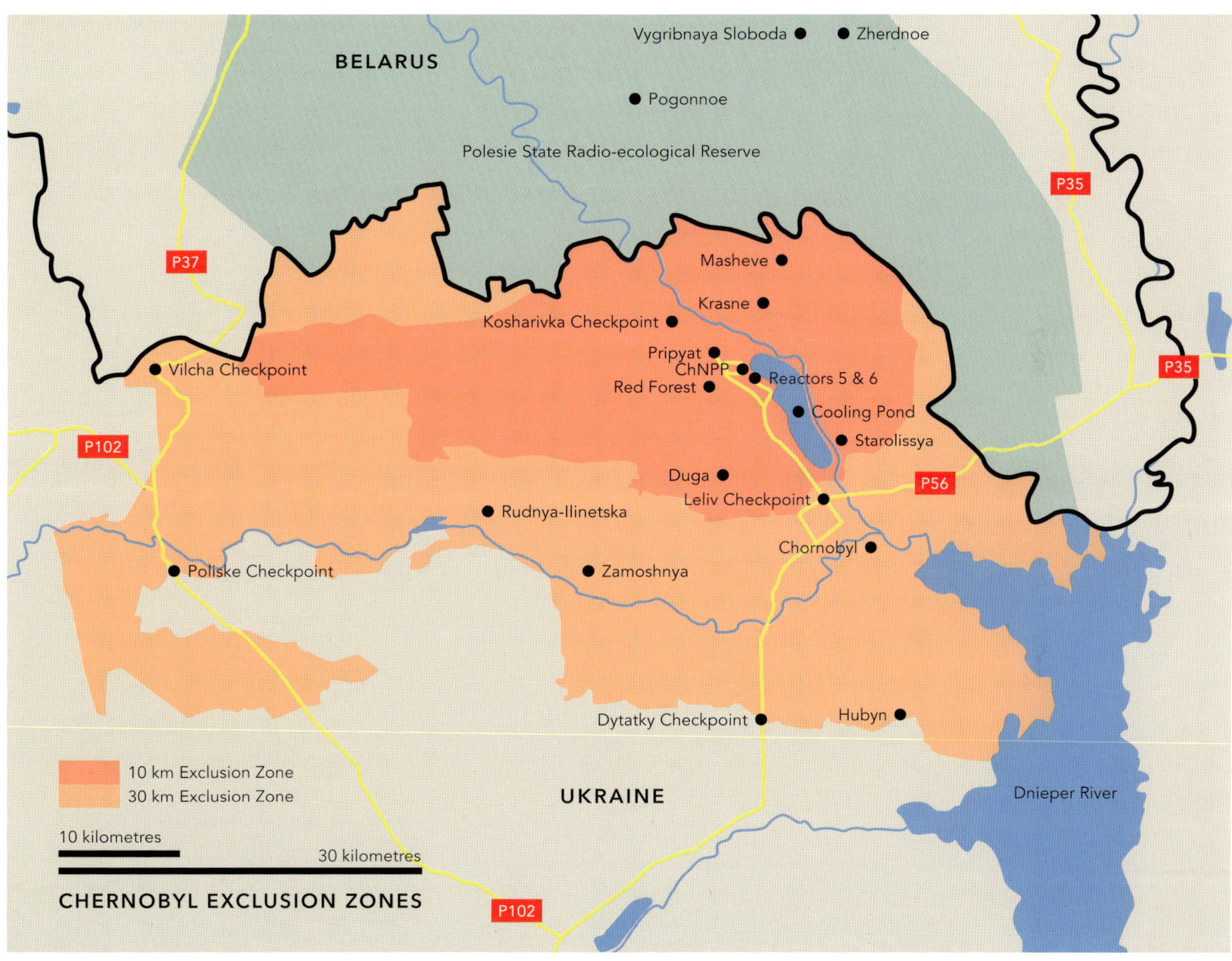

BELARUS
Vygribnaya Sloboda
Zherdnoe
Pogonnoe
Polesie State Radio-ecological Reserve
P35
P37
Masheve
Krasne
Kosharivka Checkpoint
Pripyat
ChNPP
Reactors 5 & 6
Red Forest
Cooling Pond
Starolissya
Vilcha Checkpoint
P35
P102
Duga
Leliv Checkpoint
P56
Rudnya-Ilinetska
Chornobyl
Poliske Checkpoint
Zamoshnya
Dytatky Checkpoint
Hubyn
10 km Exclusion Zone
30 km Exclusion Zone
UKRAINE
Dnieper River
10 kilometres
30 kilometres
CHERNOBYL EXCLUSION ZONES
P102

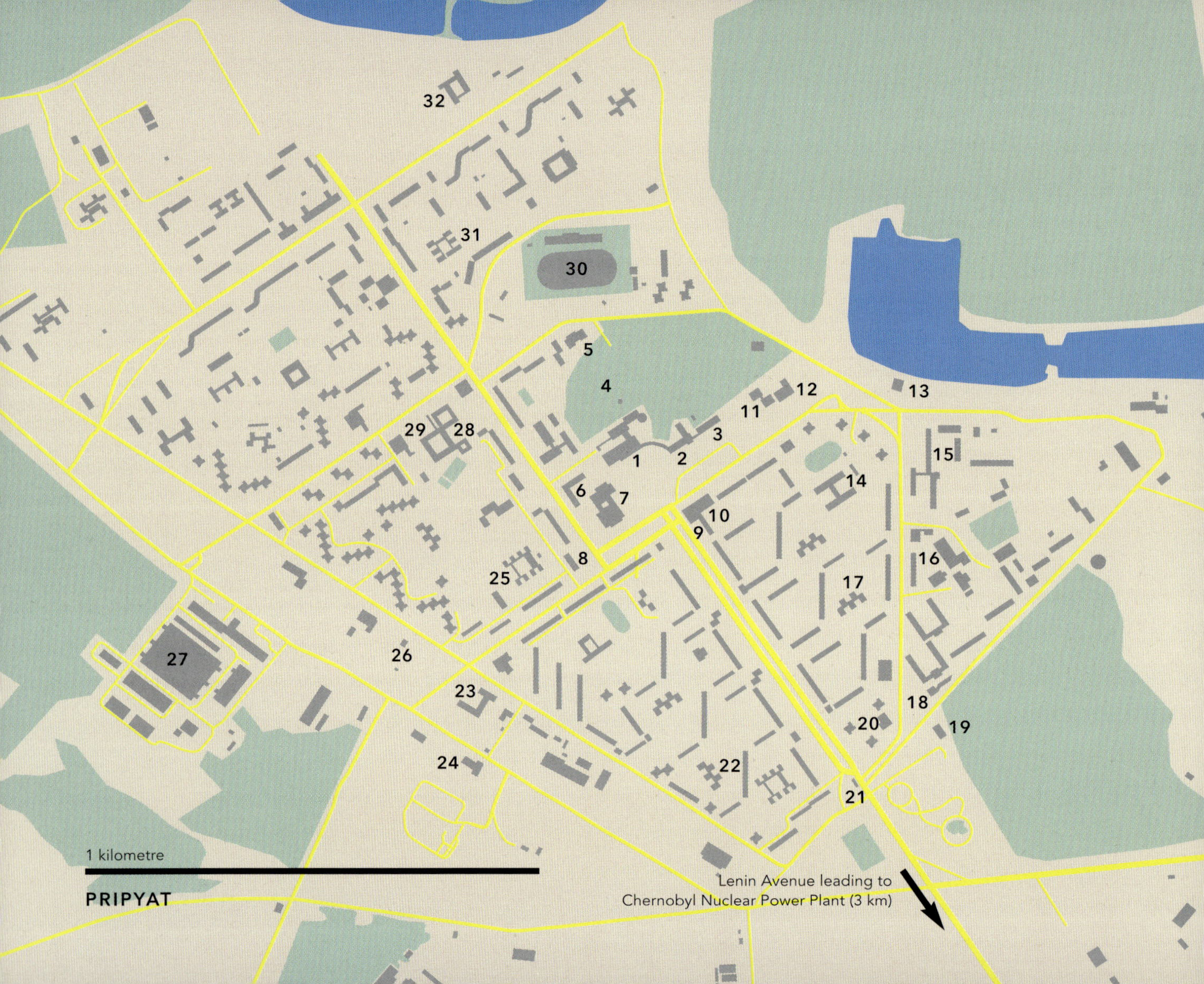

PRIPYAT
1 kilometre
Lenin Avenue leading to
Chernobyl Nuclear Power Plant (3 km)

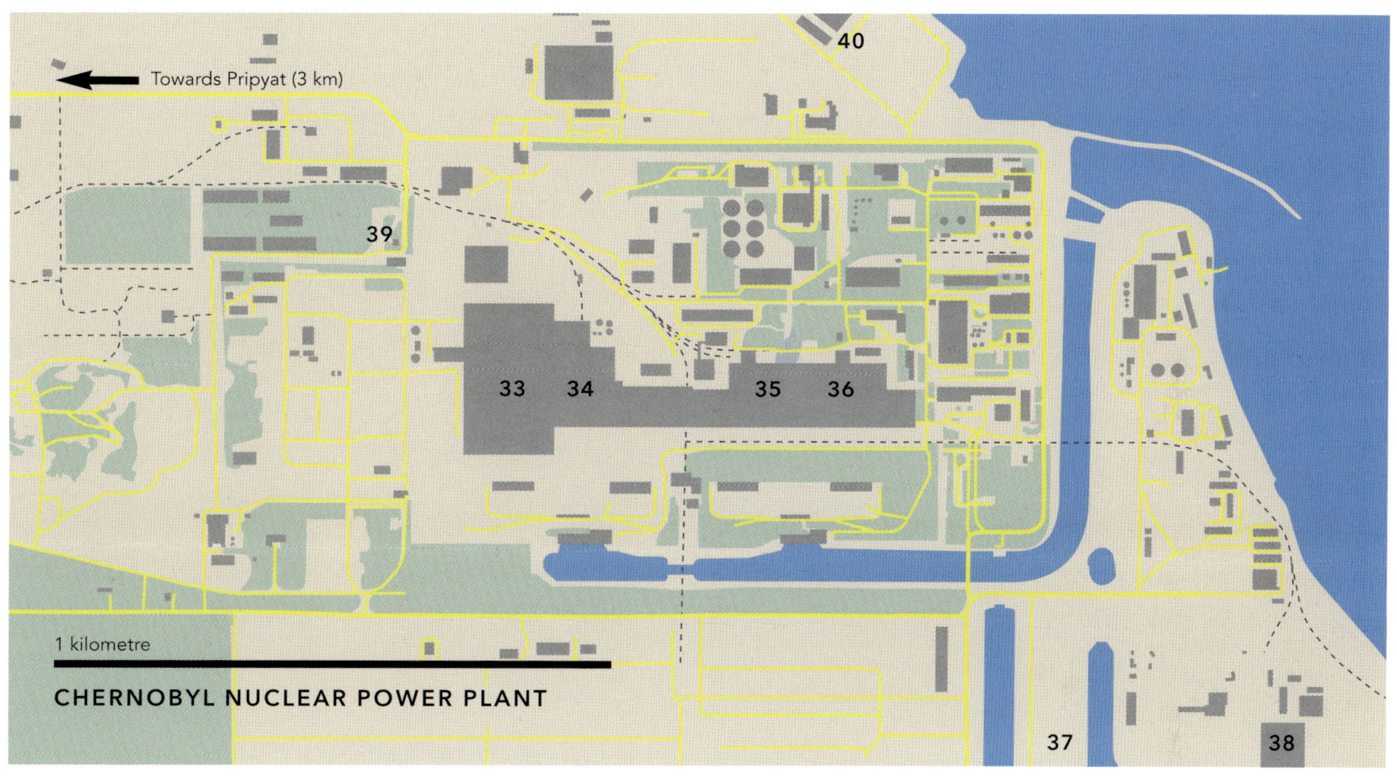

1 'Energetik' Palace of Culture
2 'Polissya' Hotel
3 City Administration
4 Amusement Park
5 'Olympia' Café
6 Post Office
7 Department Store
8 Hammer and Sickle Building
9 'Raduga' ('Rainbow') Supermarket
10 'White House' Building

11 Music School
12 'Prometheus' Cinema
13 River Port and Pripyat Café
14 Middle School No.1
15 Hospital
16 'Avangard' Sports Complex
17 Kindergarten No.2 'Ivy'
18 Friendship of Nations Monument
19 Bus Station
20 House of Books

21 Pripyat Checkpoint
22 Kindergarten No.5 'Teddy Bear'
23 Police Station
24 Fire Station
25 Kindergarten No.7 'Golden Key'
26 State Security Committee (KGB)
27 'Jupiter' Factory
28 Middle School No.3
29 'Lazurniy' ('Azure') Swimming Pool
30 'Avangard' Stadium

31 Kindergarten No.10 'Cheburashka'
32 Palace of Pioneers (unfinished)
33 New Arch over Reactor Block 4
34 Reactor Block 3
35 Reactor Block 2
36 Reactor Block 1
37 Cooling Canals
38 Reactor Blocks 5 and 6 (unfinished)
39 Monument to the Liquidators
40 Semikhody Railway Station

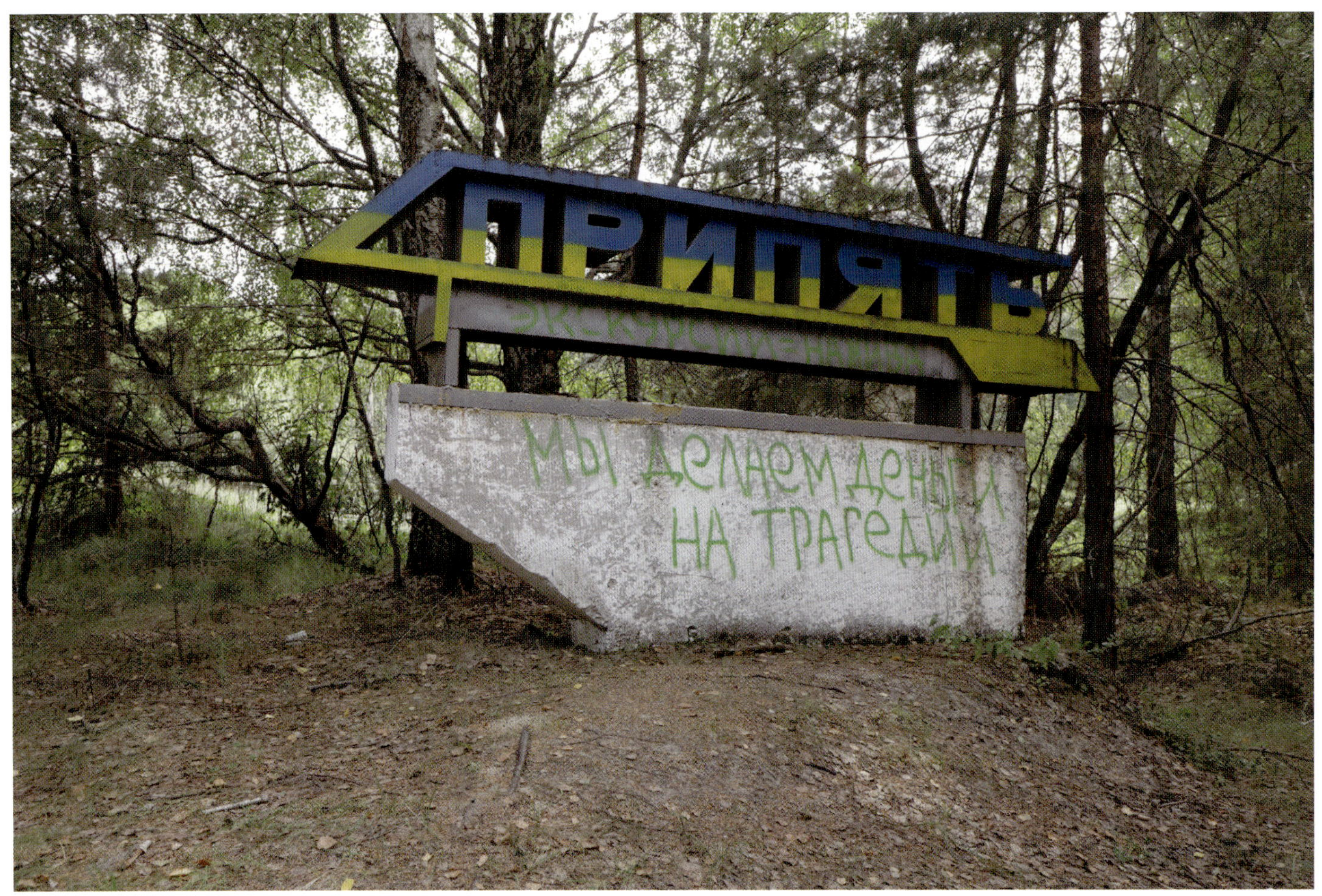
ПРИПЯТЬ
ЭКСКУРСИИ НА ВЫ
МЫ ДЕЛАЕМ ДЕНЬГИ
НА ТРАГЕДИИ

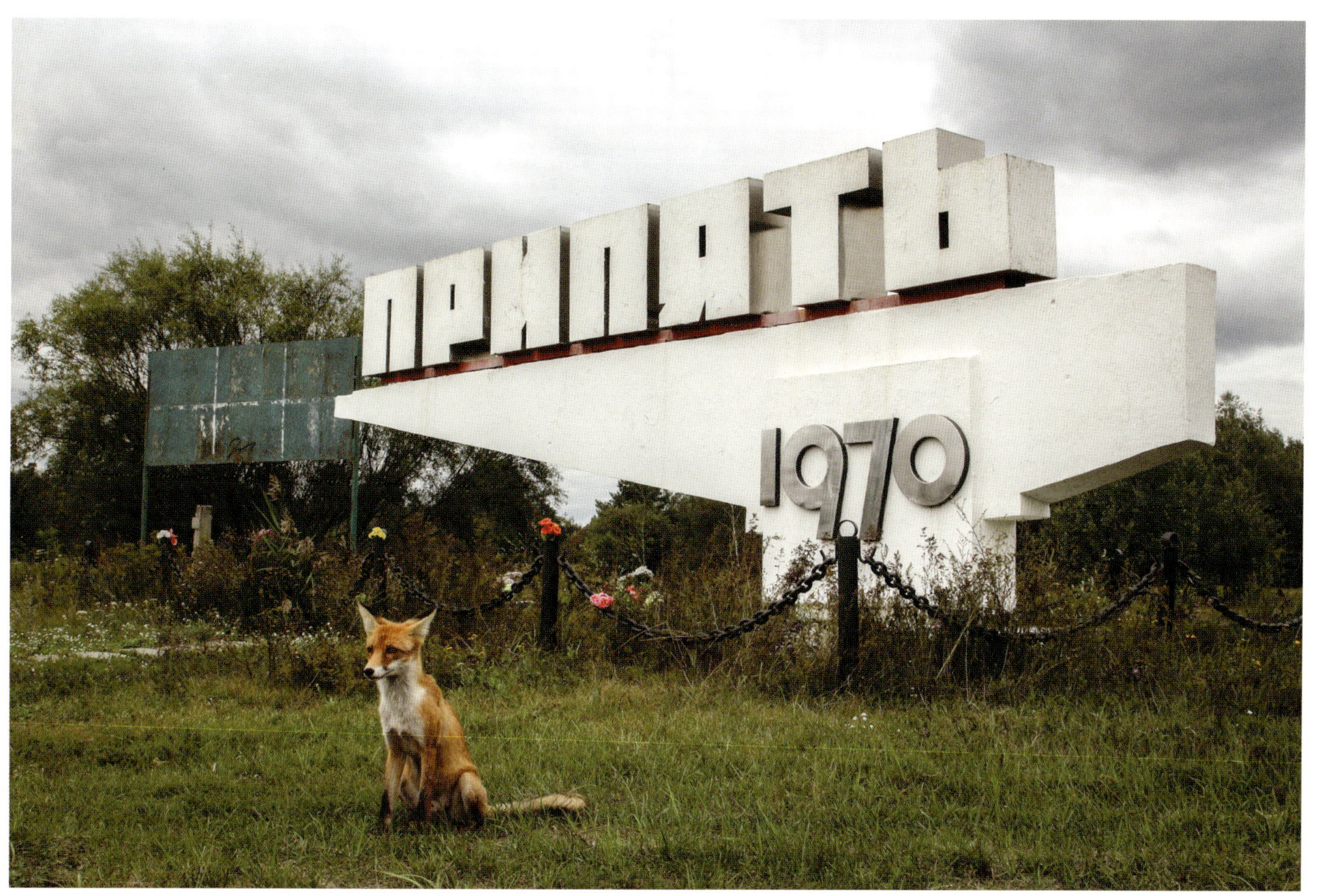
ПРИПЯТЬ
1970

There are two Chernobyls: a place, and an event.

Historians have explored every detail of the Chernobyl *event* – the nuclear disaster of 1986 – determining who pressed which button and when, who gave what orders, how many were evacuated and at what time, and the part all this played in the looming collapse of the great Soviet empire. The event has filled television screens with its smoke and flames, tragedy and death; its story is told in dank industrial corridors, in clandestine assemblies, and in hospital wards where radiation-burned flesh slews from the bones of hapless fire-fighters.

In the wake of such horror and upheaval, 'Chernobyl' became synonymous with death: a poisoned landscape, a 'radioactive wasteland'. For most people, Chernobyl the *place* is defined solely by what they know of the *event*. When journalists label those travelling to Chernobyl as 'disaster tourists', it is because the Chernobyl they relate to is the one that happened thirty years ago. But those images of disaster burned into the public consciousness bear little resemblance to the Chernobyl of today, a region that is visited by tens of thousands of international tourists every year.

Chernobyl today is a place of greenery and life, of branches sagging under overripe fruit, and of wild animals that in the decades of our absence have begun to lose their distrust of humans. Foxes will eat bread from the palm of your hand, while all around, ponderous symbols of the former regime give way to flowers, berries and ants. It is a place where the humble might find inexhaustible beauty, and

where the curious may glimpse nature's future order in a post-human world.

It would be too simple to say that one Chernobyl is past, the other present. Time cannot be so conveniently partitioned, not while victims of the accident live on and while radioisotopes continue to haunt these fecund forests. Chernobyl's history began hundreds of years before the Soviet Union was born, and its legacy will remain long after we ourselves have gone. Time seems to work differently inside the Chernobyl Exclusion Zone – and while it was curiosity about the *event* that first drew me in, over the years it has been the *place* itself that has kept me coming back.

It is midnight, one Saturday in August 2018, and I'm sitting on the rooftop of an abandoned tower block in Pripyat – the city built for the power plant's workers – with three friends and our guide, a 'stalker' of the Exclusion Zone. Other rooftops rise up around us like lily pads opening in the moonlight, with the floors beneath them – row after row of empty apartments – vanishing into the inky darkness below. There is a city down there somewhere, or at least the sunken bones of it: shops, schools, hospitals, sports halls, a cinema and a police station. Yet now, the only sound is of the wind through the trees. After just three decades, Pripyat no longer feels like a place built for humans. Tarmac roads have narrowed to ribbons smothered by bushes. Monuments collapse, murals disintegrate, new trees sprout from roofs. One by one the rectangular buildings lose their shape, slumping into hills and barrows, little more than mineral piles, while down among the ruins lie the broken

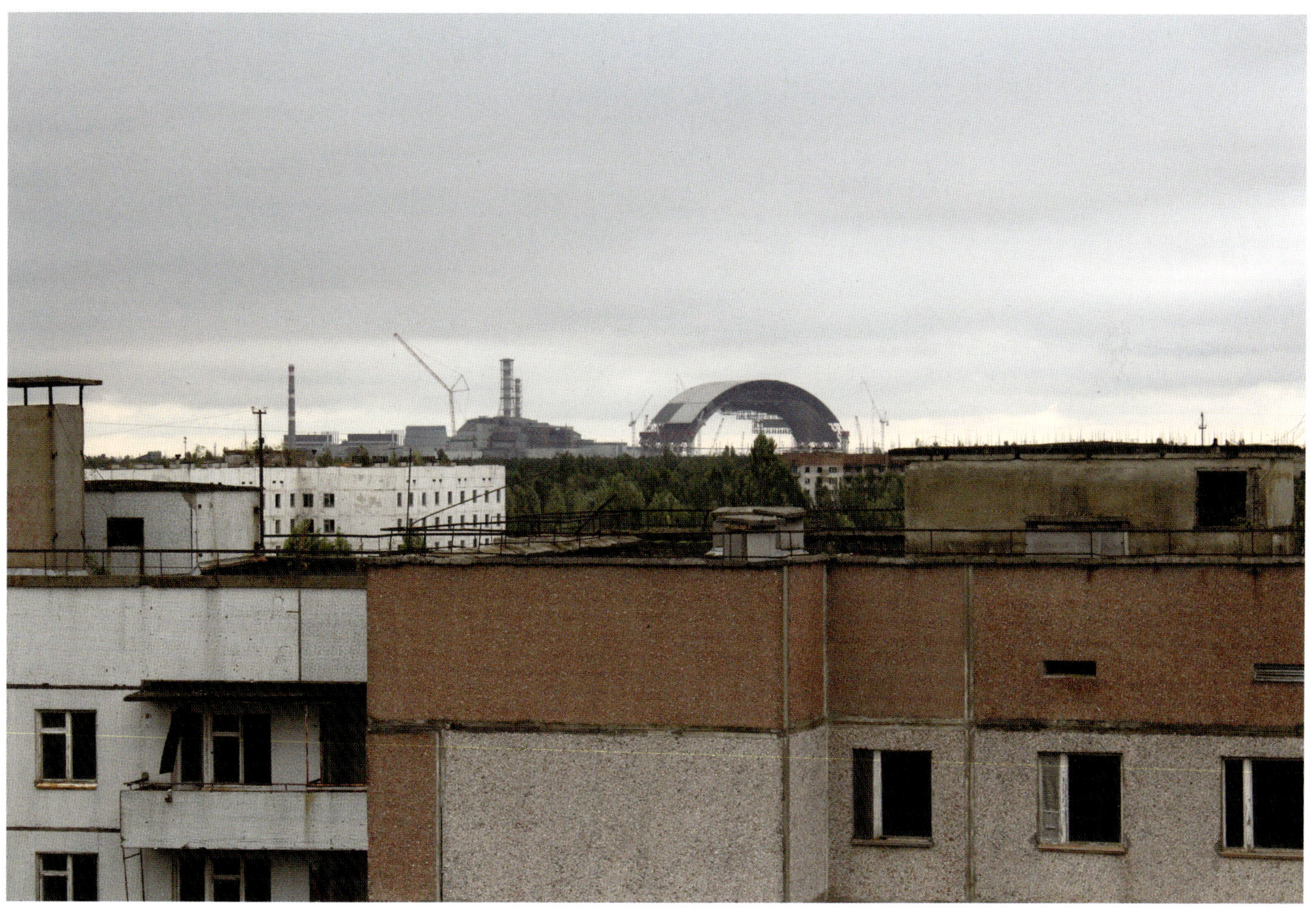

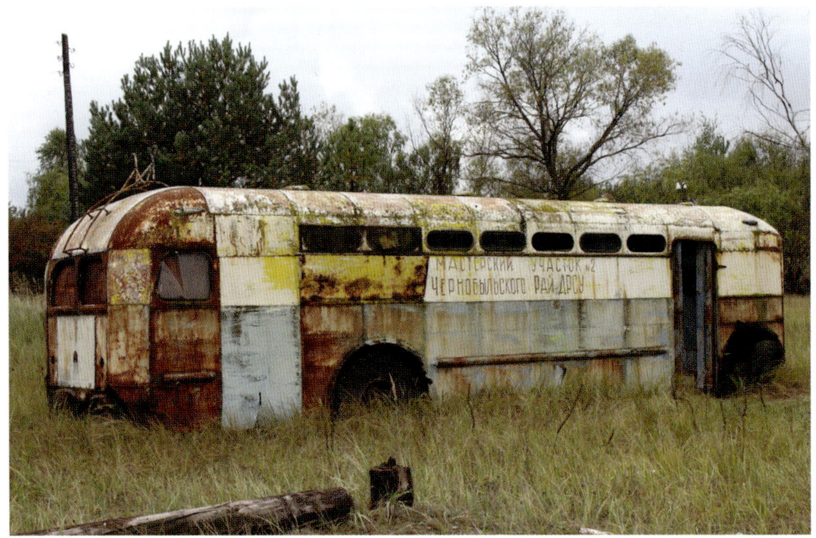

page 13: A view from 2013 across Pripyat rooftops towards the ChNPP. The New Arch is still under construction, while the old sarcophagus enclosing Reactor Block 4 stands to its left.

left: Abandoned trolleybus, Kopachi, Chernobyl Exclusion Zone. This highly contaminated village was mostly bulldozed after the disaster. In April 2020 this vehicle was severely damaged by forest fires.

right: Central Square, Pripyat. The 'Energetik' Palace of Culture (left) is attached to the 'Polissya' Hotel (right) by a covered walkway.

overleaf: Kurchatov Street, Pripyat, archive photograph, 1970s. The 'Prometheus' Cinema stands on the right.

emblems of a political regime that once believed it would conquer the stars.

Below our rooftop, city and forest can barely be differentiated – but on the horizon ahead looms the unique spectacle of an unnatural silver vault rising out of the flat landscape, glistening with power as lightning dances around it. Installed in 2016, the New Arch is taller than Big Ben's clock tower and serves to entomb perhaps the most dangerous object on earth: a devastated nuclear reactor leaking some 200 tons of radioactive fuel – a sickness of mythic proportions.

This is a book about a mythopoetic landscape that authors, artists and filmmakers had been dreaming of long before the Chernobyl disaster itself had happened. It is therefore a study of Chernobyl not as a dead zone where history was suddenly halted in 1986, but as a new Eden populated by scientists, settlers and scrap-metal thieves; where hordes of tourists come by day to explore a living memorial to the fragility of civilisation; and where 'stalkers' conduct their own nocturnal quests: rites of passage born from a blend of post-Soviet counter-culturalism, sci-fi escapism, and perhaps a yearning for spiritualistic self-discovery. Here then is the wild and timeless Chernobyl, a land of forests, swamps and hidden villages, haunted by old superstitions and Cold War-era conspiracies, where humankind's poisonous legacy to the earth may yet outlast everything else we will ever have accomplished.

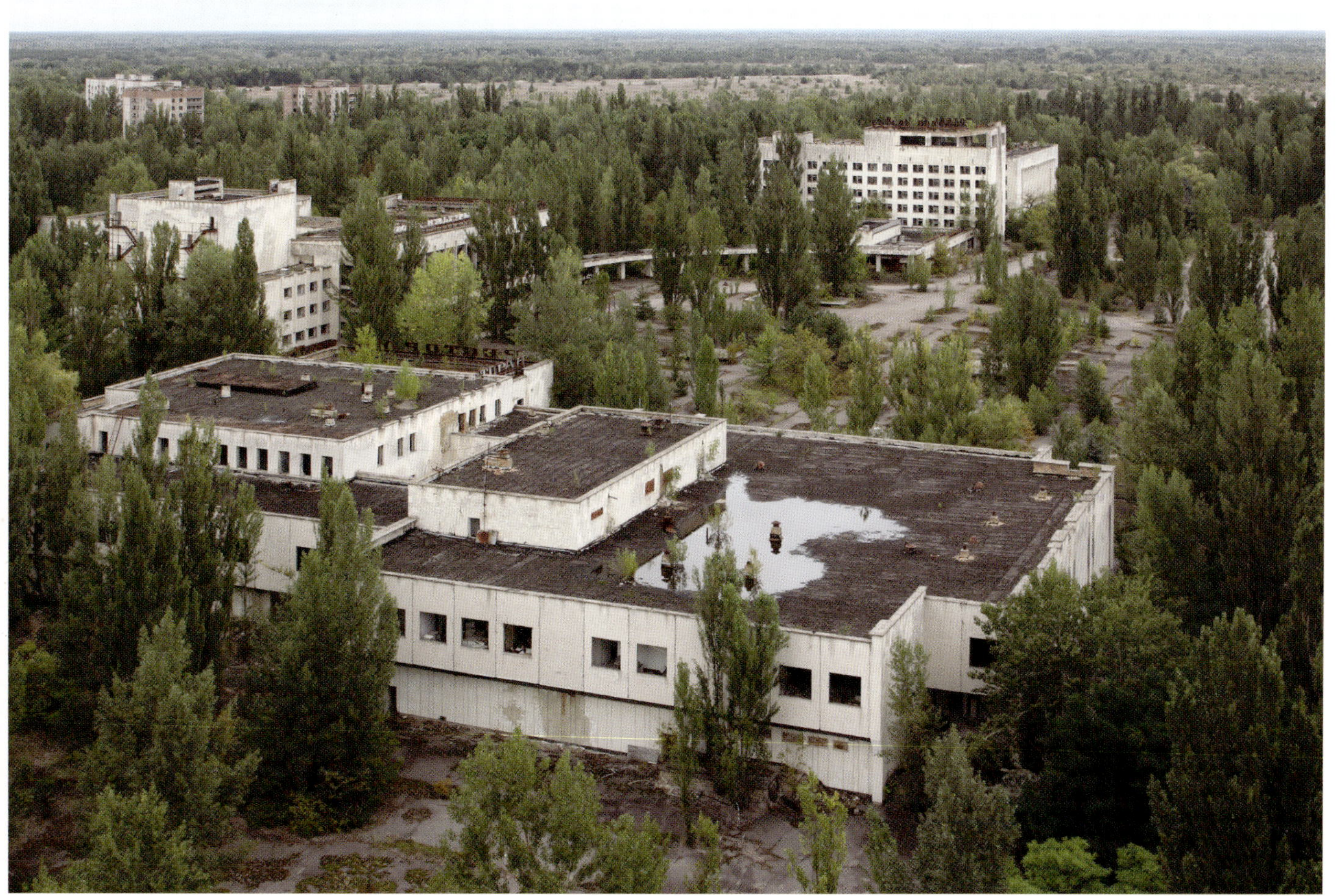

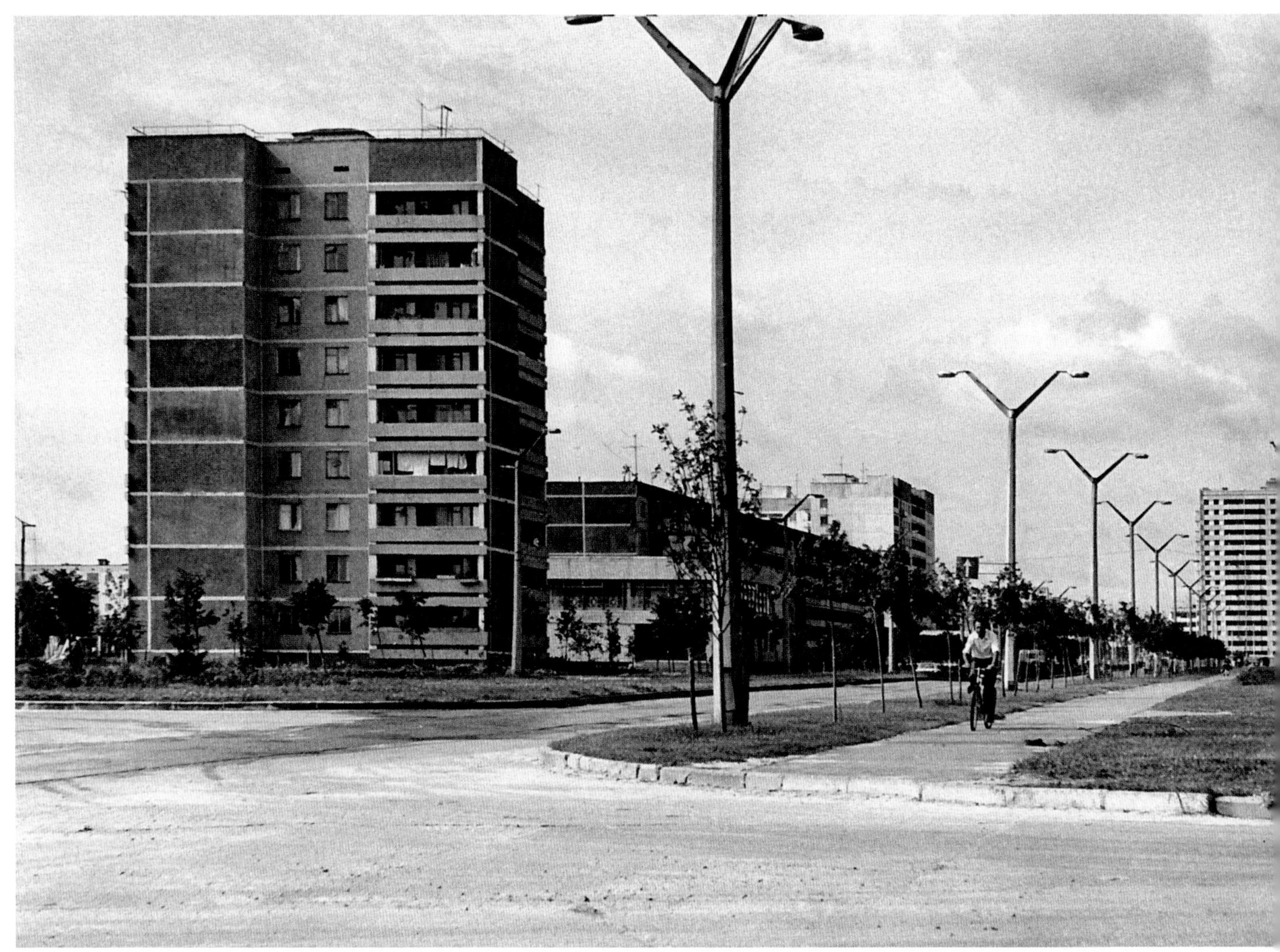

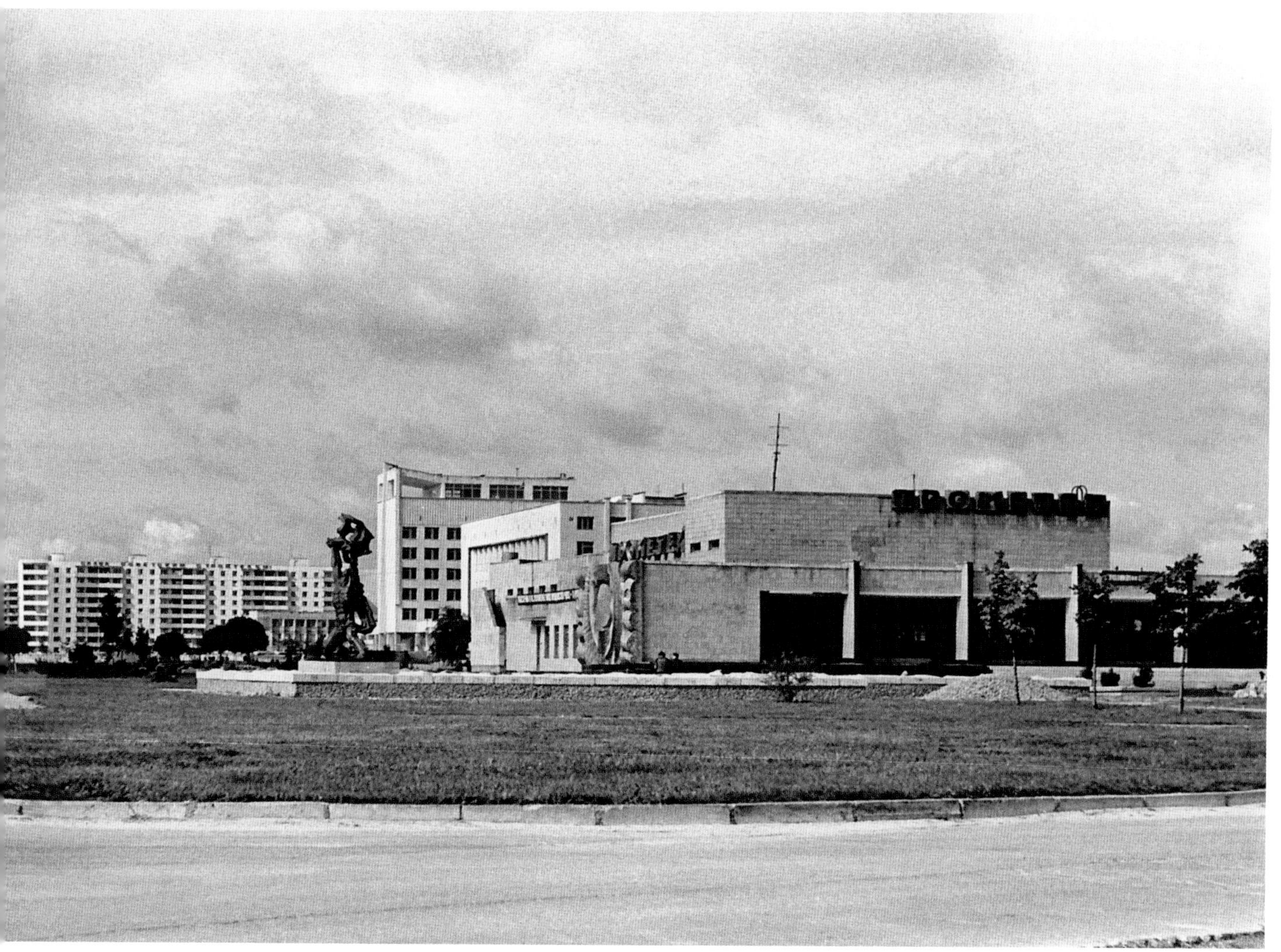

1. NIGHTMARES AND PREMONITIONS

ATOMIC CINEMA

Had it been a work of fiction rather than a real-life event, by 1986 the Chernobyl disaster might almost have seemed clichéd, so perfectly did it manifest the Cold War insecurities of the time. Cinema did not predict Chernobyl, but it did a lot to prepare a place for it in the public consciousness.

What we refer to now as the 'Atomic Era' began with an event too small to be seen by the naked eye: the smallest unit of matter, a single atom, was smashed apart. The power it released ruptured other atoms around it so they too burst, causing a chain-reaction release of raw, boundless energy. The detonation of the world's first nuclear bomb – the Trinity test – took place at Alamogordo on 16 July 1945. The blast was felt from a hundred miles away, with witnesses describing a ball of light glowing purple, green, and then white. A mushroom-shaped cloud rose 7.5 miles high above the desert of New Mexico. Just weeks later, on 6 and 9 August, similar nuclear fission bombs were detonated over the Japanese cities of Hiroshima and Nagasaki. In Hiroshima, more than 70,000 people were killed by the blast and the fires that followed. Most of the city's buildings were destroyed. The bomb that fell on Nagasaki killed tens of thousands more and the ensuing sickness would linger for a generation.

On 14 August 1945, Emperor Hirohito announced the surrender of Japan: 'the enemy has begun to employ a new and most cruel bomb, the power of which to do damage is indeed incalculable, taking the toll of many innocent lives. Should we continue to fight, it would not only result in an ultimate collapse and obliteration of the Japanese nation, but also it would lead to the total extinction of human civilization.'[1]

The world had witnessed the birth of a power unlike any seen before and it was quickly harnessed. The X-10 Graphite Reactor at Oak Ridge, Tennessee, first generated electricity in 1948. The Soviets developed their own atom bomb in 1949 and by 1954 their Obninsk Nuclear Power Plant was the first to be connected to a national power grid – followed two years later by Calder Hall in England. Still, it wasn't until 1957 and the creation of the Shippingport Atomic Power Station in Pennsylvania that a nuclear reactor was built *solely* for the purpose of energy generation: all previous reactors had also produced weapons-grade plutonium.

As nuclear-generated electricity made its way into people's homes, American cinema developed a morbid fascination with the implications of splitting the atom. Radioactive mutants became the film antagonists du jour. In *Them!* (1954), fallout from the Trinity tests created an army of mutated, 18-foot ants; in *Tarantula!* (1955), the monstrous mutant was a spider, while *Beginning of the End* (1957) featured locusts bloated to gargantuan scale by the use of radioactive fertiliser. The stakes were apocalyptically high, and films such as *The Day the Earth Stood Still* (1951) and *The War of the Worlds* (1953) – both based on earlier novels

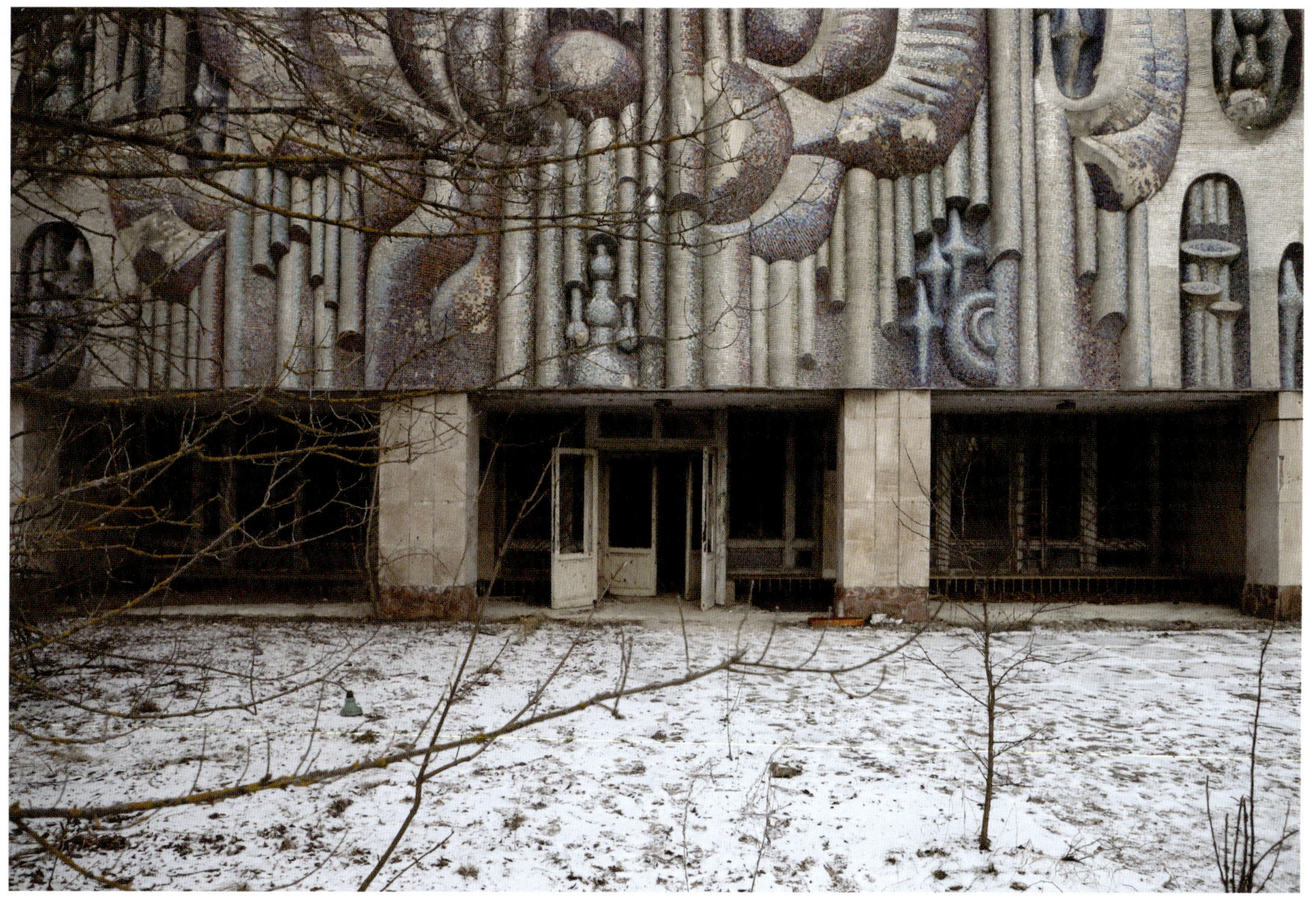

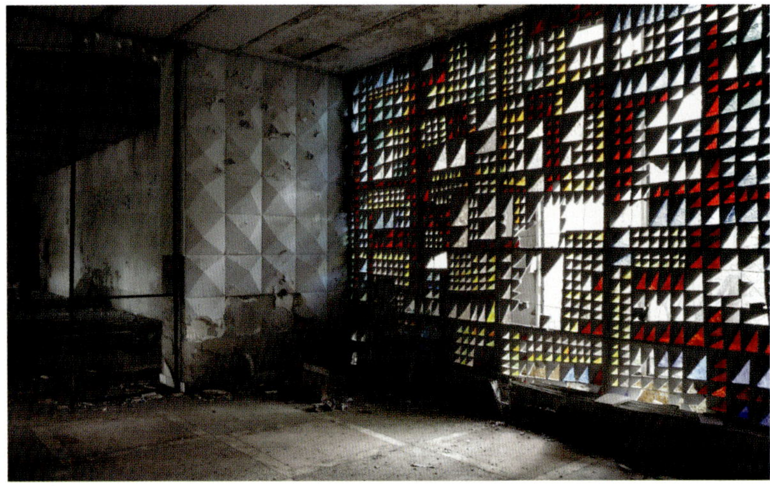

– were suddenly filling cinemas with visions of destruction on a previously unimaginable scale. 'Modern historical reality has greatly enlarged the imagination of disaster,' wrote the philosopher Susan Sontag in a 1964 essay deconstructing Cold War influences on science fiction, 'and the protagonists – perhaps by the very nature of what is visited upon them – no longer seem wholly innocent.'[2]

Comics also found ways to address contemporary atomic fears. In Issue No.1 of *The Incredible Hulk* (1962), Bruce Banner, a brilliant nuclear physicist, is accidentally exposed to radiation from an experimental gamma bomb and subsequently metamorphoses into the Hulk, a chaotic, destructive force of nature. The parallels to J. Robert Oppenheimer, theoretical physicist and 'father of the atomic bomb', were hardly subtle. That same year, *The Amazing Spiderman* introduced to readers a high-school student who developed superhuman powers after being bitten by a radioactive spider. 'With great power comes great responsibility,' would become an enduring motto of the franchise.

While American stories about nuclear technology were often concerned with side effects, or the responsibility demanded of those wielding the power, Japanese cinema of the period – understandably, perhaps – focused on the cost of nuclear war. In Ishirō Honda's 1954 blockbuster *Godzilla*, an ancient creature of incredibly destructive power is disturbed from its deep-sea habitat by the testing of underwater hydrogen bombs. At the end of the film, the protagonist warns us that another Godzilla may some day arise if nuclear testing is not stopped. In *Rodan* (1957), the Japanese city of Fukuoka is devastated by another monster,

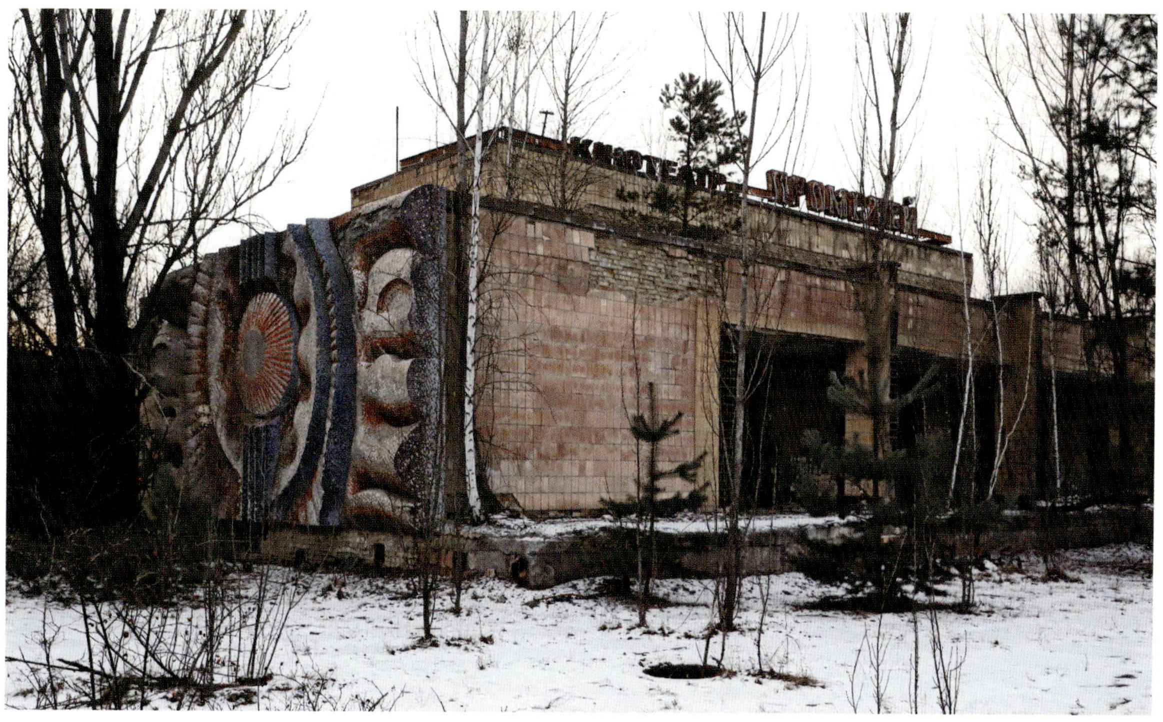

similarly awoken from its age-old slumber by nuclear-weapon tests. In *The Mysterians* (1959), Japan comes under attack from an alien race whose own planet has been crippled by the fallout from nuclear war. 'One gets the feeling,' writes Sontag of these Japanese films, 'that a mass trauma exists over the use of nuclear weapons and the possibility of future nuclear wars. Most of the science-fiction films bear witness to this trauma, and, in a way, attempt to exorcise it.'[2]

Over the next decade that trauma escalated. The Cuban Missile Crisis of 1962 saw two nuclear powers enter a bitter standoff, with potentially devastating global implications. Nobody was safe anymore. While Sidney Lumet's *Fail Safe* (1964) dramatised the atomic showdown between the US and USSR, Stanley Kubrick satirised the insanity of 'mutually assured destruction' in *Dr. Strangelove or: How I Learned to Stop Worrying and Love the Bomb* (1964). Elsewhere, Western cinema considered what it would be like to be on the receiving end of a strike – exploring themes of post-nuclear wastelands, contamination, and the collapse of society. In 1968, *Planet of the Apes* left cinemagoers with a disturbing twist when its final scene revealed the setting to be our own earth, centuries after the death of our current civilisation. Richard Matheson's 1954 post-apocalyptic novel *I Am Legend* proved so reflective of the zeitgeist that it spawned two film adaptations, *The Last Man on Earth* (1964) and *The Omega Man* (1971). Both *A Boy and His Dog* (1975) and *Damnation Alley* (1977) explored the ruins of America in the wake of devastating nuclear conflict, while the dystopian action film *Mad Max* (1979) depicted a future Australia where humans lived like barbarians in the aftermath of what was implied to have been the war to end all wars.

Some representations hit closer to home. A British television production dramatising the aftermath of nuclear conflict, *The War Game* (1965), was initially withdrawn, the BBC believing it 'too horrifying for the medium of broadcasting.'[3] By 1984, however, the BBC itself co-produced *Threads*, a film that took an unflinching look at how nuclear war might play out from the perspective of ordinary citizens. Set in Sheffield, the film opens with scenes of normal life over a backdrop of Cold War news reports about mounting nuclear tensions, when suddenly the unthinkable happens, the bomb falls and the city is reduced to rubble. The rest of the film is delivered with the grim matter-of-factness of a documentary: burning bodies, food shortages, riots, panic, cholera outbreaks and complete societal breakdown. When the bulldozers run out of fuel, the film states, the UK's surviving population will be left to live in the ruins alongside 10-20 million unburied corpses.

All-out nuclear war was not the only thing to fear, and some films entertained the possibility of even supposedly benign electricity-generating nuclear plants having the potential for deadly malfunction. *The China Syndrome* (1979) detailed the near-catastrophic failure of a US nuclear power plant. In one scene, an energy official tells Jane Fonda's character that a meltdown at this fictional Californian plant, 'could render an area the size of the state of Pennsylvania permanently uninhabitable.' Just twelve days after the film's release, in real-world Pennsylvania, a partial meltdown occurred at the Three Mile Island Nuclear Generating Station. Over the course of the five-day incident, thousands of residents were evacuated from the area. In the same way as the Cuban Missile Crisis had served to validate cinematic anxieties about global nuclear war, the incident at Three Mile Island gave weight to fears of an accidental nuclear disaster. However, of all the cautionary fiction produced during the Atomic Era, it was a novel by two Russian authors, and its subsequent screen adaptation, that would provide the uncanniest foreshadowing of the disaster to come.

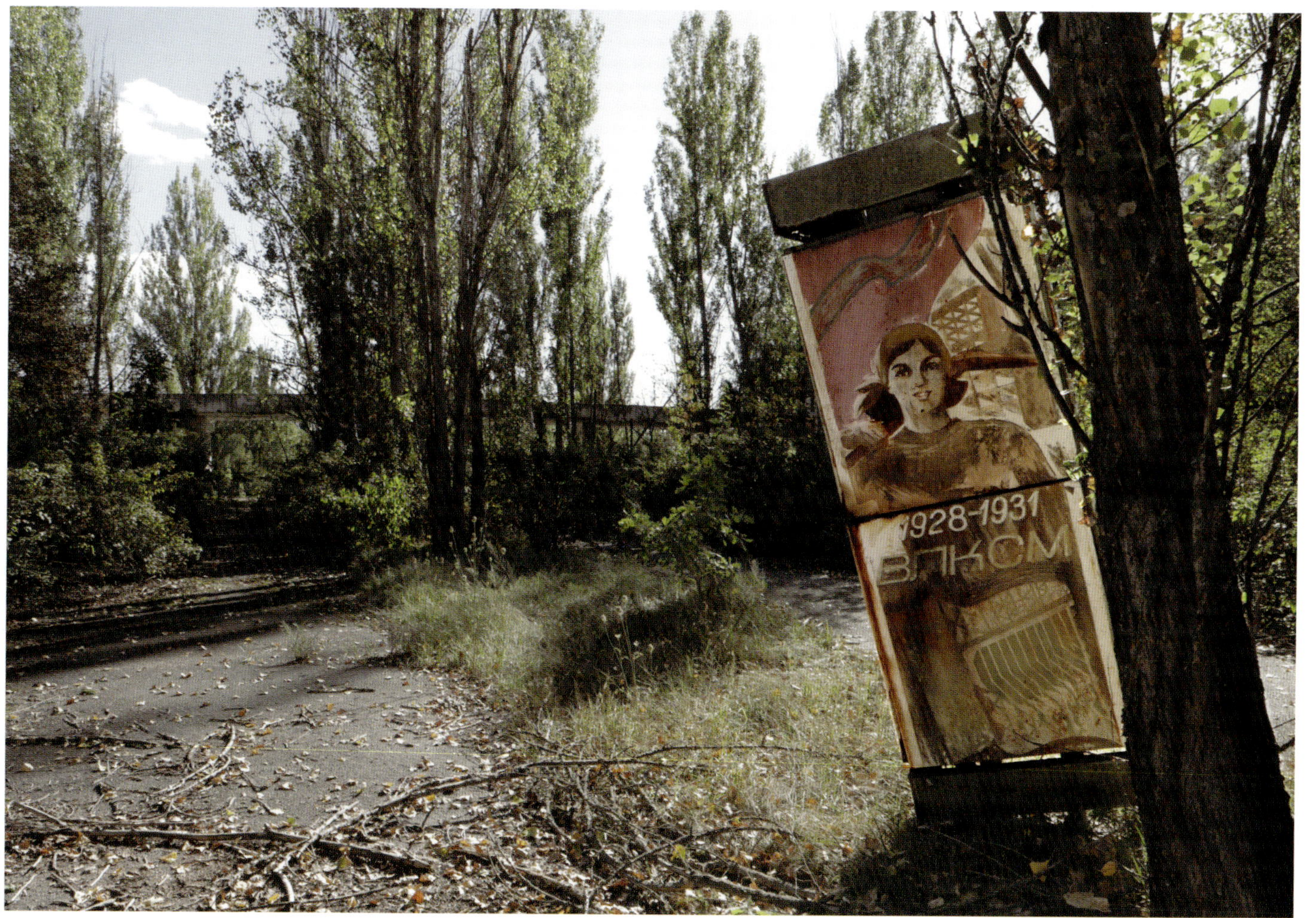
1928-1931
ВЛКСМ

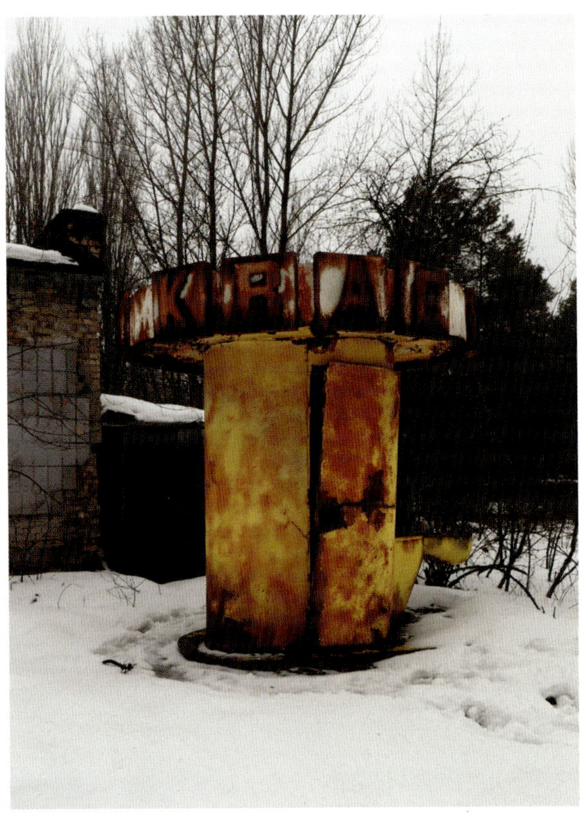
Kiosk, Pripyat Bus Station. A strikingly designed kiosk used to sell *kvass* (a popular alcohol-free malt drink).

ROADSIDE PICNIC

Roadside Picnic, written by brothers Boris and Arkady Strugatsky, was published in 1972. The story is set in our own world, in the wake of some unexplained intergalactic event. It is suggested that extraterrestrial beings have arrived, but rather than making contact with the human race, they simply pollute large areas of the planet's surface before moving on. A scientist in the novel hypothesises that these visitors might have landed to perform maintenance on their craft – or even, for a 'roadside picnic'.

The novel's titular visitation leads to the creation of secure, military-guarded Zones which are littered with bizarre alien 'artefacts', as they are called – ranging from everlasting batteries to strange devices with the potential for weaponisation. The Zones also harbour a deadly assortment of visible and invisible traps, including flesh-eating 'hell slimes', and localised gravitational anomalies capable of crushing a human body to viscous pulp. The novel's protagonist, Redrick ('Red') Schuhart, is a 'stalker' – a looter who enters the Zone illegally, risking his life to search the uncanny landscape for artefacts to sell on the black market. Red is shown to have a deep connection to the Zone, to be infected by it even: his own offspring is born genetically mutated with fur. Among the artefacts Red seeks is the fabled 'Golden Sphere', an object with the power to grant wishes. It is his hunt for this sphere that drives the novel's climax.

Roadside Picnic was not the first science-fiction novel to imagine a hostile wasteland populated with unnatural dangers. *Rogue Moon* by Algis Budrys (1960) explores a deadly alien labyrinth discovered on the moon, while Philip K. Dick's *A Maze of Death* (1970) follows human colonists attempting to survive on a seemingly sentient planet full of bizarre, invisible traps. What distinguished *Roadside Picnic* was that it was published in the USSR. The Soviet cultural policy under Stalin had permitted only near-future science fiction – works that commented directly and literally on the tangible achievements of Soviet science – but relative liberalisation under the Khrushchev regime, combined with the new confidence bought by the growing prestige of the USSR's post-Gagarin space programme, permitted the Strugatskys to look a little further afield. Their early novels (beginning with *The Land of Crimson Clouds* in 1959) were uncontroversial tales of space adventure that adhered to the popular Soviet trends of the genre: futuristic communist utopias and what the German science-fiction author and Strugatsky expert Erik Simon identifies as 'class struggle in outer space, involving American agents and/or extraterrestrial capitalists.'[4] Even so, the strength of their writing and ideas set them apart, and by the mid-1960s the Strugatskys were amongst the most popular contemporary Soviet science-fiction writers.

In the late 1960s, the Strugatskys shifted towards satire. 'The Strugatsky brothers were not blatant, and never… directly critical of their government's policies,' wrote Ursula K. Le Guin in her foreword to the 2012 English edition of *Roadside Picnic*. 'What they did, which I found most admirable then and still do now, was to write as if they were indifferent to ideology – something many of us writers in the Western democracies had a hard time doing. They wrote as free men write.'[5]

The brothers' waning enthusiasm for Party ideology began to raise eyebrows among Soviet censors, and many publishers refused to work with them. Nevertheless, when *Roadside Picnic* was serialised in issues 7-10 of the literary magazine *Avrora*, it proved to be one of the Strugatskys' most successful works. In contrast to their earlier utopian fiction, this was the story of a dystopia, one that they were careful to locate on the far side of the planet, as 'dystopian conditions could exist, by definition,' writes Erik Simon, 'only in the world of parasitic, degenerate capitalism.'[4] So the story purportedly takes place in Canada, where the fictional town of Harmont serves as a staging ground for the stalkers' forays into the Zone.

It is hard not to read politics between the lines of *Roadside Picnic*. Released just a year after the USSR launched Salyut-1, the first space station, it was surely a bold satirical move to hypothesise a universe in which extraterrestrial species might consider the USSR, and all its achievements in space, to be of no interest whatsoever – treating the Soviet home planet as little more than a toilet break on the way to somewhere more interesting. The novel's final words then read like a humanist manifesto. Red discovers the Golden Sphere, only to realise that he has no idea what to wish for. In frustration he cries out, 'I am an animal, you see that. I don't have the words, they didn't teach me the words. I don't know how to think, the bastards didn't let me learn how to think. But if you really are... all-powerful... all-knowing... then you figure it out! Look into my heart. I know that everything you need is in there. It has to be. I never sold my soul to anyone!'

Roadside Picnic might also be read as an ecological critique of the Soviet nuclear industry. The novel was developed from the authors' earlier short story *The Forgotten Experiment* (1959), in which a mysterious accident at a remote Russian power plant leads to the evacuation of nearby villages and the establishment of a high-security Exclusion Zone. Only two years earlier, a similar incident had taken place at the plutonium-producing Mayak nuclear facility in Chelyabinsk Oblast. The 1957 'Kyshtym disaster', as it became known, occurred when cooling system failures caused a chemical explosion in a waste-storage tank. The tank burst with the force of over 70 tons of TNT, spreading hot particles across an area of some 52,000 square kilometres and necessitating the evacuation of 10,000 citizens from at least twenty-two villages.[6] According to 'Boris Komarov' (the pseudonym of a 1970s Soviet whistle-blower), 'all crops, all animals, and houses were destroyed, and the population was evacuated 200 and more kilometres from the point of the explosion.'[7] At the time, Kyshtym was the worst nuclear accident the world had ever seen (it now ranks third, behind Chernobyl and Fukushima). It left behind a contaminated zone known as the East Urals Radioactive Trace, and for thirty years the Soviet regime attempted to keep the episode secret.

How much the Strugatskys could have known about the Kyshtym disaster by 1959 is impossible to say; but what *The Forgotten Experiment* reveals – with its focus so much closer to home – is that all the ideas of evacuation, invisible poison, and genetic mutation that would eventually come to characterise *Roadside Picnic* initially grew out of a fear of radio-ecological disaster within the USSR.

right: Entrance doors, 'Prometheus' Cinema.

page 28: Kurchatov Street, Pripyat. A hammer-and-sickle motif on a lamp post is still visible through the trees.

page 29: The 'White House', Central Square, Pripyat. This building once housed Party officials and plant bosses, while the ground floor contained the 'Raduga' ('Rainbow') Supermarket.

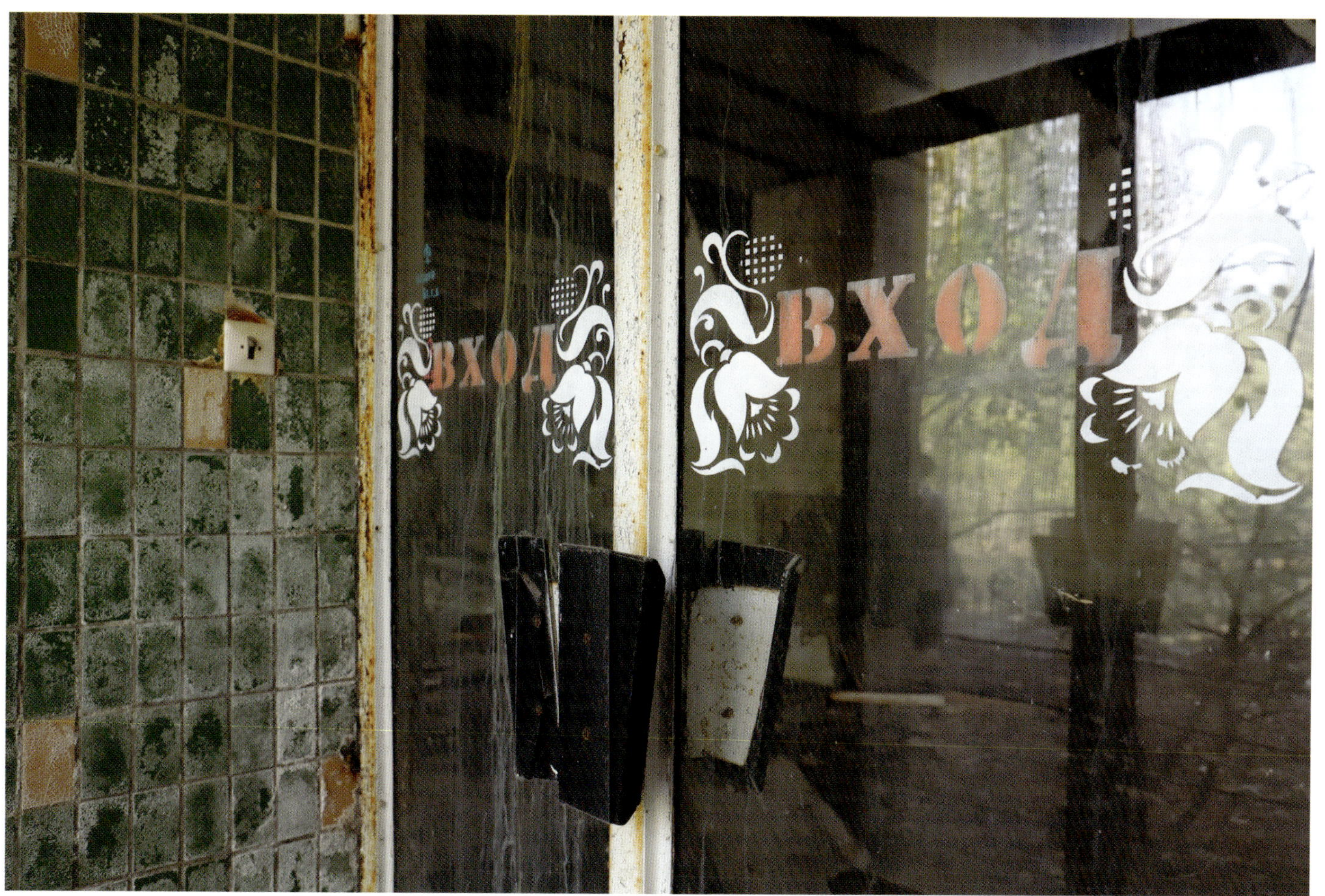

ВХОД
ВХОД

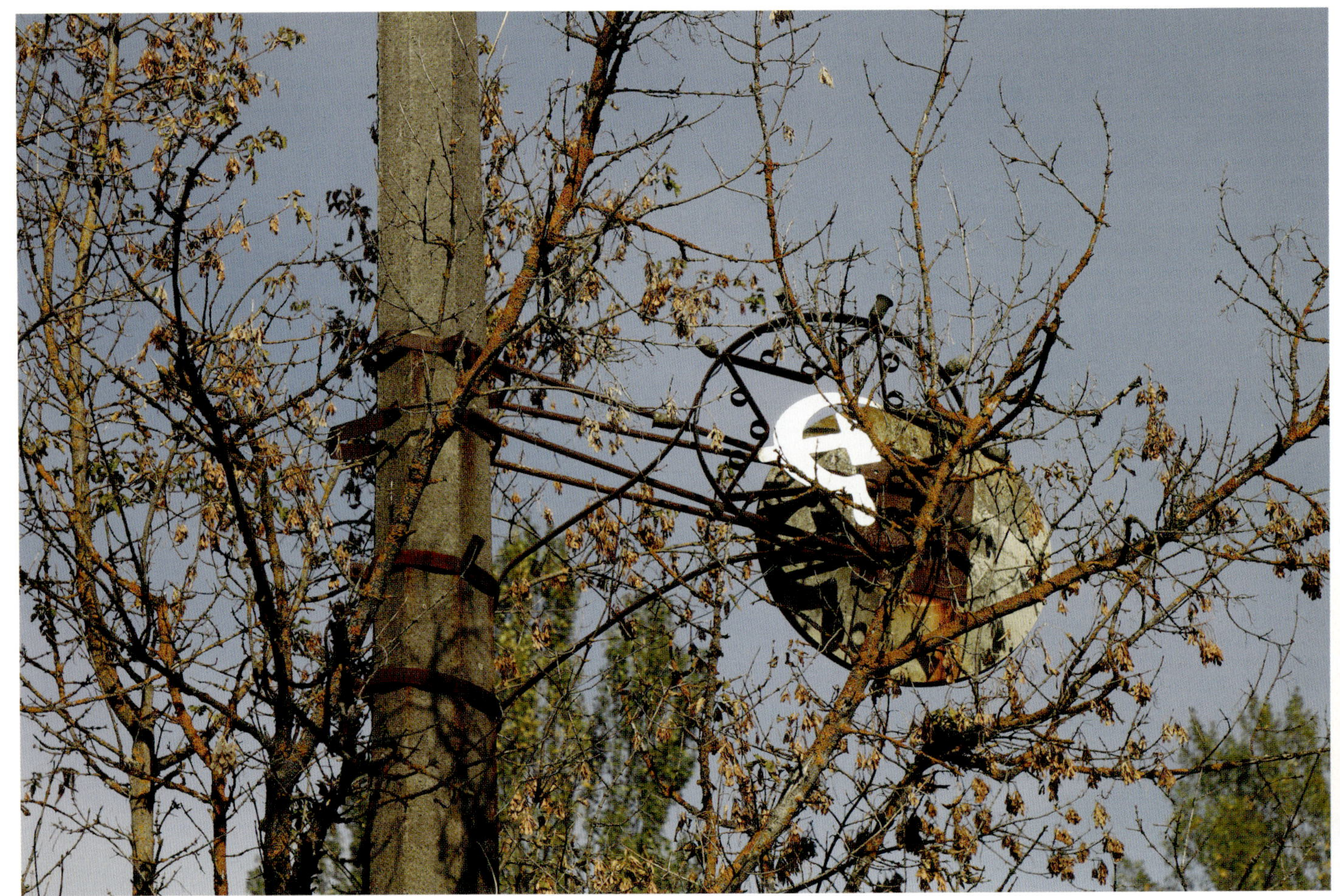

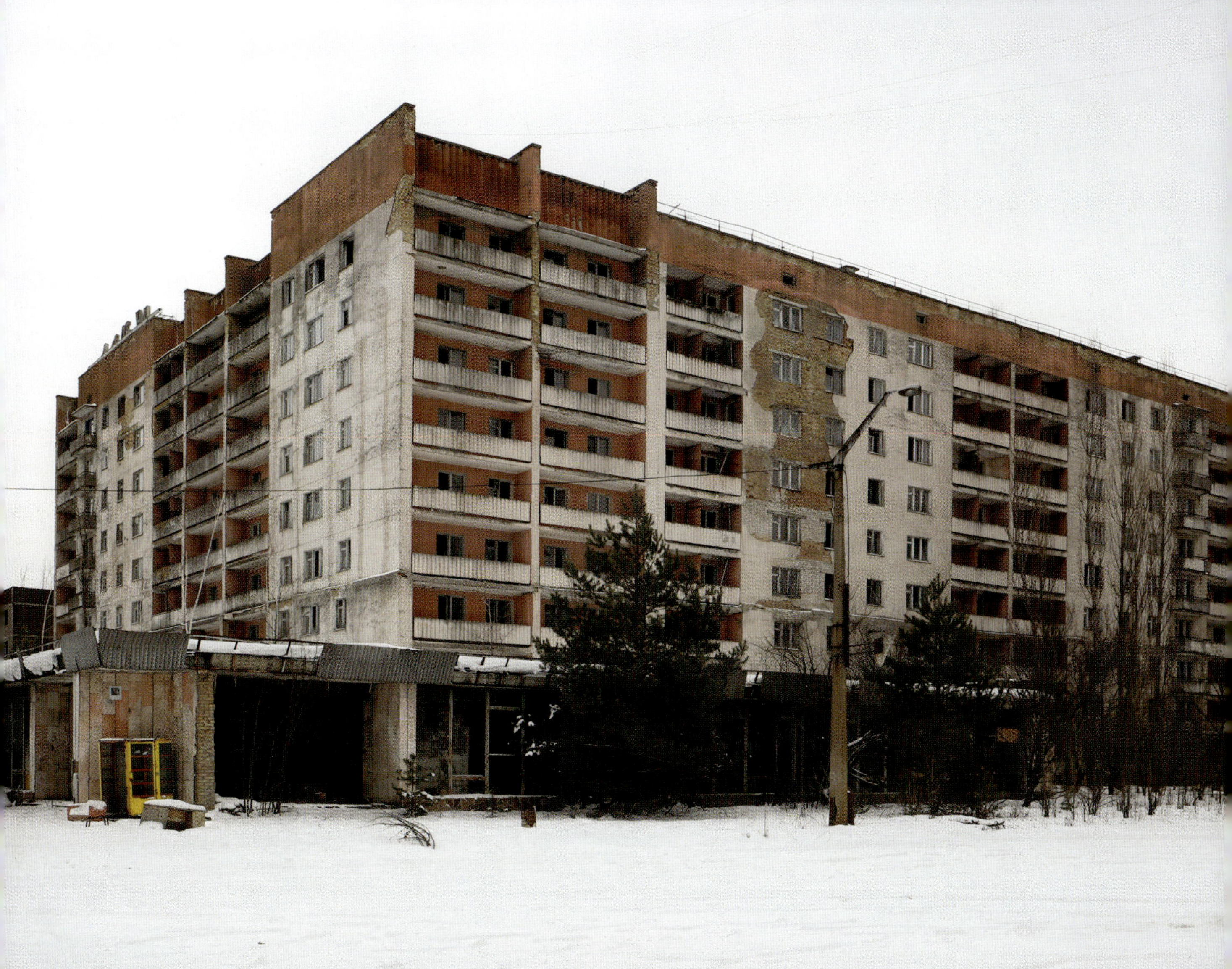

STALKER

Andrey Tarkovsky's film *Stalker*, based on *Roadside Picnic*, was released in 1979, with the Strugatskys writing a screenplay for what they thought would be a science-fiction feature. However, Tarkovsky ended up making extensive changes. In his hands, the story of *Roadside Picnic* became less dystopian narrative science fiction, and more shamanic journey into ideas of spirit, faith and communion.

Whereas for decades Japan and the US had been making films that explored the idea of nuclear apocalypse, Soviet censors had ensured that their cinema, much like their literature, presented only wholesome scenarios that upheld the notion of present and future Soviet success. *Stalker* was something very new. Tarkovsky's work had been scrutinised by Soviet officials in the past (*Andrei Rublev* faced aggressive censorship in 1966, being deemed 'too negative, too harsh, too experimental, too frightening, too filled with nudity, and too politically complicated'[8]), yet despite its controversial subject matter, *Stalker* was approved. Tarkovsky's reputation for winning coveted international film awards had surely helped appease the censors; Western film companies were already agreeing distribution rights for *Stalker* before the film finished production.

Tarkovsky, like the Strugatskys, set his dystopia on foreign soil: *Stalker*'s opening text crawl introduces 'our little country,' immediately differentiating this place from the sprawling USSR. However, where *Roadside Picnic* had named its protagonist before chronicling his life both in Harmont and on multiple trips into the Zone, *Stalker* focuses on one trip only and its protagonists are known by their professions. Stalker, a guide, has agreed to take Writer and Professor into the Zone. Their destination is a place called the 'Room,' which has the power to grant the wishes of those who enter. The Room is a stand-in for *Roadside Picnic*'s Golden Sphere, but with a significant difference: the Sphere can be stolen and taken out of the Zone, whereas the Room cannot.

Tarkovsky described his filmmaking as 'sculpting in time' and time itself – in a dilatory form – is used to powerful effect throughout *Stalker*.[9] Scenes outside the Zone are shot in black and white, creating mundane margins around the film's strange main events. Here the 'real world' feels dull and futile, and indeed the very first dialogue is an argument about a watch – an object that predicts and regulates a given order. Our protagonists first meet in a bar, then, following a brief car chase, they break through the military cordon surrounding the Zone. The film switches to colour as the trio enter the Zone proper, riding a handcar along train tracks. At this point the action slows to a drifting cruise among the damp fields, rivers, and abandoned buildings of the Zone. The laws of nature are inverted, and the landscape itself adopts a strange kind of sentience.

Sigmund Freud called dreams the 'royal road to the unconscious,' manifesting unspoken fears or desires.[10] In the dreamlike Zone, it becomes apparent that Tarkovsky's protagonists are living out their own wish-fulfilment fantasies, each seeking that which his life lacks: Writer searches for inspiration, Professor for knowledge, and Stalker, perhaps, for redemption. The film begins to echo *The Wizard of Oz*, except that here, Tin Man, Scarecrow and Cowardly Lion have to travel without Dorothy to the centre of the Zone, to the place where all wishes come true, in search of their missing heart, brain and courage. With titles rather than real names, Tarkovsky's characters feel more like archetypes than individuals, and it is surely no coincidence that only three names from elsewhere are mentioned in the film: Shakespeare and Einstein – a writer and a professor from the real world – and Chingachgook (the fictional Mohican chief from the novels of James Fenimore Cooper), a guide with a spiritual connection to the earth. Throughout the film, Tarkovsky presents Stalker as a man more bound to this Zone than to the world outside. Insects seem drawn to him here, as is the black dog (its sleek head and pointed ears reminiscent of Anubis, the Egyptian god who guards the entrance to the underworld) that follows and eventually leaves with him. When Stalker prays, he puts his head against the ground itself as if praying to the Zone.

It is established that the Room doesn't necessarily grant the wish that is asked of it, but rather, the deepest unconscious desire of whoever enters it. Stalker talks about his friend Porcupine, who entered the room hoping to save his brother but instead was granted riches. Porcupine hanged himself

after that, unable to live with the implication. In his analysis of *Stalker*, the cultural theorist Slavoj Žižek calls such an attitude 'religious obscurantism', the idea that wishes will only be granted, 'on the condition that you are able to formulate them. Which, of course, you are never able.'[11]

By the end of the film, at the very threshold of the Room, each character's narrative arc is subverted. Writer decides not to enter, and thus avoids exposing his soul to scrutiny (this is not so much redemption as a first step in recognising the need for it). Professor, who ostensibly came here seeking knowledge, reveals he has smuggled a bomb into the Zone and intends to destroy the Room – or 'Bunker 4', as we learn his scientific peers have named it. 'This place obviously won't bring anyone happiness,' he says, though in the end he neither enters nor destroys the Room, instead defusing the bomb and tossing its components into a puddle. Stalker, meanwhile, who appeared at first as a stoic, mysterious leader, breaks down and cries when Writer knocks him to the floor, chastising the sobbing guide as a 'hypocritical louse,' and later a 'holy fool.' Stalker is revealed as a parasite, a weak man unfit for the real world, who instead plays power games here, juggling his customers' lives in the Zone. He is not the Zone's master, but its subject: it inhabits his tired-looking body and also his home. The black dog, a messenger from the Zone, joins his household, and while Stalker's daughter isn't covered in fur, the final scene implies she does have telekinetic ability – as if the Zone's influence had triggered a genetic, evolutionary leap forward (much as radiation did for 1960s superheroes).

It is a wonder that *Stalker* was ever made. Behind the scenes there were dramatic fall-outs and firings, added to which the initial set of film negatives was damaged, resulting in the loss of almost the entire first shoot. A second shoot was deemed unsatisfactory and it wasn't until the third attempt, on location in an abandoned factory in Estonia, that Tarkovsky finally secured his footage. *Stalker* was the last film Tarkovsky made in the USSR before moving permanently to Italy in 1982, where his films received far less censorship. 'I am not a Soviet dissident,' he declared, and though he maintained he had no political quarrel with his homeland, he acknowledged that if he went home, he 'would be unemployed.'[12]

In December 1986 – eight months after the Chernobyl disaster – Tarkovsky died from lung cancer. He was fifty-four years old. There were rumours claiming that he had been assassinated by the KGB in retribution for his role in creating 'anti-Soviet propaganda', but his sound editor Victor Sharun later wrote: 'Up the river was a chemical plant and it poured out poisonous liquids downstream. There was even this shot in *Stalker*: snow falling in the summer and white foam floating down the river. In fact it was some horrible poison. Many women in our crew got allergic reactions on their faces. Tarkovsky died from cancer of the right bronchial tube. And Tolya Solonitsyn [who played Writer] too. That it was all

connected to the location shooting for *Stalker* became clear to me when Larisa Tarkovskaya [Tarkovsky's wife, and assistant director] died from the same illness in Paris.'[13]

In *Stalker*, Tarkovsky left behind a film that seemed to simultaneously condense and invert all preceding themes of post-apocalyptic fiction. The Strugatskys' novel had detailed the chaos and mutation that followed a colossal ecological catastrophe, the creation of a militarised Exclusion Zone to keep out trespassers, and the stalkers who nevertheless ventured inside on treasure hunts. It showed that borders, even those created to keep a population safe, could be transgressed and how those with the strength to survive beyond might just find their wishes granted. However in Tarkovsky's retelling, the Zone became not an enemy to overcome but rather a teacher, while a mysterious building – the 'Room' or 'Bunker 4' – was introduced as the geographical and figurative heart of this sentient terrain. He showed how the Zone's dangers could be overcome, not by cunning or brute force, but by stripping the ego away in a process of spiritual purification. Tarkovsky's Zone was a place that could make you a better human, if you let it.

right: Apartment rooftops Pripyat, view from the sixteenth storey

overleaf: River Port, Chornobyl. This post-Soviet mural with its pastoral painting illustrates a section from the 1994 Ukrainian Forest Code.

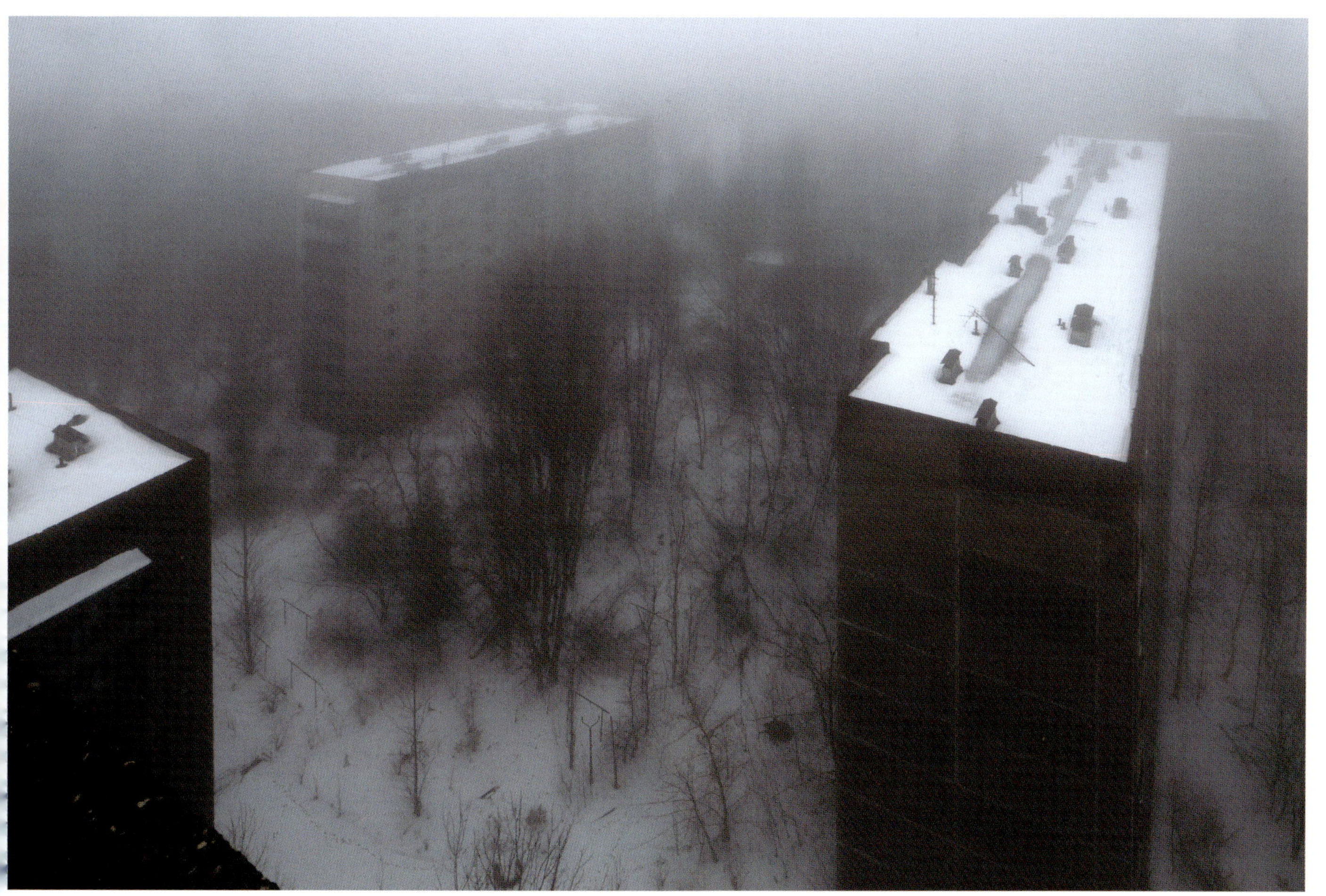

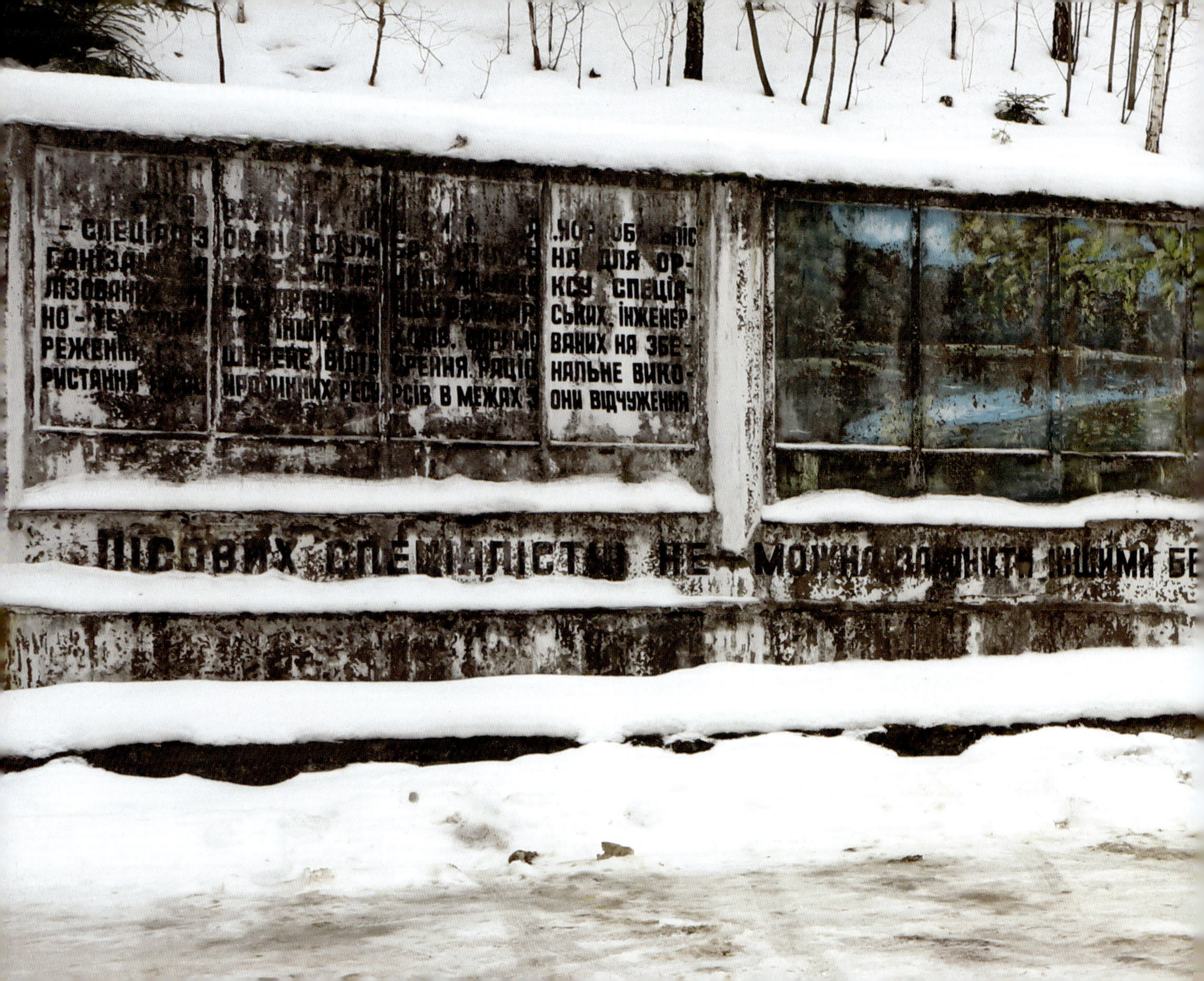
ЛІСОВИХ СПЕЦІАЛІСТІВ НЕ МОЖНА ЗАМІНИТИ ІНШИМИ Б

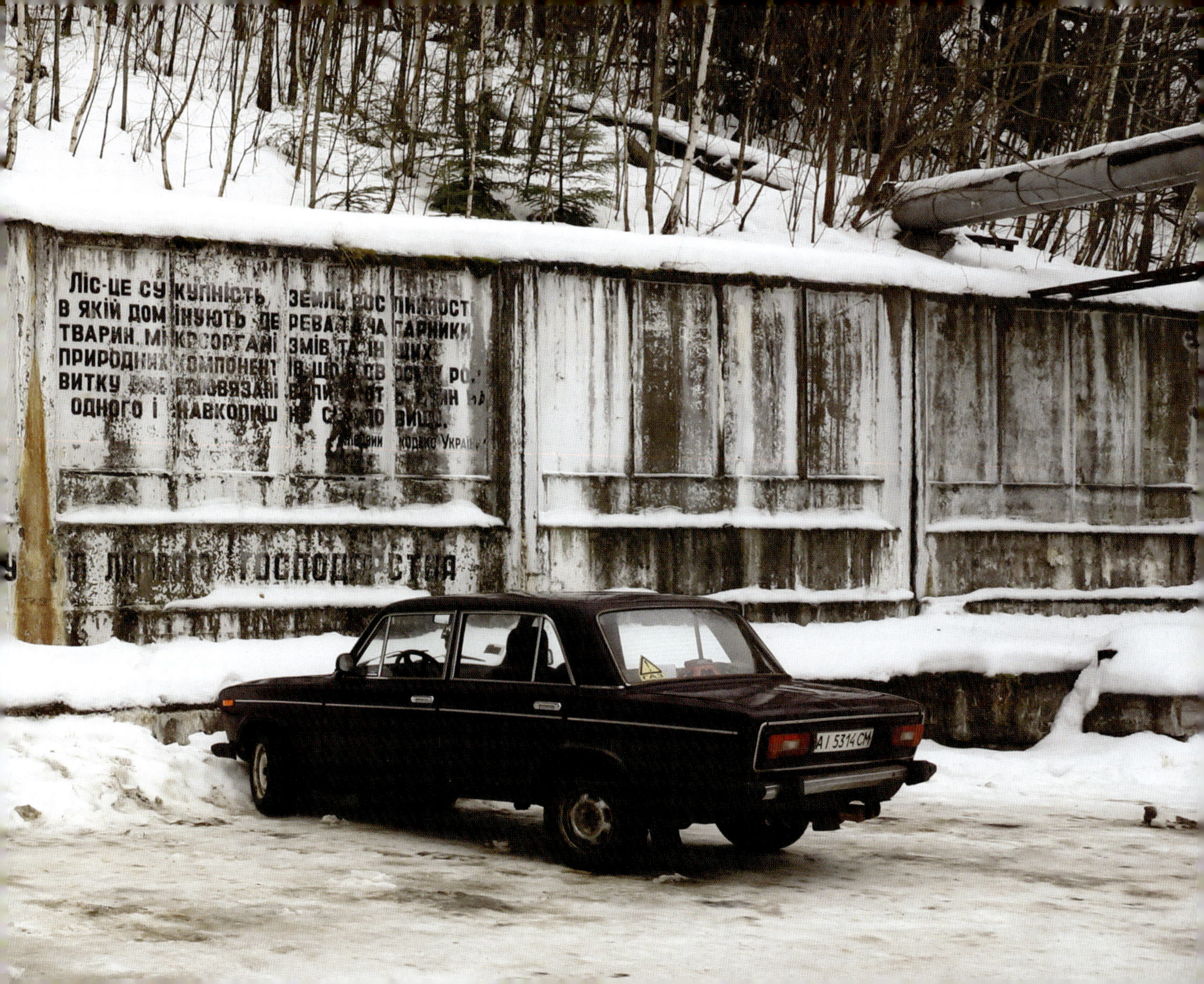

Ліс-це сукупність земл, рос линості
в якій домінують, де ревала на гарники
тварин. мікроргані змів та ін ших
природних компонент ів що я св осму ро
витку зовязані вли ют ь ин на
одного і навкориш не ся ло вищ.
кодекс Украї
АІ 5314 СМ

A TOURIST

I was born a couple of years before the disaster at Chernobyl, and I grew up on a diet of atomic science fiction – I adored Isaac Asimov and Philip K. Dick, and read comics whose characters possessed radiation-enhanced powers. My favourite film, for a very long time, was *Back to the Future*. I didn't identify with the young hero Marty McFly, though: I wanted to be Christopher Lloyd's mad-scientist character, Dr. Emmett Brown, stealing plutonium from terrorists to fuel a fission-powered time machine. By the time I saw Tarkovksy's *Stalker,* I had already watched a dozen other films inspired by it, inspired by the real-life Chernobyl Zone, or often a combination of the two.

In 2013, I encountered my first real stalker in the derelict lobby of Pripyat's 'Polissya' Hotel. He was in his late thirties, with his hair tied back in a wiry ponytail. He wore a Megadeth T-shirt tucked into camouflage trousers and was leaning in a doorway as casually as if this had been his living room. Between hard puffs on his electronic cigarette, he gave me a friendly nod. 'Alyosha!' called his friend from somewhere out of sight, and the stalker smiled and left, his head bobbing like a pigeon as he slunk into the ruined city.

I was backpacking across Europe and Asia that summer and my hosts in Kyiv had offered to book me a tour of Chernobyl. At that time, the Exclusion Zone received around 10,000 tourists a year, a tenth of the number it gets now. I knew a handful of photographers who had been and ever since I heard it was safe I had wanted to visit it for myself. Few destinations carry such historical significance; but it was more than just a location, it was an idea: the post-apocalypse, the world without us, the real-life case that embodied (and later, inspired) so many of the stories I consumed as a child. Some kids grew up with fairy tales, then got to realise them in Disneyland. I suppose Chernobyl was my equivalent.

We were picked up from a Kyiv train station at dawn, in a bus branded with a radiation sign. On the two-hour drive, we watched a film about the disaster and signed our names beneath a list of rules. No shorts. No sandals. Long sleeves at all times. No souvenirs to be taken home. No food to be consumed in the open. No alcohol. No drugs. In the more contaminated centre of the Zone we were told: touch nothing, sit nowhere and absolutely no smoking. Despite these apparently categorical regulations, our own tour guide – a burly Ukrainian named Nikolai – would break half of them in the space of a morning, explaining they were really more like 'recommendations'.

I had joined a Russian-language tour. This was before 2014 saw new hostility between Russia and Ukraine, and my group had members from both countries. The itinerary was stressful: thirty people on a bus, being herded from one photo stop to the next, with barely enough time to focus a camera. It felt like a mechanical tour of the visual highlights, without actually experiencing any of them. I was also surprised by the behaviour of some of the guests. Litter

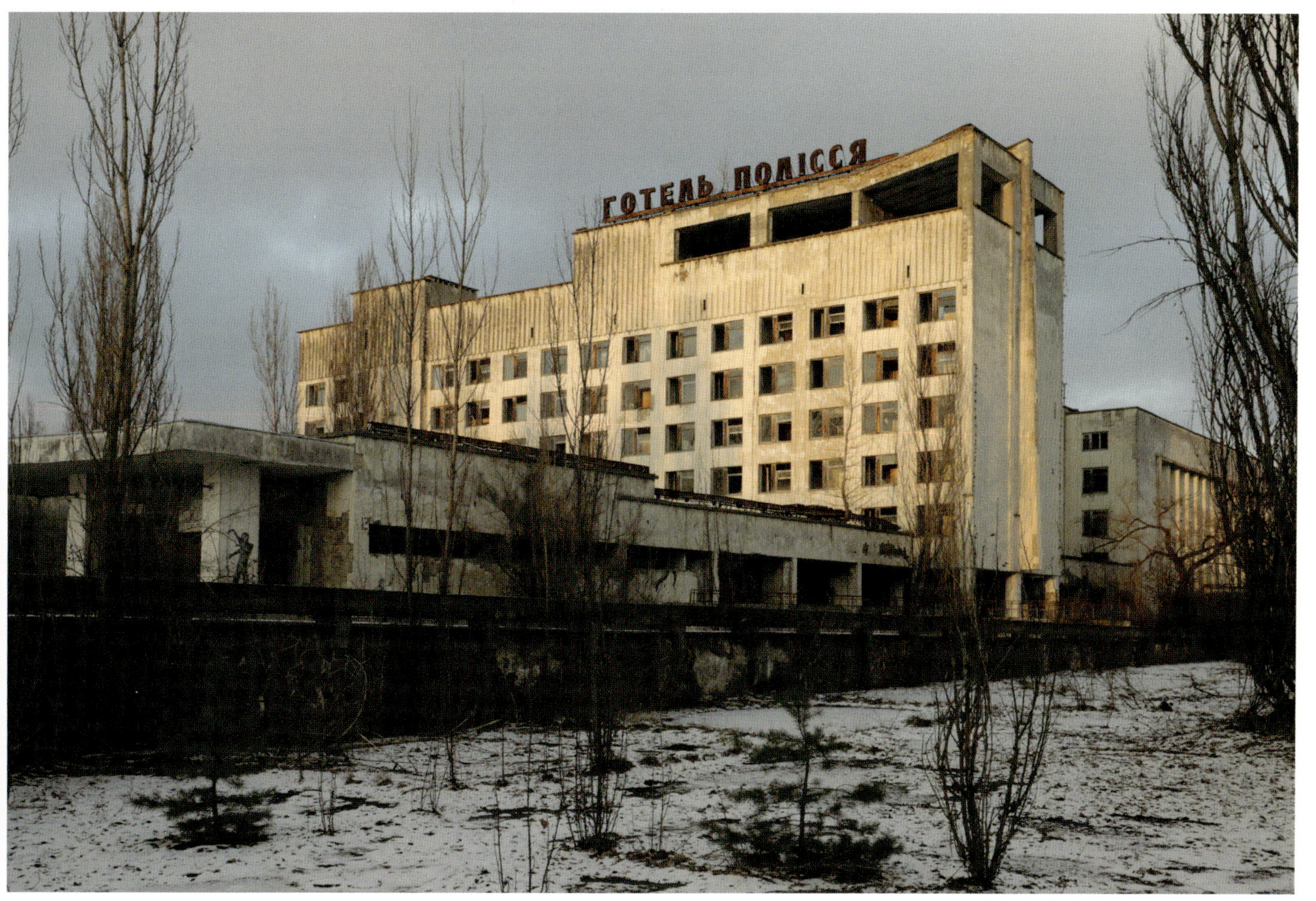
ГОТЕЛЬ ПОЛІССЯ

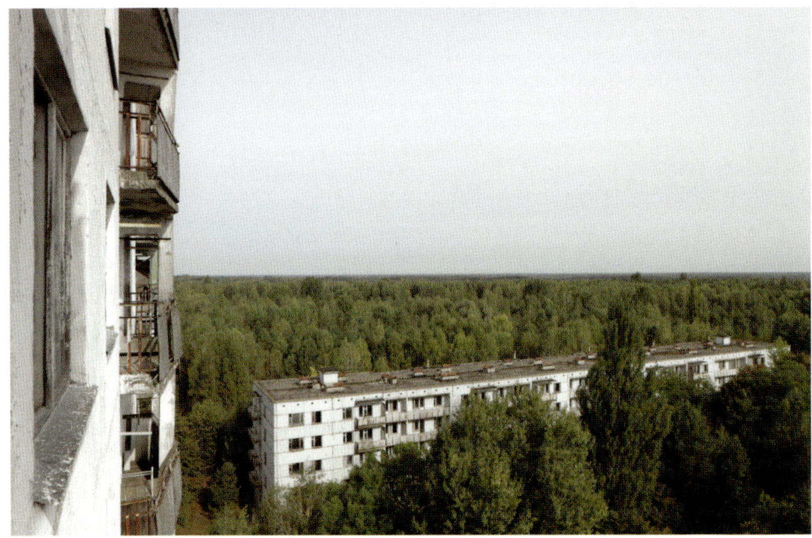

was dropped, glass was smashed, names scrawled in dust. A trio of loud, brash, young Russian men even smuggled in their own stash of beer. At one point a Ukrainian girl scolded them for leaving empty bottles in the bushes.

Before the trip, I was nervous about radiation. The habitual line from Chernobyl guides is that you'll typically receive more radiation from a transatlantic flight than you will from two days in the Zone. (The other is that alcohol thins the blood and prevents radiation sickness, so drink up!) All the same, I felt better when Nikolai let me operate the dosimeter and I took some readings for myself. At the time of the Chernobyl disaster, the Soviets measured radiation in roentgens; but today Chernobyl has largely switched to the international standard unit for measuring ionising radiation dosage – the sievert. A dose of 3-5 sieverts in an hour is potentially enough to kill, but on this tour we were counting millionths of a sievert – known as microsieverts – per hour (µSv/h). For comparison, cities like London, Rome and New York have background radiation in the region of 0.1 to 0.3 µSv/h[1]; while an airliner flying at an altitude of 35,000 feet hits something like 3 µSv/h.[2] Most of the places we visited in Chernobyl measured no more than 0.3 µSv/h, comparable to the average developed city. There was the occasional 'hotspot' though – for example, the dosimeter crackled into life and started beeping as we approached the scrapyard where clean-up vehicles had been buried after the disaster.

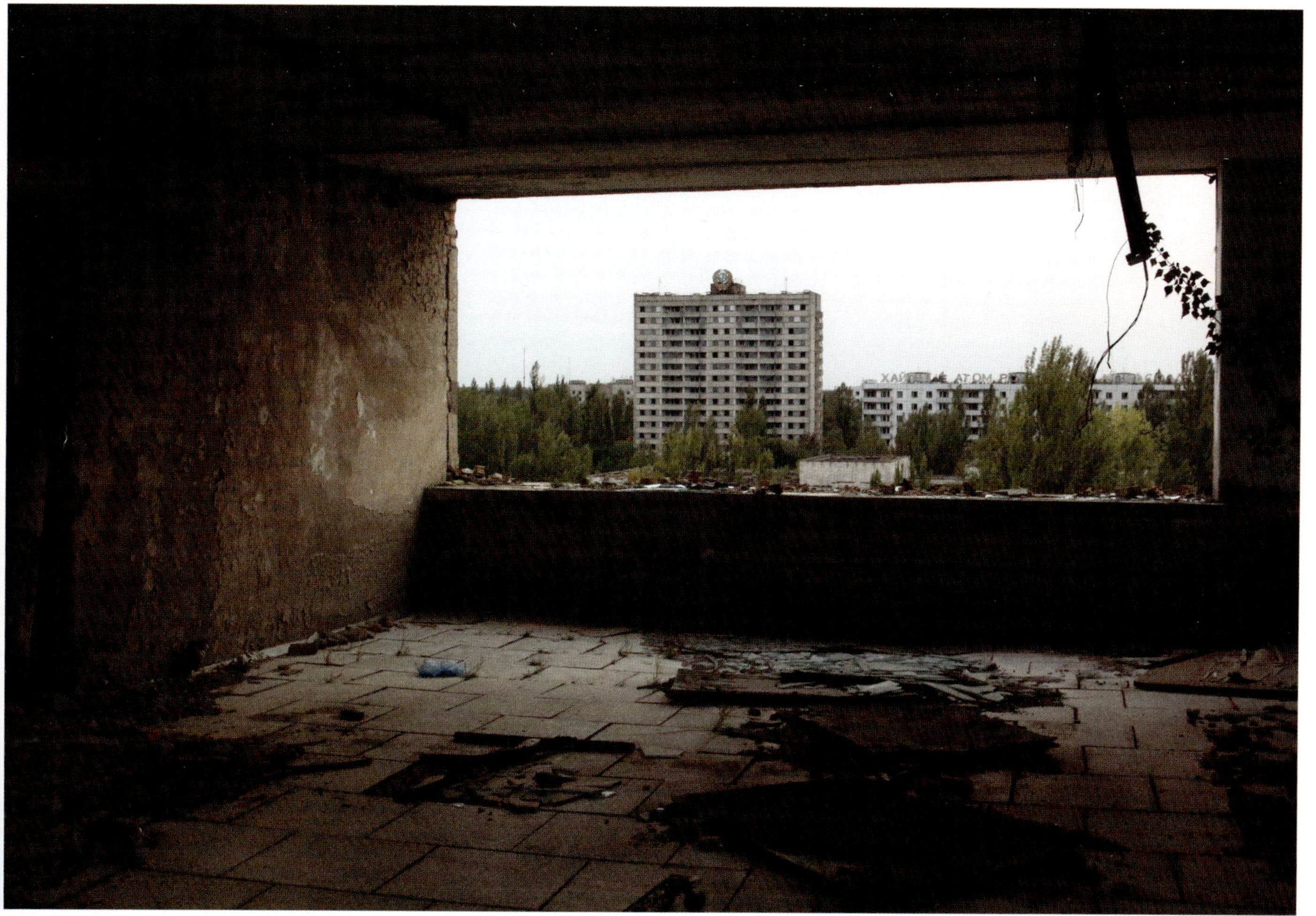

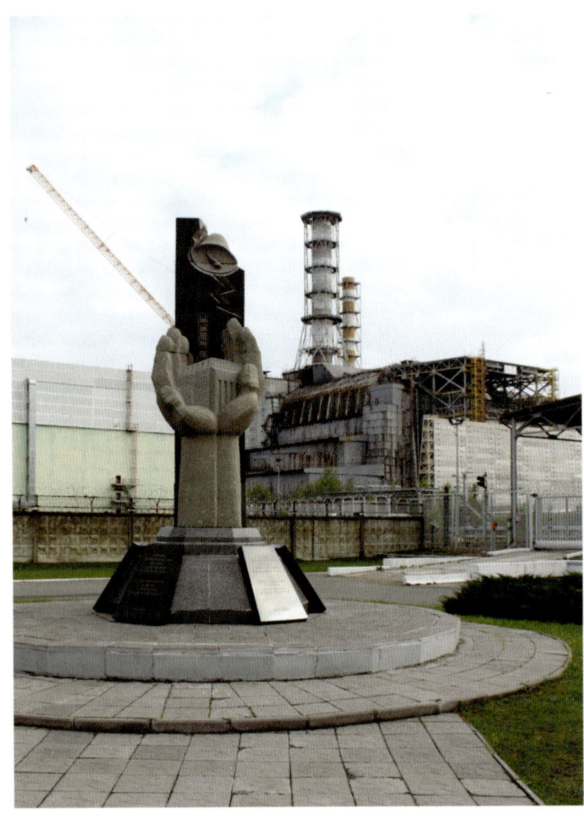

A discarded crane claw showed a reading of 2 millisieverts – that's thousandths of a sievert – per hour (mSv/h), 8,000 times more radioactive than the background level in London. Thankfully such hotspots were infrequent, and easily detected. We were also regularly scanned ourselves: twice a day we stepped into ancient heavy-duty full-body radiation detectors, waiting for the green light to shine for 'Chisto' ('Clean') as the magnetic barriers unlocked with a reassuring clunk.

The Chernobyl Exclusion Zone consists of an inner and outer ring. The innermost part – called the 10 km Zone – is the area of highest contamination, the land within a 10-kilometre radius of the power plant. The outer 30 km Zone was evacuated too, though on the whole it's much cleaner than the centre of the Zone and mostly serves as a buffer area. Over the course of two days, we spent time exploring each – stopping at ruined villages and rural schools in the 30 km Zone, before crossing Leliv Checkpoint (named after a former nearby village) into the 10 km Zone. There we saw the power plant itself: stopping to photograph the vast and dirty blue-grey sarcophagus containing the ill-fated Chernobyl Reactor 4. Alongside it rose the gargantuan silver arch of

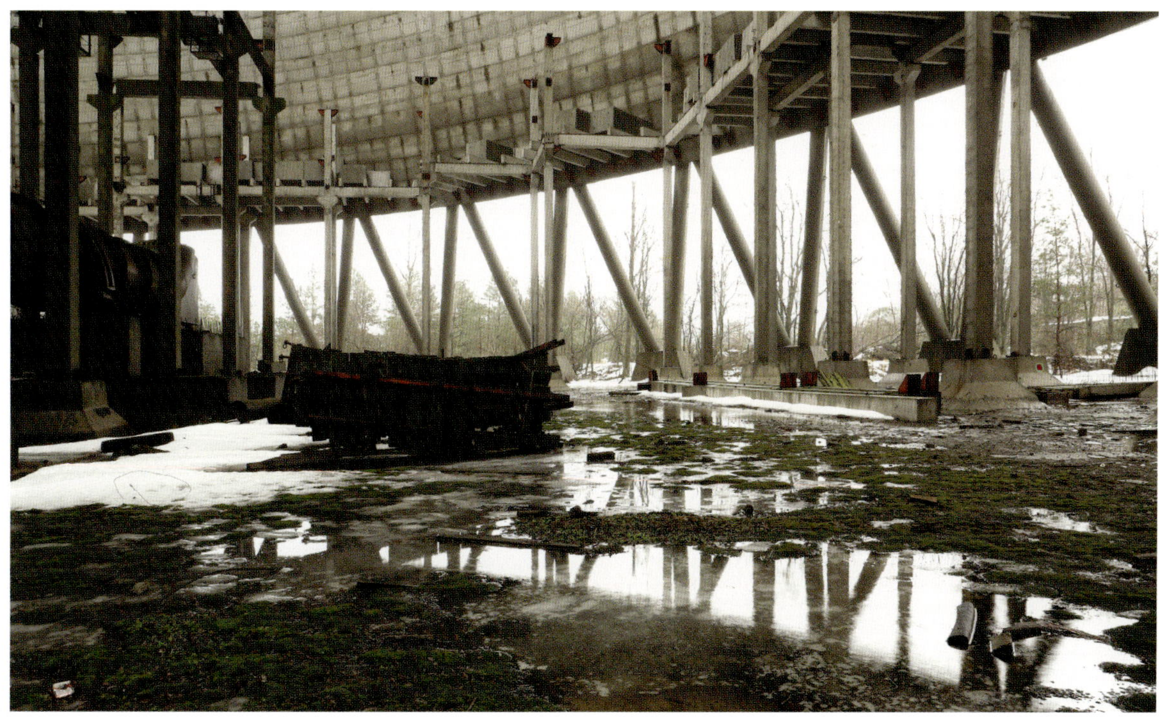

the New Safe Confinement (which was still under construction at this time). At more than 100 metres in height and weighing 31,000 tons, this protective cover was designed to slide on rail tracks neatly over the top of the fourth reactor block.[3] 'The largest movable object ever built,' said Nikolai, proudly.

Standing in the shadow of the power plant, I had to keep reminding myself where I was. The reactor block looked even bigger than it did in photos, yet the complex around it was surprisingly pleasant. I had imagined an industrial hell-gate, a radioactive Mount Doom, but instead here were neatly mown lawns, Modernist sculptures and the busy sounds of ongoing work. It was hard to imagine that beneath this steel and concrete, in the basement of Reactor 4, lurked perhaps the single most dangerous object on the planet:

the so-called 'Elephant's Foot'. The lava-like remains of the molten core (silicon dioxide, titanium, zirconium, magnesium and uranium, mixing to form a new substance the scientists had named 'corium') were said to emit as many as 10,000 roentgens per hour – the equivalent of more than 4.5 million chest X-rays.[4]

The unfinished cooling tower was another visual – and auditory – highlight: an immense concrete cylinder, tall enough that the distant upper rim, still clad in scaffolding, was partially lost to the mist. We walked inside beneath the walls, along the bed of what would have been a cooling pond had the structure been finished. The slightest noises echoed, rippled and bounced around the sheer interior walls. One Ukrainian on our tour, an amateur soprano, suddenly broke into a gutsy rendition of *The Phantom of the Opera*. Inside the cooling tower, the song swelled and boomed to unearthly proportions; the group fell silent, before enthusiastically applauding at the end.

Away from the reactors and other visual reminders of the deep sickness contaminating the earth, the Chernobyl Exclusion Zone struck me as remarkably unremarkable. Its lanes, forests and meadows were green and filled with nature, while the warm sun that shone throughout that trip did a lot to dispel any lingering sense of disease. The Zone's administrative centre in Chornobyl town, though sparsely inhabited, had the same sleepy atmosphere and the same shabby utilitarian architecture as any other provincial Soviet town. ('Chornobyl' is the Ukrainian spelling of this place-name. While the Russian form, 'Chernobyl', was officially used for the plant and has become synonymous with the disaster, throughout this book the Ukrainian spelling of 'Chornobyl' will be used to specify the town, as it remains an active settlement and this spelling is typically preferred by those who live there.) Our state-run hotel was just off the main street, along which could also be found a canteen, sports club, post office, police station, and a statue of Vladimir Lenin. Chipped murals decorated building façades, their colours long since drained of energy. Outside the market, where workers stood and smoked and drank espresso from paper cups, the once fresh 1970s signage had faded almost to illegibility.

The abandoned villages of the broader Zone were indistinguishable from empty villages I had seen elsewhere in Eastern Europe. Nikolai told me how Ukraine's population had dropped by 10 million since its independence from the Soviet Union. Young Ukrainians had moved to the cities, or left to work abroad, while the rural villages grew old then faded to ruins. He told me that even if the disaster had never happened, many of these villages would have looked like this by now. Pripyat was the exception: in the new city built to house the power plant's workers, the sheer scale of abandonment was unlike anything I had seen before.

I didn't realise we were in Pripyat until we had almost reached its centre. What was once a broad two-lane

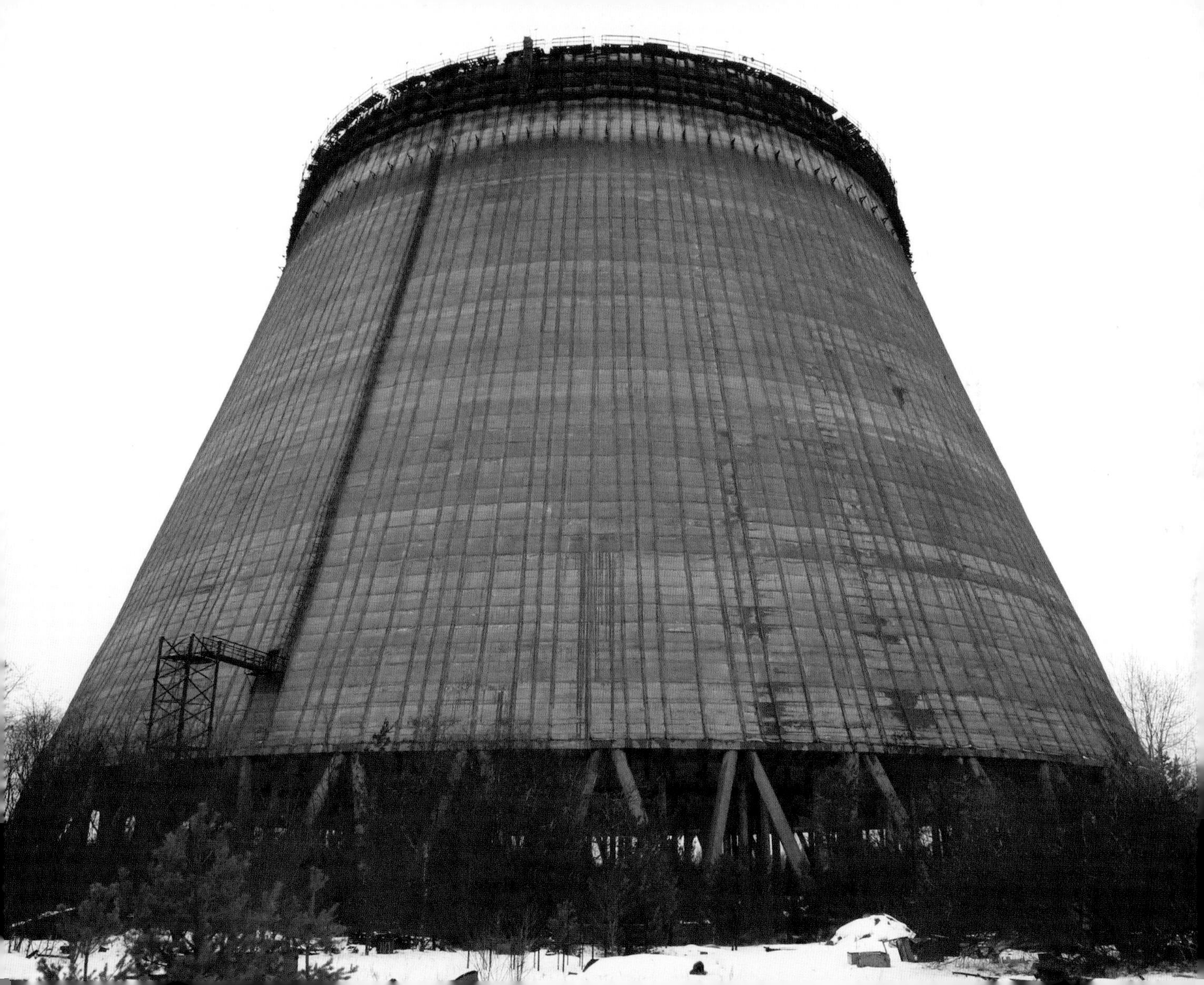

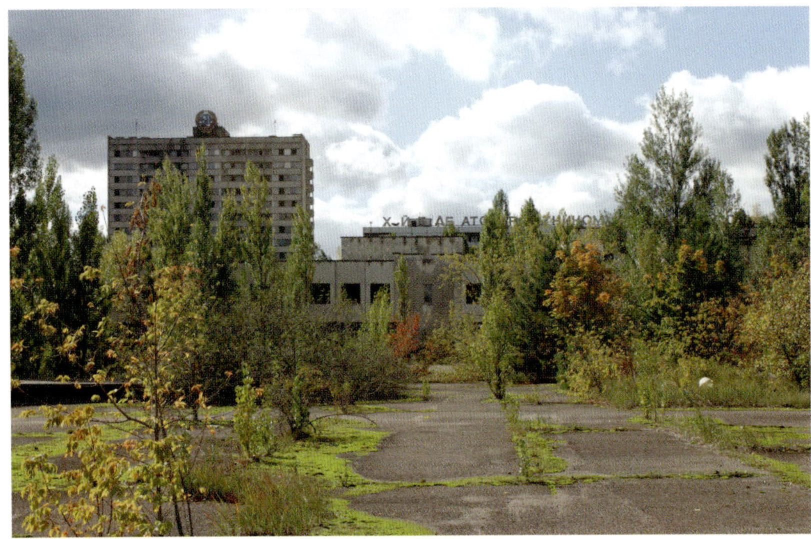

boulevard flanked by wide pavements and grass verges had been reduced to a single-lane track between trees. It was only as I peered through the bus window into the hedgerows that I began to spot the walls of buildings hidden behind the greenery. As we pulled into the main square, the space suddenly opened up to reveal an entire abandoned city. Even in this state of decay, Pripyat had personality, an immediate sense of place and identity: the bold, angular shapes of the buildings, the marble tiles and textured surfaces of bush-hammered concrete, the subdued palette of greys and magnolia. Ahead of us across the weed-infested plaza rose the Modernist bulk of the former Palace of Culture, with 'Polissya' Hotel to our right, and to our left, a sixteen-storey tower block topped with a giant hammer and sickle. It was the most thoroughly sovietised city I had ever seen, and yet in being so besieged by the forest, it also felt somehow removed from history altogether.

The bus doors popped open and our group tumbled out, spreading across the square with cameras rapidly clicking. The bodies moving through this space enabled me to make more sense of its scale, and I tried to picture it as it must have been three decades ago, with chairs and tables spilling out of busy cafés, and young families strolling through the city centre. Like everyone else, I had expected to find a dystopia here, but it was quite the opposite of this – the bittersweet ghosts of a would-be utopia – that greeted me instead.

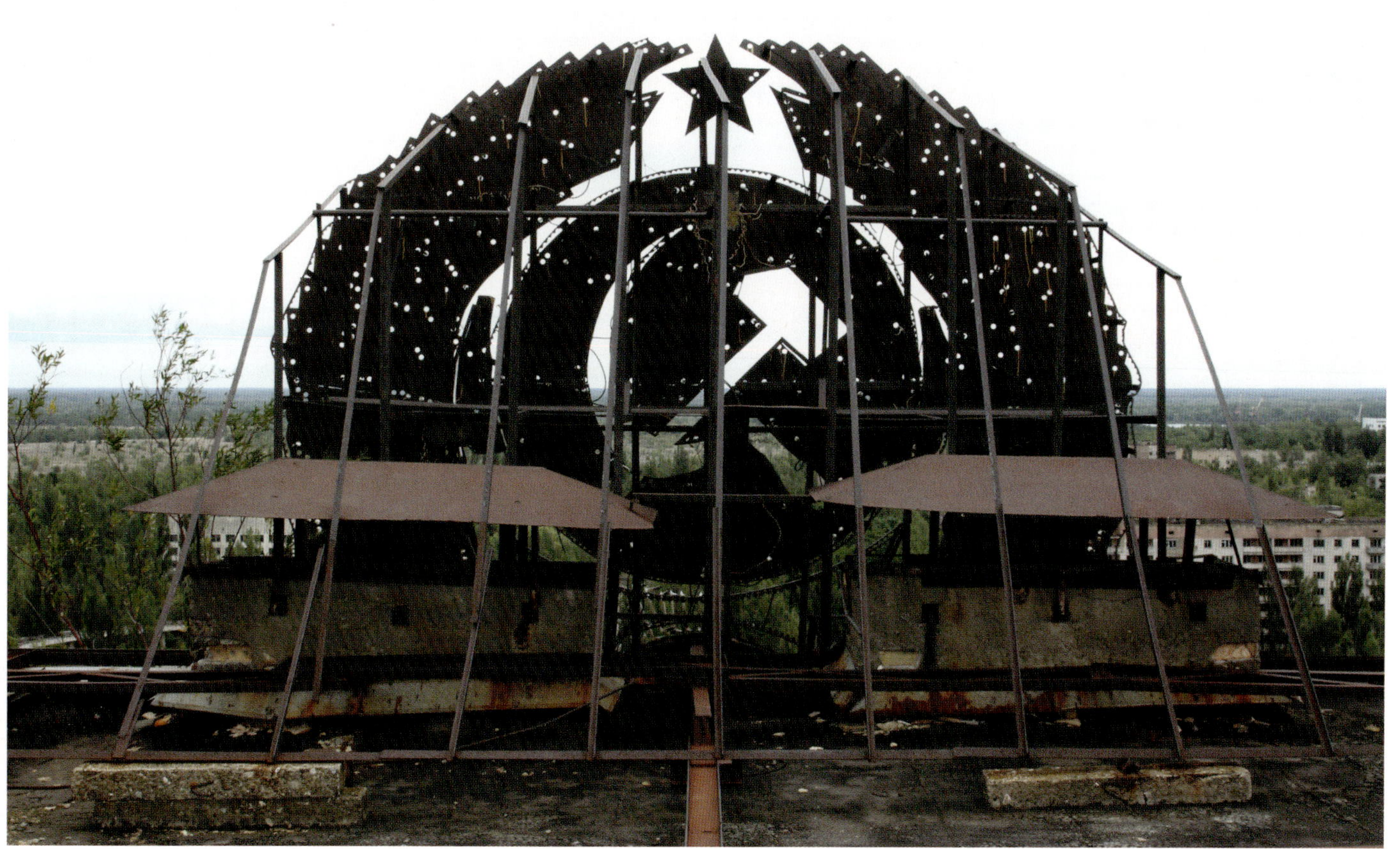

A CITY FOR MARX AND PROMETHEUS

The city rose up all at once from the marsh. Where storks and frogs and snakes had held dominion, there appeared a proud new utopia, purpose-built to serve the needs of the socialist proletariat in their pursuit of atomic science.

Founded on 4 February 1970, Pripyat was what the Soviets called an 'atomgrad'. These were atomic cities, dedicated to nuclear research, power generation and, more often than not, weapons manufacture. Typically they were closed, military-guarded cities, impossible to enter or leave without permission. Many had coded addresses instead of city names and some didn't even appear on maps. The first atomgrad, Chelyabinsk-40 (later called Chelyabinsk-65, and now Ozyorsk), was founded on 9 November 1945 near Chelyabinsk in Russia; its plutonium-producing reactors would establish it as the home of the Soviet nuclear-weapons programme for years to come. It was swiftly followed by new atomgrads such as Krasnoyarsk-26 (its city crest depicting a bear tearing an atom apart in its claws); Arzamas-16, Tomsk-7 and Tryokhgorny; Krasnoyarsk-45, equipped with three nuclear reactors and a gaseous diffusion enrichment plant, built inside tunnels excavated using Gulag labour; and Chelyabinsk-70, home to the Institute of Technical Physics, where nuclear warheads were developed.[5]

Pripyat was the Soviet Union's ninth atomgrad. It was built in the marshes close to the Ukrainian-Belarusian border, on the site of the Kalinin Collective Farm at Semikhody, an old village near the regional town of Chornobyl. The location had a good supply of water, with space for growth and reasonable proximity to three national capitals. This new atomgrad housed the workers of the V. I. Lenin Nuclear Power Plant – later more commonly referred to as the Chernobyl Nuclear Power Plant, or ChNPP – whose first reactor began producing power in 1977. Three more reactors followed (in 1978, 1981 and 1983), capable of producing 1,000 Megawatts electric (MWe) each. Purportedly the plan was to build eight more, so that the complete complex would have consisted of twelve reactors whose output – had such a plan been realised – would have exceeded that of the largest nuclear plant in the world today.

Pripyat, whose name derives from the river that flows through the marshlands, was given official city-status in 1979. Like many Soviet atomgrads before it, its architecture was festooned with atomic symbolism. Atom signs appeared in mosaics and murals, and were worked into the wrought-iron fences around schools and laboratories – they became as ubiquitous here as the stars, hammers and sickles that decorated regular Soviet cities. However, unlike most other atomgrads, Pripyat was never a closed city: its residents were free to come and go. Wages were higher than the Soviet average, and Pripyat's shops were stocked with 'exotic' foreign foods, high-quality homeware and consumer electronics. Pripyat had a young population, with an average age of twenty-six, and a thriving social scene: it had two

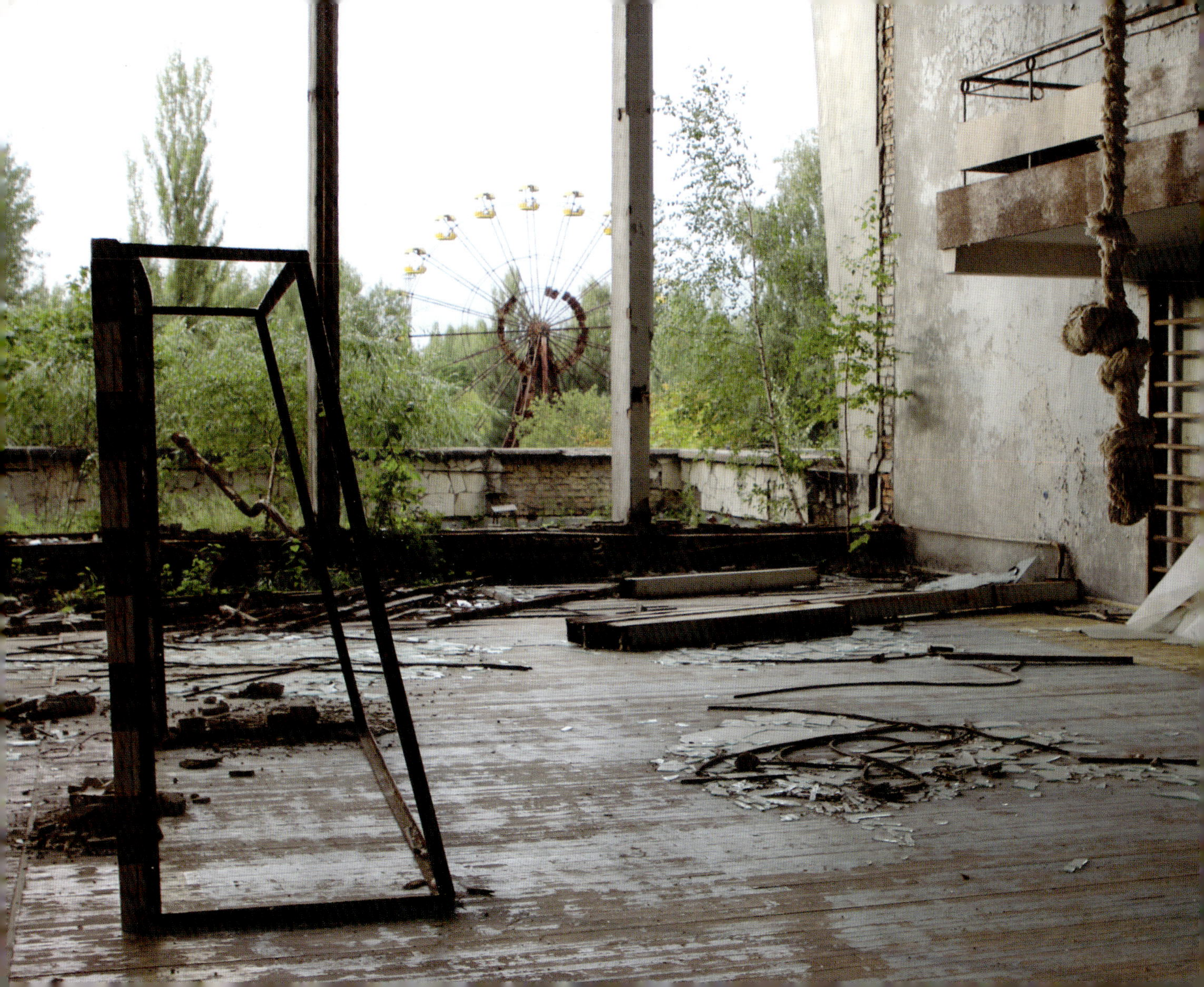

sports stadiums, three indoor pools, a cinema, ten gyms, twenty-seven dining venues, and the 'Energetik' Palace of Culture.[6] The city even fielded a respectable football team, FC 'Stroitel' Pripyat – 'the Builders' – who in 1981 appointed the former USSR international striker Anatoliy Shepel as their manager.[7]

Pripyat was also a fundamentally Marxist city. In older cities – Moscow or Kyiv – the Soviets had planted their stars on top of the palaces of former regimes; but Pripyat provided an opportunity to build a new system from the ground up, and the design of the atomgrad reflected a radical new vision for the organisation of society. Public facilities were distributed with an almost algorithmic logic. Each of the city's five micro-districts consisted of utilitarian housing blocks clustered around a nucleus of shops and parks. These were tessellated around a central plaza featuring the Palace of Culture, 'Pollisya' Hotel, and the city's administrative buildings. Each micro-district had its own secondary school, while the provision of fifteen kindergartens reflected a culture where both parents would go out to work, with childcare considered a community concern. Residents invariably worked at the nearby power plant, in hospitality trades, or at one of the four factories surrounding the city – the largest of which was the Jupiter Factory, producing audio equipment and electrical components.[6]

The atomic city stood out against the flat horizon of the marshlands, and in many ways was completely at odds with the surrounding communities. The official language at the plant was Russian, whereas many locals spoke Ukrainian at home. Pripyat was the very epitome of a modern Soviet city – atheist and utilitarian – yet lifestyles in nearby villages had changed relatively little in a century, and many still had an Orthodox church at their centre. However, Pripyat was not entirely without its own mystical dedication. Near the river stood the 'Prometheus' Cinema, outside of which in the plaza rose a 6-metre bronze statue of Prometheus himself, the Titan of Greek mythology, holding aloft a burst of fiery, plasma-like energy.

According to myth, Prometheus stole fire from the gods and gave it to mankind. However, Zeus, the king of the gods, was displeased, punishing Prometheus by binding him to a rock where an eagle would descend and peck out his liver, only for it to grow back again each day so the cycle of torture would be repeated. The Titan was linked to communist ideology as early as 1841, when Karl Marx wrote: 'Prometheus is the most eminent saint and martyr in the philosophical calendar.'[8] For Marx, Prometheus was code for seizing the means of production from the bourgeoisie. Sociologist Victoria E. Bonnell explains: 'whereas Hercules served to symbolize the sans culottes in the iconography of the French Revolution, the Russian proletariat sometimes became associated during the Civil War years with the Titan Prometheus... The sovietization of the Prometheus myth had the proletariat bound to the rock of capitalism and

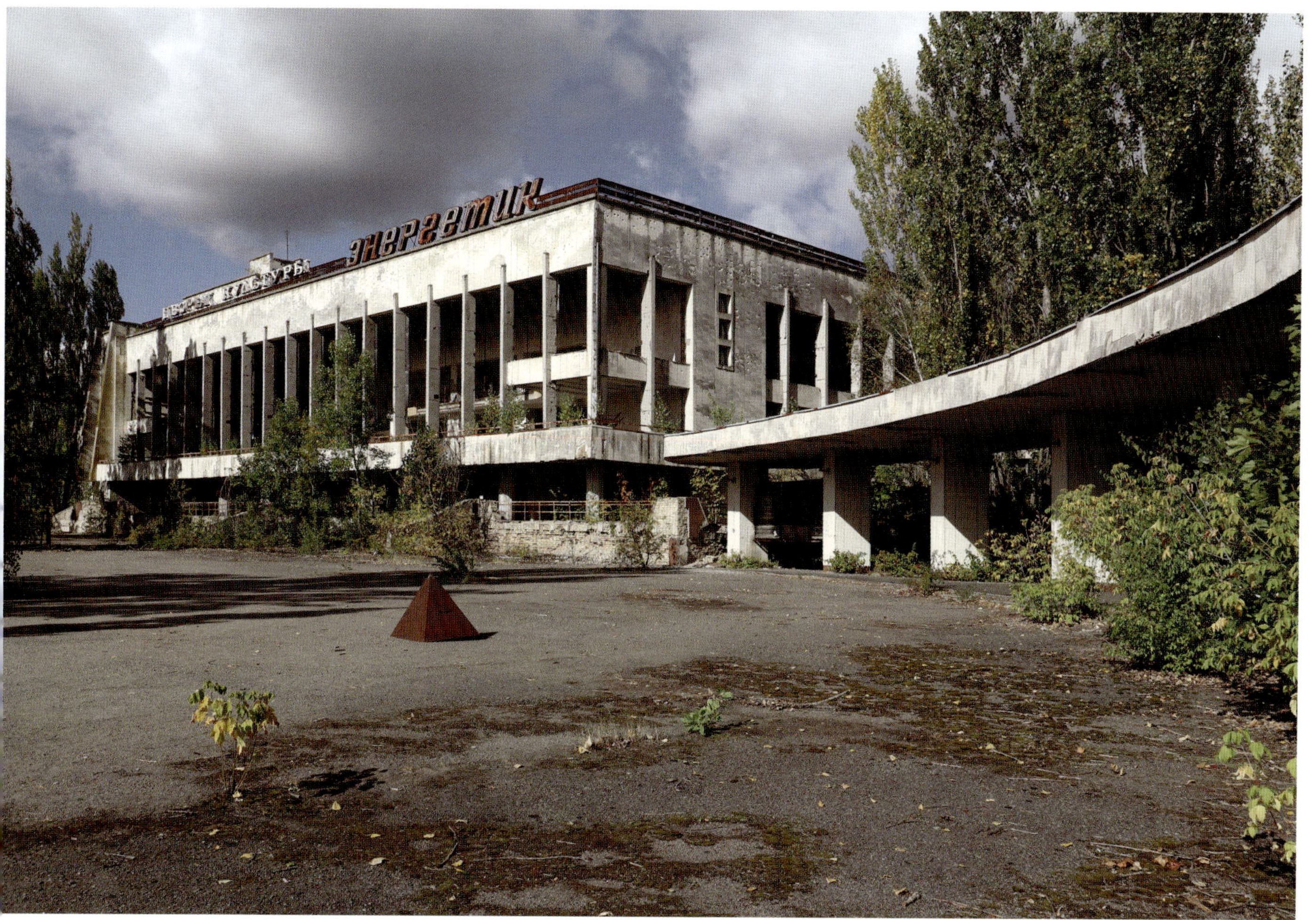

ЭНЕРГЕТИК
ДВОРЕЦ КУЛЬТУРЫ

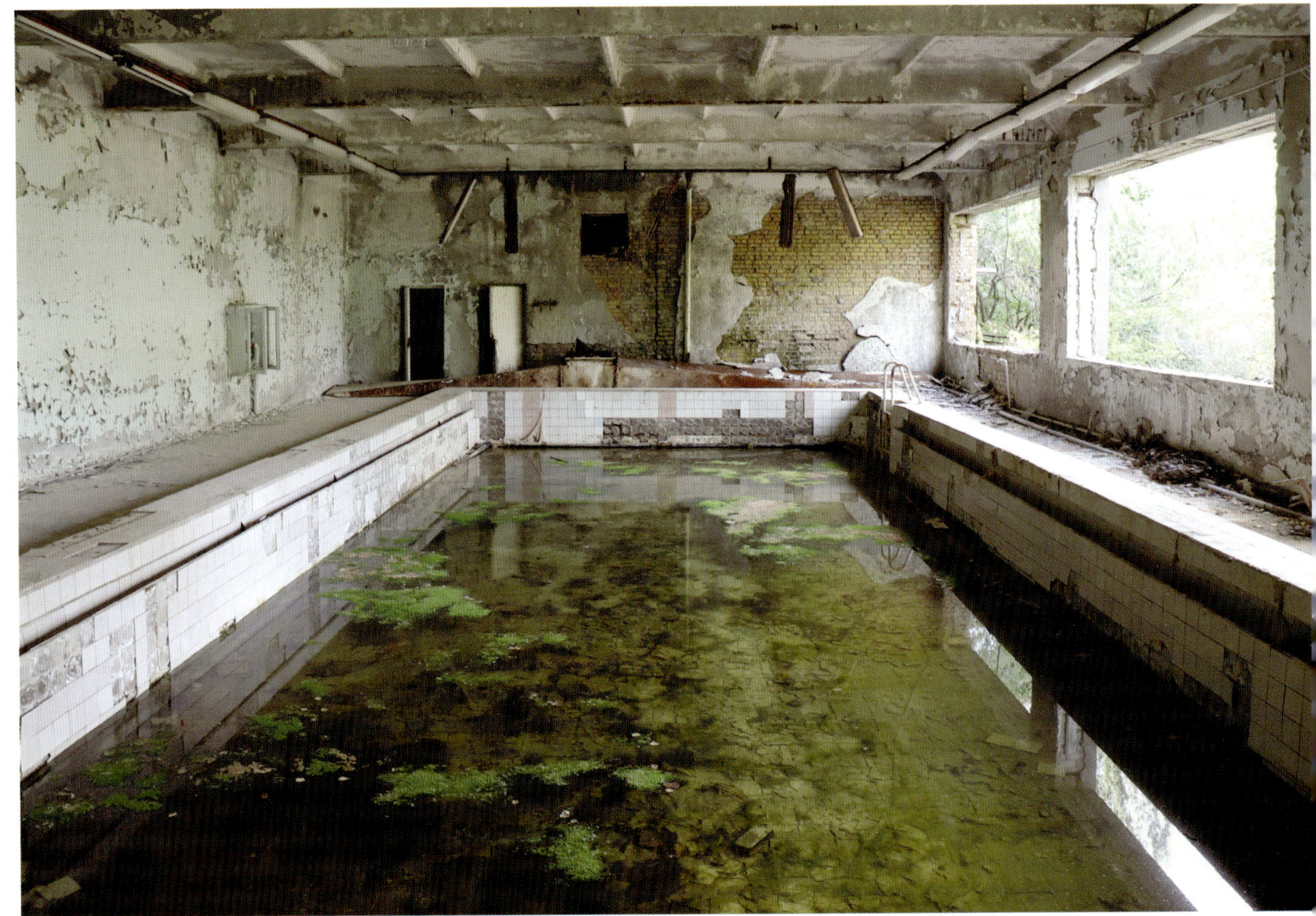

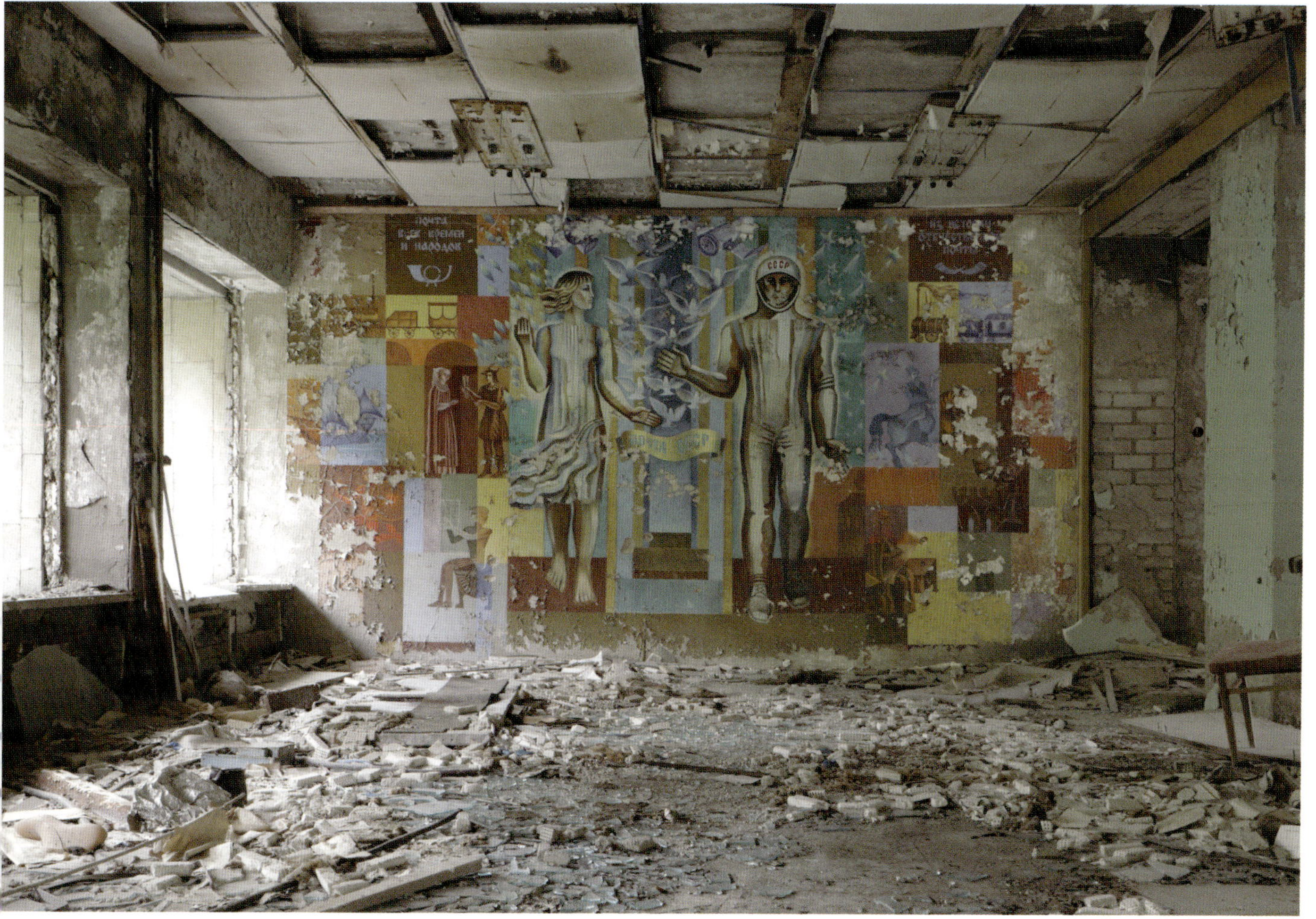

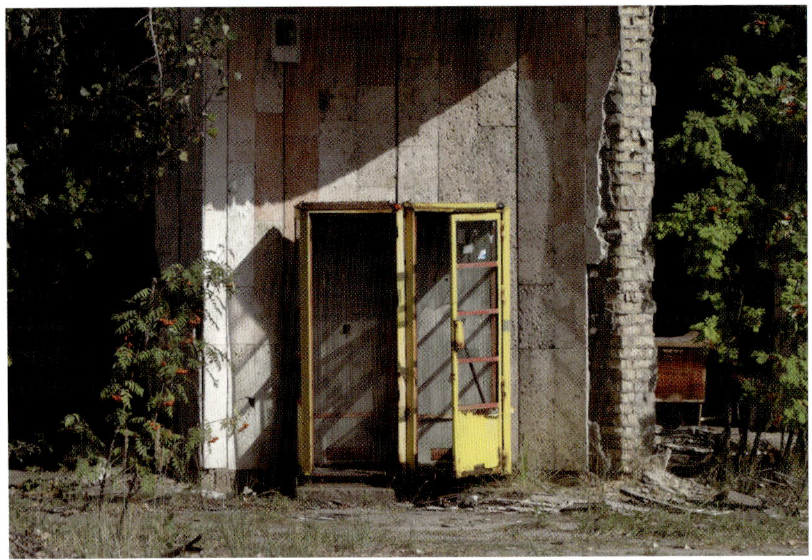

attacked by an eagle, the official emblem of the old regime.'9

Symbols of Prometheus appeared in architecture throughout the Communist bloc. At Dniprodzerzhynsk (now Kamianske) in Ukraine, a monument titled *Prometheus Unbound* – with the Titan holding a torch and broken chains – was raised on the fifth anniversary of the October Revolution at the entrance to a metallurgic plant. He was often associated with the generation of power, places that 'stole fire from the gods'. In Ceauşescu's Romania, a Prometheus monument was erected above Vidraru Hydroelectric Dam. Another guarded the nuclear power plant at Novovoronezh in Russia, while in the Estonian SSR, a statue of him was raised in the centre of Sillamäe, a closed city involved in the extraction and enrichment of uranium for use in Soviet nuclear power plants and weapons facilities. In the story, the Titan's stolen flame had brought warmth and light to the homes of men, but it had also fired their blacksmiths' forges. In Sillamäe, Prometheus held an atom instead of a flame, while the Pripyat Prometheus suggested that in this new Soviet atomgrad, as in Ancient Greece, military might and self-determination were inextricably linked.

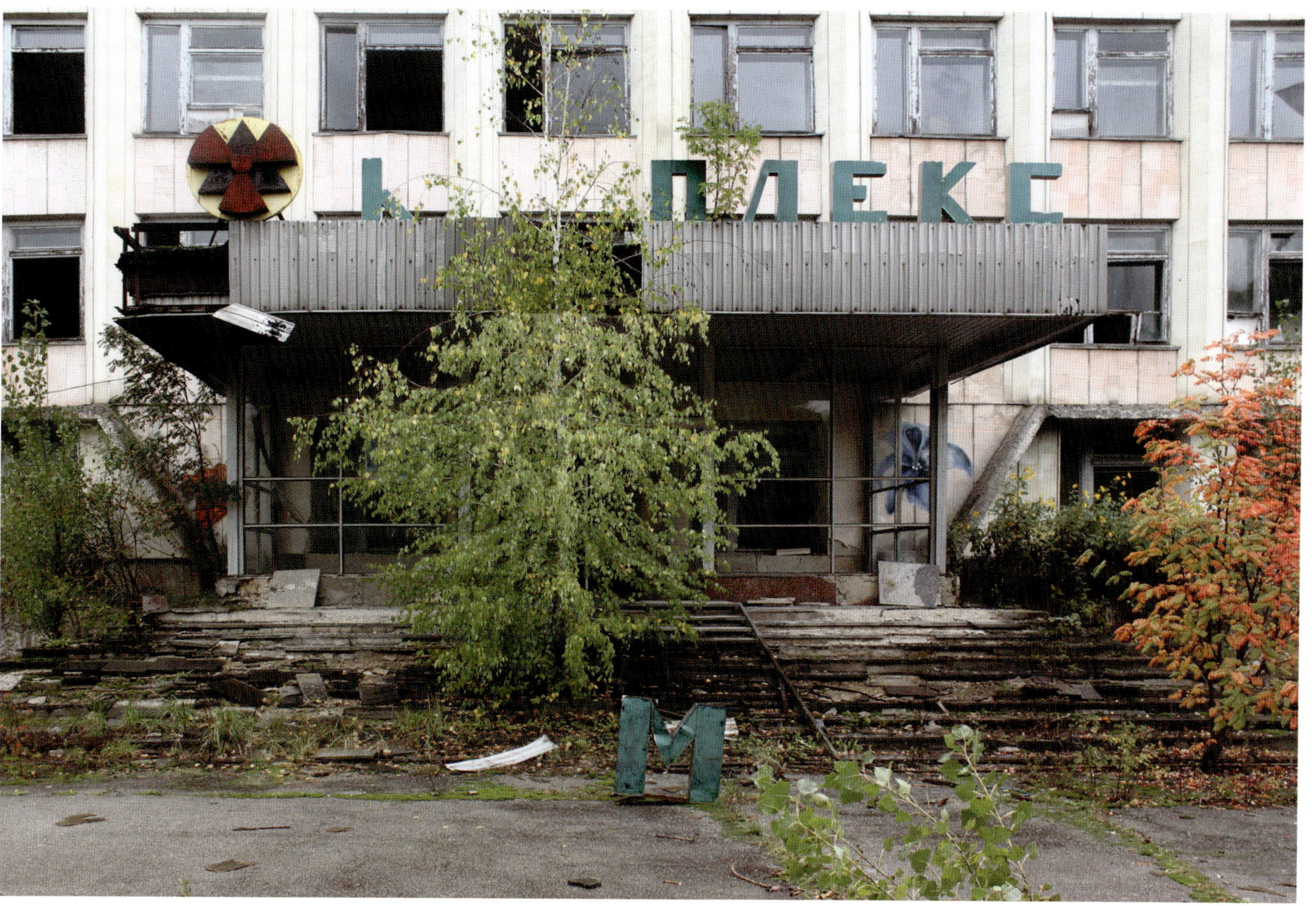

ПЛЕКС

THE PRIPYAT MYTH

What surprised me most about Pripyat's shops, schools and hospital wards was how inauthentic they felt. Gas masks dangled from light fittings. Dolls and other toys sat propped in creepy poses on wireframe beds, like B-rated horror movie props. Prior to my visit, I had read an article that described how 'children's dolls are scattered about, left where their young owners dropped them in a hurry a quarter of a century ago.'[10] I watched my own group wade through the ruins, cameras in hand, constantly rearranging the artefacts to create new and original compositions. I imagined these actions multiplied by thousands of photographers each year, and suddenly the notion of an untouched Pripyat seemed laughably naive. There were moments of plausible truth along the way (miniature, self-contained stories, like the upright piano abandoned on the seventh floor of an apartment building, too big for the elevators, too heavy to drag down the stairs), but for the most part, the interior spaces of Pripyat looked like bad taxidermy.

This wasn't purely the work of tourists. In *Voices from Chernobyl*, Belarusian journalist Svetlana Alexievich quotes a local man as saying: 'Newspaper reporters flocked to us, took photographs with cheap effects. The window of an abandoned home: they would put a violin on the sill and call it Chernobyl Symphony. There was no need to invent anything.'[11]

I wondered if some of these objects hadn't even originated from Pripyat. Some of the books and stuffed animals, in particular, seemed far too fresh to have weathered twenty-seven winters here. I asked my guide if the tour companies ever arranged these scenes themselves, but Nikolai dismissed the question. 'Maybe the stalkers do it,' he said, defensively. 'Who knows?'

In a sense though, the promise of Pripyat was always, essentially, a lie. 'Let the atom be a worker, not a soldier,' read a slogan facing down onto Pripyat's central square. However, the Chernobyl plant had been specifically equipped with RBMK reactors capable of producing large quantities of weapons-grade plutonium, and plant workers, if not the population at large, would presumably have recognised such slogans for hypocrisy. Even the Jupiter Factory, it was later rumoured, had used consumer electronics as a smokescreen for its production of military-use semiconductor components.

As the Soviet Union's westernmost atomgrad – culturally as well as geographically – Pripyat served as a Potemkin village (a deceitful façade) for the whole atomgrad programme. Outsiders who came to visit this open city would marvel at the blessed lives of these Soviet nuclear engineers, while in reality the workers in those atomgrads not marked on maps often lived in incredibly hazardous environments. For example, one 1992 study stated that 8,015 people had been killed over three decades as a result of the 1957 Kyshtym disaster at Chelyabinsk-40.[12] Even the correctly functioning atomgrads were toxic, as Boris Komarov warned:

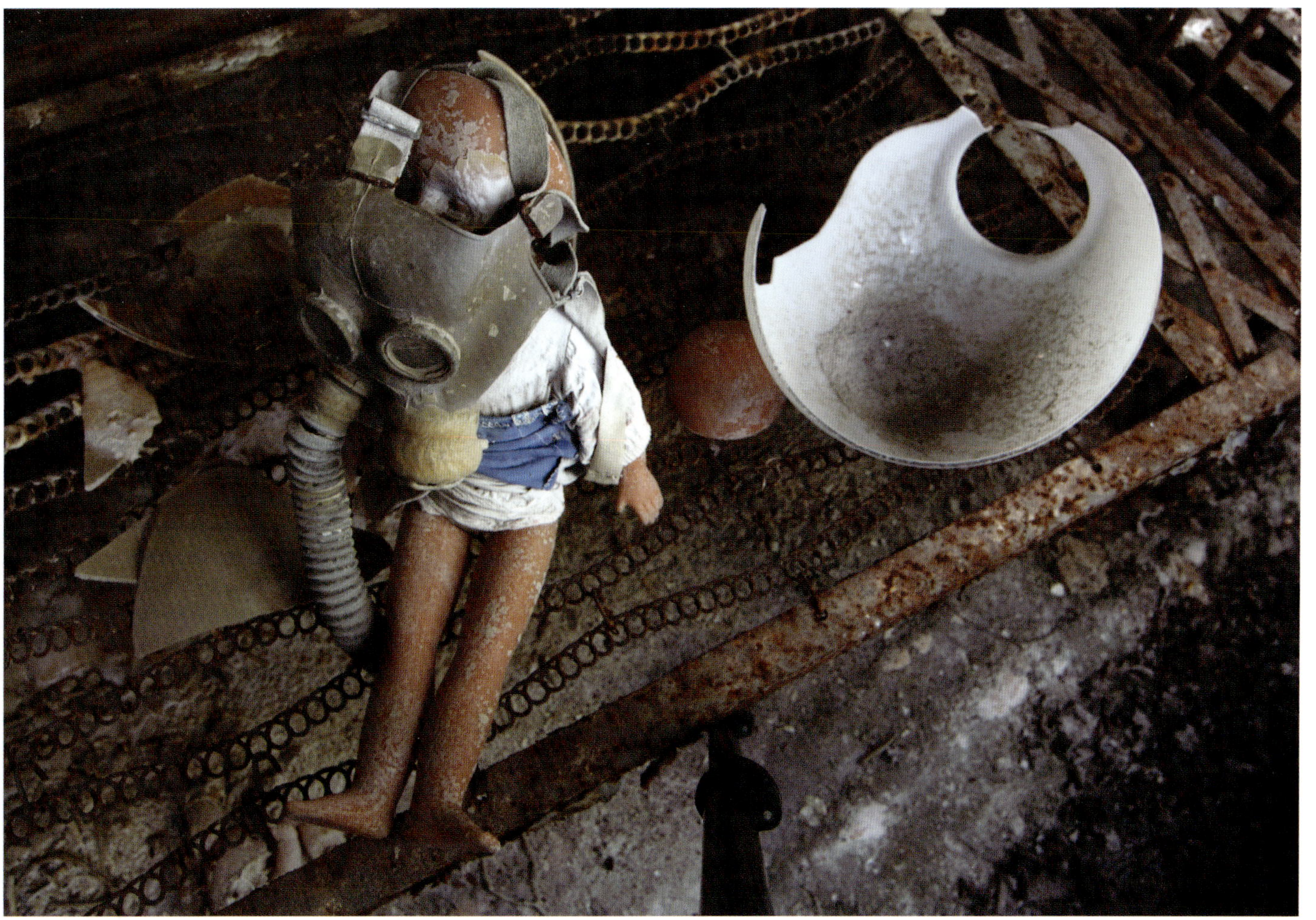

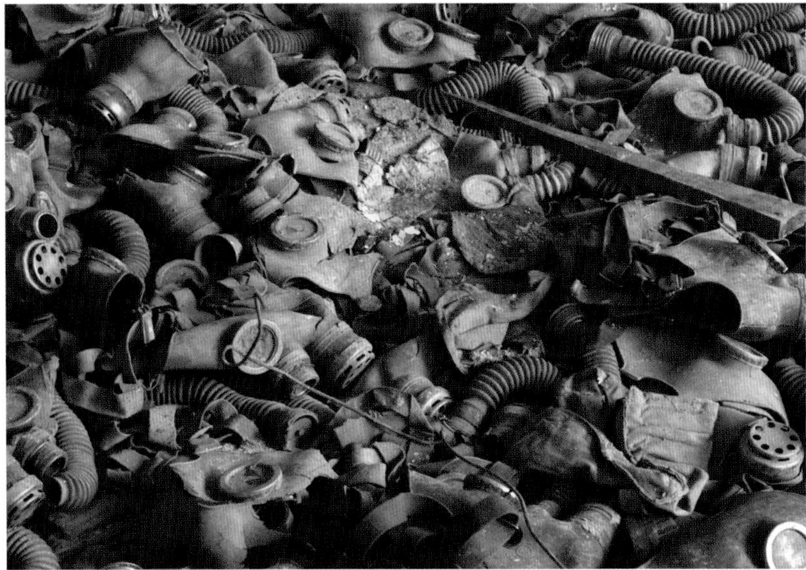

left: Middle School No. 3, Pripyat. These gas masks were not used during evacuation. Some have been dismantled by looters, in the belief that their filters contained trace amounts of silver. Others have been added to the pile by visiting photographers.

right: Fire Station, Chernobyl-2 military-scientific complex. This scale model of the Duga array and its surrounding buildings was used by firefighters for training purposes.

'To concentrate uranium requires thousands of tons of sulphuric acid… Before it even produces one kilowatt of energy, an atomic power plant is more costly to the natural environment than all other forms of energy production.'[13]

Anatoli Alexandrov, a Russian physicist and director of the Kurchatov Institute (the leading Soviet nuclear-research centre) once claimed that a nuclear reactor was as safe as a samovar – and Pripyat was the PR-friendly atomgrad that opened its doors to prove this to the public. However, for all this supposed transparency, ChNPP was also powering something far more secretive.

Deep in the forest, 9 kilometres from the plant, stood a secret, closed city known only as Chernobyl-2. Despite officially not existing, the settlement had a permanent population – barracks for soldiers and apartments for officers, scientists, and their families – with a school, fire station, shops, and a club, all contained within a high-security perimeter fence. Secret or not, Chernobyl-2 couldn't help but draw attention to itself as, rising out of this military base, the sinister, skeletal form of a vast radar array broke through the trees to dominate the surrounding landscape. Measuring 150 metres high by some 750 metres in length (as tall as a

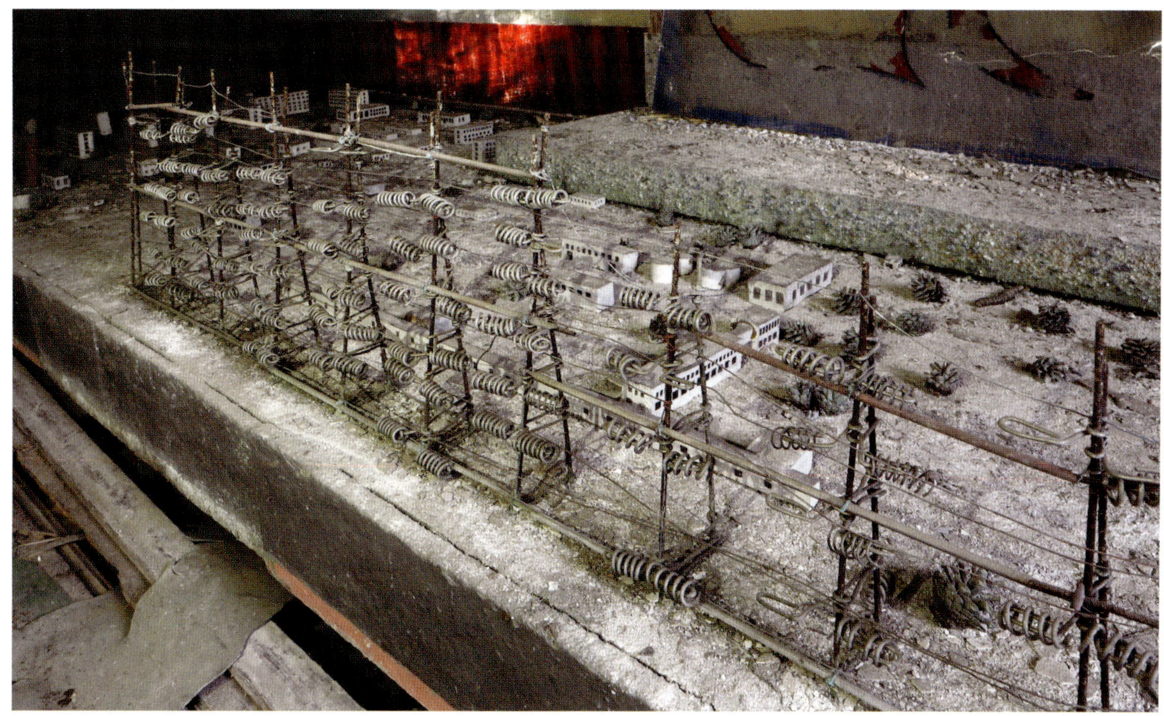

skyscraper, as long as seven football fields), the radar installation pointed north-west and was known – at least, among those authorised to know – by the codename 'Duga-1' (the Russian word for 'Arc'). The radar was one of three installations which at that time represented the pinnacle of the Soviet anti-ballistic missile early-warning network. The original site, 'Duga-N', was a smaller array located in southern Ukraine near Mykolaiv. A third installation, 'Duga-2', was erected near Komsomolsk-on-Amur in the south-eastern most part of Russia. All the arrays faced outwards, listening for American missiles.[14, 15]

'No one called it *Duga* back then, just *Antenna*. Though on maps it was marked *Abandoned Pioneer Camp*,' says Alexey Moskalenko, formerly a chief inspector with the

Pripyat police. 'As you turned to Chernobyl-2, there was a road sign: "Entry forbidden". You could be stopped and prosecuted for trespassing on that road. Everybody knew what was there though… By 1985 it was creating interference on TV sets in Pripyat. When we used our police radio, all the citizens could hear us through their television sets, as if we were broadcasting to them.' Moskalenko also said that post and other deliveries to the radar station were addressed to Korolyova Street, Chornobyl, 'but Chornobyl had no such street.'

The Duga-1 radar consisted of two sites that worked in tandem: the receiver at Chernobyl-2, and a transmitter at Liubech-1, a closed city in the Chernihiv region. According to one of the Duga's chief engineers, Valery Alebastrov, the transmitter consumed 1.5 megawatts while the receiver ran at 0.5 megawatts, between them roughly equivalent to the power consumption of 1,600 homes today.[16] Using signals broadcast on shortwave radio bands, this system was able to detect launches around the globe within two or three minutes, by monitoring the disturbances that missiles made on passing through the earth's ionosphere. Alebastrov claims the team tracked more than a hundred missile launches worldwide and were developing new algorithms to help them detect aircraft movements as far away as the UK. Beginning in July 1976, the transmissions from Duga-1 could be heard in the 5 to 28 megahertz frequency range, a short, sharp tapping noise that led shortwave radio hams in the West to nickname the unidentified source the 'Russian Woodpecker.'[14, 17, 18]

Meanwhile in the atomgrad, residents got on with their lives: they knew better than to ask questions. When they weren't working at the Soviet Union's most prestigious new energy-production plant, these atomic citizens would spend their days in cafés by the riverside, watching sports fixtures or taking in theatre performances at the Palace of Culture. By spring 1986, the city was at peak growth, with almost 50,000 residents. With a thousand more born in Pripyat hospital every year, two new housing districts were already under construction. Banners and decorations had gone up to mark the 27th Congress of the Communist Party of the Soviet Union (held in Moscow, from 25 February until 6 March), and these would stay up until International Workers' Day on 1 May. The city was in festival mode. The power plant's director, Viktor Bryukhanov, had 30,000 rose bushes planted down the main boulevard, and a brand new Ferris Wheel stood waiting for its grand holiday opening.[19] Pripyat's citizens counted down the days to the celebration.

Duga-1 radar array, Chernobyl-2, detail showing the bowtie-shaped 'vibrators' on this colossal Soviet over-the-horizon radar receiver.

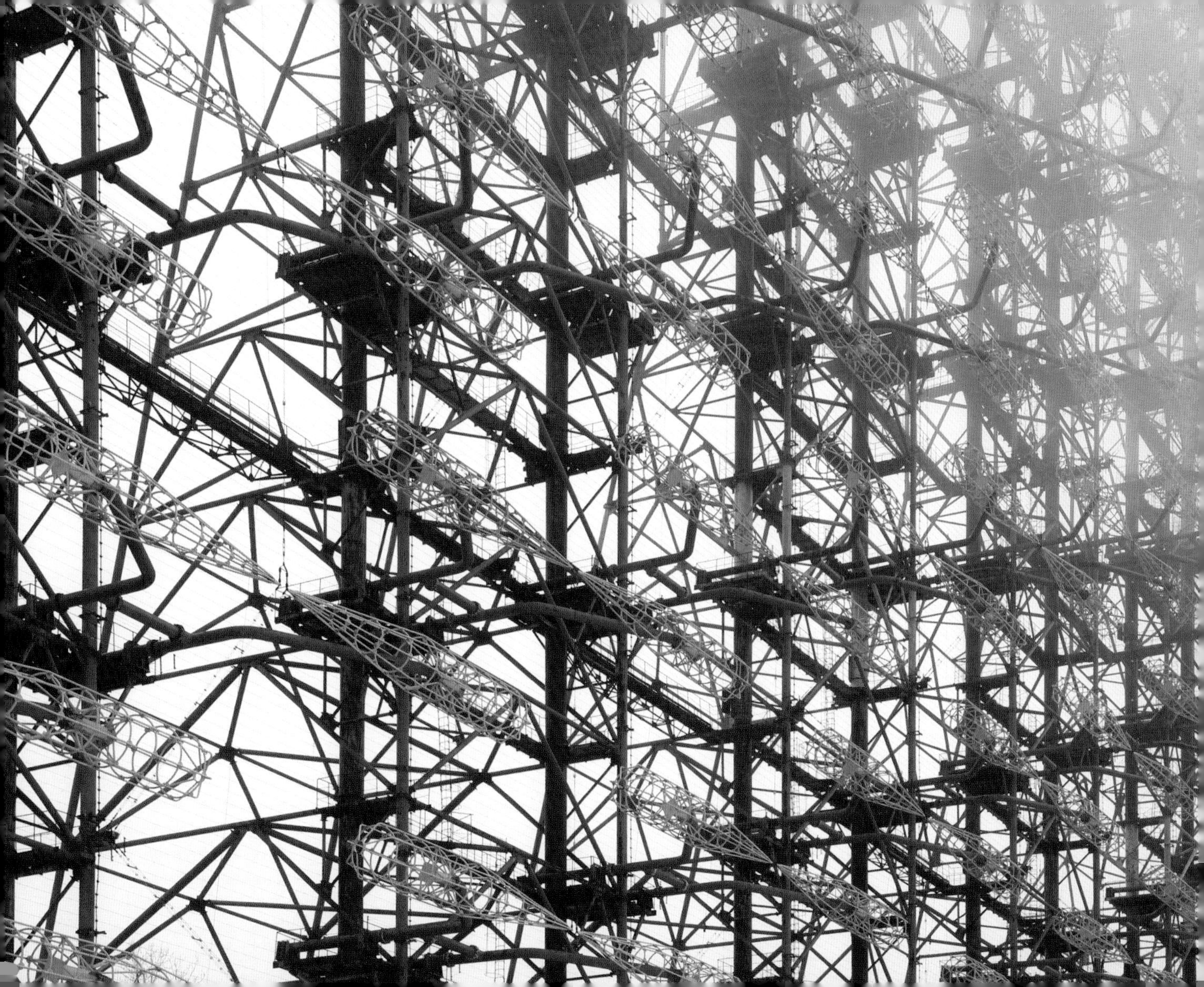

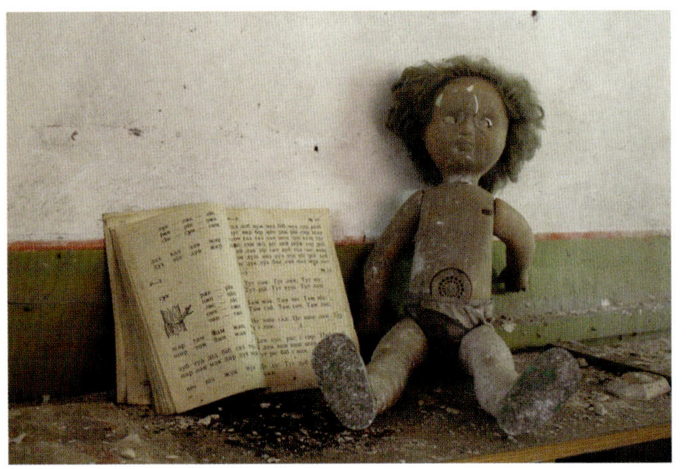

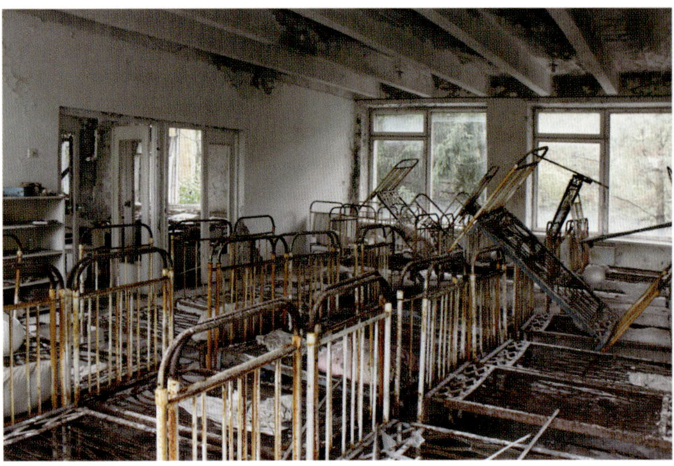

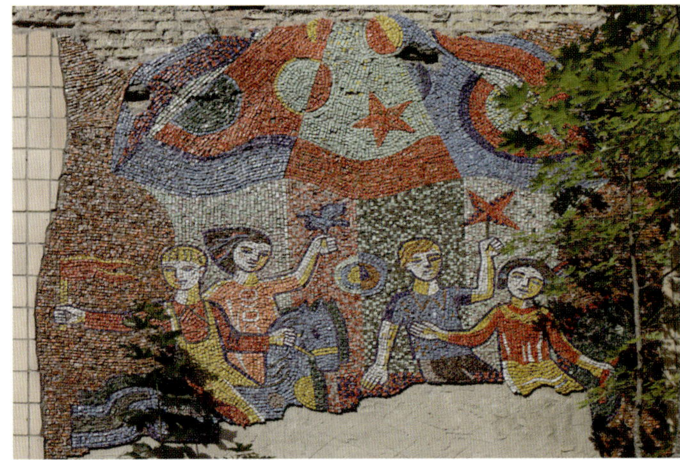

top left: Kindergarten, Kopachi village.
top right: Kindergarten No.7 'Zolotoy Klyuchik' ('Golden Key'), Pripyat.
bottom: Kindergarten No.5 'Medvezhonok' ('Teddy Bear'), Pripyat, a mosaic on the outside wall.

top right: Duga-1 radar array, Chernobyl-2, views from the radar's base, and from a maintenance gantry halfway up the structure.
bottom right: Pripyat Bus Station, Pripyat Café.

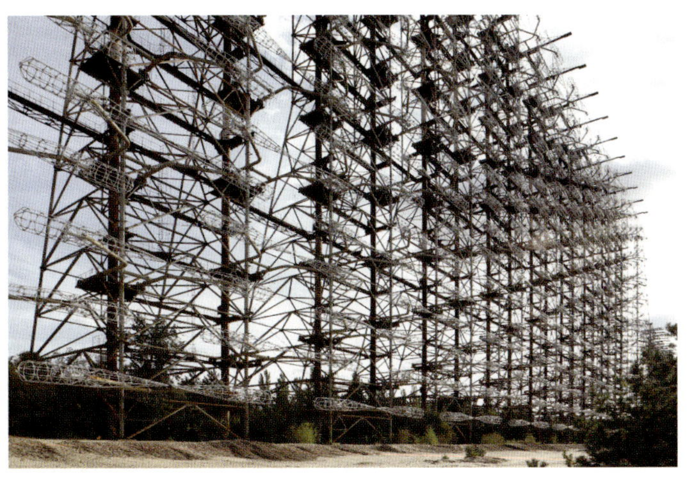
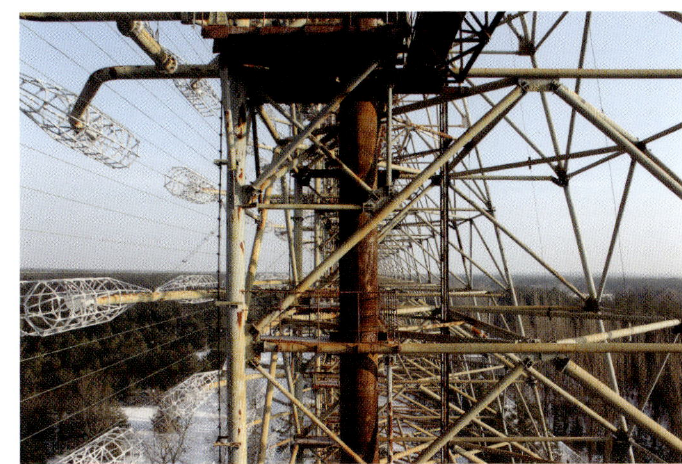
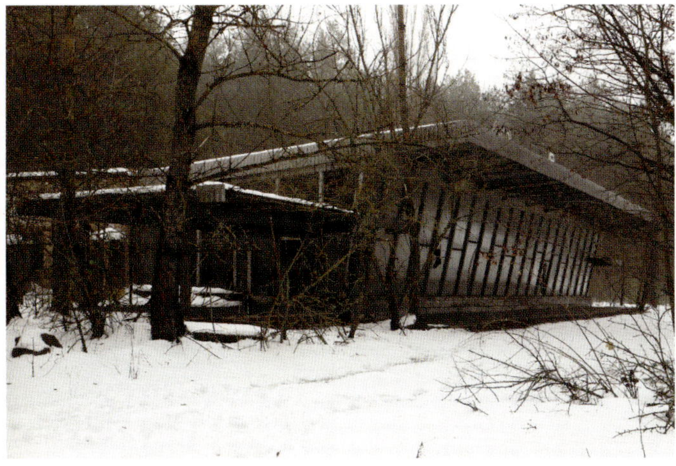
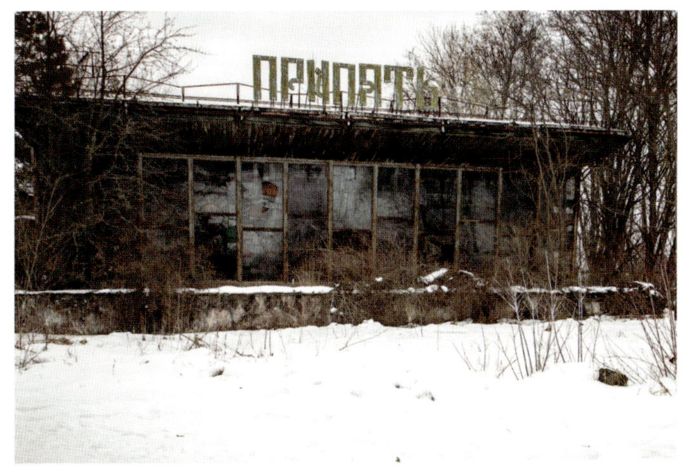
ПРИПЯТЬ

3. WORMWOOD STAR

THE PROPHECY

Seven hundred and seventy-seven years before the founding of Pripyat, Chornobyl was first mentioned in a charter of the Kievan Rus of 1193. Its name came from the plant that grew profusely in the region: *Artemisia vulgaris*, which the locals called 'polyn', as well as 'chornobyl' or 'chornobylnik' (derived from the Ukrainian words for 'black' and 'stalk'). In English the same plant is known as mugwort or wormwood.

Chornobyl would change hands over the centuries, alternating between Lithuanian, Polish and Russian control. By the late 18th century the population was largely a mixture of Ukrainian Orthodox Christians and Polish Catholics, with a growing community of Hasidic Jews. The Chornobyl Hasidic dynasty was founded by Rabbi Menachem Nachum Twersky – the 'Maggid of Chornobyl' – and under his leadership the town became an important centre of Judaism in the region.

Outsiders are quick to associate the town of Chornobyl with the disaster in 1986. However, in terms of the number of lives lost, that nuclear meltdown and its aftermath were only the third-worst thing to befall the Chornobyl region in the 20th century. During the years 1932-33, Ukraine fell victim to what is referred to as the 'Holodomor', a mass famine that many historians contend was deliberately engineered by Stalin (an understanding that was passed into law by the Ukrainian parliament in 2006, when the denial of Holodomor was criminalised). This act resulted in the deaths of millions (including by execution, when they 'stole' from the fields to feed their starving families),[1] and hit agrarian communities like Chornobyl particularly hard. Then, just eight years later, the area fell under Nazi occupation, with the majority of local Jews being arrested and sent to various concentration camps in the region. Brigades of Red Army partisans fought against Nazi occupation from hidden bases established in the forest surrounding Chornobyl.[2]

Deep in the same forest stood an old pine tree in the shape of a cross, with horizontal boughs sprouting at right angles from either side of its trunk. The tree, already fully mature by the time of the Great Patriotic War (1941-45), was important to local Christians as it recalled for them a particular story from the Orthodox tradition: the three angels of the Old Testament who announced to Abraham the imminent destruction of the sinful cities of Sodom and Gomorrah left their staffs with him, and he in turn gave them to his nephew Lot, who planted them in the ground outside Jerusalem where they grew into a triple-trunked tree composed of three types of wood – cedar, pine, and cypress. King Solomon later had the tree cut down, while building his great temple. It was also said that wood from this same tree was used to make Christ's cross.[3] During the wartime occupation, Chornobyl's cruciform tree became a symbol of sacrifice in its own right, with local stories of the Nazis using it as a gallows for captured partisans.[2]

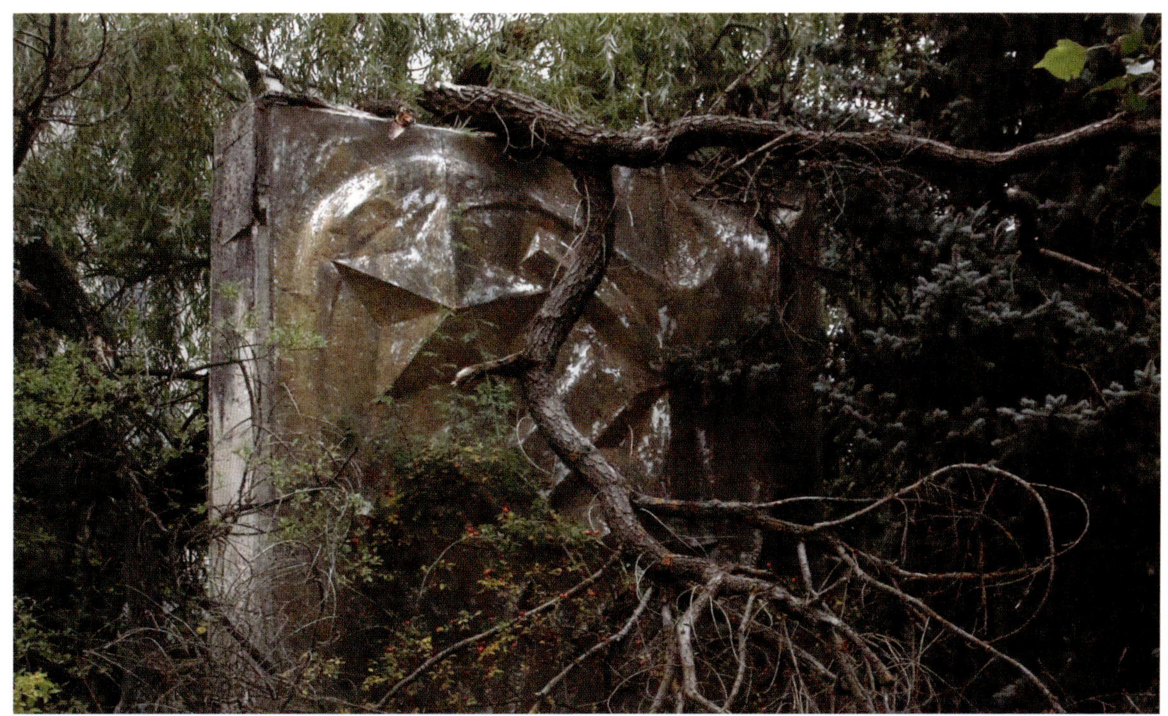

By the end of the war, the majority of Chornobyl's Jewish population had been killed. 'Antifascism' became a new political buzzword which the Soviet leadership used to unite the disparate republics of the Eastern Bloc. The actions of Nazi Germany were framed as anti-Soviet rather than anti-Semitic, and particular discussion of the Jewish experience was discouraged. As a result, the significance of the Holocaust was downplayed, and the universal Soviet proletariat was presented as the chief victim of the war. Monuments were built to commemorate the victims of Nazi occupation, the Soviet Red Army, and the antifascist partisans, but no special emphasis was placed on the Jewish victims – even in Chornobyl, a once significant Jewish settlement. The town's main synagogue was repurposed as an administrative office

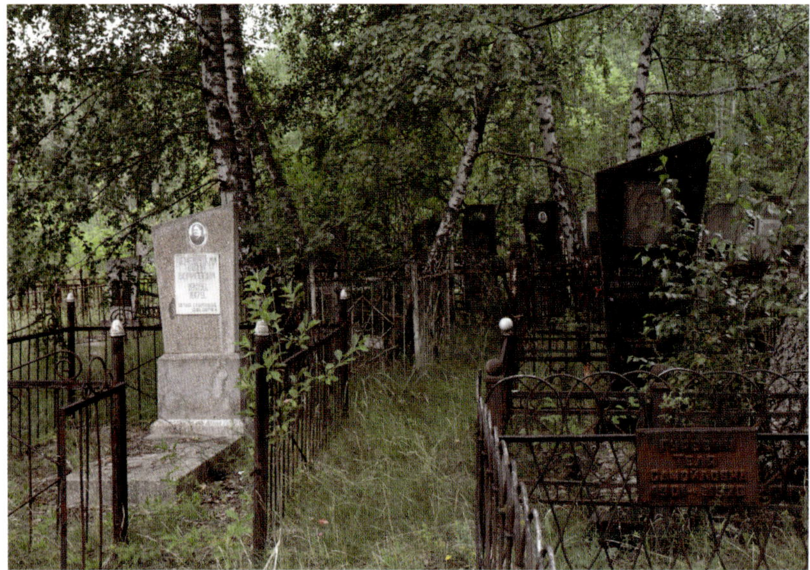

for military recruitment, and all that survived of the Chornobyl Jews were their graves.

The Chernobyl Nuclear Power Plant was constructed just 2 kilometres from the cruciform tree in the forest. It was a site that carried a tremendous weight of history, much of it tragic, and although Pripyat was officially an atheist atomgrad, Chornobyl remained a largely Christian town. Archimandrite Sergius, rector of Chornobyl's Church of the Prophet Elijah, recalls an omen that was seen on 26 April 1976, ten years to the day before the disaster: 'Many locals saw a cloud fall to the ground so that the outline of the figure of the Blessed Virgin Mary became clear on it… In her hands She held bunches of dry wormwood, which we call *chornobyl*. The Mother of God dropped wormwood over the town… Only years later, after the accident, did it become clear what this sign foreshadowed.'[4]

Ten years later, the sky was again filled with peculiar phenomena. The orbit of Halley's Comet brings it past the earth once every seventy-six years or so, and it has long been viewed by the superstitious as a harbinger of disaster. Its sighting in 66 CE was said to have heralded the destruction of the Second Temple of Jerusalem a few years later;[5] in

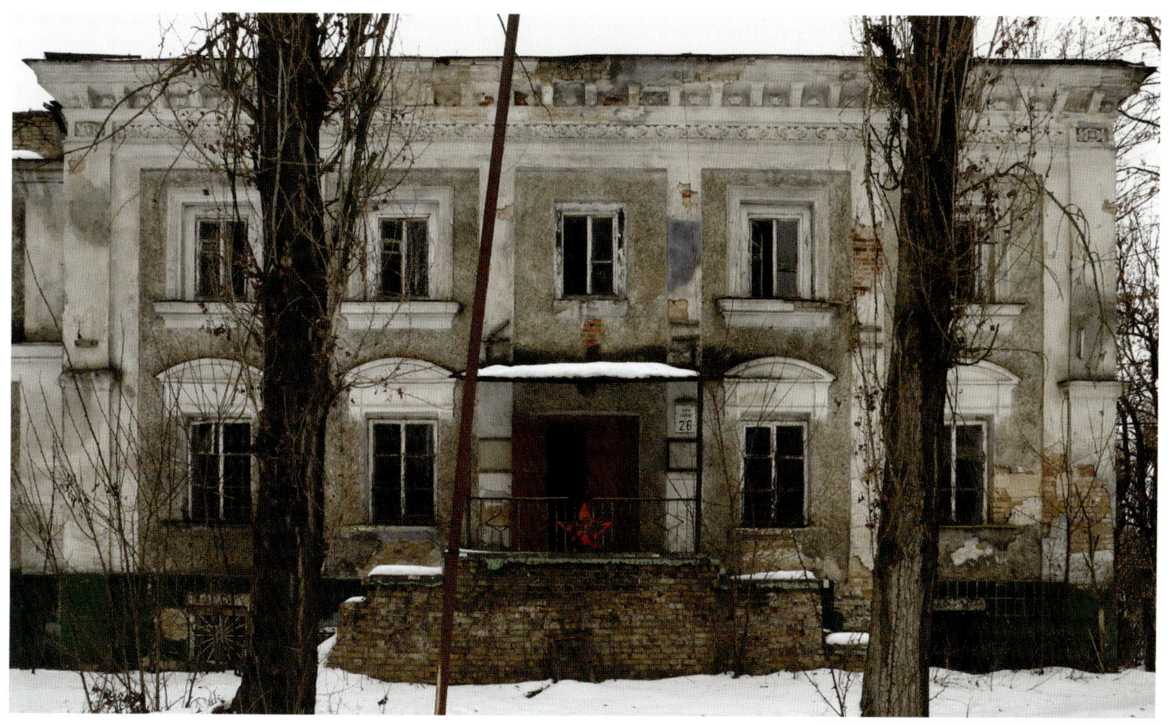

1066 it preceded the Battle of Hastings by a few months. Prior to its appearance in 1910, many were gripped by comet paranoia. Medicine men even peddled 'anti-comet pills' to those who feared imminent destruction by celestial forces. In March 1986, the Soviet Vega-1 space probe took the first ever photographs of the nucleus of Halley's Comet, and it reached its closest position to the earth on 11 April. On 24 April, the moon disappeared in a total lunar eclipse – another traditional omen of doom – and two nights later, the Chernobyl Nuclear Power Plant exploded.

Amidst the chaos that followed, the government remained tight-lipped about the catastrophe – and many citizens turned to more traditional sources of information. Omens and prophecies were reconsidered. As the evacuations began

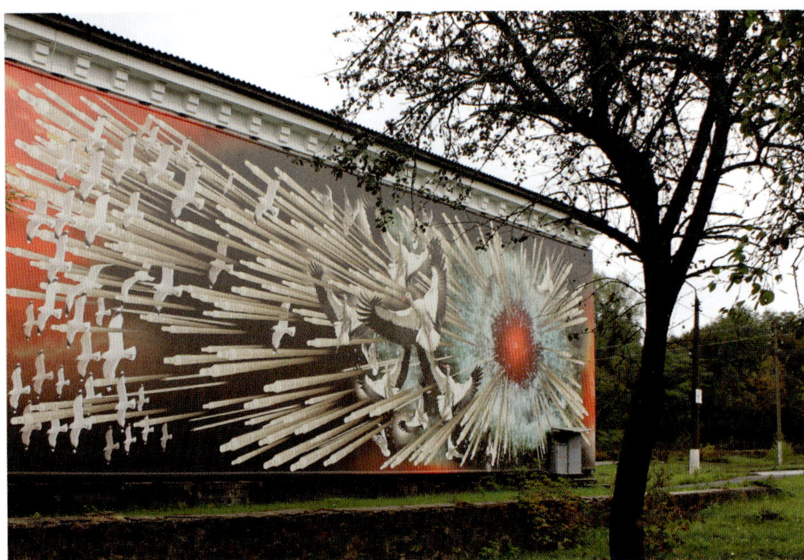

and the state warned of an invisible danger stalking the fields and hedgerows, the religious took to prayer, and those who read the Bible would find in the Book of Revelation the passage that reads: 'And the third angel sounded, and there fell a great star from heaven, burning as it were a lamp, and it fell upon the third part of the rivers, and upon the fountains of waters; and the name of the star is called Wormwood: and the third part of the waters became wormwood; and many men died of the waters, because they were made bitter.' (Revelation 8:10–11, King James Version)

Years later a new monument was raised in Chornobyl to commemorate the disaster. Designed by People's Artist of Ukraine, Anatoly Gaydamaka (who also designed the candle-shaped Holodomor Memorial in Kyiv), the sculpture, titled *The Third Angel*, takes the form of a celestial being with a trumpet raised to its lips. And in Chornobyl's Church of the Prophet Elijah hangs an Orthodox icon titled *Chornobyl Spas* (*Chornobyl Saviour*), depicting Jesus holding the scroll of Revelation, flanked by the Virgin Mary and Archangel Michael. Beneath them the Chernobyl 'liquidators' (as the disaster clean-up workers were called), and the victims of the disaster, gather around the blackened shape of a

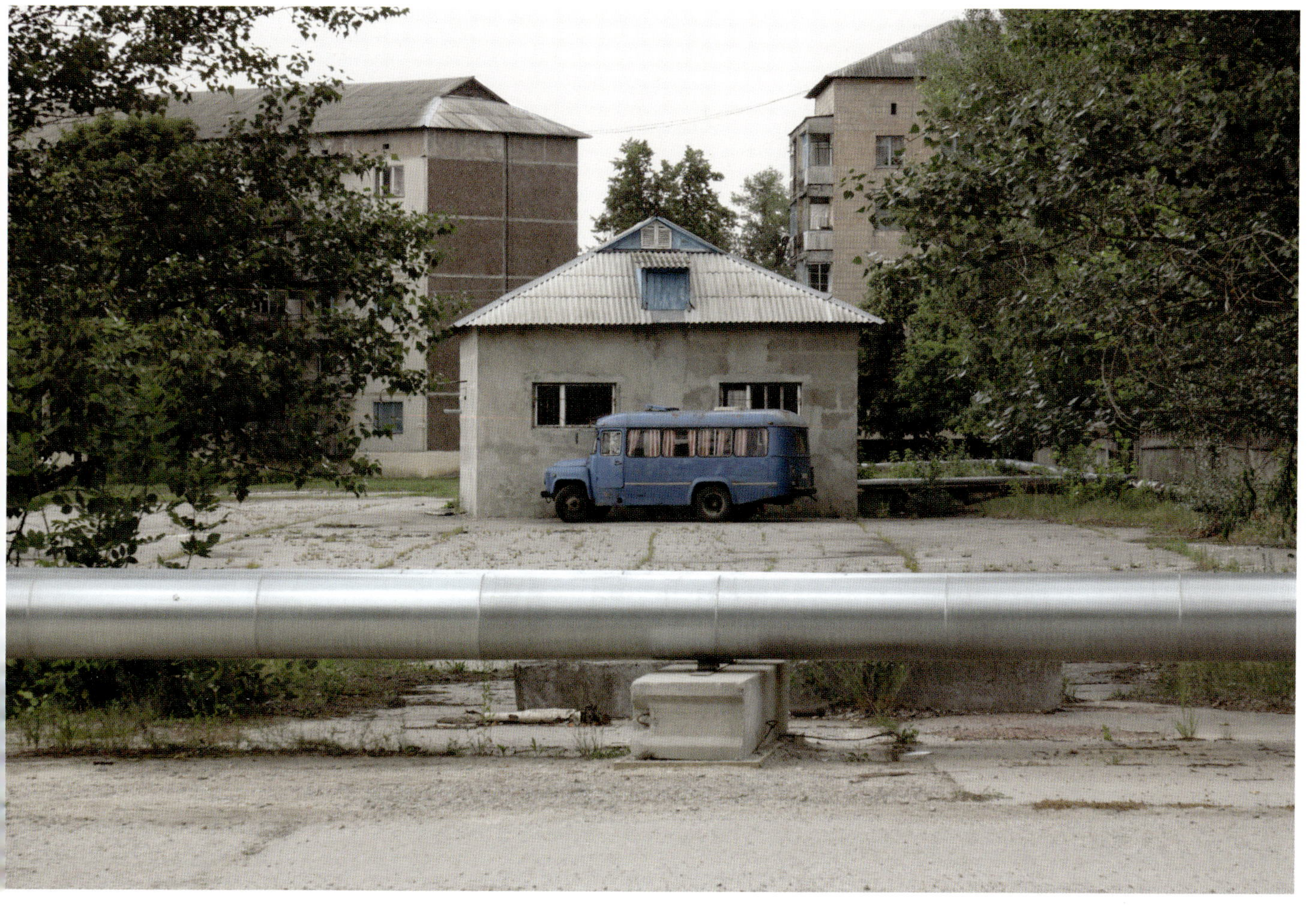

cruciform tree. In the background, across a poisoned, barren plane, the Chernobyl Nuclear Power Plant is silhouetted against a burning comet arcing across the heavens.

THE DISASTER

On 25 April 1986, a balmy Friday night, Chief Inspector Alexey Timofeevich Moskalenko of the Pripyat police was on patrol near the power plant with four other officers. At half past midnight there was an emergency release of radioactive vapour from Reactor 1, hinting at some clumsy work in the control room. 'We joked about it,' Moskalenko says, 'because for those engineers, if an emergency steam release occurs on their shift, the whole shift loses their bonus. So we were joking that their bonus was now floating in the air.'

I have taken the train to Slavutych – the new city built to house evacuees from Pripyat – to meet with Alexey Moskalenko and hear his first-hand account of the disaster. He is in his seventies now, but could pass for a fifty-year-old. A tall man, with a smooth, kindly face, and a ruddy glow in his cheeks, he's drinking vodka faster than I can drink my beer. That night in 1986, he tells me, right after the emergency steam release from Reactor 1, the police noticed two men down by the cooling pond, unloading something from an inflatable boat.

'It was about 1.20am,' Moskalenko remembers. 'They were poachers – illegal fishermen. The moon was very bright so it was easy to spot them. But as we got out of the car, we heard two bangs behind us. Not very loud, not as loud as the emergency release from the other block a little earlier. But there was a cloud of steam… It turned and seemed to move north, towards Belarus. Some kind of ash was falling on us. It smelled like burning cable insulation – a really heavy smell.'

An announcement over their radio ordered all personnel to gather immediately in Pripyat. 'The plant itself was guarded by troops from the Ministry of Internal Affairs of Ukraine,' Moskalenko explains, 'but around the power plant, everything else was under the control of us Pripyat police.' At the time, he was dressed in his civilian clothes, so he had to fetch his uniform from home – where his wife, a plant employee, made him take off his ash-covered clothes in the corridor outside. 'We arrived at the police station at 2am, and the entire Pripyat police force was gathered in the assembly hall. At the time of the accident we had 126 officers between all departments. Everybody was called in that night, even those officially on holiday. As we walked in they all noticed us, saying: "Hey, your faces are white!" I could feel it too – it felt like my face was burning.'

None of the police knew it yet, but at precisely 01.23:40 that morning, what should have been a routine test of ChNPP's Reactor 4 had gone seriously wrong. The plant's first two reactors were of an older design, which could release built-up steam into the atmosphere whenever pressure rose too high inside (as Moskalenko had observed, that same

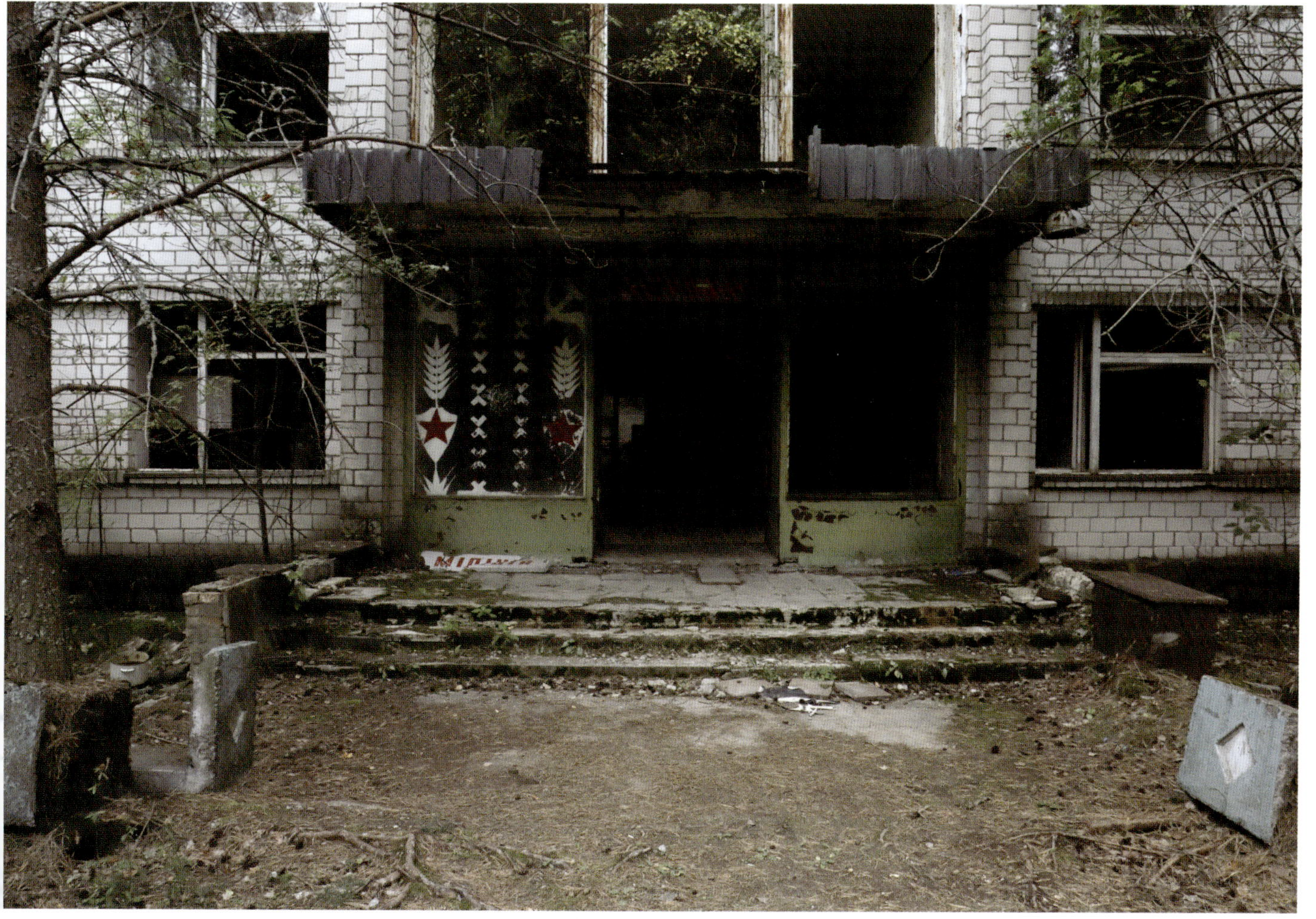

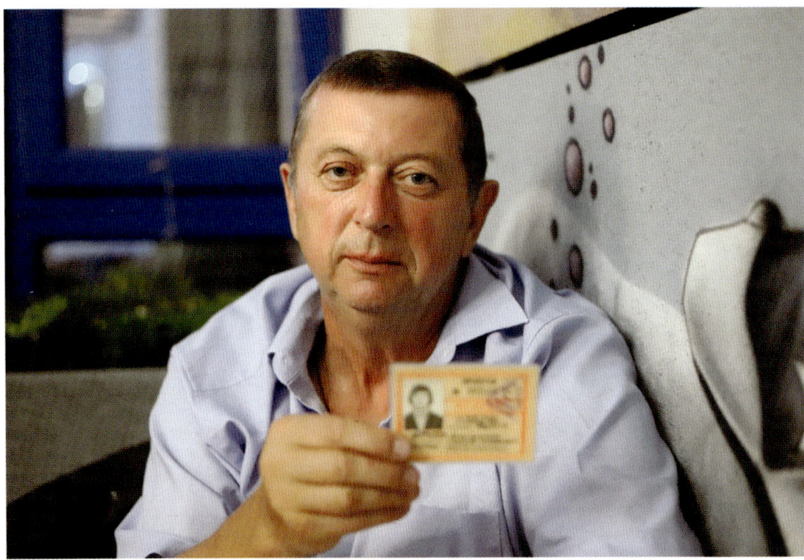

Alexey Timofeevich Moskalenko, former Chief Inspector, Pripyat police. Slavutych, August 2019.

evening). In Reactors 3 and 4 steam was channelled through pipes into a chamber known as the bubbler pool. Here the radioactive steam hit water, condensed, and the liquid was then siphoned off for safe storage as radioactive waste. In the event of a power failure, it would take around one minute for the backup generator to kick in, and the test in Reactor 4 that night was supposed to establish safety procedures for maintaining cooling systems in the interim. However, the test had been delayed by ten hours, putting it in the hands of a less experienced nightshift team. During the test the reactor began behaving erratically, with a sudden power drop, and then when control rods were reinserted into the core it caused an unexpected power surge (later found to be the result of a reactor design flaw). The coolant water was instantly vaporised, and its explosive force blasted off the reactor's cover plate, exposing the core, which caught fire and began releasing radioactive contamination into the sky.

Two of the plant's staff were killed instantly. Others died later in hospital. The first emergency teams to arrive were fire-fighters, many of whom had been given little or no briefing about the nature of the accident. One of those men, interviewed on the scene, described a feeling like pins and needles, accompanied by a metallic taste in his mouth; twenty-eight of the emergency responders would die soon

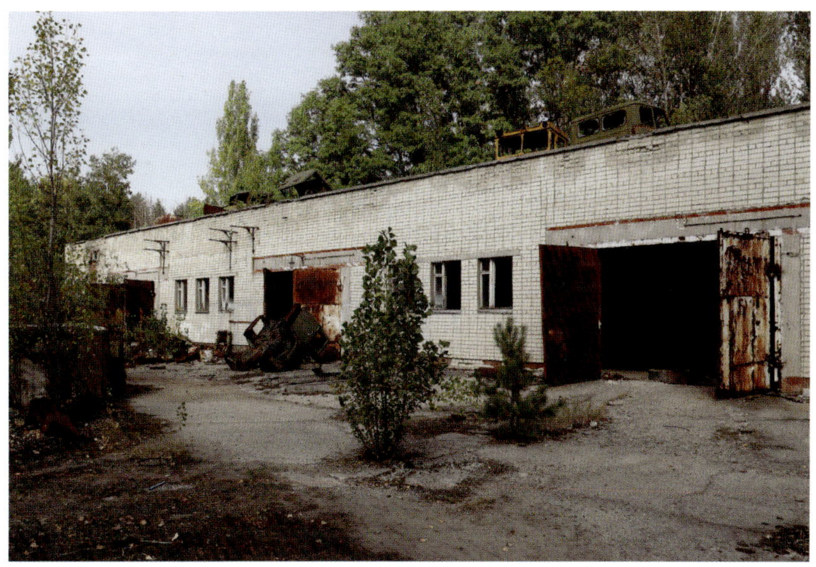

SVPCh-6 Fire Station, Pripyat. On the night of the disaster, a crew of first responders was mobilised from this station under the command of lieutenant Victor Kibenok. Kibenok himself died on 11 May 1986, and was posthumously honoured with the 'Hero of the Soviet Union' award. Local rumour claims the doors have remained open ever since the fire engines left.

after from acute radiation exposure. The Pripyat police set up roadblocks and began restricting access to the area around the plant. Moskalenko remembers how two women, police employees, had been posted near the plant that night. They called the station shortly after the explosion, saying they felt sick and needed help. He sounds sad as he recalls: 'I took another officer and went to the plant looking for them. But as we approached, the steam was already condensing into a damp fog – we had to use the wipers because we couldn't see anything. We never found those women. Later, an ambulance that went through carrying firemen found them and picked them up. They both died in Moscow, in Hospital No.6. They were called Luzganova and Ivanenko – their names are on our monument now.' Moskalenko gestures across the clean, Modernist plaza, to the Chernobyl memorial that stands tucked in among the trees outside Slavutych's Minsk Shopping Mall.

As Saturday 26 April rolled on, citizens of Pripyat were generally aware there had been some kind of accident at the plant – but even while clouds of radioactive dust drifted across the landscape, life continued as normal. 'There were six weddings in the city that day,' says Moskalenko. 'They put a few bags of boric acid in the watering machines to clean the street – it's a sorbent, which binds radioactive dust. All five schools in Pripyat were open and when the kids were sent home after their third class, the weather was so hot, they all went playing in those puddles instead.'

On Sunday morning the police intercepted a car on the edge of Khotiv village, near Kyiv, which was found to be 5,000 times over the safe radiation limit. Its driver, a Pripyat resident named Ivanitskiy, said they had left the city at six that morning for a day of recreation in the forest. The vehicle and its passengers were escorted to the Institute of Nuclear Research for decontamination. It wasn't until a full thirty-six hours after the explosion that a public announcement called for the evacuation of Pripyat:

'Attention, dear comrades! The City Council informs you that due to the accident at Chernobyl Power Plant in the city of Pripyat, the radioactive conditions in the vicinity are deteriorating. The Communist Party, its officials and the armed forces are taking the necessary steps to combat this… Comrades, on leaving your residences temporarily please make sure you have turned off the lights, electrical equipment and water and shut the windows. Please remain calm and orderly during the process of this short-term evacuation.'[6]

Chief Inspector Moskalenko and his colleagues oversaw the evacuation, while trying to keep the population from panicking. They told them: 'Everyone should leave town for three days. But we're coming back.' Citizens were given two hours to pack while the state mobilised every bus, boat, and train at their disposal (many of these vehicles were later scrapped because of contamination). More than 100,000 people were evacuated from the most contaminated areas, with arbitrary lines drawn on a map to establish an Exclusion Zone the size of Luxembourg. Though its shape would change over the years, initially it was a circle with a radius of 10 kilometres around the plant, incorporating Pripyat and most of the areas worst affected by the fall-out, with a second circle with 30-kilometre radius intended to contain the broader spread. But it was by no means a perfect system. Some towns and villages inside the 30 km Zone had shown no signs of contamination, yet were evacuated all the same; meanwhile, there were numerous areas of significant contamination outside the Exclusion Zone, such as Naliboki Forest, in Belarus, which had been directly in the path of the radioactive clouds.

At the plant, radio-controlled bulldozers were deployed to clear the contaminated debris. However, their electronics were quickly damaged by radiation and the radio-control systems failed. In the end, the bulk of the waste had to be cleared by hand. The military referred to these workers as 'bio-robots'. The reactor core burned until 10 May: more than 5,000 tons of clay, lead, sand, and boron (to smother the flames and impede the reaction) were dropped from helicopters before Chernobyl's Block 4 could be sealed inside a steel and cement containment sarcophagus.[7] An army of liquidators was recruited – some 240,000 workers

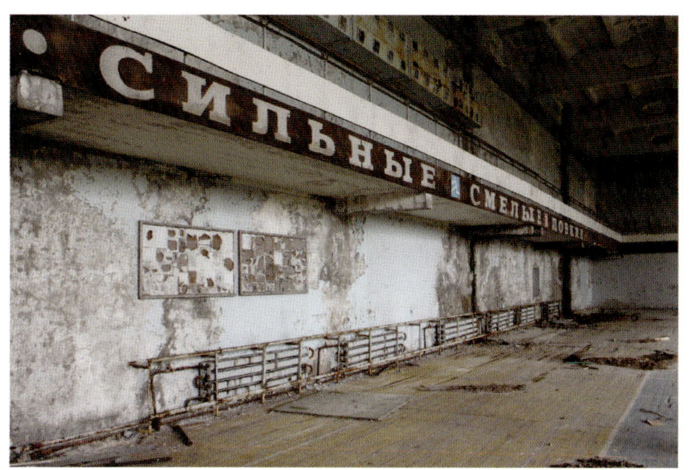
СИЛЬНЫЕ СМЕЛЫ ЛОВКАЯ

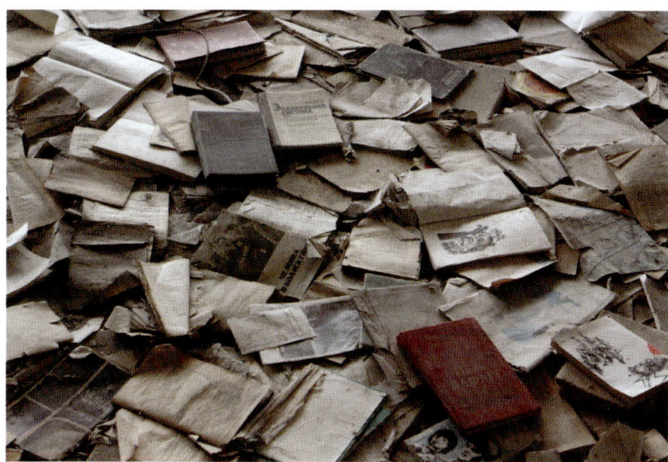

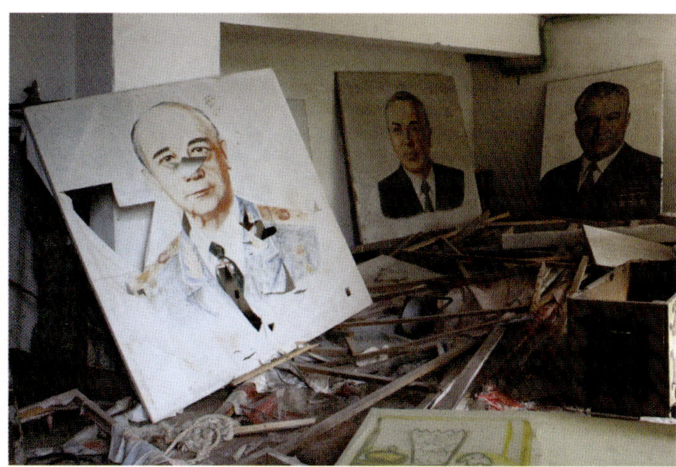

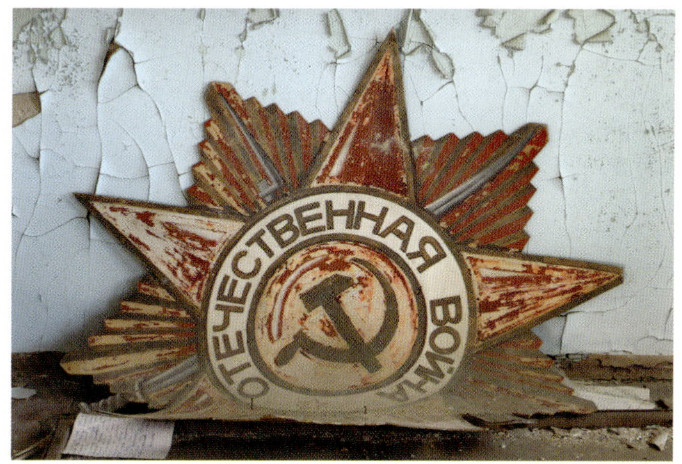
ОТЕЧЕСТВЕННАЯ ВОЙНА

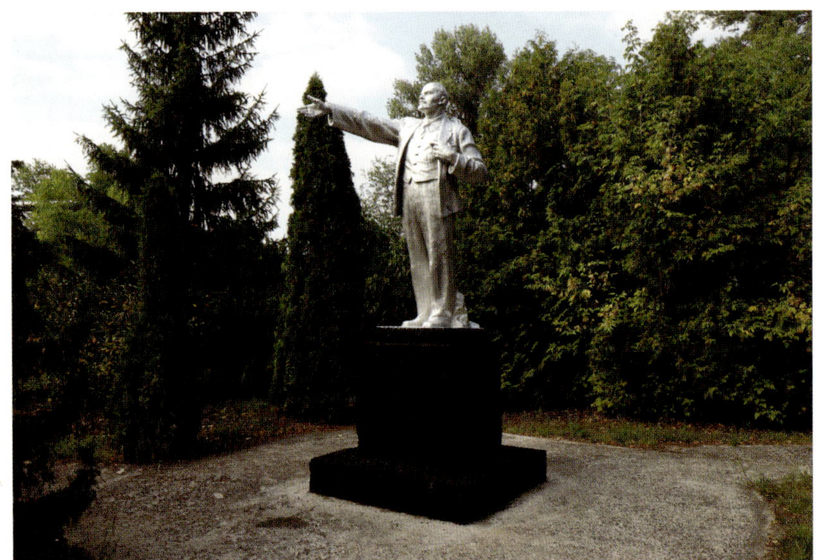

left: Former shipyard, Chornobyl. A statue of Lenin still stands on this territory, which is now controlled and guarded by the local forestry commission. Because of radiation, the Exclusion Zone has inadvertently escaped the decommunisation laws that have seen the eradication of many such Soviet relics from the rest of Ukraine.

right: Monument to the Liquidators, Chornobyl outskirts, created in 1996 as part of an unfinished memorial complex. The stone reads: 'Here, on the 10th anniversary of the accident at the Chernobyl Nuclear Power Plant, the Memorial Park "Green Murmur" was unveiled, in memory of the dead, and the victims of the largest industrial disaster in the history of mankind.'

in 1986-87 alone, according to the World Health Organisation – and tasked with containing the worst of the contamination.[8] Many of them stayed in makeshift lodgings established at the 'Skazochniy' ('Fairy Tale') Pioneer Camp, a forest complex full of sculpted dragons and dolphins, where plant employees had once sent their children for summer breaks.[9] Later, large boats were brought up the river to accommodate these clean-up crews.

Moskalenko had received acute radiation poisoning from his proximity to the explosion at Chernobyl – an estimated 3-4 sieverts, which could easily have proved a lethal dose. He was diagnosed with vegetovascular dystonia, and spent time in the oncology ward at Kyiv's Clinic No.25: 'We were there for three weeks like laboratory rabbits… They tested new kinds of drugs on us.' He made an impressive recovery, then successfully applied for a job and an apartment in the new city built for the refugees. 'In January [1987] the chief of the security police department came to visit me, and said: "Go build Slavutych".'

Located 45 kilometres north-east of the power plant, most of Slavutych's buildings were constructed in 1987 and inhabited from 1988. Architectural teams from eight Soviet republics each designed a city district and these 'quarters' were named after their respective capitals.[10] It was advertised

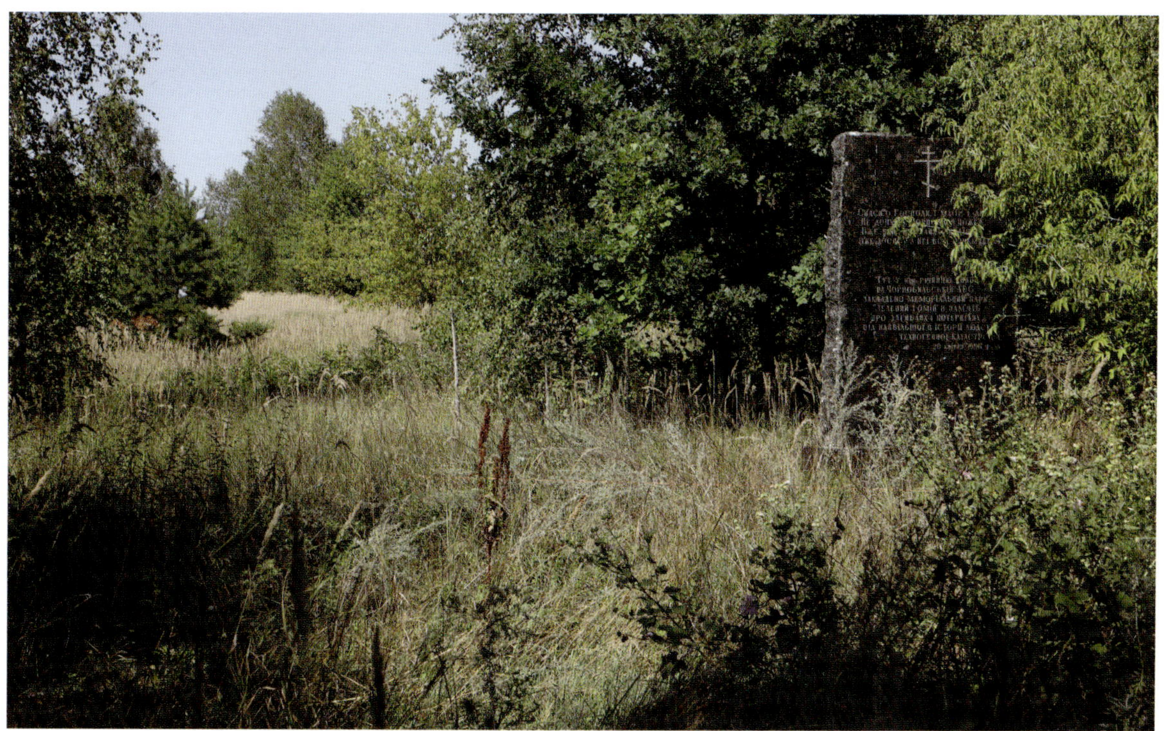

as a clean refuge for evacuees from the newly formed Exclusion Zone, but according to Moskalenko, Slavutych was built on plutonium-tainted ground. 'In 1987,' he says, 'soldiers were still scraping irradiated bark from these trees with special shovels. If you go down to the Dnipro River, where the city's water is pumped from, there are wells going 400 metres deep to the ground water, and radiation-warning signs everywhere.'

Moskalenko explains that this site was the eighth location proposed for the city. 'The best idea was to build it in Chernihiv,' he says – a plan that would have seen Slavutych added as a new district to an older city, some 40 kilometres away. 'Slavutych is beautiful, but it's not Pripyat,' he sighs. 'Pripyat had time to grow, but they built Slavutych in just one year. Citizens of Pripyat were proud of their city. And even though we've got all this architecture here, the newest projects from all these different republics, Pripyat was still more beautiful. Everyone who lived there would say this.'

A few years after the accident, Moskalenko was visited by two familiar faces: the illegal fishermen he had arrested on the night of the disaster. 'They found me in 1989, here in Slavutych,' he laughs. 'Those two were drunk [when we arrested them], so we locked them in a drunk-tank located in what is now the Red Forest… where they were exposed to a high dose of radiation. They wanted me to confirm that I saw them poaching at the moment of the explosion, near Reactor 4, so they could apply for disability pensions.'

THE EXCLUSION ZONE

When Pripyat fell, authority in the region deferred to the older town of Chornobyl, now situated inside the 30 km Zone. Chornobyl had shown little sign of contamination, despite its proximity to the plant (a fact the local Christian community interpreted as a reward for their unwavering faith). The town became a staging post for soldiers, fire-fighters, scientists, biologists, and construction teams – a Ukrainian version of *Roadside Picnic*'s Harmont.

Today Chornobyl has around 500 permanent inhabitants, with apartments converted into dormitories capable of housing several thousand more temporary workers. Workers wear personal dosimeters and typically spend two weeks out of the Zone for every two weeks on duty. Chornobyl has four working shops, three canteens, a bus station, a police station, and a post office. Its three bars serve alcohol, but only between the hours of 7pm and 10pm. It is in one of these establishments – the aptly named 'Roadside Picnic Grill Bar' – that I meet with Vladimir Verbitski one summer day in 2019.

Verbitski has the face of a retired army general: strong features, a silver buzz-cut, and mischievous eyes that make you feel he's never quite telling you everything he knows. He's dressed head to foot in camouflage, with a radiation sign stitched on his shoulder like an epaulet. Before the disaster, Verbitski worked in the power plant's metals laboratory.

'Chernobyl was the only plant in the Soviet Union that didn't provide power for internal consumption,' he tells me. 'Only 7 per cent of its output went to Ukraine… The rest was exported to the Comecon countries [the Soviet-led Council for Mutual Economic Assistance]. Really, its most important task was making weapons. That was the whole point of building this type of reactor, with a single cooling circuit. Electricity was just a by-product. After the fuel was burnt at Chernobyl, it was moved to Kola NPP [in north-west Russia] or to Beloyarsk [a nuclear plant near Yekaterinburg].

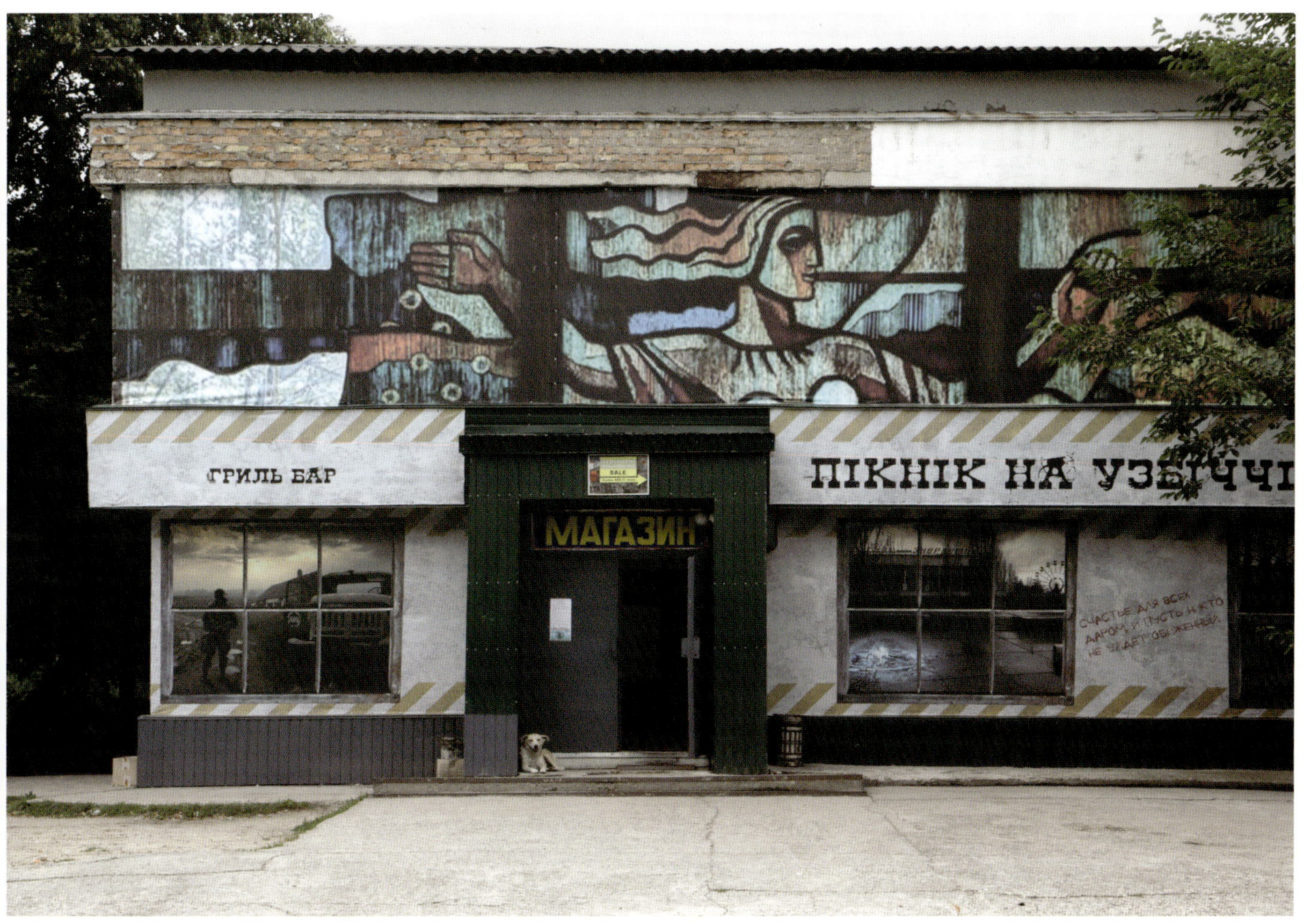
ГРИЛЬ БАР
ПІКНІК НА УЗБІЧЧІ
SALE
МАГАЗИН
СЧАСТЬЕ ДЛЯ ВСЕХ
ДАРОМ И ПУСТЬ НИКТО
НЕ УЙДЁТ ОБИЖЕННЫЙ

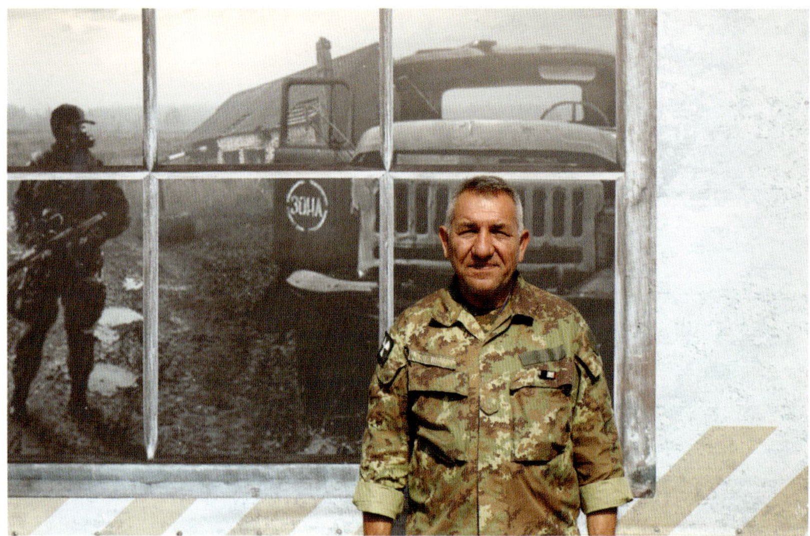

left: Vladimir Verbitski, former laboratory worker, Chernobyl Nuclear Power Plant. Chornobyl, August 2019.

right: Duga-1 radar, winter view from the rooftop of its control building.

They had fast neutron reactors – we called them "dirty" power plants – that took this second-hand fuel, and generated weapons-grade plutonium from it.'

In 1986, the KGB ran an investigation into the causes of the accident, returning a verdict of 'operator error'; it was only later that the RBMK reactor's design flaws were officially acknowledged. 'We have a theory,' Verbitski says, leaning in closer and lowering his voice. 'The KGB had already predicted the collapse of the Soviet Union, and they knew that Ukraine was capable of independence. We had massive natural resources, we produced everything from needles to space rockets, and had the third-largest nuclear arsenal in the world! Ukraine could have joined the EU without any conditions – but the EU cannot admit a country that's suffering a nuclear catastrophe.' He smiles, allowing the implication to sink in. 'Then thirty years later, we reach the stage where we can say we've almost completely overcome the consequences of the disaster. But a country with border disputes can't join the EU, or NATO. So what does Big Brother do now? He suddenly annexes one of our territories.'

In 1987, Verbitski was transferred to the dosimetric control department: the team responsible for the hundred permanent stations monitoring radiation levels across the Zone, as well as maintaining dosimetric controls at checkpoints. He explains how the Zone was divided between three security forces: 'The SBU [Security Service of Ukraine] provides security at

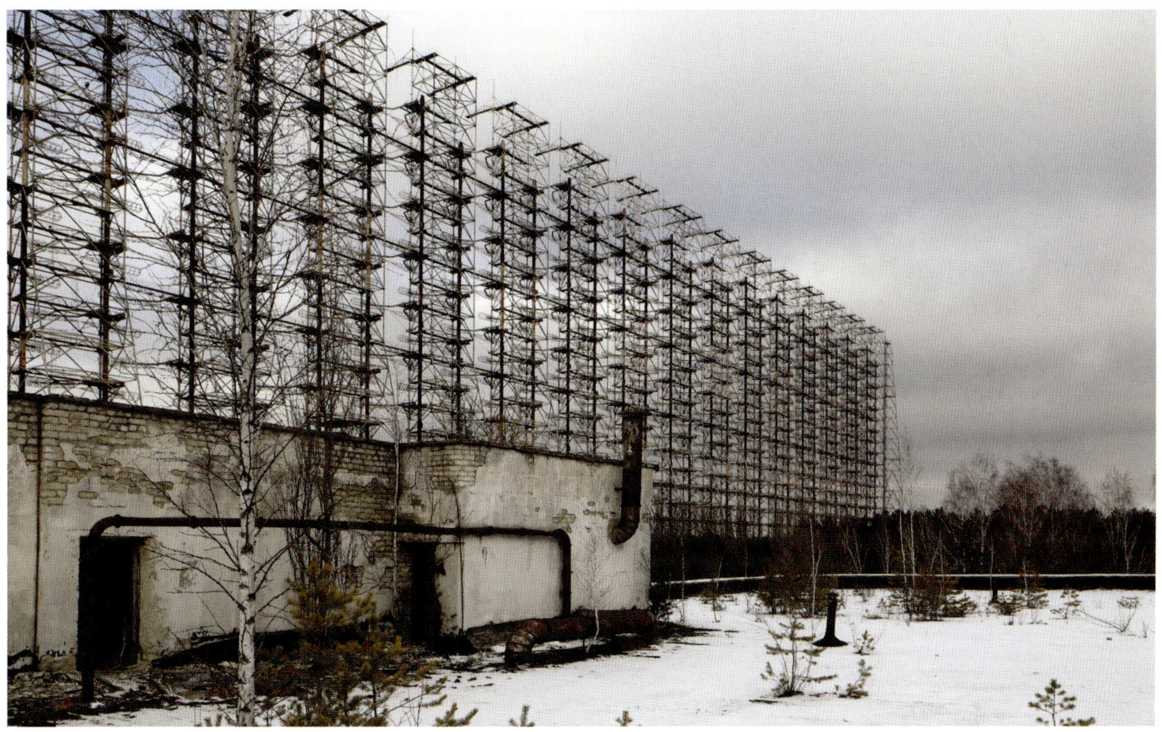

the power plant with a department that issues documents for the tourists. General security in the Exclusion Zone is provided by the regular national police. Then the 154-kilometre border we share with Belarus, that's covered by two border detachments from Zhytomyr and Ivankiv.'

The Duga-1 radar was deactivated just hours after the explosion at the plant, as its ventilation systems were shown to be sucking radioactive dust inside the facility. It would never work again. Chernobyl-2, the closed military town built to contain it, had its civilian population evacuated on the same day as Pripyat – though a military presence would remain on-site for years to come.[11] The base had been a repository for high-tech state secrets and contained some of the largest and most advanced radar systems ever devised. It wasn't somewhere that could be abandoned overnight. A team of soldiers systematically ransacked the Duga's control rooms – whatever could be moved was packed up and sent to Russia. Any equipment of no value, or that couldn't be taken away, was dragged outside and destroyed. Later, looters masquerading as liquidators would further strip the remains for any materials of value. According to rumours, a back-up control room, built in a large bunker beneath the complex, was collapsed, flooded and sealed with concrete. By the time the soldiers left, Chernobyl-2 was a ghost town, and the Duga a skeleton without a brain, towering impotently over the forests, the wind whistling through its lifeless cables.

When the 'Russian Woodpecker's' signal was first heard in 1976, Western intelligence agencies had investigated the possibility that the Duga might be some kind of new experimental weapon. They studied its potential effects, considering everything from climate interference to mind control. One U.S. Department of Defense consultant allegedly commented: 'The Russian Woodpecker signal is the most powerful source of electromagnetic radiation ever created by man. Ten pulses per second, 40 million watts, it is psychoactive! It is emitted from the Soviet Union and permeates everything in the US. It is caught by electric wires and flows into our homes through them.'[12] While experts and amateur radio hobbyists worldwide soon established

the Duga's true purpose as an over-the-horizon radar system, conspiracy theories would continue to circulate for decades (eventually receiving a detailed treatment in the 2015 documentary *The Russian Woodpecker*).

Verbitski doesn't believe these stories, though he does wonder what else Moscow has kept hidden about the project. 'The night of the accident,' he says, 'apparently the Duga station was running for the first time ever at full power. I know this from my colleague, who worked on the computers there. And they normally mention only three objects [Chernobyl's Duga-1, the prototype Duga-N, and Russia's Duga-2], but the commander of the Chernobyl-2 military unit once told journalists that there are eight of them! So where are the rest?'

As for Pripyat, the atomgrad didn't die all at once. Both the Jupiter Factory and the 'Lazurniy' ('Azure') Swimming Pool were still in use until 1996. Liquidators and scientists working at the plant would swim in Pripyat to relax after a hard day's work. Signs of this later use are still evident today – the boot-wash station by the front door and the thick plastic sheeting lining the stairwells to protect swimmers from radioactive dust. (Eventually though, it failed a health inspection and had to close.) Both Pripyat's laundry and its water-treatment plant remain in use even now: the power plant still required a clean water supply and its staff needed clean uniforms. Decontaminating these existing facilities was far less work than building new ones, or laying new

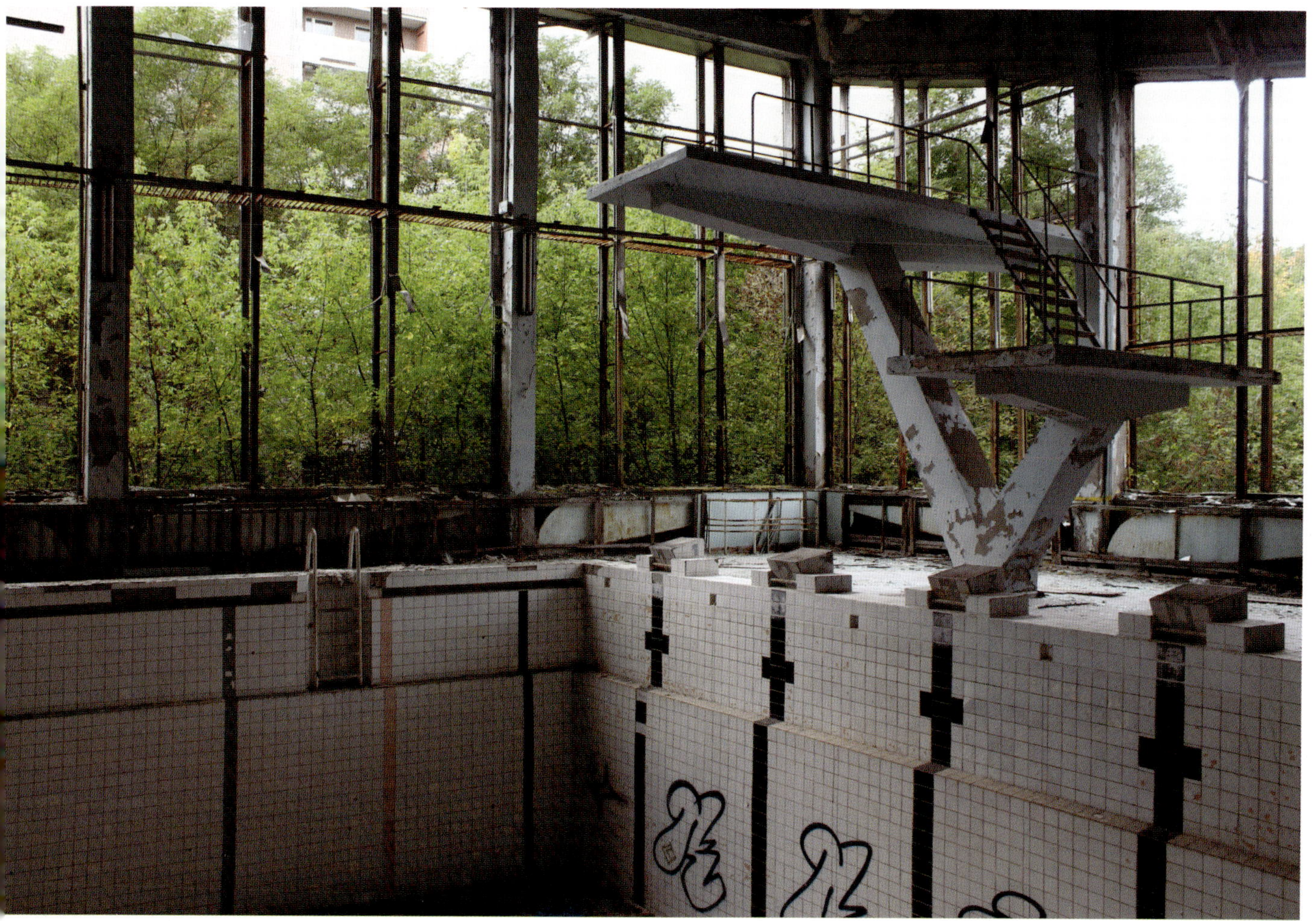

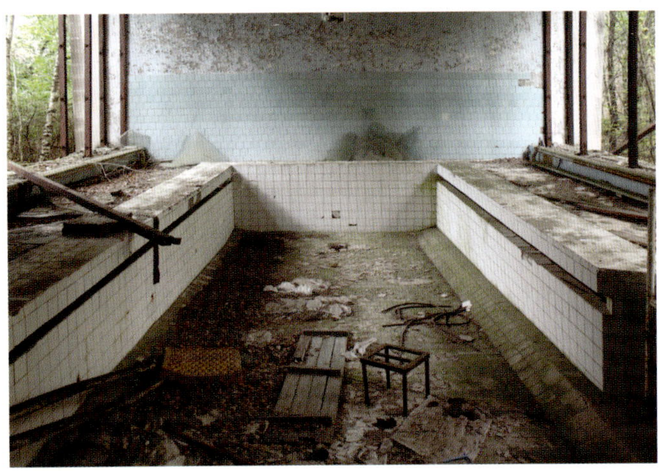 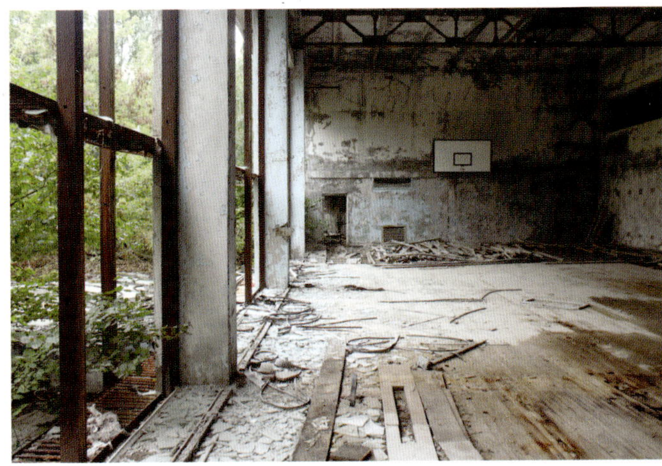

water pipes in contaminated soil. However, the once open city had closed. A security fence went up around Pripyat, with a guard post placed on the main road into the atomgrad.

When it became apparent that this was not the three-day temporary evacuation that had initially been announced, Verbitski says some citizens were allowed back for a few hours to collect their belongings – but only what they could carry, and they would still need to pass through radiation control. A number of buildings were stripped of furniture by the military, and the liquidators raided Pripyat as well. According to Verbitski, 'the state barely spent any money on accommodation for liquidators, so we had to improvise by fetching furniture from Pripyat ourselves. A city meant for 50,000 people and

we numbered 80-100,000 people in just one shift! We'd go to the Pripyat guards and say we needed furniture – then they'd lead us to some abandoned building, disable the alarm, and we'd drag out all the furniture from the apartments. We could pick up ten to thirty beds in one trip.'

The collapse of the Soviet Union in 1991 meant funding was suddenly reduced and the Zone's security teams drastically scaled down. Looting became easier, and more prolific. At Middle School No.3 on Pripyat's Sportivnaya Street, a cache of child-sized gas masks was broken open and scattered. The masks had never been worn, but looters had heard their filters contained trace amounts of silver. 'Some looters came in big boats from Belarus,' remembers

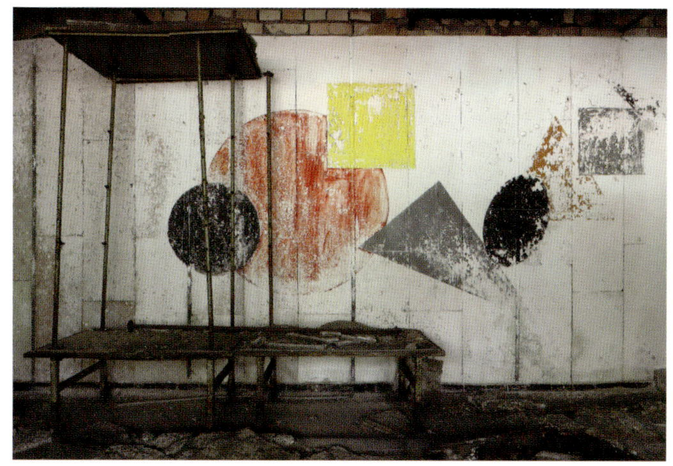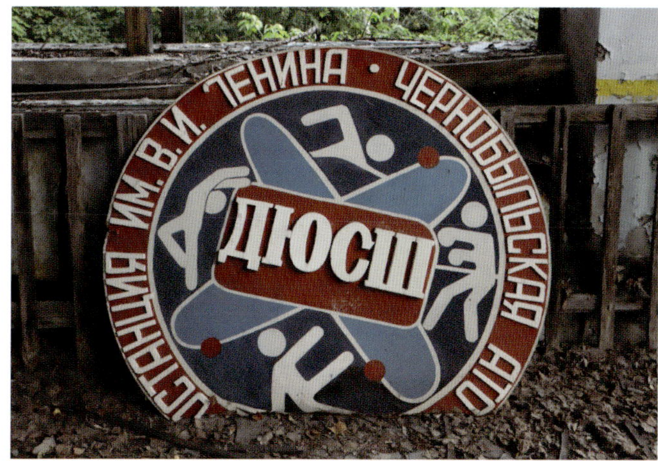

Verbitski. 'They'd smash the windows in the nearest building, get inside and grab anything they could.'

Near the entrance to Pripyat, a Christian cross was erected in memory of the victims; and Prometheus, the former champion of the atomgrad, was moved out of the city to a new location at ChNPP. Chief Inspector Moskalenko told me the bronze Prometheus statue was removed so the looters couldn't steal it for scrap… but according to Verbitski, the Titan came to the power plant as a warning. 'He was chained to the rock as punishment for his rebellion. In boxing, the most painful blow is to the liver, and so that's what happens to rebels – your liver is punished for eternity!' he laughs. 'They took Lenin down because he's meaningless now, but Prometheus is still there as a warning to would-be rebels.'

In 2006, in a district of Kyiv that would become populated with Pripyat refugees, a memorial park was dedicated to the 'Heroes of Chernobyl'. Here, surrounded by plaques that list the evacuated villages of the Zone, a new statue of Prometheus was raised, but this post-Soviet Titan was different from those which had preceded it. Erected in a place of mourning, this Prometheus is surrounded by the symbols of his punishment and raises his flame to the sky in a gesture that locals describe as giving the fire back to the gods – suggesting a satirical inversion of the sovietised myth, as if Prometheus himself were saying, 'I'm sorry, they were not ready.'

4. NUCLEAR TOURISM

'Visit the atomic Mecca. Affordable prices.'

Svetlana Alexievich, *Chernobyl Prayer*

THE INDUSTRY

In October 2019, the State Agency of Ukraine for the Management of the Exclusion Zone – the 'Chernobyl State Agency' – reported that the number of paying visitors to the site had already exceeded 100,000 that year, a figure that was double the former population of Pripyat (80 per cent were non-Ukrainian, with the largest groups from Britain, Poland, Germany, and the US, followed by Czechia).[1] Unsurprisingly, numbers like this have a profound physical and economic effect on the Zone. With each visitor typically paying upwards of $100 per person per day, Chernobyl tourism has become a multi-million dollar industry.

Sergei Franchuk is one of the most experienced guides working in the Chernobyl Exclusion Zone today. He leads private tours for groups from Poland, Czechia and the Baltic states, including large numbers of Lithuanians. 'The Lithuanians come twice a month, and soon it'll be four groups a month,' he tells me. We are sitting at a picnic table outside a café in Ivankiv, a small town of some 10,000 citizens that serves as the administrative centre of Ivankiv region and, by extension, of much of the nearby Exclusion Zone too. 'There are twenty-five people in each group, and my job is to keep them safe. I show them the unusual stuff that goes unseen by the thousands of other tourists.'

Franchuk was a farmer before starting work in the Zone, and in 2017 he was flown to Fukushima in Japan where he talked at press conferences about the long-term effects of radioactive contamination on the land. Since then, he has also guided Japanese groups in Chernobyl. 'Last time, farmers from Fukushima came to see me,' he says. 'This time it's a delegation from Japan's Ministry of Ecology.'

His involvement with the Exclusion Zone began in the 1990s. 'With the break-up of the Soviet Union and the independence of Ukraine, they stopped paying my salary at the collective farm. But you could still earn a wage in the Zone,' he says, going on to explain how he took a construction job in the Chernobyl Zone in 1996, and was part of the team that installed the fire-fighters' monument in Chornobyl. I ask him who was visiting the Zone back then, before the first tour companies appeared. 'Official delegations, photographers, journalists, and scientists, in addition to us workers. The *samosely* [the local term for those re-settling the Zone] had already begun returning by the end of 1986, beginning of '87, and various organisations were sending them humanitarian aid. I delivered some myself. There were religious programmes too, even Jehovah's witnesses.'

As tourism began to pick up, it offered far more lucrative employment. 'Sometime around 2002-03, the company Pripyat.com was the first to conduct actual tours, for Russian and Ukrainian customers. But it wasn't technically a tour company. Legally they had to call it a "study trip". After that, Chernobyl Tour was founded, then Solo East – and then came the tourism boom in 2006-07.'

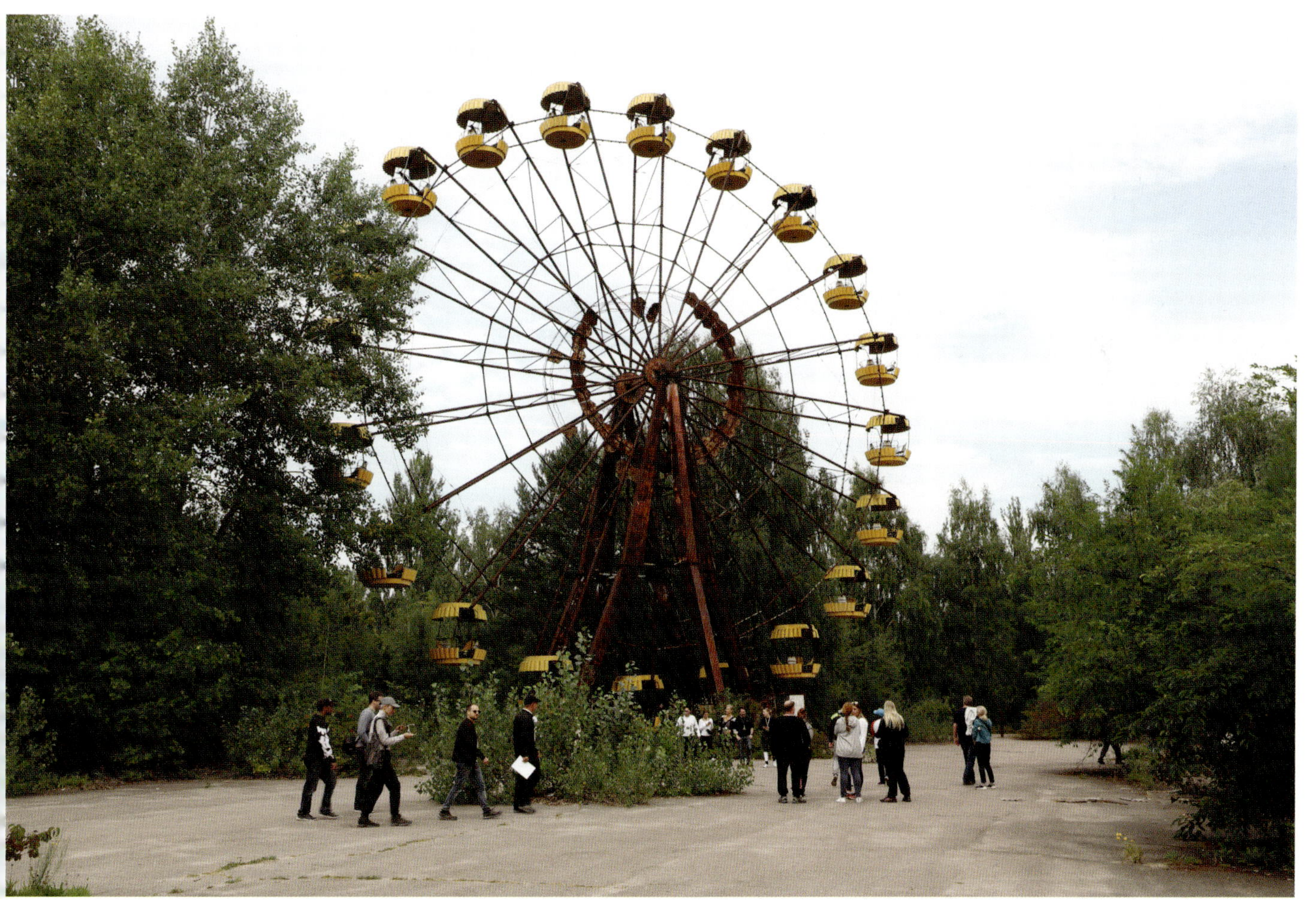

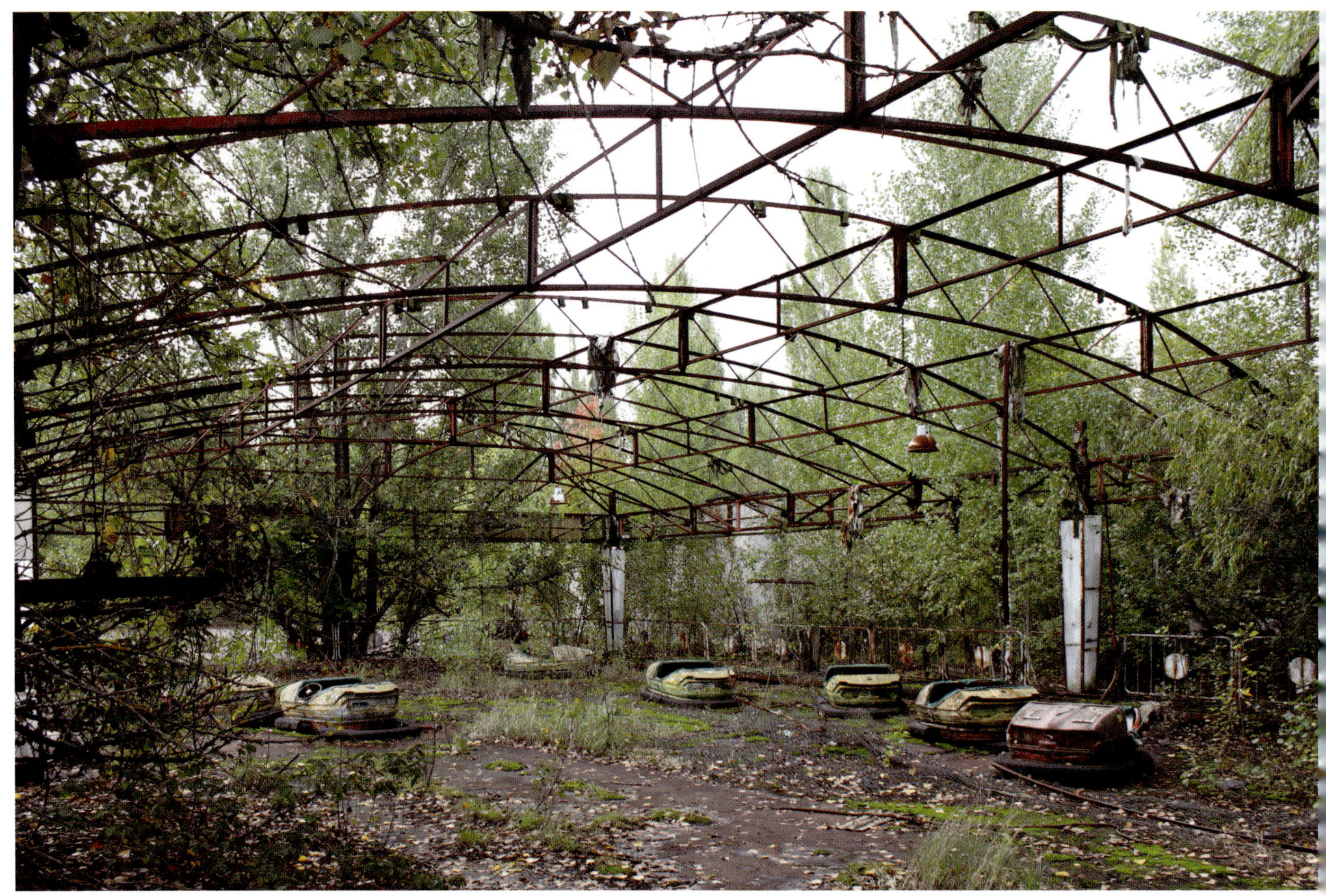

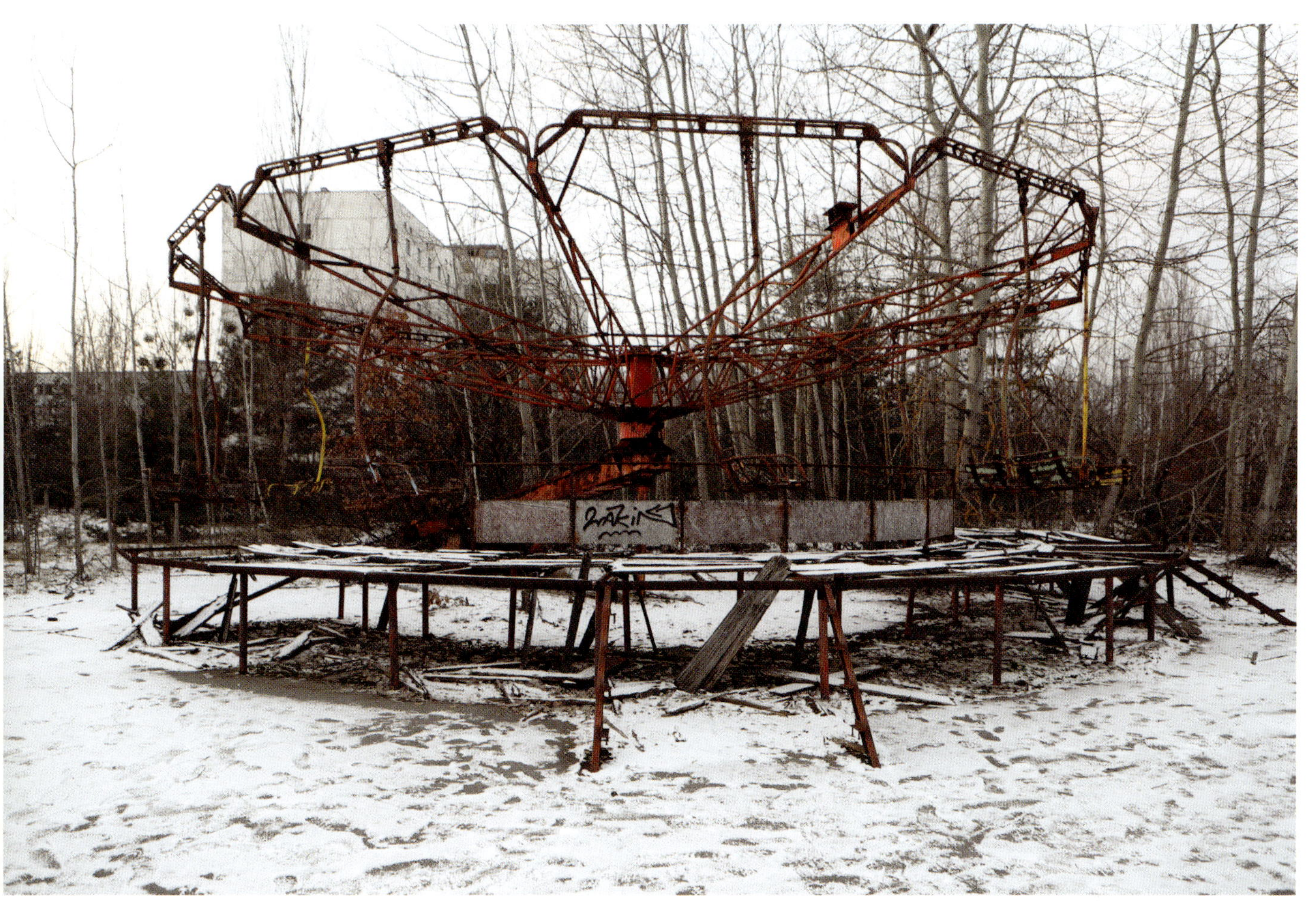

Jim Alston is an Australian who visited in 2008 with Solo East. At that time, online bookings were made through a basic and already outdated webpage. 'There was about twenty of us in an old, old coach,' he tells me. 'We spent way too long stopping at each checkpoint. The group was mostly Americans, a few Chinese, us Aussies, and some Ukrainians.' Priced at $120 for the day, the itinerary was roughly the same as what is offered now – except that in Pripyat, the group was given free rein to explore. 'We had an hour to go wherever we wanted. They told us to stay on the concrete and to "Come back when you hear the bus horn". As you can imagine, we ran around like headless chickens.'

In 2004, the Exclusion Zone received 870 paying visitors. By 2009, that had risen to 7,500. A report in 2011 showed an increase to 10,000 visitors, although the industry came under scrutiny that year, as Ukraine's Emergencies Ministry (the political body responsible for managing the site) was accused of profiteering. Alexander Ampleev, speaking on behalf of Ukraine's Prosecutor General's Office, said: 'We urge the ministry to inform the government of every dollar earned from these trips. We know that a lot of money has been made – but we have no idea in whose pockets it ended up. Why not put the money into the budget and use it to solve the Zone's problems?'[2] A Kyiv court briefly banned tours to Chernobyl, ruling that the Ministry of Emergencies could not authorise visits without gaining permission from the Ministry of Internal Affairs. The dispute was resolved by bringing tours under closer state observation – and the entry price was significantly increased, so that the profits might spread more readily around various governmental departments.

Following Russia's annexation of Crimea in 2014, and the ensuing conflict in the east, Russian tourists largely stopped visiting Chernobyl – but the number of Western tourists was rising. The new Ukrainian government felt no obligation to protect Soviet military secrets and added the Duga-1 radar to the standard tour itinerary. Then in 2015, Ukraine issued a 'decommunisation' law instigating the state-sanctioned mass removal of Soviet-era monuments and political symbols. More than 50,000 Ukrainian street names were changed (no more Lenin Boulevards, or Karl Marx Squares), along with over a thousand city and village names.[3] Outside the breakaway territories of Donetsk and Luhansk in the east, Chernobyl was the only region where Soviet-era art and architecture wasn't placed under immediate threat of demolition. From the perspective of Western tourists, Ukraine was growing rapidly more accessible, while in heritage terms Pripyat was becoming something quite new and unique: a Soviet Pompeii.

Despite the increase in visitor numbers, the tour experience on offer changed little. Most visitors were taking day trips, which meant losing four hours being ferried from Kyiv and back. Once delivered to the Zone, they would visit the Lenin monument in Chornobyl, stop for a photo beside the power plant, have lunch at the workers' canteen, then take a quick walk through Pripyat, with perhaps a glimpse of the Duga. Judging by the photographs that tourists posted online, the itinerary was essentially the same as the tour I'd taken back in 2013 – practically room for room. The Exclusion Zone covers 2,600 square kilometres, yet the tour buses were all queuing for the same five attractions along a single 45-kilometre stretch of road. I knew almost nothing about the wider Zone back then, but I'd heard it contained nearly a hundred abandoned villages, along with factories and collective farms, and I began to wonder what they would be like to visit. More than anything, I craved authenticity, the sensation of touching history. I figured there was more to be found on the back roads of the Exclusion Zone.

In 2015, I got into tourism myself, leading trips to communist heritage sites in Bulgaria, where I was living at the time. I had started visiting Ukraine more often too, as had my Australian friend, the travel writer Nate Robert, who was already leading his own tours in Iran. In 2016, Nate asked if I wanted to put together a Chernobyl tour with him. That same week, I received an email from a licensed Chernobyl guide named Orest. He had read my article about my 2013 trip and offered his services as a fixer should I ever decide to return. From that point on, everything seemed to fall into place quite naturally.

Working through itineraries with Orest, it soon became clear that the default Chernobyl tour route was far from the only experience available. It just happened to be the easiest and it stopped at all the places locals assumed foreigners would want to see. Tourists didn't ask for anything different, because they didn't know what else was possible; and so each tour followed in the footsteps of the last, with more buses joining each year. However, if there was one thing I'd learned from my travels, it was that locals don't always understand the value of what's right in front of them. Some of the most breath-taking sights I ever saw – the underground river beneath Moscow, abandoned theme parks in China, mine shafts in the mountains of north Wales – were places that native inhabitants might never have thought to take a guest. Sometimes it takes a foreigner to know what other foreigners will find most interesting.

The people who signed up for our trips were often fascinating themselves. Many had a specialism that drew them in: radiologists, architects, historians, biologists, and veterinarians – we even had a satellite-communications engineer. Other visitors – tourists of Polish, Lithuanian, or Ukrainian descent – had ancestors from the region. One couple, who were American Jews, wanted to visit the Jewish Cemetery in Chornobyl and say a traditional prayer for the dead. Another visitor was a nuclear specialist with the U.S. Department of Defense. In *Manual for Survival* (2019), the nuclear researcher Kate Brown dismisses the new breed of visitors to Chernobyl as 'disaster tourists', but having myself guided over a hundred visitors between 2016 and 2020, that term feels grossly misplaced.[4] A number of these people

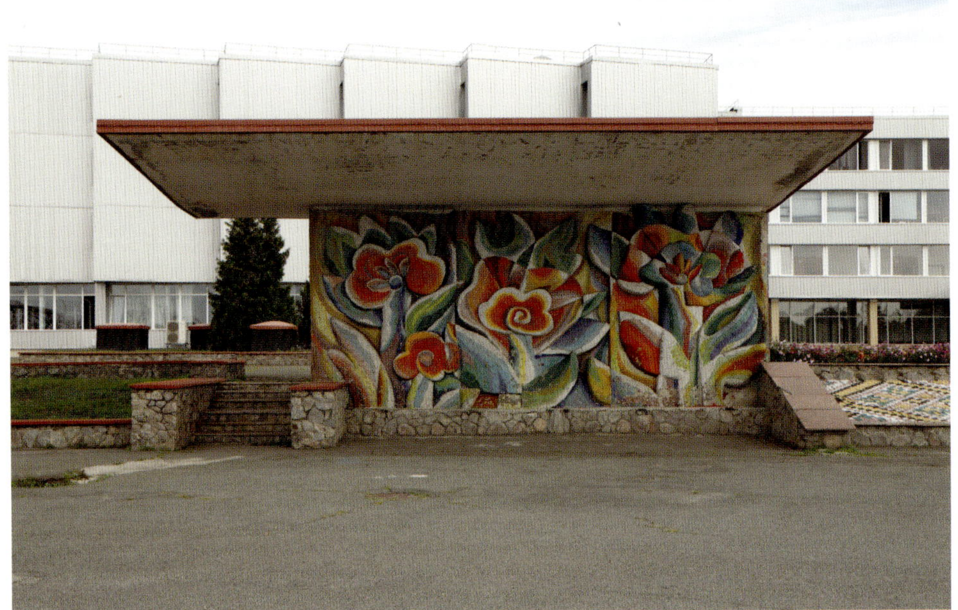

Bus stop, Chernobyl Nuclear Power Plant. The drop-off point for plant employees arriving by bus.

have worked in the nuclear industry for longer (and at higher clearance levels) than Brown herself. Moreover, the idea that a visit to Chernobyl can never be anything other than disaster tourism suggests an understanding of the Zone preoccupied with the events of 1986. Of the people I met, more had come to see scenes of life and progress, than of disaster.

We created routes that focused on village life and tradition, public art (murals, mosaics, and monuments), and overlooked works of architecture, often to the bemusement of our Ukrainian colleague. 'Are you *sure* they want to see this?'

Orest would sometimes ask, as we stopped to admire another utilitarian concrete bus stop. 'Every Soviet village had one back in the day…' But British and American tourists often found the small-scale ephemera of Soviet-era life more interesting than the well-documented landmarks of Chernobyl. Together we ran more than a dozen multi-day tours, taking groups to the farthest corners of the Zone. We saw churches, factories, farms, and village clubs – a world that felt so different to the narrowly prescribed Pripyat experience. We drank *samogon* (moonshine) with the

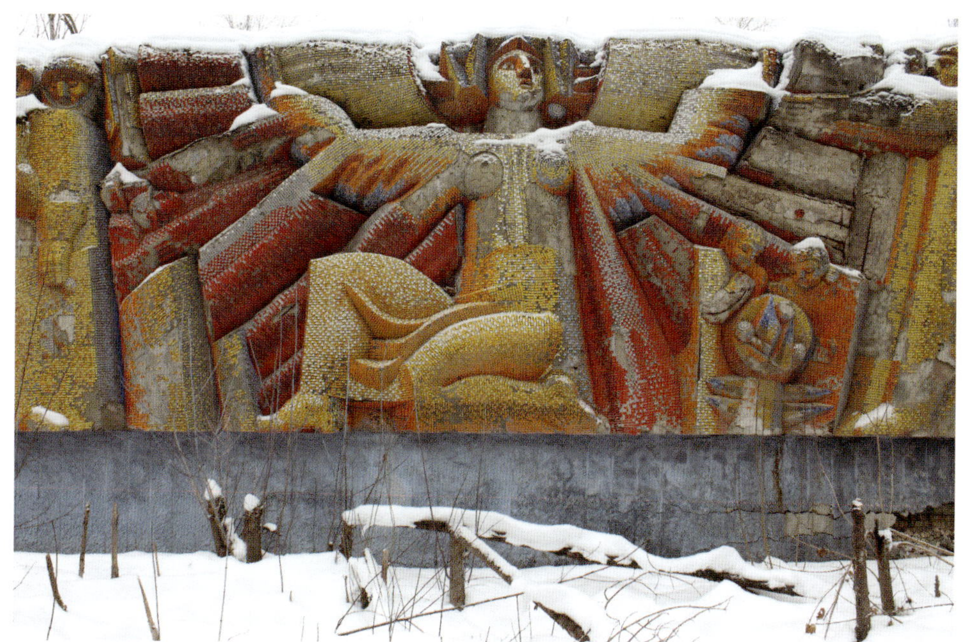

Demetra (1982), by Ivan Semenovych Lytovchenko. Mosaic mural, Lenin Avenue, Pripyat. Sculpted mosaics by this artist decorate a number of buildings in Pripyat.

samosely, slept in locals' homes, and ate packed lunches on the road rather than losing an hour each day at the canteen. On one January tour, we saw more moose than tourists.

It didn't always go smoothly, though. On the very first tour we ran, the bus broke down as soon as we entered the inner Zone. Had it happened a few metres back, we'd have been able to sit down and relax while we waited to be rescued. As it was, we shifted uneasily under the watchful gaze of the checkpoint guards for a long sixty minutes. Here we were subject to the more stringent rules of the 10 km Zone: no sitting outside, no eating or drinking, no smoking, and despite the late September heatwave, on no account could we take our jackets off. 'Well this fucking sucks,' said Nate with his typical Australian charm, as he fingered his cigarette lighter. Eventually we were saved from this limbo by a police car. Our whole group was told to pile in with the officers, five in the back, three in the boot, squashed in so tight against the Chernobyl security police that I had a handgun poking me in the ribs all the way to the power plant.

RULES OF THE ZONE

Soon I was spending three months a year in Ukraine, entering the Zone as often as ten times a month, during which I got a good look behind the scenes of the tourism industry, and witnessed a lot of changes. The canteen and checkpoint queues got longer. In 2018, tourists began hanging 'love locks' on the Pripyat Ferris Wheel, and it became such a popular spot that on Saturday afternoons, sometimes five or six groups would arrive at once. It almost looked like a normal amusement park then – even more so in August 2019, when stalkers cut the anchor cable and for a few days the Ferris Wheel turned morosely in the wind. Meanwhile, the amateur *tableaux mourants* in the schools and kindergartens of Pripyat grew ever more absurd: no longer were the children's dolls merely posed beside the gas masks, they were now wearing them.

The number of tour companies increased every year. The cheapest budget trips didn't even cover the cost of meals for their own staff. At the other end of the scale, Chernobyl Tour seemed to be building an empire. Their advertisements could be seen on billboards around Kyiv, they had signs at the airport, and they opened a souvenir stall at Dytyatky Checkpoint. Here tourists could purchase mementoes of their trip from a motley array of goods, while a speaker system played music from the post-apocalyptic mutant-killing *Fallout* games. Gas masks, mugs decorated with radiation-warning symbols, glow-in-the-dark Chernobyl-branded condoms, even novelty containers of 'Air from Chernobyl': the merchandising opportunities appeared limitless. They later opened a second stall across the road. Indeed, so prolific was Chernobyl Tour's marketing that tourists would occasionally ask me if they owned the Zone.

The industry was now making millions of dollars each year and even the most trivial Chernobyl stories were like catnip to the Western press. In summer 2016, the *Pokémon Go* craze opened a debate on the ethics of playing augmented-reality games at sensitive real-life locations. I published an article about Pokémon in Chernobyl, and my inbox promptly exploded with interview requests (the *New York Post* introduced me as a 'Pokémon enthusiast'). In November 2017, a Belarusian stalker fell to his death while climbing the Duga. The story was not widely reported in the world's press, but it wasn't hard to imagine the media attention should an American or British tourist ever die in the Exclusion Zone. So as tourism revenue multiplied, the safety rules became increasingly strict.

Although it was always officially forbidden to enter buildings in the Zone, for a long time the authorities didn't really seem to care. On our tours, Orest only had one rule: 'If it's dirty, we stay away.' So long as his dosimeter never hit the danger threshold, he'd let us sneak into any building in any off-limits corner of the Zone. He would take us up to the top level of the unfinished Reactor 5 building to stand between towering, rusted cranes – abandoned mid-

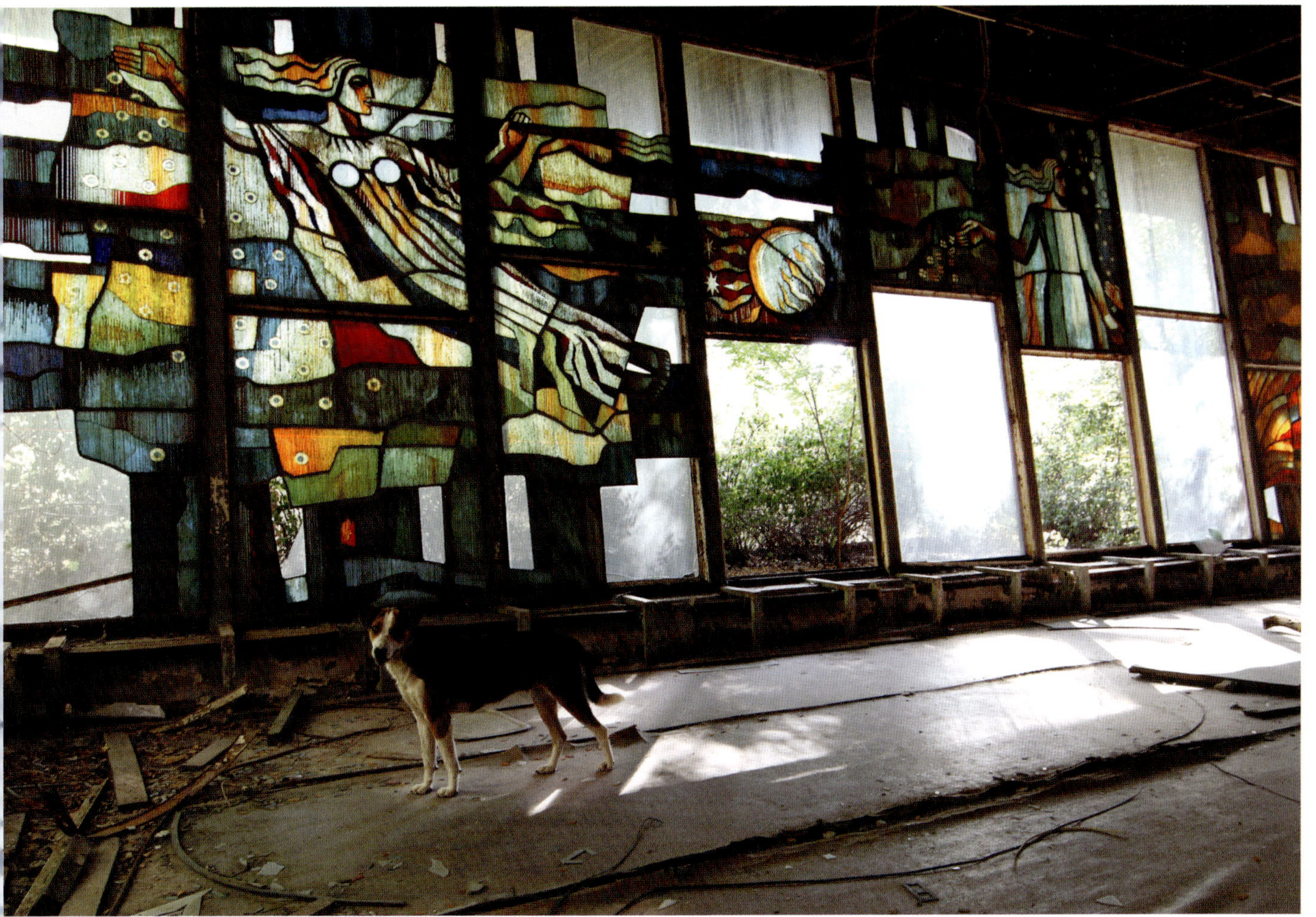

construction – and look down over the entire power-plant complex. He let us climb the Duga radar too, up sturdy ladders just high enough to clear the tree line and see the power plant on the horizon. But as tourism increased, that all began to change. On one trip, the police caught our group climbing ladders in Pripyat and Orest spent that night filling in paperwork at Chornobyl police station; he escaped with a one-month ban from guiding.

The Chernobyl experience was getting safer, but it was starting to feel more sterile, corporate, and manufactured. It got harder too for locals to cash in on tourism revenue. One villager complained to me that the administration wouldn't let her operate her private Chernobyl guesthouse anymore. The authorities preferred tourists to stay in the state-run hotels of Chornobyl, where an ambulance could reach them faster should the need arise (and the state could keep the booking fee itself). In late 2018, the entry process at Dytyatky Checkpoint – which previously had been a clumsy, old-fashioned routine of clipboards and check-lists – was completely revamped. Tourists were all given barcodes to be scanned on entry, thus vastly increasing the number of buses that could be admitted to the Zone each hour.

In addition, from 2019, every tourist was issued with a personal dosimeter, while guides had to carry a GPS tracker, making it easier for the authorities to enforce the no-interiors rule. Naturally, Orest would leave his on the bus and one quiet morning, sans tracker, he led our group inside the off-limits Pripyat hospital. When a vehicle pulled up outside, he motioned us to be silent. Footsteps approached the building and stopped for a while by the entrance. Orest burst into laughter when a fellow tour guide walked in. 'I thought you were the police!' he said to his colleague, with relief. The situation was repeated when a third group arrived and in the end all three groups, each from different companies, explored the hospital together, their guides taking turns to watch the road for patrol cars.

CHERNOBYL AFTER *CHERNOBYL*

The drama series *Chernobyl* launched in May 2019 on the HBO network. Spread over five hour-long episodes, it was eaten up by viewers. It garnered rave reviews, becoming one of IMDb's most highly rated television programmes ever. While it was praised by many for its authenticity, there were nevertheless certain aspects of the plot that differed quite significantly from historical events. In a crucial scene in the first episode, it is discovered that the reactor's bubbler pool must be manually emptied to prevent the melting corium from coming into contact with the water and causing a second steam explosion. In the dramatised version, vice-chairman of the Council of Ministers, Boris Shcherbina (played by Stellan Skarsgård), needs volunteers for this suicide mission, which he pitches with a passionate Hollywood-style speech to a roomful of engineers: 'You'll do it because it

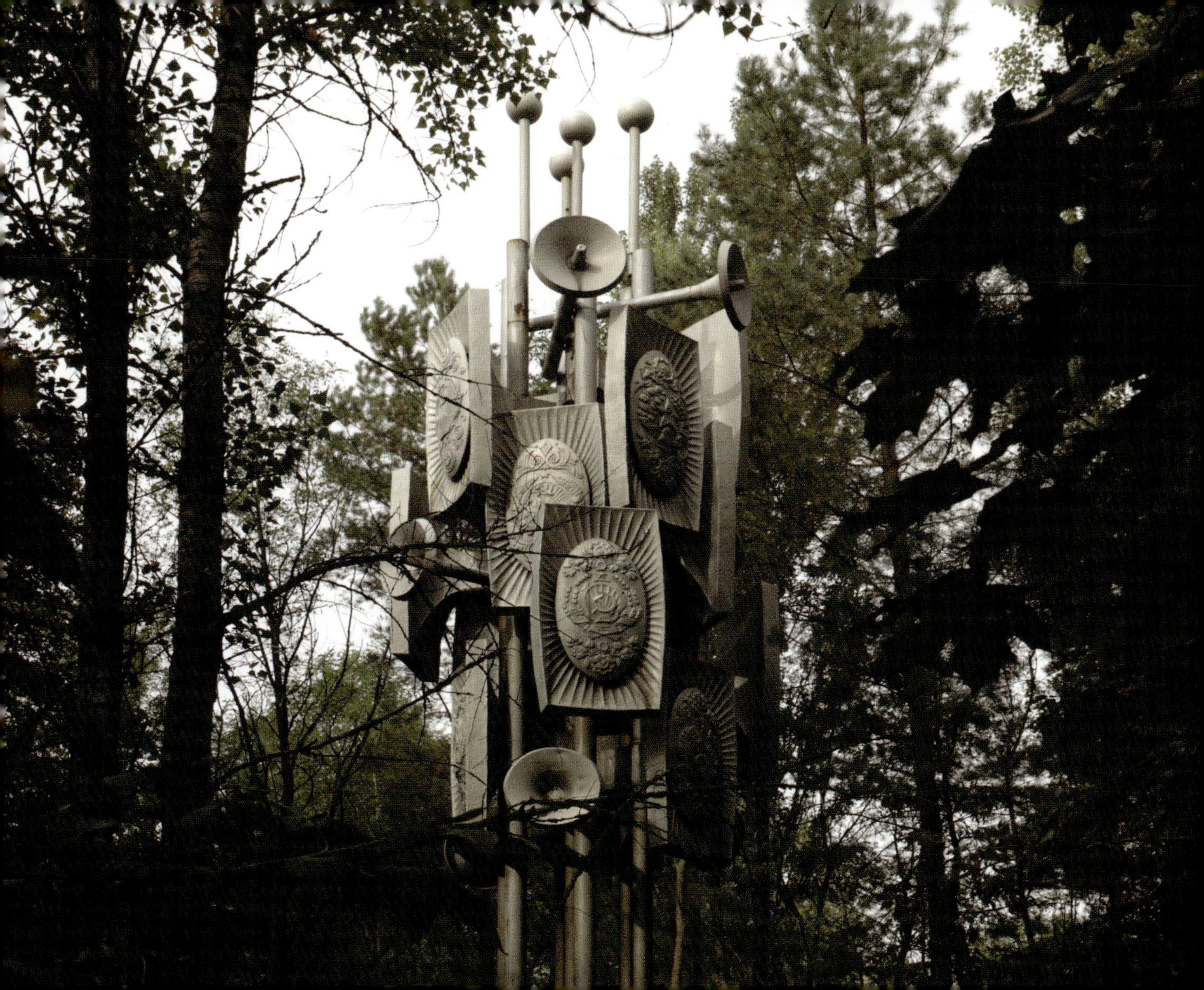

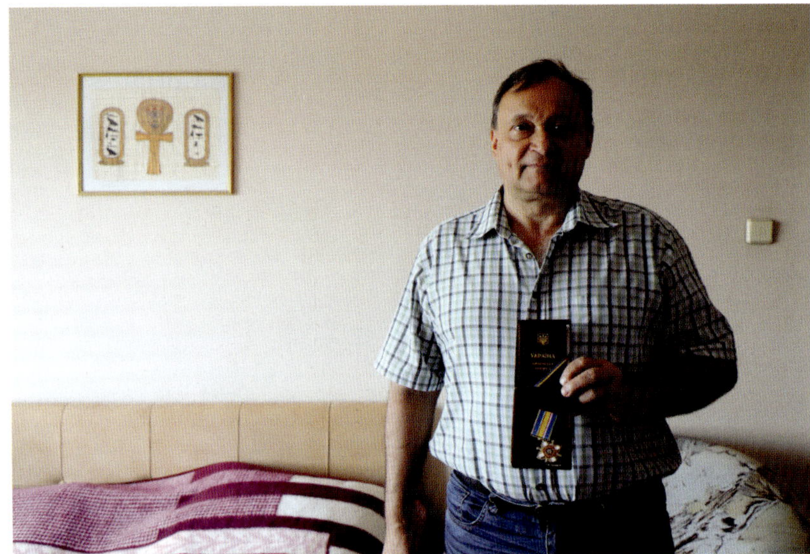

left: Alexey Ananenko. The former Chernobyl Nuclear Power Plant worker holds the Order of Courage medal he was given in 2018 for his actions during the disaster. Kyiv, September 2019.

right: Komsomol Monument, near Chernobyl Nuclear Power Plant. This monument celebrates the Lenin Youth teams who assisted in the construction of the power plant. Once an official entrance to the plant complex, the original welcome sign has since been removed.

must be done. You'll do it because nobody else can. And if you don't, millions will die. If you tell me that's not enough, I won't believe you. This is what has always set our people apart. A thousand years of sacrifice in our veins.'

Three volunteers stand and announce their names: 'Ananenko!' 'Bezpalov!' 'Baranov!' The last we see of them are their silhouettes disappearing into the murky depths of flooded tunnels beneath the power plant, to the sound of their dosimeters going haywire. The speech scene made for fantastic television, but it never actually happened.

'American people think like that,' Ananenko tells me when I visit him a few months after the series aired. 'They presented it in the way *they* would have done things had it happened over there. But here, things are a bit different.' All three of the men on that mission survived long after the disaster, with shift supervisor Boris Baranov the first to die, in 2005, from heart failure (as the series notes, in the closing credits). As I sit with Alexey Ananenko and his wife Valya at their apartment in a suburb of Kyiv, he explains what really happened that day.

'They called me and said I had to go down and flush the bubbler pool. I called Baranov, the shift supervisor. I asked

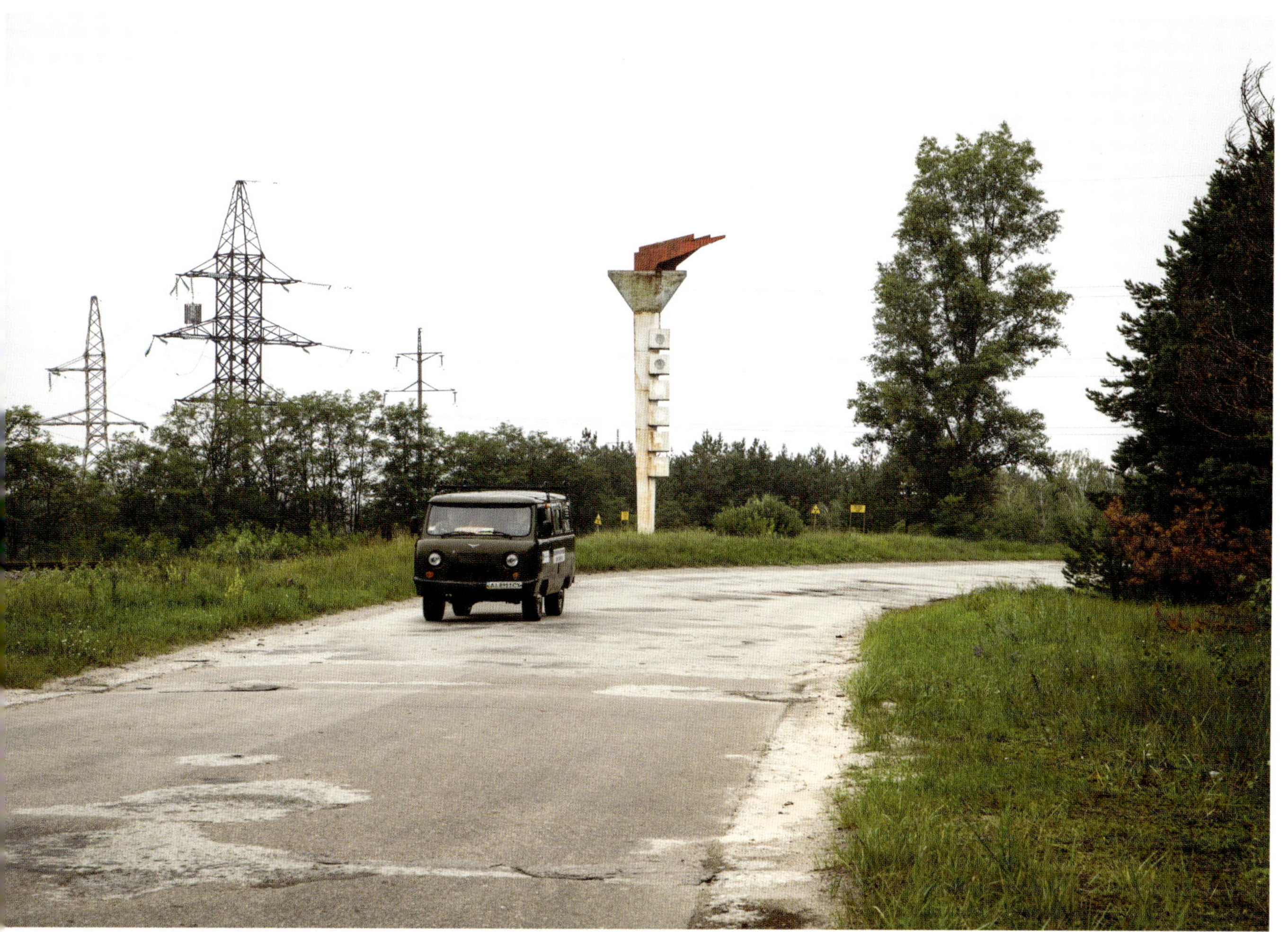

for one more person to come with us [Bezpalov], because we needed to open two valves. I don't remember the readings, as they weren't bad enough to be memorable. The water only reached our knees because the firemen had already pumped some out. We didn't want to walk in it, but there was a pipe running above the water – so we walked on that instead. I never thought it might mean death, and they only sent me because I knew how to do it. They couldn't have sent anyone else!'

Generally though, Ananenko approves of the dramatisation. 'They made everything their own way, but I'm not against them. If it wasn't for HBO, nobody would know about us! One thing though,' he adds with his characteristic humour, 'the man that plays me isn't me at all. Why? Because I have nothing here,' he says, pointing to his clean-shaven upper lip 'and this guy has a big moustache!'

That summer, newspapers claimed the miniseries had caused a huge surge in visitors to the real Exclusion Zone. 'HBO show success drives Chernobyl tourism boom,' announced Reuters.[5] But this was not some new phenomenon that could only be explained by outside factors, such as a TV show. The final count for 2019 was 124,000 visitors – a new record in total numbers, but still only the third-greatest annual growth seen in the past five years. Chernobyl visitor numbers grew by 90 per cent in 2015 (from 8,400 to 16,000 people); by 125 per cent in 2016 (to 36,000 people); by 36 per cent in 2017 (to 49,000 people); by 47 per cent in 2018

(to 72,000 people); and then by 72 per cent in 2019.[6, 7, 8] The HBO miniseries had the effect of putting the industry into the spotlight like never before – but in reality, the tourism boom had already been going strong for several years before it aired.

Nevertheless, with renewed demand for Chernobyl content, the Zone was now crawling with foreign television crews. Many aspects of the Chernobyl experience, which had been quietly going on for years, would suddenly become front-page news. When a company with an English-language website started selling vodka made in the Zone, it was heralded by Western newspapers as 'Chernobyl's first homebrew vodka' – even though the *samosely* had been making their own ever since the disaster.[9] Journalists would typically join the cheapest, most sensationalist day-tours on the market, then write articles describing the Chernobyl experience as cheap and sensational. One writer called it 'messy and morally queasy,' and much of the coverage that followed reflected only the basest consumer experience on offer, as well as fostering widespread misunderstandings about the nature of the region as a whole.[10]

This sanctimonious reporting peaked with the moral panic over Chernobyl selfies. A selection of images circulated in the media showing tourists 'inappropriately' posed in the empty streets of Pripyat – smiling, laughing, even baring flesh. One young woman was dressed in only her underwear and a hazmat suit that was more off than on. This image was later revealed to have been taken thousands of kilometres

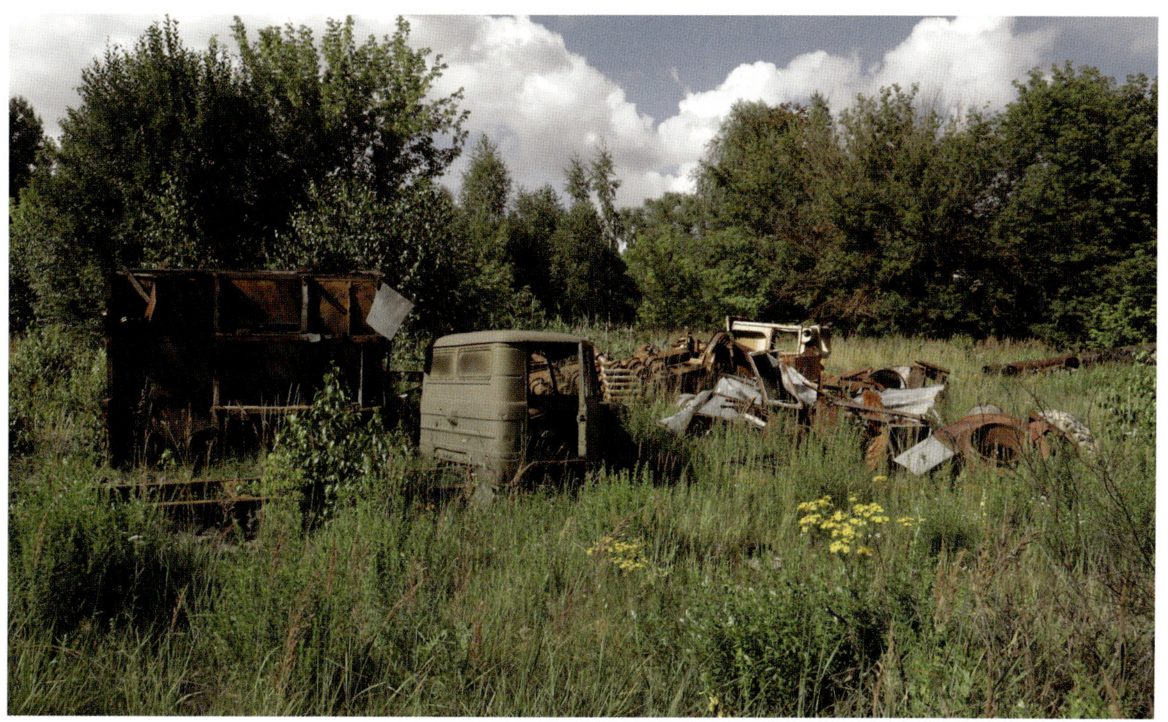

away, at a fashion shoot in Russia – despite being tagged 'Pripyat'; another offending image had actually been taken in London. However, these facts did nothing to mitigate the ensuing storm of outrage, with several of the photographers later claiming to have suffered severe online abuse as a result of their public shaming in the press.[11]

Inhabitants of the Zone, meanwhile, seemed a lot more laid back about it. 'Oh, let them have their fun,' said Maria Kravchuk, who lives alone in her house in a sparsely inhabited village. Her husband had worked as a liquidator after the disaster, but died five years ago. 'Silly pictures never hurt anyone,' she told me. 'As long as they learn something too, and bring more money to the area, why should I worry if they want to be naked in Pripyat?'

'We are grateful that people are coming,' said Sofia Bezverhaya – or Baba Sofia, as we knew her – when I asked what she thought of the tourists. Sofia lives in the village of Kupovate, where before the disaster, she had been mayor. Of some 450 former residents, she is one of only fifteen remaining *samosely*. Sofia didn't mind tasteless photos, she said, or morally queasy souvenirs: 'If that's what sells, let them sell it. Let people buy it and show the rest of the world that they came to Chernobyl and bought it here. I think it's good.'

That summer I watched as foreign journalists attempted to impose their own sensibilities onto a place that was largely indifferent to them. There appeared to be a basic misunderstanding of what Chernobyl is (an error epitomised by comparisons of the Chernobyl Zone with fundamentally different sites such as Auschwitz). When Westerners talk of Chernobyl, it is almost solely in terms of the accident. They imagine the whole 2,600-square kilometre Zone should be treated as a memorial to the events of 1986. However, from a local perspective, that disaster wasn't even the deadliest in living memory to strike Chornobyl, having claimed fewer lives than either the Holodomor or the Holocaust. Besides, the tourist experience is a tiny aspect of life in the Exclusion Zone, and is largely confined to a fraction of the area. Around 6,000 people enter the Zone every day, and on average fewer than 5 per cent are tourists. The vast majority are normal commuters getting on with their working lives, alongside roughly 700 full-time residents. And it has been from the people who live there that I have heard the most 'inappropriate' Chernobyl jokes. It seems that for many, outrageous humour is just part of the healing process.

THE FUTURE

Tourism in Chernobyl, as it exists today, is simply not sustainable. Pripyat and its surrounding villages are falling apart. Buildings collapse, spilling into roads; plants tear up tarmac. Eventually, even some of the current tourist hotspots will be rendered inaccessible. The radioactive particles released into the atmosphere at the time of the disaster are heavier and denser than earth and so they sink into the topsoil (I've heard guides say they sink one centimetre deeper each year). Consequently a law was passed that forbids digging in the Zone. This makes construction or renovation very difficult, yet unless more facilities can be built – hotels and restaurants especially – the Zone will soon struggle to cater for its growing number of tourists.

The company Chernobyl Tour are not without their critics; whether that's journalists taking issue with their 'tasteless' souvenirs, or other tour companies accusing them of overly aggressive business practices. Nevertheless, they are the indisputable industry leaders – so if I wanted to know what the future of Chernobyl tourism might look like, then there really couldn't be anyone better to ask.

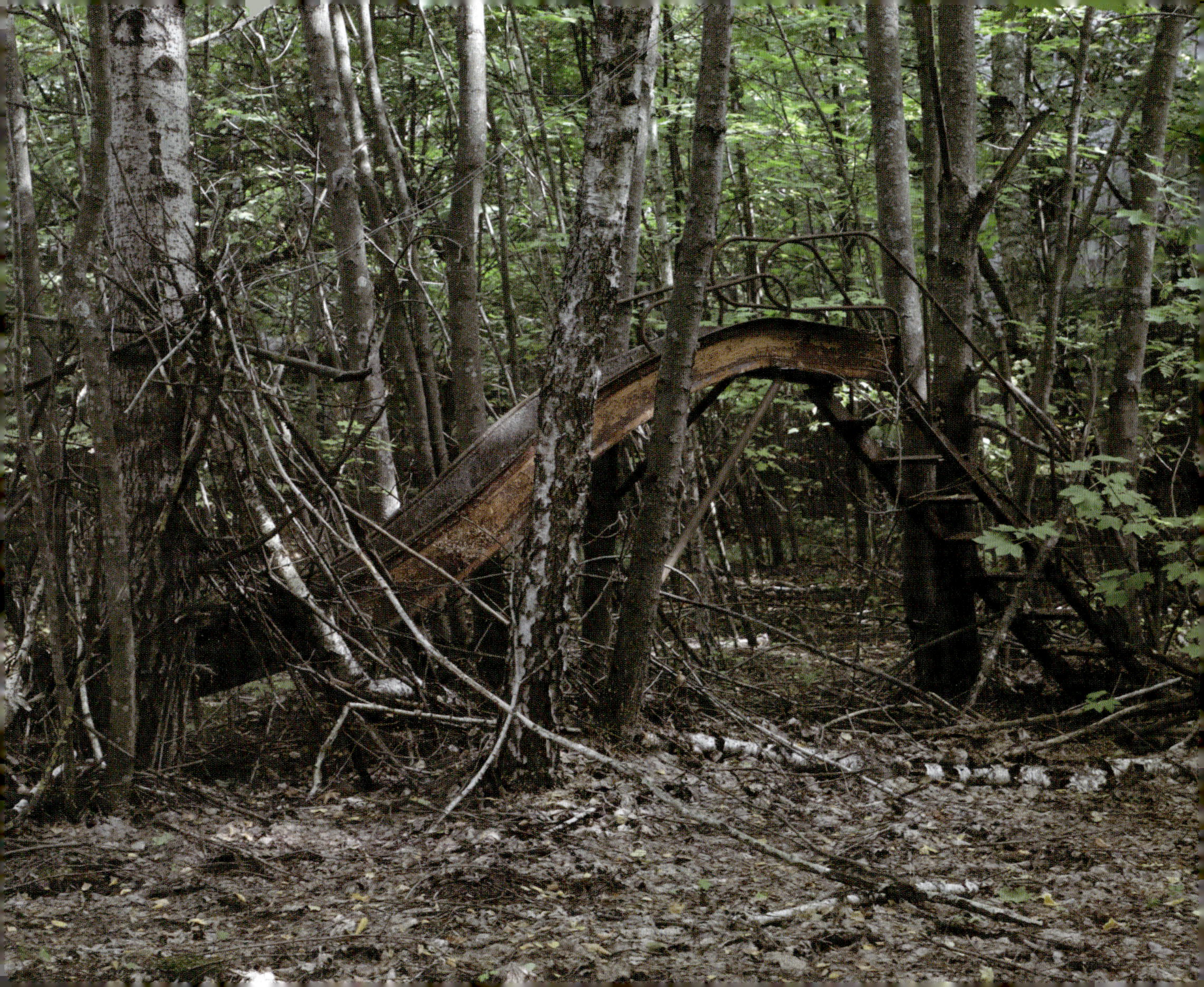

The wall behind the reception desk in their Kyiv office is decorated with framed awards. A glass cabinet in the corner displays a selection of Chernobyl souvenirs, like a miniature version of the stall at Dytyatky Checkpoint. The place has a buzz about it. A receptionist answers a never-ending series of calls in a clipped, professional Ukrainian accent; I can hear more voices down the corridor, and eight or nine employees walk past in the short time before I am invited through to the manager's office.

The room is decorated in a refined, almost classical style. An ornate wooden desk bears a black and yellow radiation-warning symbol inside a carved inlay that might once have borne a monogram. Behind it, Chernobyl Tour's co-founder, Yaroslav Yemelianenko, stands to greet me. He wears a fashionable blue suit jacket over a 'Chernobyl Tour'-branded T-shirt, and has the disarming smile of a television talk-show host. He continues working on new tour routes on his computer, while his chief deputy, Kateryna Aslamova, answers my questions.

'Our company was founded in 2008,' says Kateryna, inviting me to sit on a green leather couch by the window. She is young, with dark hair and bright eyes, and her English is fast and fluent, spoken with the enthusiasm of someone who is passionate about her work. 'At that time, Yaroslav was an investigative journalist at one of the biggest Ukrainian TV channels. But he was also a gamer. I guess you've heard of the Ukrainian video game *S.T.A.L.K.E.R.*?'

S.T.A.L.K.E.R. is a first-person shooter video game with survival horror elements, created by Kyiv-based GSC Game World. Lead developer Sergiy Grygorovych had been inspired by the 'Zone' described in *Roadside Picnic* – but used environments based on real locations in the Chernobyl Exclusion Zone. Released in 2007, the name is a type of intentional acronym known as a 'backronym' – *Scavengers, Trespassers, Adventurers, Loners, Killers, Explorers and Robbers* – allegedly created in order to avoid copyright issues with the Tarkovsky estate. *S.T.A.L.K.E.R.* and its sequels became something of a cultural phenomenon, allowing players to explore the Zone from the safety of their armchairs.

'Yaroslav was playing the game,' says Kateryna, 'then he realised, the real Zone is just nearby, so he decided to go and see it.' Yaroslav joined a tour with a busload of former Pripyat residents, though where they saw tragedy, he was was moved by the beautiful nature of the Exclusion Zone. He got talking with the guide, a former liquidator named Sergii Mirnyi, about how it might be possible to change Chernobyl's image. They ended up co-founding Chernobyl Tour together.

The Chernobyl Zone wasn't recognised as an official tourist attraction until 2019. Earning that recognition has taken hard work and time, during which Chernobyl Tour has grown to accommodate a workforce of more than sixty employees. That includes the staff in the souvenir stalls (or as they call them, 'Tourist Information Centres'), who are usually recruited from local villages where, as Kateryna says, 'there's no industry and no work. So for them, this is a great opportunity.'

'We just opened a centre in the canteen too,' adds Yaroslav, turning his monitor to show me a live camera feed of tourists arriving for their lunch. 'And this is Dytyatky Checkpoint,' he says, switching to a camera at the entrance of the Zone.

I ask about the future and how the company plans to adapt in light of Chernobyl's limited facilities and failing infrastructure. 'Variety' is the answer. Yaroslav tells me about a new route they're offering through the Zone, travelling 18 kilometres downriver in kayaks: 'You don't see anyone,' he says, 'it's amazing.' Chernobyl Tour already offers nature hikes, and also aerial tours by plane or helicopter, while another solution is using Slavutych, rather than Chornobyl, as a tourism hub.

'Chornobyl has limited accommodation,' says Kateryna. 'It's already overcrowded, and it's not as comfortable as some people might like. So we've started taking guests to Slavutych on the workers' train [from the power plant]. It's outside the Zone so everything is easy. It's full of interesting people, experts, and eye-witnesses to the disaster, plus there are plenty of good restaurants and hotels.'

After the popularity of HBO's *Chernobyl*, Chernobyl Tour launched an itinerary inspired by the miniseries. 'It discusses the same stories, but in more depth,' says Kateryna. 'People want to see where things happened and they always ask how much of it was true.' She agrees, however, that HBO did not cause the current tourism boom: she mostly puts that success down to the hard work of locals. 'We visit a lot of international travel fairs – in Berlin, London, New York, Warsaw, and Singapore. All around the world, tour operators and press are realising that it's safe to visit the Exclusion Zone. Every year more people visit, and share their impressions with friends.' She explains that the growth so far has been entirely organic, though she anticipates a slow-burn HBO effect: 'People didn't just watch the miniseries and visit straight away, but I think we might see more HBO fans next season.'

The company's HBO tour includes a visit to the apartment of Deputy Chief Engineer Anatoly Dyatlov, who was in charge on the night of the accident and features prominently in the miniseries. The administration's policy forbidding tourists to enter buildings is a blanket rule, imposed to prevent accidents. However, Kateryna points out that many buildings remain safe to enter, and suggests a better system would involve assessing their safety on a case-by-case basis – opening up more possibilities for tourism, as has been the case with Dyatlov's apartment.

In this way, she hopes that some of the Zone's structures might end up being preserved for future generations. 'Our co-founder, Sergii Mirnyi, is in charge of the preservation of the Duga. It's thanks to him that it hasn't already been

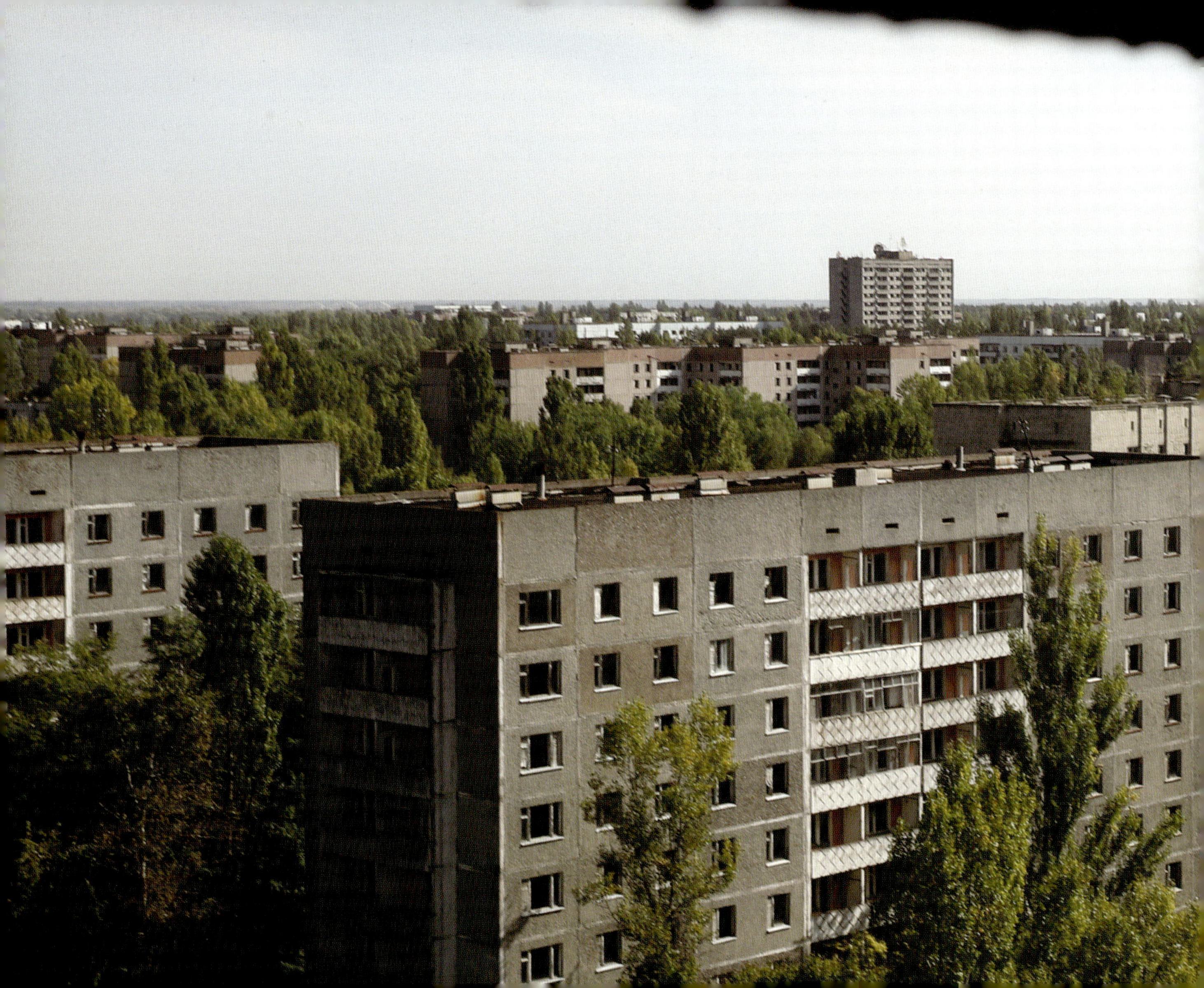

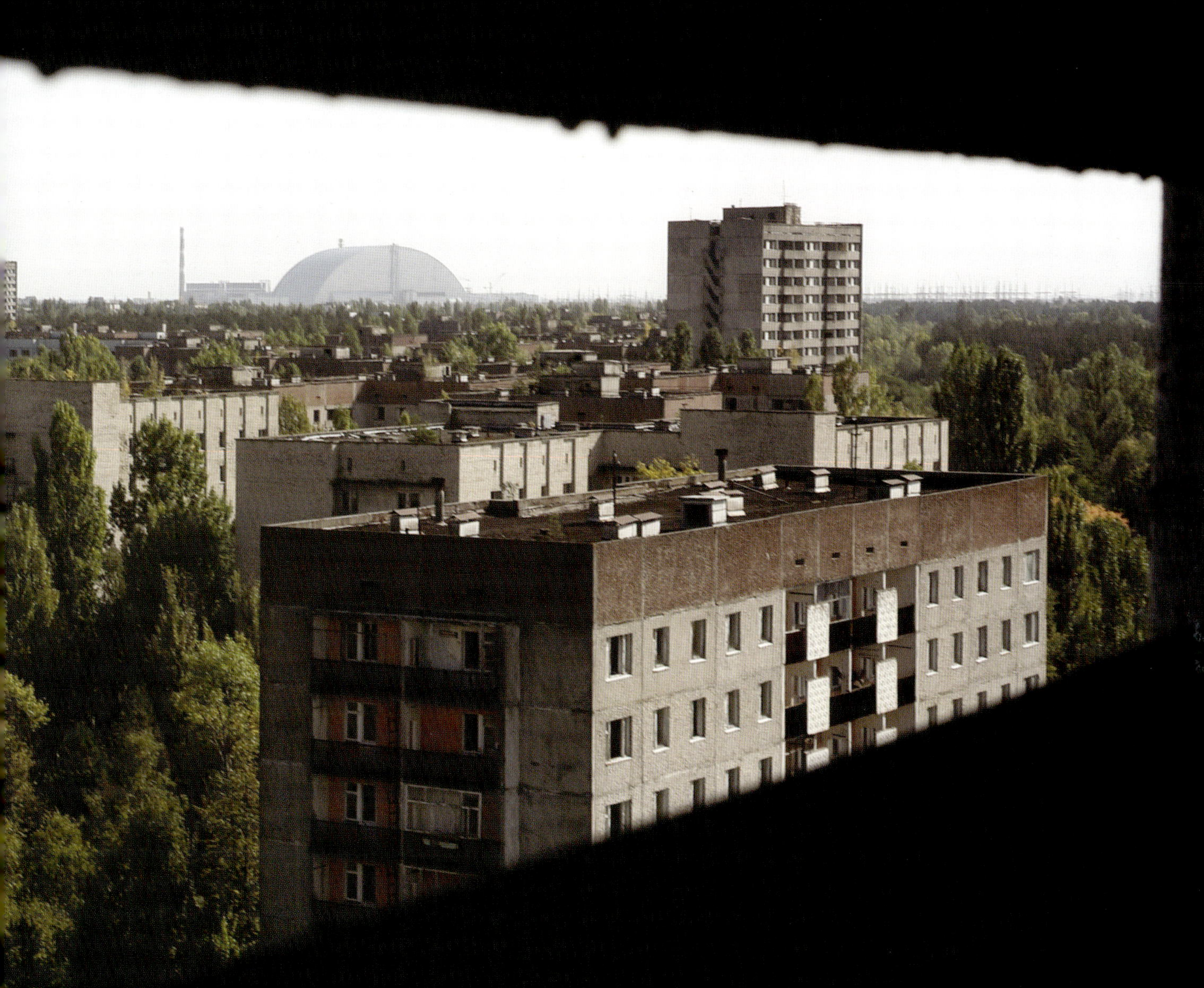

dismantled. And in 2016 we began the process of submitting some parts of the Exclusion Zone, including Pripyat, for protection by UNESCO. It's a long process,' she adds, 'but it's getting urgent now. These places are not just suffering from age and lack of maintenance, but also because the Ukrainian National Guard has been allowed to use them for training.' (Journalists have reported the bullet-holes peppering some of the walls around Pripyat, and I have also seen them myself.[12]) 'We really hope the Exclusion Zone can become a protected UNESCO site – survive as a nature reserve, and an open-air museum.'

As much as I appreciate hearing talk of preservation, I can't help feeling that Chernobyl Tour's slick, branded, exit-through-the-gift-shop approach stands at odds with what many visitors consider to be the appeal of the Zone, which is its quality of unpolished, Soviet-era authenticity. Yaroslav says his interest in Chernobyl was sparked by the *S.T.A.L.K.E.R.* games, but I wonder if the programme of tours he has created would appeal to other gamers or potential stalkers. Kateryna believes so: 'I think in many cases, people enter illegally to visit the places they can't see on regular tours. Imagine you want to see the Zone at night, for instance. Occasionally I have ex-stalkers on my tours, and now, with all the choice we offer, they realise there's no longer a reason to go in illegally.'

Despite her conviction, however, there is also the issue of economics: Chernobyl Tour's half-price trips for Ukrainians are still expensive for those living on the country's $200 monthly minimum wage. Presumably, many would struggle to visit the place in the 'correct way' even if they wanted to, and I find myself wondering what the stalkers themselves have to say about it.

previous page: Pripyat rooftops, view through a ventilation slot in the roof space of a residential tower block. The power plant, complete with the New Arch, can be seen on the horizon.

right: Audio-visual shop at 27a Kurchatov Street, Pripyat. Broken television sets have been replaced on their wooden shelves.

overleaf: 'Izumrudniy' ('Emerald') Holiday Camp, near Chornobyl. Once a popular spot for summer holiday breaks, these rustic wooden chalets, painted with characters from cartoons and fairy tales, were completely destroyed by forest fires in April 2020.

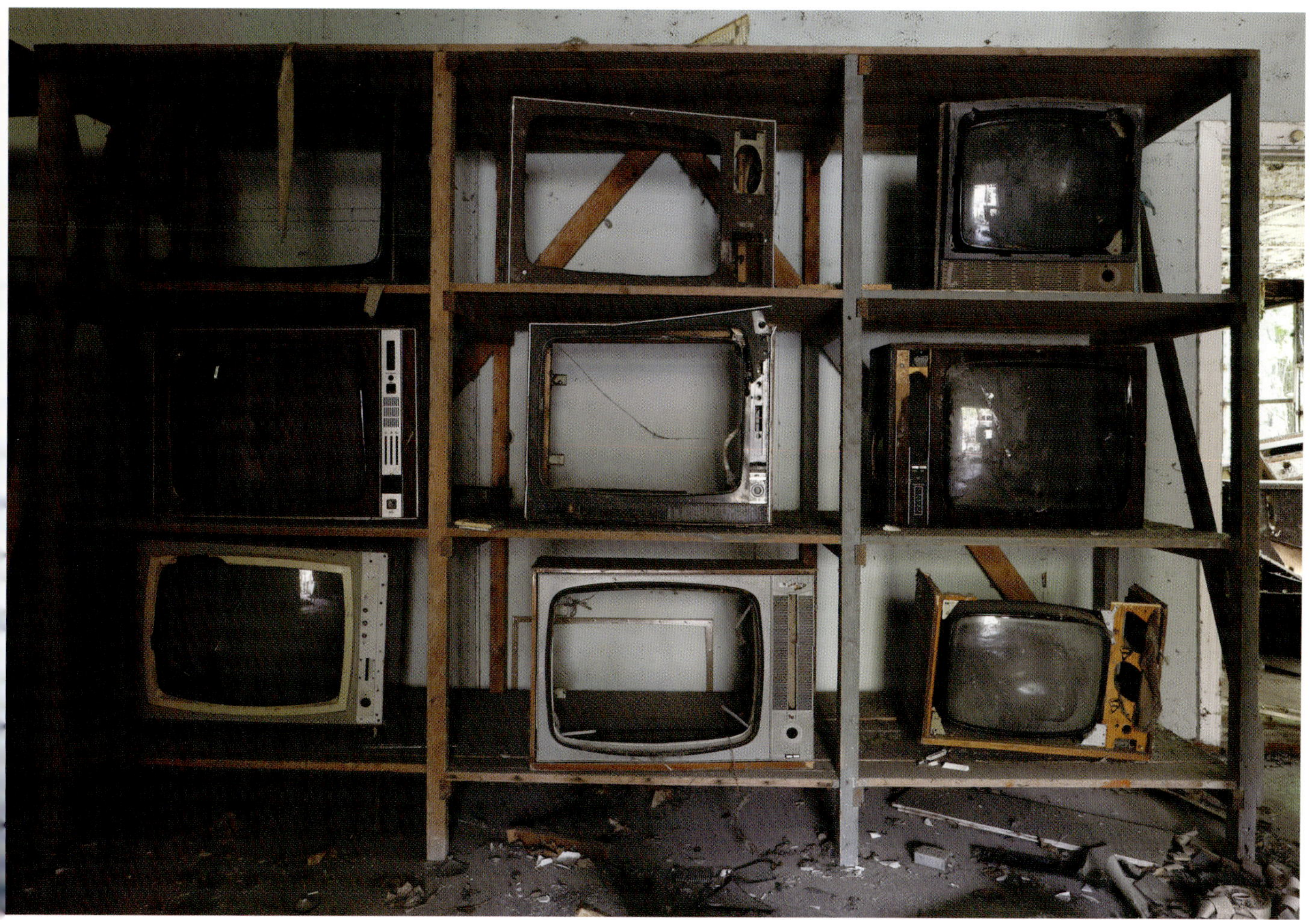

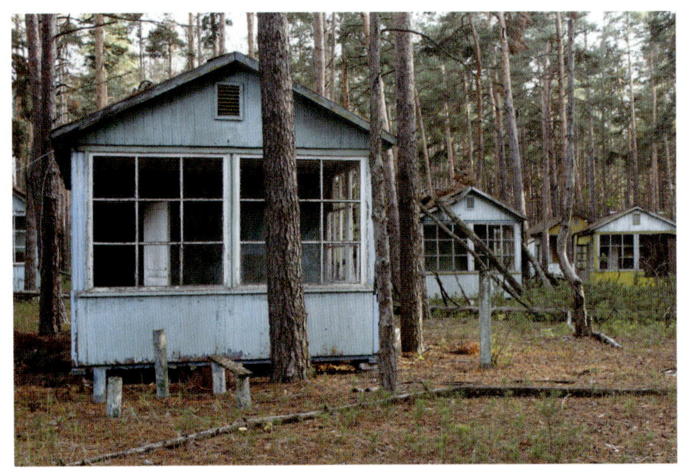
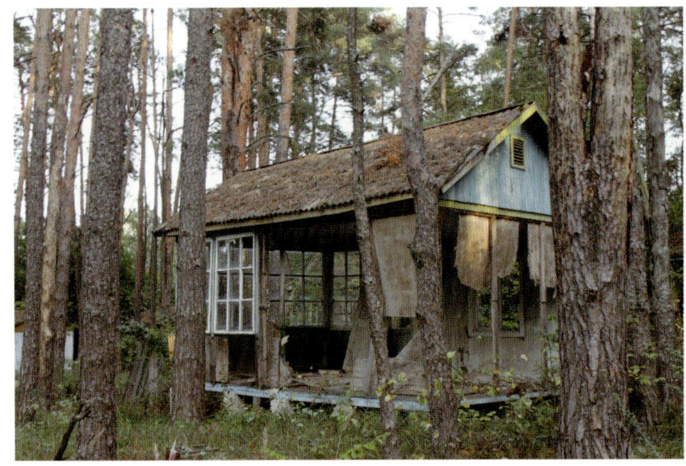
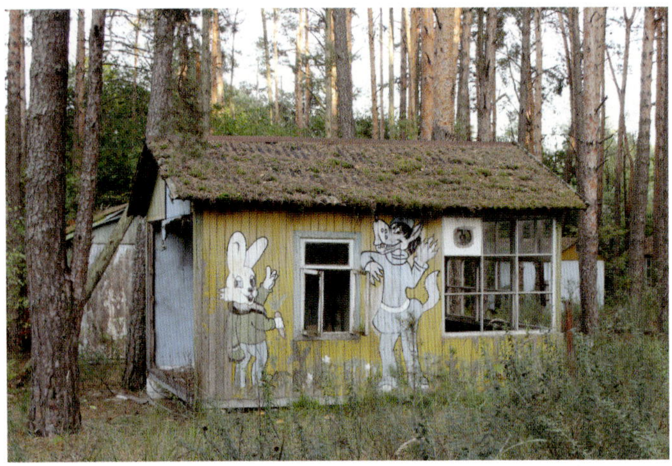
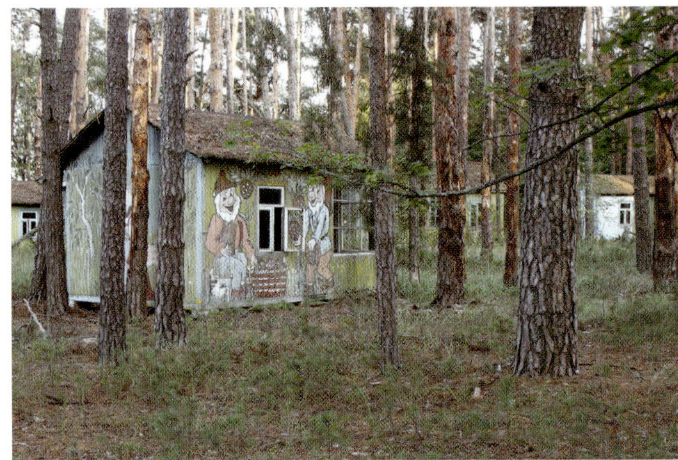

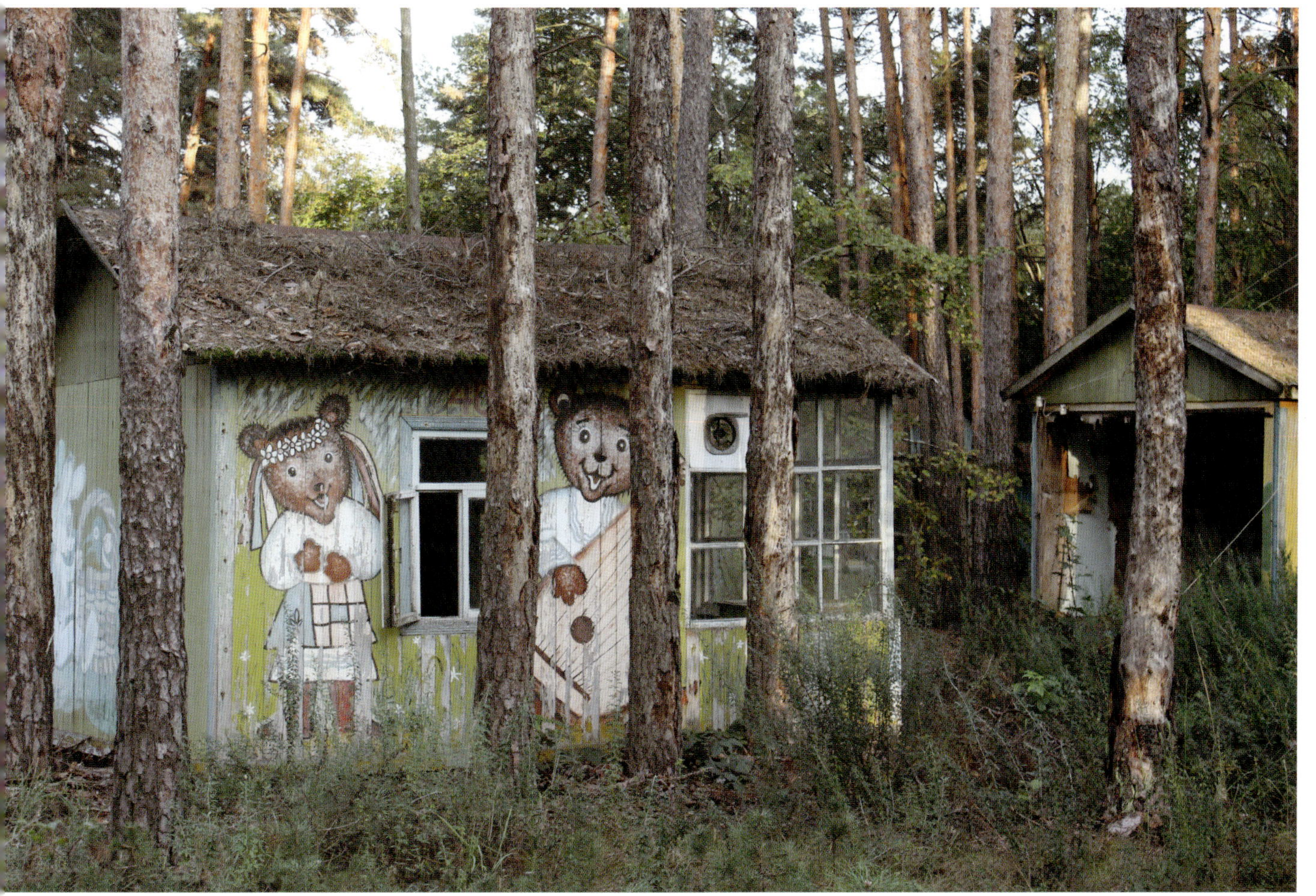

'... from death in valleys preserve me, O Lord.'
Robert Macfarlane, *Mountains of the Mind*

THE STALKERS

One morning, driving from Kyiv to the Zone with my Ukrainian friend Anton, we stop for coffee at a roadside motel. 'You're going to Chernobyl?' asks the matronly woman behind the counter. It must have been obvious – us out here, speaking English, and few other destinations on this road. 'Well if you're interested, I do tours to unusual parts of the Zone,' says the woman, who for the sake of discretion I'll call Snezhana. She tells us there's a vehicle graveyard in the process of being exhumed: 'at Buryakivka you can see cars buried two deep in the ground.' Carefully avoiding the word 'illegal', Anton, a lawyer by training, asks Snezhana if she enters the Zone through the official checkpoint – or by some detour. 'A detour,' she confirms, with a smile. 'I drive everywhere. I know every part of the border, where and when to enter.'

Snezhana says that she guides groups three or four days a week, using back roads to bypass security checkpoints. She takes her clients to the scrapyards, an airfield, and to an active monastery where the monks sell homemade Chernobyl cheese. Snezhana also claims that she can drive groups into Pripyat itself. She worked in the Zone for twenty years before opening her motel, knows everyone there, and insists that she's never encountered any problems with the police. Her last group, from Poland, paid her 1,000 Ukrainian hryvnias ($40) in total for a single-day tour for six people.

'Do you want to eat something, maybe?' she asks. 'We have fresh borscht. Or cabbage dumplings.' We order dumplings and eat them by the window. Watching the road, I count twenty mini-buses and three large coaches in just thirty minutes, all headed towards the Zone. Around a quarter of them display the Chernobyl Tour logo.

'Today we had a bus full of Hasidic Jews at 6am,' says Snezhana when she comes back to take the empty plates. 'Then two double-deckers full of Turks. The checkpoint opens at 8am, so they have breakfast here. I asked how much their tour costs – $1,500 per person, they said! I told them they should have gone with me.'

Snezhana seems intent on selling us one of her illegal tours. 'Come with me next time,' she says. 'I can show you the Przewalski's horses.' I had seen some of these peachy-faced wild creatures already: they roam the Zone and can sometimes be spotted in the overgrown fields beside the road into Chornobyl. Przewalski's horse is a rare and endangered breed originating from Central Asia. In 1998 and 1999, scientists introduced a total population of thirty-one horses to Chernobyl, and within a decade more than a hundred foals had been born in the Zone.[1] 'I'll show you the place near one of the checkpoints, where the horses stay after they're captured,' Snezhana says. *Captured?* Anton asks her, and she whispers: 'For the sausages. Come again, and I'll feed you some very nice horsemeat sausages. They bring them to me and I butcher them,' she boasts. Slightly stunned, I ask her how these poachers manage to smuggle

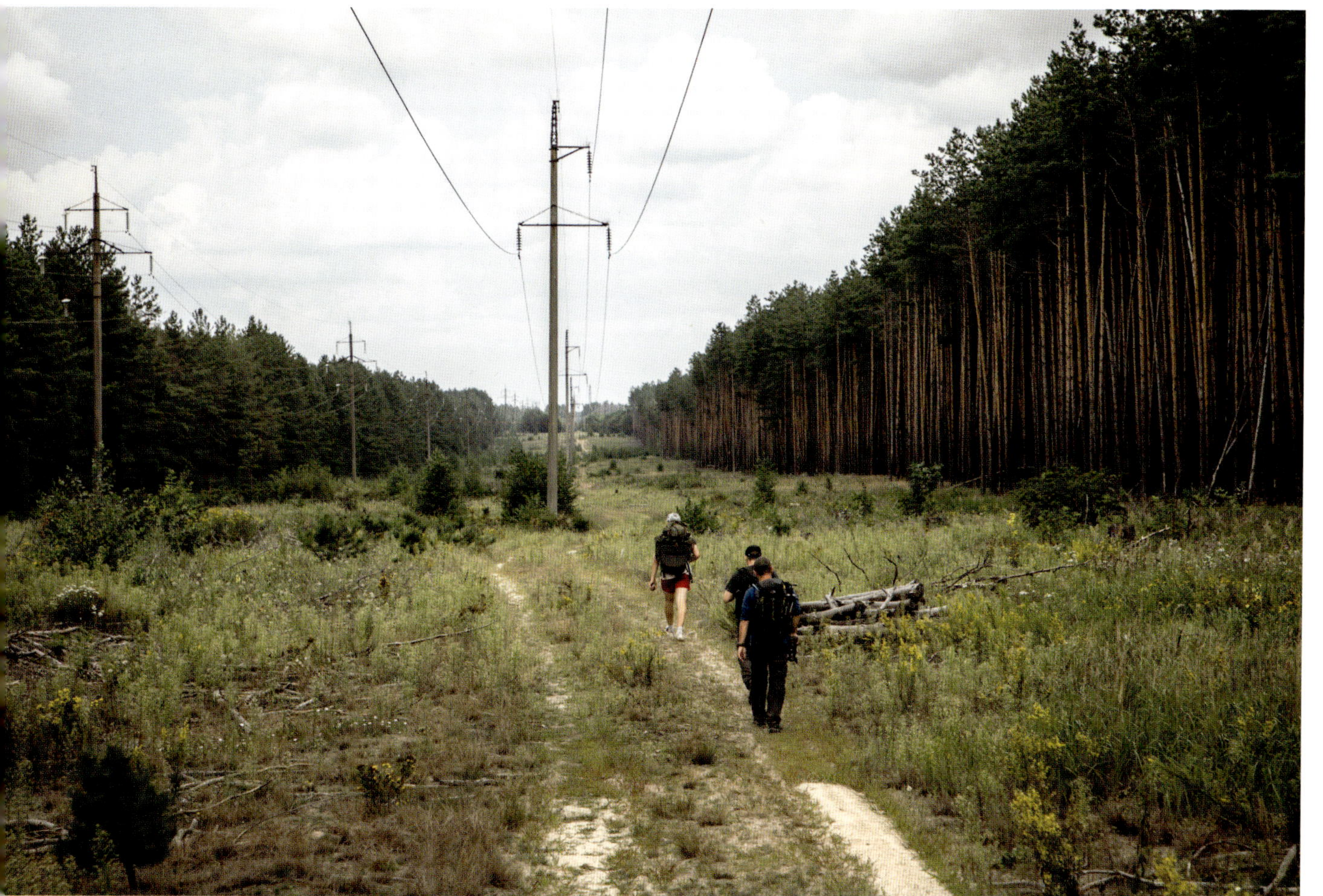

dead horses past the checkpoint police. She looks at me like I'm slow on the uptake, then spells it out: 'The police *are* the poachers.' I ask where the sausages go, dreading the inevitable answer: 'Kyiv, of course – Demiyivskyy Market.'

Before we leave I ask Snezhana if she would call herself a stalker. 'I suppose I am,' she says, and laughs. A formidable hotelier in her fifties, Snezhana does not conform to the standard picture of a stalker – young, male, fit, possibly a vandal, and careless of personal safety. However, Snezhana does fit the *Roadside Picnic* definition of a stalker as well as anyone I have met.

At the opposite end of the spectrum is Alina Filatova. 'Since childhood I dreamed of visiting the Exclusion Zone,' the red-haired twenty-six-year-old tells me. 'I watched a lot of films about the Chernobyl accident, read books and collected rare photographs.' Alina had already explored the drains and underground rivers beneath Kyiv, when in 2015 one of her friends offered to take her into the Zone. Alina's parents helped pack her bags that first time, and she has returned every summer since. 'I am drawn there,' she explains. 'Everywhere they write that it's a dead city, but Pripyat is alive. It has its own strange soul, laws, and quirks. The bustle of city life is forgotten. Only there am I truly calm.'

Alina says she has seen Tarkovsky's *Stalker* five times. But while she loves the film's strange beauty, she says it has little connection with what she does. I ask what the term 'stalker' means to her. 'For me, that word is very powerful,' she says.

'It signifies a person who enters the Exclusion Zone illegally, but who also protects the Zone, someone who loves it sincerely and unquestioningly. To hike more than 100 kilometres with a heavy backpack through the thickets of the forest, hiding from police patrols, your feet blistered and sore, even in rain or hail – this can only be a masochist or a stalker.' Alina has encountered wolves, boars, and vipers in the Zone. She once suffered serious injury: 'I broke my leg on our way back, and still had to walk more than 40 kilometres. I didn't want to give myself up to the patrols, so decided to test my strength. It ended well: I proved to myself that I could do it.'

Alina packs a first-aid kit for her trips, though when I ask about dosimeters, she quips: 'We have a stalkers' saying, *No dosimeter – no radiation!*' I press her on this, and she relents: 'Most stalkers have a good understanding of dosimetry and radiation. We check the places where we sleep, eat, and so on… There is an understanding of what is really dangerous and what is not.'

Alina disapproves of official Chernobyl tourism, however. 'It's a business built on bones, on tragedy, and it's getting worse – they made a circus out of Pripyat. There is no soul, only business, trash, and crowds of tourists.' Other stalkers share the same opinion: graffiti left by an illegal visitor in Pripyat's Microdistrict 4 reads, 'Tours = profit. We make money from tragedy.'

Vladyslav Suvorow also began his illegal visits four years

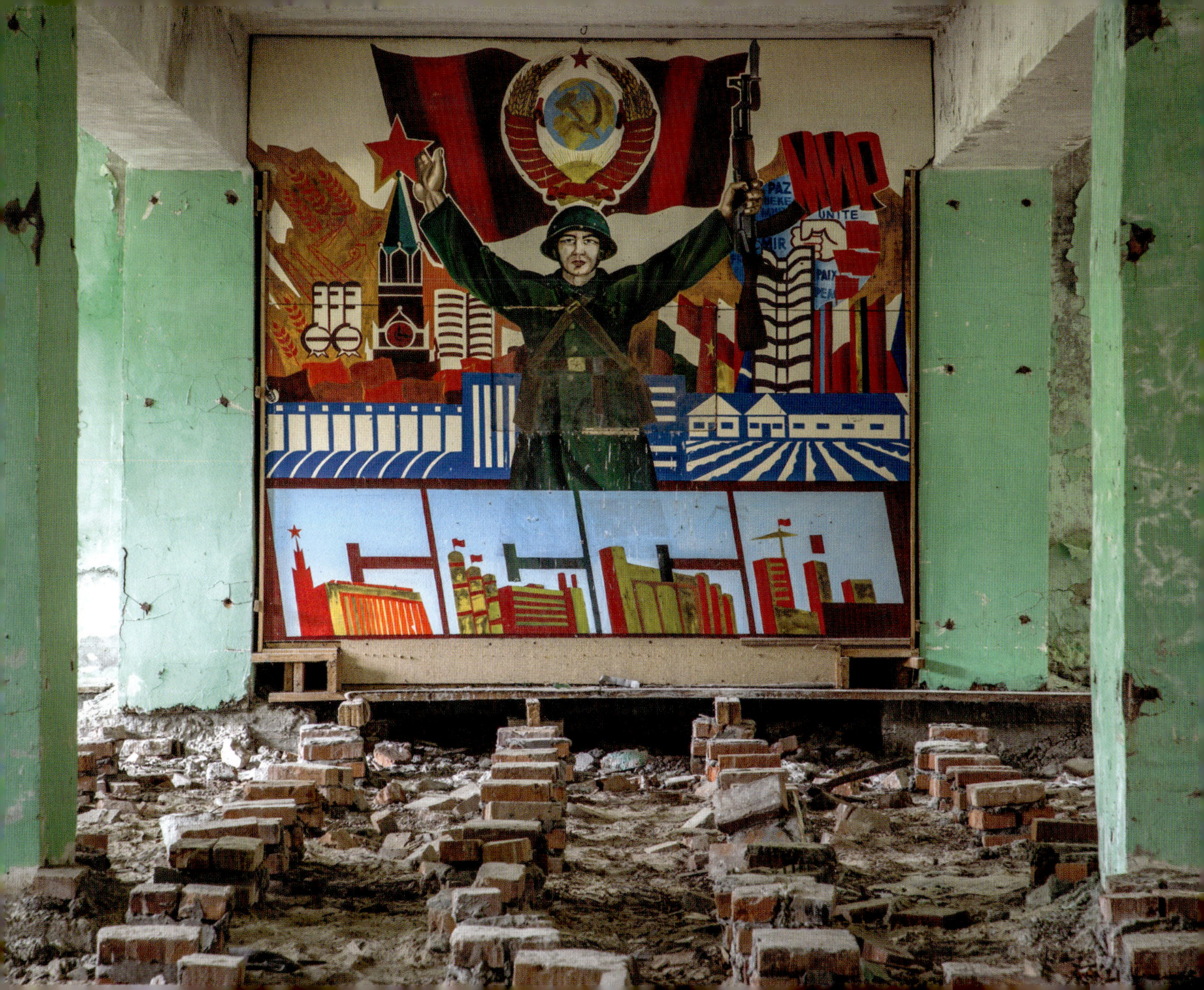
МИР
PAZ
BEKE
MIR
UNITE
PAIX
PEACE

ago. The first time, he went without a guide. Although he's made ten illegal trips into the Zone, he doesn't refer to himself as a stalker. His interests are global. He tells me about recent trips he's made to the Exclusion Zone around Fukushima and hiking across the Kazakh desert to see abandoned Soviet shuttles at the Baikonur Cosmodrome.

'Some stalkers go into abandoned factories, looking for the elements out of filters,' says Vladyslav. 'Tiny flakes made of gold and platinum.' He shows me a photo on his phone: a pair of hands, cupped together around a small pile of green shards. 'That handful is worth $300 dollars,' he says. 'These guys, if they're good, can earn up to $10,000 a night.'

Over the last few years Vladyslav has been selling illegal Chernobyl tours online – connecting curious foreigners with experienced local stalkers. Usually these trips are trouble-free, he says, though recently a French group were the first of his clients to get caught. 'It was their own fault. They disobeyed the guide. They were told not to climb the Duga in daylight, but they did it anyway.' Their punishment was a fine of 340 hryvnias (around $14), along with having their ninety-day Ukrainian entry permits reduced to five days: enough time to pack up and leave. However, there was no restriction placed on them making future visits to Ukraine, so they left and returned the same day, picking up fresh ninety-day permits on their way back in. Illegal tourists, if caught, are often blacklisted from joining future official tours; though for most stalkers this isn't a relevant concern.

I ask Vladyslav if he's taking a risk by advertising illegal tours online. He tells me the Zone administration don't look at websites. 'Anyway, they don't really care what we do. Their only concern is that someone is making money, and it isn't them.' I tell Vladyslav that I'd like to sign up for one of his trips.

THE RIVER

We drive through fields of darkened sunflowers, silent lightning flickering blue-white on the horizon. It is July and even at night the warm air is thick enough to choke on. Almost two hours out of Kyiv, we take a turning off the highway. The road gets worse, the storm passes, then we arrive at a back-road destination you'd struggle to give directions to without knowing the GPS co-ordinates. We kit up in near silence: five of us standing in a sandy lane between hedgerows, pulling on gloves, boots and backpacks in the dark. Head torches are tested, cigarettes glow like fireflies and I nervously sip my water until our guide, Kirill, says quietly, 'Let's go.'

I have assembled a team of hardy and adventurous people. Bradley is an American geographer and research fellow with the University of Sydney, who rose to notoriety in 2012 for illegally ascending London's (then unfinished) Shard skyscraper. Aram is a British-Armenian journalist and award-winning documentary photographer. Wayne, another American, is a

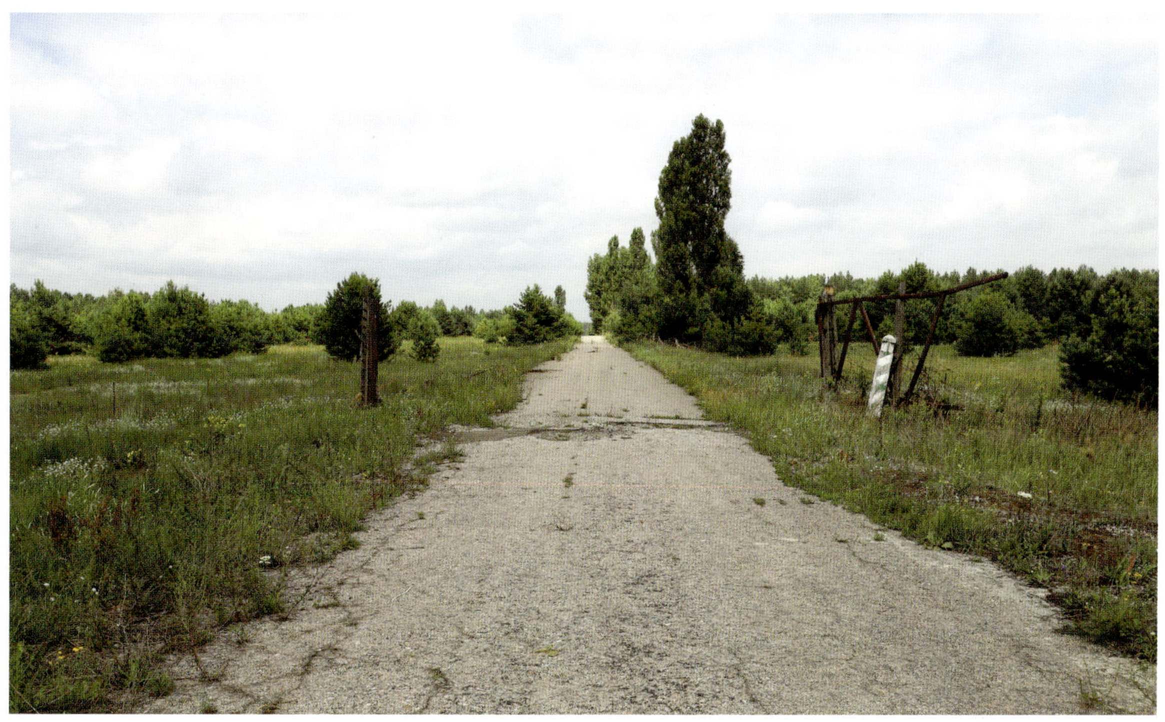

poet and a first-rate storyteller (he commemorated his divorce by cutting his wedding ring in two and throwing half into the frozen Arctic Ocean, waking a polar bear in the proecess; he's saving the other half for the Antarctic volcano Mount Erebus). None of us has met Kirill before.

Kirill is a *real* stalker, Vladyslav told me. Instead of meeting in a bar though (the way Tarkovsky pictured it), we rendezvous outside a supermarket at dusk. Kirill speaks a little English and it's the language we all have in common. Despite this he isn't much of a talker. Dressed in a white singlet and beaten-up trainers, he is wiry, with short-cropped hair and spectacles. He looks less prepared than us tourists, with our gadgets, Gore-tex and hydration packs – but with more than a hundred illegal Chernobyl trips behind him (and only a handful of those ending in arrest), Kirill is our best hope for getting through the next four nights unharmed and undetected, before our extraction from Pripyat on the final morning.

Our driver wishes us luck as he leaves. Then we are alone, taking our first blind steps in the direction of the Exclusion Zone, following each others' silhouettes in the dark, boots slipping in the sand. Real fireflies come out and I watch their lights spin until I feel dizzy. After a while Kirill hisses at us to stop: there's a police checkpoint ahead, beside the track. The light of a TV set flickers between window blinds. We creep past unnoticed, and eventually hit the river.

The River Uzh skirts the southern perimeter of the Zone before joining the River Pripyat, which in turn feeds the Dnieper, flowing south through Kyiv, and then some thousand kilometres later disgorges into the Black Sea. When the water level drops, stalkers roll up their trousers and wade through it up to their knees – but tonight the Uzh flows deep. 'We must make a little strip show,' says Kirill, as he whips off his clothes on the riverbank. He balls them into his backpack, which he hoists high above his head, and then he's wading off between the reeds, milk-white buttocks melting into darkness. I go next but I do it in my underwear – too afraid of getting spotted by police half way across, then having to flee through reeds and brambles, naked from the waist down. The river mud is like treacle, sucking at my feet and oozing over my ankles while freezing water closes around my chest. I emerge on the opposite bank as if

baptised, skin tingling in the cold air of the Chernobyl Zone. Within minutes we are all across, cigarettes are smoked, towels are dirtied and then we're walking again.

From the reeds we cross a farmyard, past barns and rusting debris. Something squeals in the darkness. There's a commotion and a stack of old metal pipes is noisily disturbed. We hear something race off. 'Probably a horse,' says Kirill. A little further on, in the centre of the ruined village, a figure in white greets us: a statue of a Soviet soldier, his stone hands raised palms upwards in a Christ-like gesture. After a few more paces, buildings in various states of disrepair emerge from the dark. Kirill points to the end one, the sturdiest, squarest of the wrecks. 'This is home.'

Inside, we unfurl camping mats onto floors thick with dust. 'Are you gonna use that?' asks Bradley, pointing to Kirill's dosimeter. Our guide shrugs before waving the meter around the room like a magic wand. It gives a reading of 0.1 µSv/h, as in any normal forest. Kirill says it will be another day's walk before we reach anywhere dirty. When stalking alone, he explains, he tends not to use a dosimeter anymore, relying instead on the map of the Zone's hotspots he has built from memory. Besides, if you are caught, your equipment will be confiscated – and dosimeters are expensive to replace.

We crack open a bottle of vodka to celebrate our successful infiltration of the Zone. Kirill doesn't drink, but he sits with us and talks. Tarkovsky's *Stalker* has a cast of

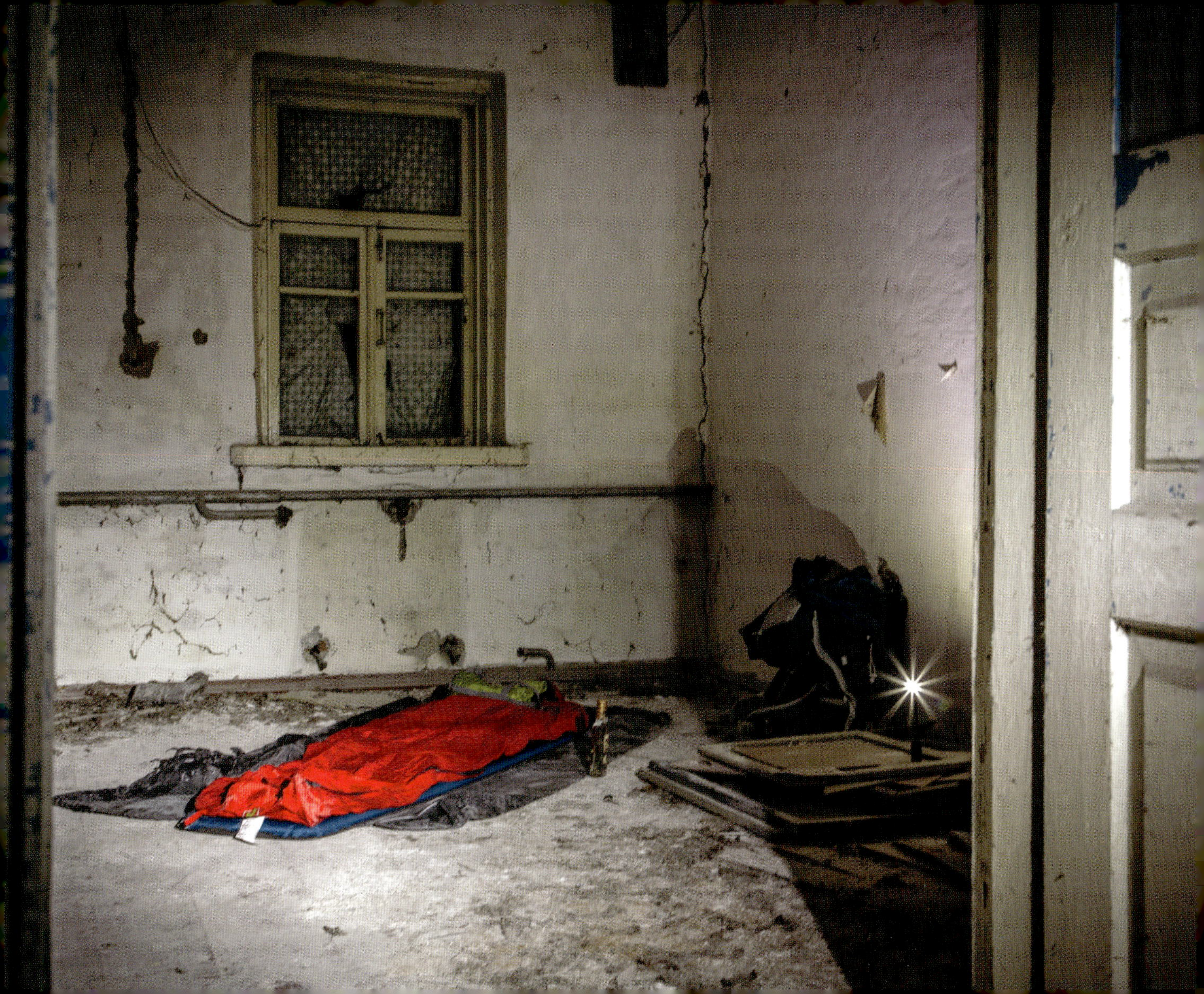

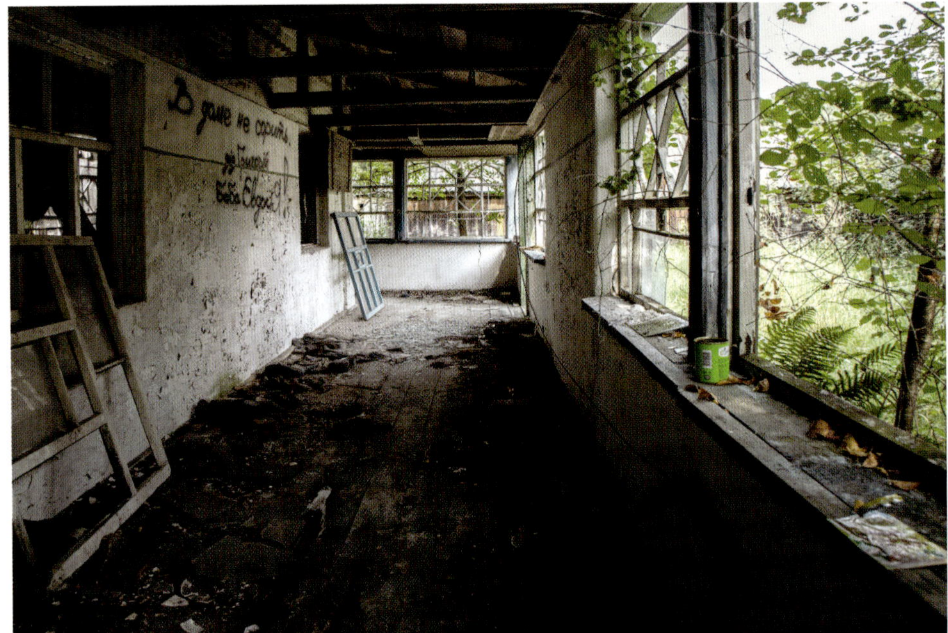

Abandoned house, Chernobyl Exclusion Zone. Houses such as these are used by stalkers as rest stops during the long hike to Pripyat.

three: Stalker, Writer, and Professor. Our group consists of one stalker and four writers, and soon poor Kirill is fielding questions from all directions at once. He previously studied for a career in cultural-heritage management, he says, and his first trip to the Zone was on an official tour in 2009. He didn't like it much – too sterilised, with no opportunity to really experience the place. Two years later he returned with friends, this time illegally. He has been coming back ever since. He says the number of stalkers entering the Zone has increased, but this doesn't bother him. 'More stalkers means more people for them to catch before me,' he jokes.

I sleep maybe for four hours, waking at dawn to find the house empty – save for the mosquitoes that have followed us from the river. The others are out, no doubt exploring the village, with Bradley habitually whispering notes into his dictaphone. Painted on the wall outside, a message in Ukrainian reads: 'This house belongs to Grandpa Grisha and Granny Dunya.'

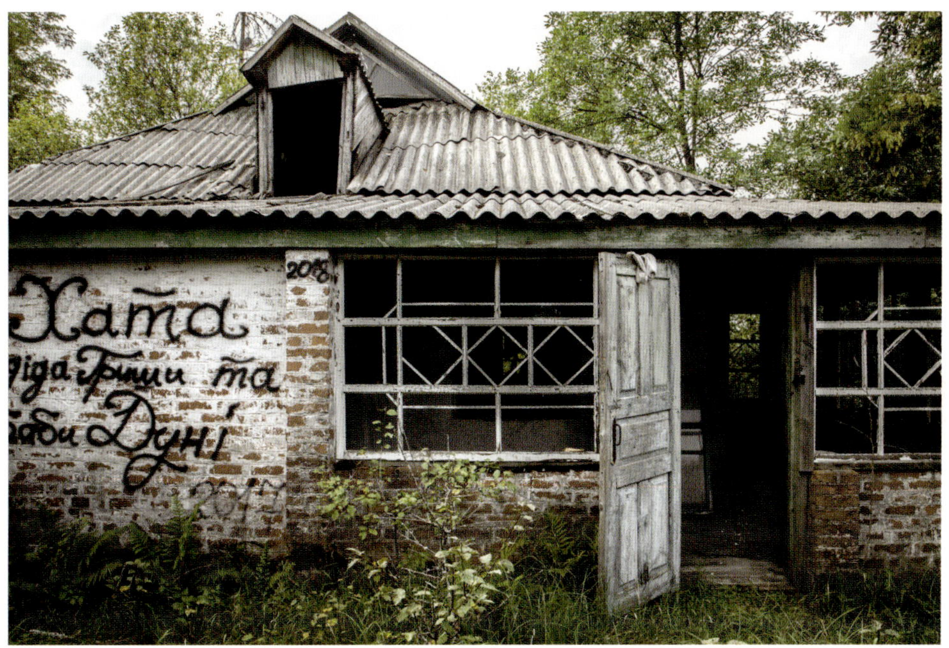

Abandoned village. Ukrainian text reads: 'This house belongs to Grandpa Grisha and Granny Dunya.'

Later, Kirill cooks breakfast as Bradley lies on his bunk reading a book. I begin to think I should have brought a book too: I packed for a Spartan adventure, but this feels surprisingly bucolic. For the next few hours I rest and wait. I brush my teeth in the old stables, now a foul-smelling stalkers' bathroom, and I clean the sand from my shoes – yet to learn the value of the water that I'm wasting.

THE WILD PLACES

At midday, Kirill runs into the house shouting 'Police!' and immediately bolts out the back door. Aram, Wayne and I are sitting on our beds. It takes a few moments to process, then panic sets in and we begin shovelling gear back into our bags. Bradley walks in, oblivious, and we tell him we need to get out. In twenty seconds we're all creeping swiftly out the back, across the overgrown garden, between the outhouses and into the dense bushes beyond. Sprinting between bushes and trees, we break into fields, then keep on running. We spot Kirill peeking back at us over the long grass, and we throw ourselves down into cover beside him. 'I need to go back,' he says. 'I need my stuff.' Wayne asks what we're supposed to do if he gets caught. Kirill shrugs. 'Cross the river and leave the Zone. Or carry on to Pripyat maybe. Whatever you like.'

Lying in the long grass I hardly dare breathe. Ants make a path across my leg. It seems like an age before Kirill returns, looping and ducking back through the bushes towards us. 'There's no one,' he says, perplexed. We ask what he saw before. 'A man in black, outside the house, talking into a radio. But I didn't have my glasses on.' Bradley, dressed in black, is getting all of this on his dictaphone. The realisation dawns on us simultaneously: we are running from our own shadows.

The mood lifts as we leave the village behind, crossing fields to follow a logging track north through the woods. The farther we get from tarmac – and deeper into the wilds – the safer I feel. Across a meadow, a regal stag watches us briefly before springing back into the forest. We see signs of boar as well, their sleeping hollows burrowed out of the scrub.

The Zone possesses a humbling power that's hard to describe. It was never quite like this with the tour bus – an umbilical cord that kept us attached to the modern world. With the bus, we were only ever *visiting* the wilds, but now we are immersed in it, breathing it in – as well as high on

adrenaline from the constant fear of being caught. Our quest to reach Pripyat, against the ever lurking threat of capture or contamination, takes on mythical dimensions in my head. I think of the 'Shimmer', the beautiful, uncanny zone of alien corruption in Alex Garland's film *Annihilation* (2018); or the rural folk horror of Ben Wheatley's film *A Field in England* (2013), its psychedelia, hedgerow mysticism and paranoid fear of sentient landscapes evoking a kind of 17th-century *Stalker*. These feelings of awe and mania intensify when we catch sight of our next destination. We cross a precarious old bridge that spans a waterway choked with dark algae and frogspawn – every creak has me glancing nervously at the water – then ahead, we see something incongruous within this wilderness: the Duga-1 radar rises in front of us, a vast steel monstrosity haunting Eden like a vision from some future Hell.

The road to Chernobyl-2 is paved with concrete slabs, designed to withstand tanks heading in and out of the base. Long, straight, and elevated, it commands an excellent view of the fields on either side. We need to get across without being seen by the tour buses and police patrols that regularly pass by. 'Hide!' Kirill suddenly commands, as we draw close to the edge. I can't hear anything, but sure enough, a car eventually passes. We wait until he gives the order – 'Now!' – and the five of us make a break for it, full tilt, towards the incline. We're only halfway across when he yells: 'Another one!' Clearing the road, we land in a comical heap behind

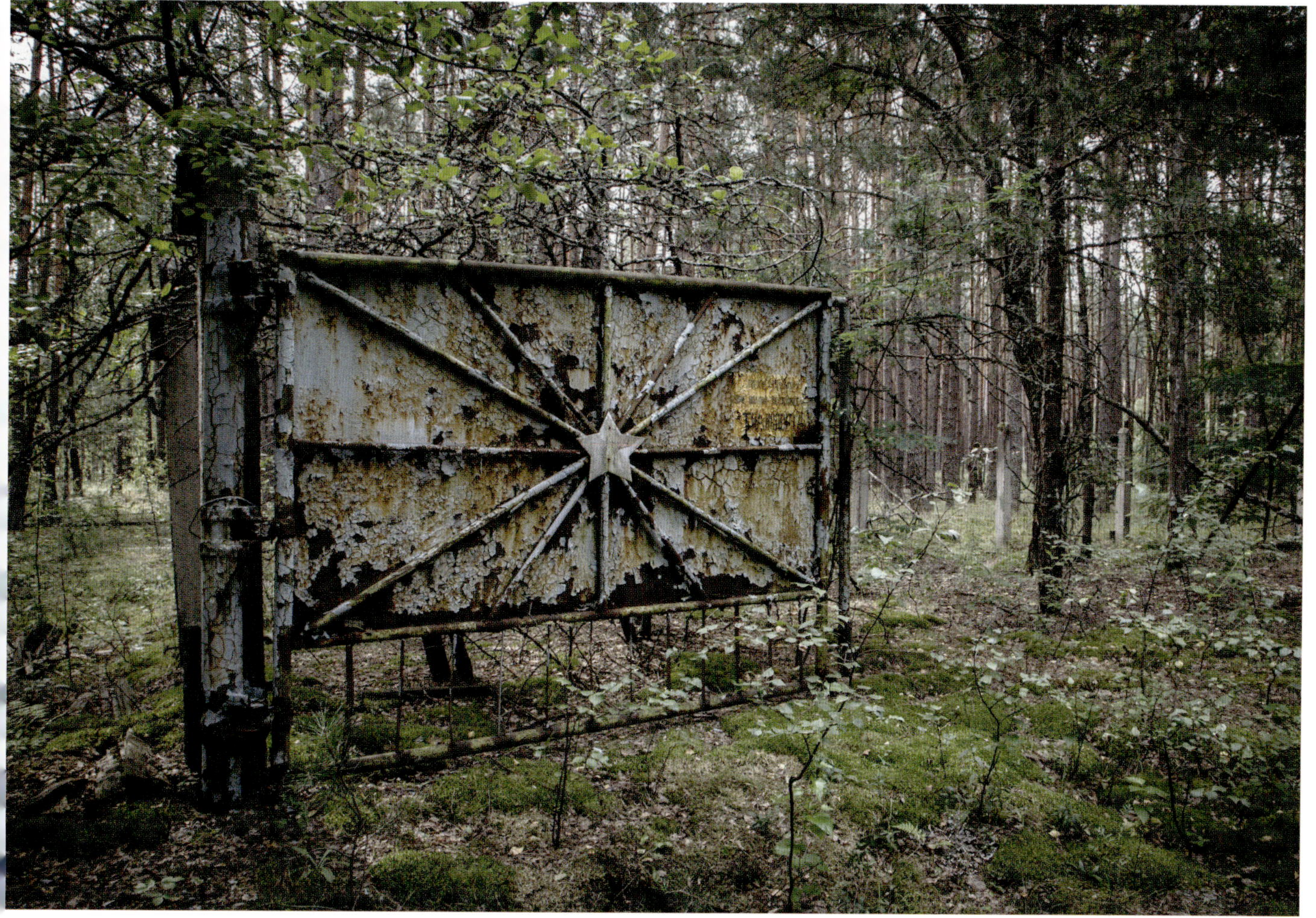

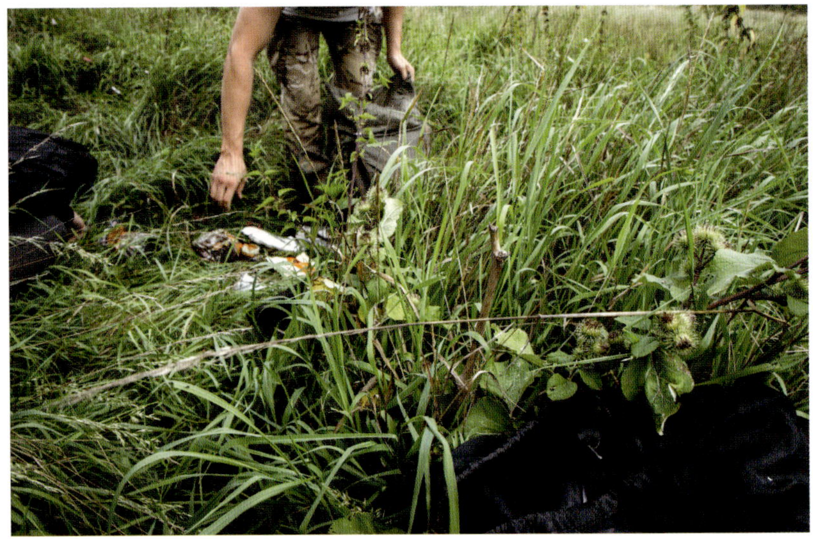

a single bush. A pair of legs protrudes from one side, and a backpack from the other. It is fortunate that the car's occupants don't happen to glance in our direction.

The last stretch is tough. The clouds part and the sun, now at full strength, has us sweating and panting as we stumble through the shifting sand at the forest's edge. Somewhere along those 14 kilometres, each of us runs out of water, and it's twilight before we arrive at the run-down pig farm where we will bed down for the night. The farm once reared pork for the soldiers at Chernobyl-2. Now, abandoned to the forest, it is virtually unreachable by car, making it a safe haven for stalkers. A picnic table outside is littered with beer cans and crisp packets, and campfire ash is scattered about.

Rather than have us carry four days' worth of food and water, a contact of Kirill's – an official tour guide – has hidden supplies for us at various locations in the Zone. Our first pick-up is at the Duga: the guide stashed black bags in the bushes there while his tourists photographed the radar. We decide to split up: Aram and myself will wait at the farm, while Kirill leads Bradley and Wayne to the drop point, using co-ordinates on his phone. They are supposed to be back in an hour.

The night is warm and we try not to think about our thirst. The hours roll by. Around midnight, we hear noises in the forest: a distant dog barking, then a crash like a heavy metal door slammed shut. My mobile signal is flickering around zero but I try to get a message to Bradley. Twenty minutes

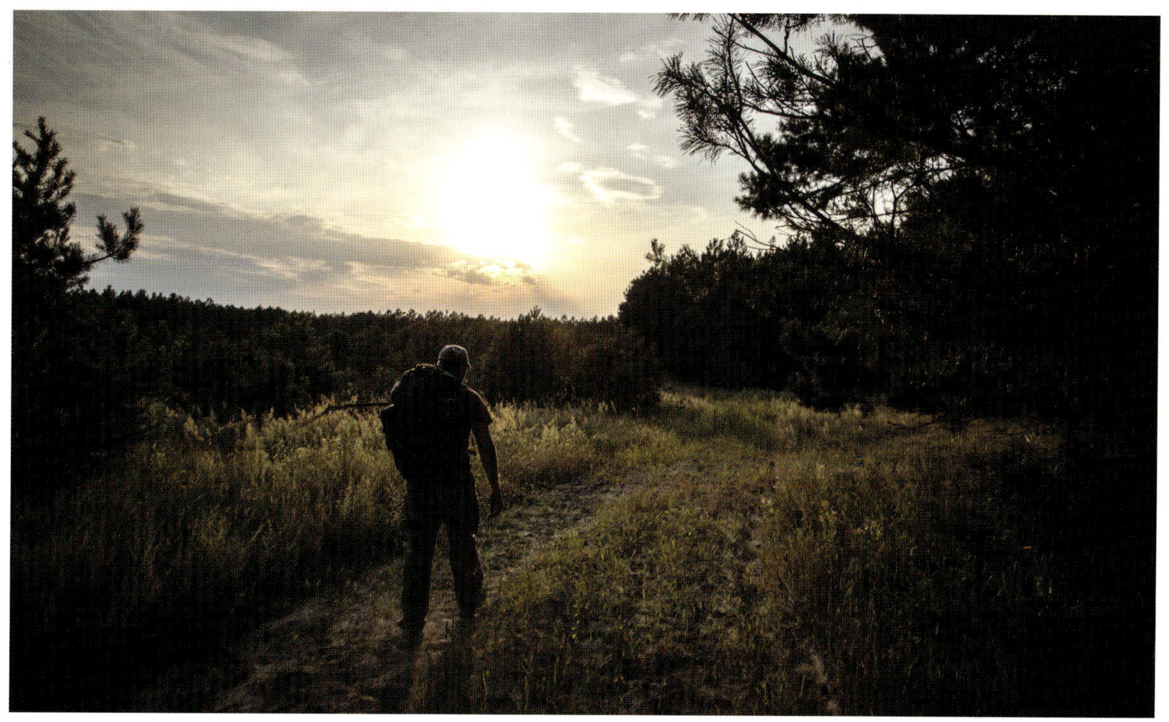

later he replies: 'No water. Guard dogs. Delayed at best.' I start to wonder if this pig farm is really the ideal hiding place. Surely the police know that stalkers come here, and the dog has already told them there's someone in the forest tonight. Even if the others get away, perhaps the police will search for us here?

'We can hide in the woods,' says Aram, sounding hopeful. 'Wait it out.' I agree – better to keep our options open than to get caught unawares. We take what we need, and push a good way through the trees before concealing ourselves in a nook between two fallen trunks. We turn off our torches. In the darkness, time seems to take an eternity to pass. It is maybe forty minutes before faint torchlight begins to illuminate the pines. The lights pause at the pig farm but we stay hidden. Finally Bradley sends me a message:

'We're here – everything's okay.'

'I hate this dog.' Kirill is cursing, more animated than I've seen him yet: 'This fucking thing.' Bradley and Wayne look broken and exhausted; but we're relieved to find they have water. Kirill's contact either got spooked or lazy. He hid our food in the agreed location, inside the floor cavity of a building near the radar, but our 5-litre water bottles never made it inside the base. Rather than smuggle them past the guard at the entrance, he had tossed them into the bushes where the buses park – the same spot where the guards chain their dog overnight.

Kirill had crawled on his belly to fetch the water, they tell us, until he was almost nose-to-nose with a snarling guard dog. When the guard came outside they ran. They heard a car start up and for a while the dog chased them. Luckily, the lone guard could only move so far away from his post; but come 9am, when the rest of the security team clock on, it's likely that hunting us will be the first order of the day.

THE WOODPECKER'S SHADOW

Kirill tells us we're safe to lie in, but none of us feels comfortable about lingering. On my bed of plastic bin liners I manage three short bouts of sleep, each interrupted by stress-induced nightmares. By 7am we're drinking watery coffee and eating vacuum-packed porridge fit for cosmonauts.

We have 8 litres of water between five of us, and a long walk in the heat ahead. It doesn't help that our stash is full of freeze-dried food, putting extra strain on our limited water resources. Ultimately, we are left with just a litre each for the hike. As we leave the pigsties behind, we hear a car door slam somewhere nearby in the forest. 'Probably loggers,' Kirill says, adding, 'could be or could be not.'

The terrain is difficult to negotiate: fallen logs rotted to mulch and overgrown with moss so thick that you never know quite where you're putting your foot. I stumble more than once. There are spiders here too: fat white orb-weavers suspend themselves at eye level across our path. Every so often one of us briefly breaks the silence when he gets a face full of spider's web. Brad tells Kirill to watch out for 'Silver Webs' – in *Roadside Picnic*, these alien strands killed off a character also named Kirill. Our Kirill doesn't respond – perhaps he didn't get the reference – and in the end it's Brad himself who's bitten, the injury quickly swelling up to the size of a ping-pong ball.

We reach the Chernobyl-2 perimeter fence, follow it behind the base, and walk the length of the Duga's shadow. Kirill asks if we want to climb it. 'Aren't they looking for us already?' asks Wayne, and Kirill gives a 'maybe' half-nod. 'So if we climb it we'll probably get caught?' He nods again.

'It's your tour,' says Kirill, 'but Duga today is maybe a bad idea, yes.'

Having passed the end of the base, we leave the towering

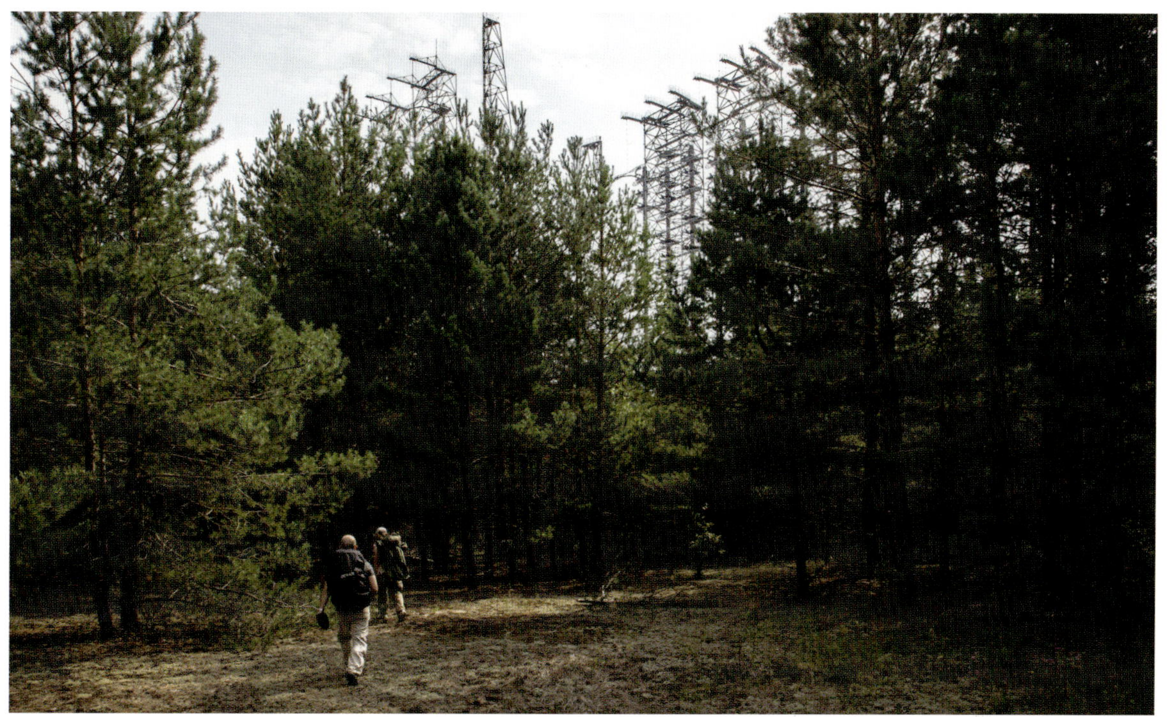

Soviet radar behind, cutting back into wild forest for a time, before finally breaking out of the trees into a vast, open corridor where pylons march towards the horizon like metal colossi, with butterflies dancing on hollyhocks between their feet. The sun's slanting rays filter through a sky filled with puffy, marbled clouds. We feel safe here, far from any road, and rest a while to eat and carefully sip our water. When we follow the pylon valley north, Kirill blasts Russian rock songs from his phone, and for the next 12 kilometres our hike feels almost normal. Halfway to our next target, though, the clouds part and an angry sun beats down on us. The grass gives way to sand, making everything more difficult, and the level of water in my litre bottle grows dangerously low – we won't pick up our next stash until Pripyat. After several hours of hard, sweaty work, I consider asking Kirill for a break; and then suddenly we arrive. We step off the sand onto tarmac, and pass through a gate into a ruined yard where buildings, pipes, and water tanks lie piled around, all rusting away into oblivion. This surface-to-air missile base near Chernobyl-2 was constructed to defend the Duga against possible air attacks. Now, with its access road long since overgrown, it has become another popular safe house for the stalkers.

Wayne and Bradley lie down on the grass, and Kirill offers us water from an old well nearby. He says he has filters, bought online, that could make the water almost perfectly clean. None of us likes his use of 'almost', and we decline – perhaps we're still closer to being tourists than stalkers. Kirill shrugs it off as if to say it's your loss, and undresses to pour buckets of cold water over himself. Afterwards he offers us a tour of the base, where mobile missile launchers were once housed in a reinforced shelter. Inside, past the heavy steel doors, stalkers have made a bonfire and graffitied the walls. Kirill inspects the remains of the fire. Trees can absorb radionuclides from contaminated dust that has settled in the soil, which are then released into the air when the wood is burned. 'The idiots who made this fire all have cancer now,' he says.

We rest for a few more hours at the base before moving on. I explore the main building, with its propaganda murals and 1970s pastel-coloured washrooms. Bradley is counting kilometres on his smart-watch. 'We walked 10 kilometres the first night, to the village,' he says, 'then 14 to the pig farm, and 11 so far today.' Our hardest walk is still ahead of us, however: the final 10-kilometre slog down the main road to Pripyat… And we'll be doing it on roughly half a litre of water each.

GROUND ZERO

At 8pm we walk to Buryakivka, a former village that now ranks as one of the dirtiest places in the Zone. More than a million tons of irradiated vehicles and pieces of machinery were buried here in concrete tombs after the disaster. Only a handful of buildings remain on the surface, and if you didn't know better, you'd assume it was just another abandoned farmyard. Kirill guides us inside a broken-down old bus where he says we'll wait until sunset. I don't like it – I've visited this place before with tour groups. I've even peered inside the very bus we're hiding in now. Out in the forests, or in places that can only be reached on foot, it feels like we're in a parallel stalker dimension. There's a surreal sense of safety, as long as we stick close to our guide; but in this familiar location I feel exposed, and painfully vulnerable. Kirill is as insouciant as ever. 'Tourists leave the Zone by 7pm,' he says, 'and the police are lazy. They won't come here.'

When the sun sets, a new constellation appears on the horizon: red lights dotted along the spine of the New Arch over Reactor 4. We stand among ruins, and gaze on one of

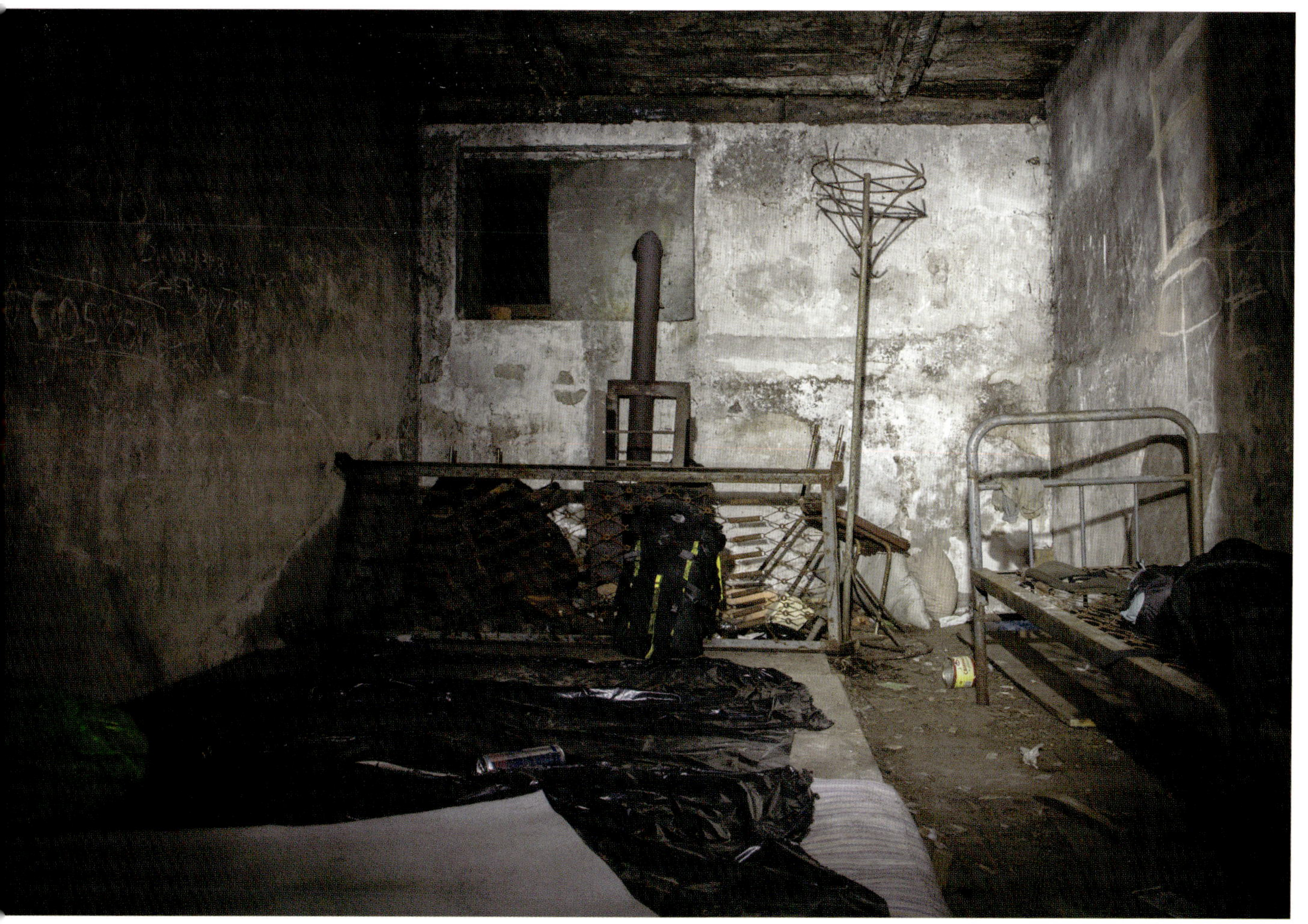

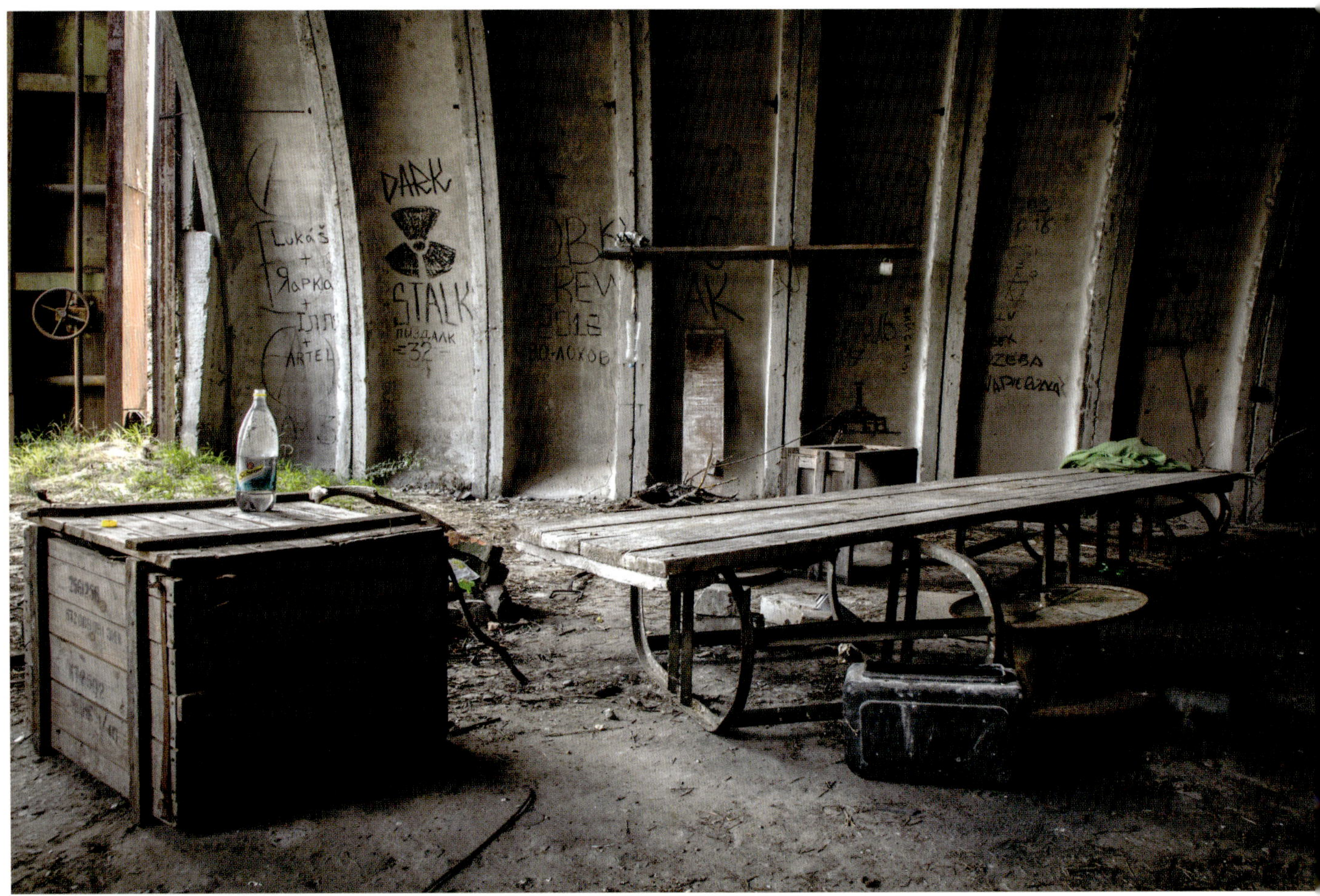

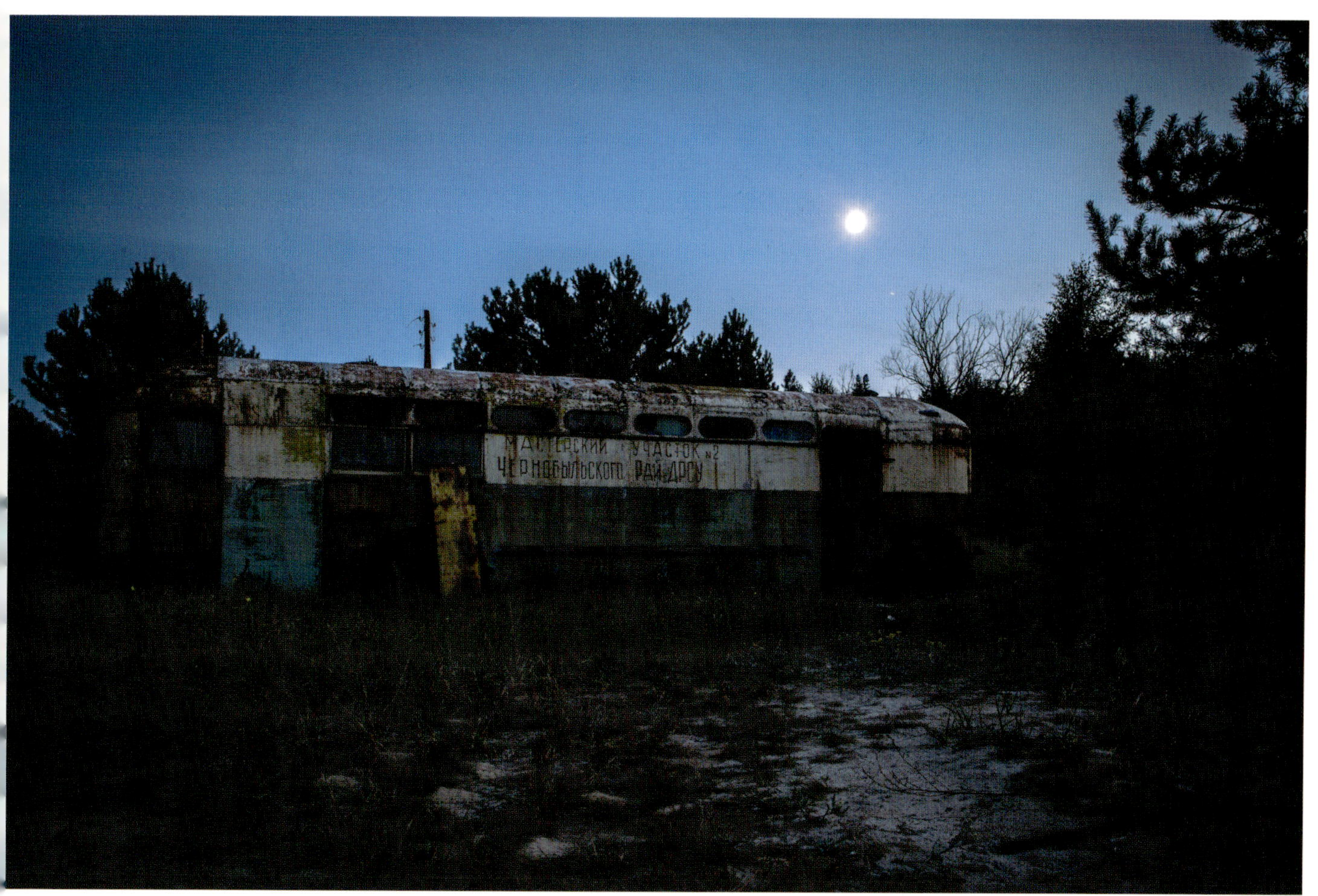
МАСТЕРСКИЙ УЧАСТОК №2
ЧЕРНОБЫЛЬСКОГО РАЙ ДРСУ

the technological wonders of the modern world. The arch will stand for a century, by which time the surrounding villages, rocket bases, and farms, will all have been swallowed up by the sand and marshes. Here is one of humankind's most advanced structures, rising from one of its most notoriously devastated regions, like a giant Pandora's Box containing all humanity's evils. Yesterday our group resembled five hobbits in a broad green wilderness. Today, we are truly beginning our final hike into Mordor.

By 10pm it is fully dark, and with the tourists either back in Kyiv or safely ensconced in their Chornobyl hotels, Kirill says the only traffic will be deliveries or police patrols – around one car an hour. We get onto the main road. Kirill takes the lead, while I bring up the rear of the column, a position that comes with the responsibility of watching for car headlights behind us. Soon my neck is aching from the constant twisting to look back down the road. Regardless of my efforts, the first time a vehicle approaches us Kirill has already heard it long before any sign of lights. We hide in bushes at the roadside and moments later a truck speeds past: a blur of red and yellow. For a fleeting moment, I see the driver's face before it's gone and we climb back onto the tarmac. Soon another car approaches and we hide again. After that comes a lorry. And so it goes on. Tonight we are in for a long walk.

Near the old village of Kopachi we reach a fork in the road. The right fork leads to the power plant, but we veer left onto a slip road that runs parallel to the railway track straight towards Pripyat. The red beacons of the New Arch wink at us through the trees, and soon we see the sodium glow of street-level lights around the power-plant complex. By now I'm wondering how much more I can take: my feet have blistered badly, my neck and shoulders ache, my throat's dry enough to crack and my dehydrated brain seems to rattle around my skull like a shrunken walnut. I only have a few mouthfuls of water left, so I pop a boiled sweet into my dried-out mouth in the hope it might ease my suffering. 'Hold up!' someone hisses. The rest of our column abruptly halts and I walk face-first into Aram's backpack. The sweet gets stuck in my throat, and for one hysterical moment I think I'm going to choke, until I use most of my remaining water to wash it down.

'See that?' asks Wayne, but all I see is darkness and fireflies dancing in the distance. Then I remember that fireflies shouldn't be blue. The lights, perhaps two or three of them, are a good distance along the road ahead.

'We must be careful,' says Kirill, in an anxious tone I've not heard him use before. He leads us off the road and up to the railway tracks, where we tiptoe carefully from one wooden sleeper to the next. Every time someone misses a step, the crunch of gravel sounds horribly loud; but we manage to give the lights on the road a wide berth. As we pass them, we see that they are in fact head torches. 'Maybe illegal workers,' Kirill explains later, 'digging for metal or something else. Still, it is best they did not see us.'

Since the law was passed that forbids digging in the Zone, urban myth has it that anything you bury here can be permanently disposed of, without the risk of it ever coming back to haunt you – and that goes for human bodies too. Whether these men were removing something (scrap metal or plutonium waste, for example), or were putting something into the ground, I agree with Kirill that we are better off not knowing.

There are no more cars after that, and I'm relieved – just keeping my legs swinging, one boot in front of the other, is hard enough. We pass the original Pripyat city sign, and follow the road beside the Red Forest: in 1986, when plutonium rained down from the sky, it petrified the trees and turned their bark red. The highly contaminated trees were bulldozed, buried, and in time a new forest grew; but from beneath the soil, the presence of the old forest can still be discerned. As we pass by it, Kirill's dosimeter hits 16 µSv/h – 160 times higher than the villages in the outer Zone.

The road to Pripyat is straight and smooth, and presently we see a light ahead: the security hut at the entrance to the city. We creep out of the darkness, getting close enough to make out the fence, the gate, and the guard post. Then we turn off the road to a track that skirts the city's perimeter. Knowing that our destination is now within reach, I drink my final drops of water.

A number of sites on the outskirts of Pripyat remain active overnight – lights are on in the laundry, the water plant, and around the Jupiter Factory. After hours of sensory deprivation, the sudden glare and noise overwhelm my brain and I begin to hallucinate. The light spilling through the factory fence takes on the shape of a chain of men in white suits, passing boxes down the hillside. When a dog barks at us from the yard, the illusion is dispelled. I'm ready to run, but Kirill just ignores the animal, so I try to do the same. The darkness envelops us again as the track leads us around the south side of Pripyat, and back in through Microdistrict 4. We pass the fire station, where first responders were mobilised in 1986. As we draw closer to the city centre, the overhanging trees begin to thin out. Above them, barely visible against the night sky, rises a seventeen-storey Brutalist housing block. We have arrived.

THE GHOST CITY

Pripyat takes on new qualities at night. The buildings, off-white, beige and concrete grey in daylight, look blue by moonlight and somehow bigger too. With visibility reduced to the arc of your head torch, the city gives the illusion of going on forever, block after block, in all directions. It feels more labyrinthine. Its edifices, no longer human dwellings, are now more like looming, featureless, glacial cliffs.

We find our Pripyat stash quickly enough, but we swear and curse when we tear open the bag to discover yet more

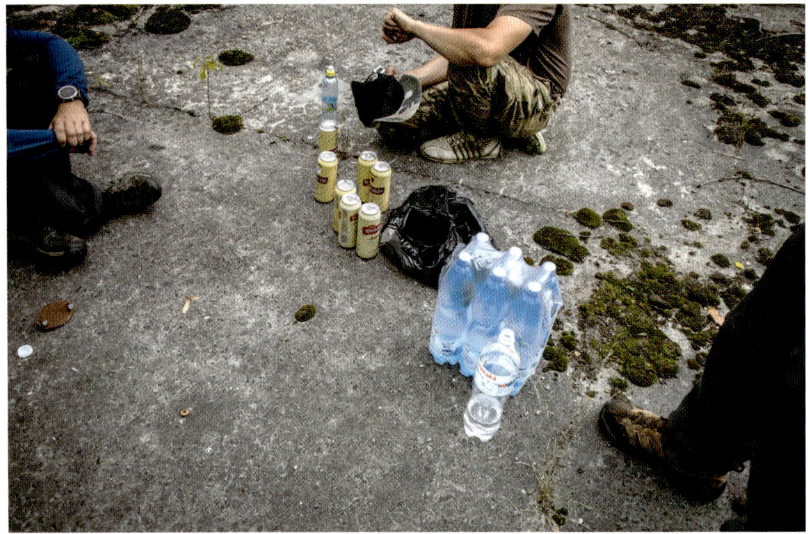

Microdistrict 4, Pripyat. After collecting an aid package hidden in bushes near a popular tour stop, stalkers celebrate a renewed supply of water and beer.

freeze-dried food. Our suppliers have included a mere 12 litres of water to share between five men. This will have to cure our current dehydration, and then last for another two days, with much of it used up in cooking all our meals. It won't be anywhere near enough. We grumble all the way to our lodgings on the fourth floor of a nondescript suburban block. Kirill opens the door into what was once someone's home. 'Welcome to our stalker flat,' he says proudly. By Soviet standards, it is spacious: two bedrooms and a kitchen-dining room, with most of the windows still intact. Previous stalkers have set up beds, and Kirill unpacks his stove in the kitchen to begin boiling water for dinner. The far end of the block, along the hall past the staircase, has been designated as toilets – a fact that is quickly apparent from the smell.

The five of us gulp water greedily, eat our food, and then turn to the bottle of chilli vodka that was included in the stash: the only welcome surprise. Kirill goes off to sleep in the kitchen while we sit on the beds like it's a sleepover, swigging from the bottle and talking nonsense. The bottle only goes back on the table once it's empty, and soon we're all dropping from exhaustion.

I sleep surprisingly well and wake up with the sun shining on my face. Tree branches scrape and claw at the window, as if nature were demanding entry to the only Pripyat apartment still resisting it. I remember that Orest, my tour-guide friend, said he would be escorting a group today, so

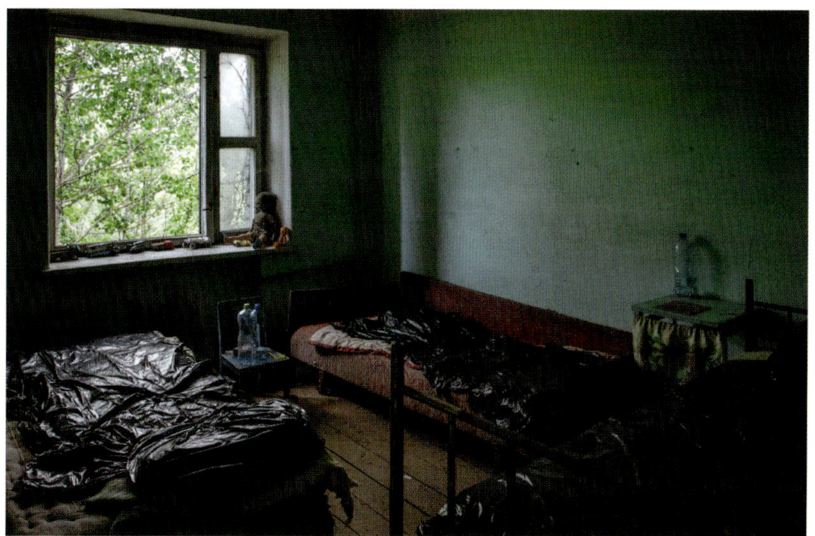

Stalker apartment, Pripyat. Out of roughly 10,000 apartments in the city, a small number have been discreetly cleaned and equipped to serve as illicit accommodation for stalkers.

I call and ask if he can bring us water. He says he'll try.

Being an illegal in Pripyat is both comforting and terrifying. Our hideout feels safe: there are 10,000 apartments in the city, and tourists are forbidden from entering them. The chance of anyone finding us by accident is slim. All the same, it's unnerving to hear tour buses outside the windows, and I remember Vladyslav telling me that the police had got more serious about looking for stalkers. Sometimes they camped beside the roads at night. Others disguised themselves as stalkers and prowled the city streets around dawn to lure out trespassers. When we head out to explore in the late morning, Kirill tells us not to leave our valuables behind. He says there's a scrap-metal thief they call the Metal Man, who knows how to spot stalker hideouts and makes a good living from stolen cameras and passports.

One of Pripyat's kindergartens is so overgrown that there's no way to get into it that doesn't involve a messy scramble through bushes. For this reason it is dismissed by official tours, making it prime stalker territory. The place is filled with the usual staged clutter: dolls, bears, and tricycles. Wayne is seeing this for the first time and as we plough through the decorative debris, he muses on the way these items have lost their original purpose, instead becoming building blocks in the expression of new ideas – raw material for making art, or shrines. 'The ontological cages have sprung open. Everything is pure materiality,' he says, stopping before a row of children's blocks that have been lined up to spell 'Chernobyl'. 'It's like a cargo cult turned inside out.'

We climb up through a hatch to the roof, but the building is so engulfed by trees it doesn't offer much of a view. The black asphalt is tacky underfoot and Kirill warns us not to sit down: 'It gets sticky in the sun. Dust sticks to it… radioactive dust too. These roofs got very dirty after the disaster.'

To leave the kindergarten, we need to evade Pripyat's daytime traffic. Dodging tour buses and police patrols on a grid of tight city streets feels a lot like playing a video game. Exhaustion has put me in a spacey, dreamlike state of mind and, suddenly untethered from the heavy backpack I've carried until now, my every step feels like bouncing on the moon. We hop fences and sneak through parks and gardens. After exploring a radiological lab, we ascend to the roof of a nine-storey residential block. Occasionally we hear the chatter of tourists, but we never see them, and they never see us – exclusive worlds coexisting in one city. I receive a message from Orest with an address for the package he's hidden for us. It's an apartment on Sportivnaya Street, near the swimming pool, and there are celebrations all round when we arrive to find 10 litres of water and two four-packs of beer wrapped up in a black bin liner.

Halfway back to our hideout a helicopter passes overhead. We duck into cover and for just one crazy second I'm convinced it's looking for us, but then it circles away – just some wealthy foreigners on their VIP tour. Finally we get

inside and start cooking. I wash my face in clean water, then settle down to hot risotto with a beer: I've never appreciated a meal so much. We rest for the afternoon. Our extraction is scheduled for 9am, but tonight – after the tourists go home – the city is our playground.

We walk down Kurchatov Street at twilight. The city looks empty, but Kirill reminds us that no one is ever alone in Pripyat: 'There could be fifty people here. Stalkers are always here, hiding everywhere.' We play it safe, keeping torchlight to a minimum and avoiding the hospital, post office, and swimming pool – places where guards could more easily corner us. Instead we make our way to the Ferris Wheel. It's a long time since I've seen it free of tourist crowds; it's the first time Bradley and Wayne have seen it at all. In recent decades this Ferris Wheel has come to serve as a symbol for the abandoned city of Pripyat. A thing of life and joy among the ruins, its yellow plastic capsules haven't faded like the signs and murals that surround it. Even in a midnight city of washed-out blues and greys, the capsules glimmer golden in the starlight.

There is a storm tonight, somewhere off to the north-east. The thick July air has felt electrified for days, and now the clouds boil into a thunder-and-lightning show. We hear it drawing closer and see flickers of light behind the city skyline. We decide to get up high for a better view. As we heave open the hatch to the flat roof of an eight-floor residential block, Chernobyl Nuclear Power Plant rises in

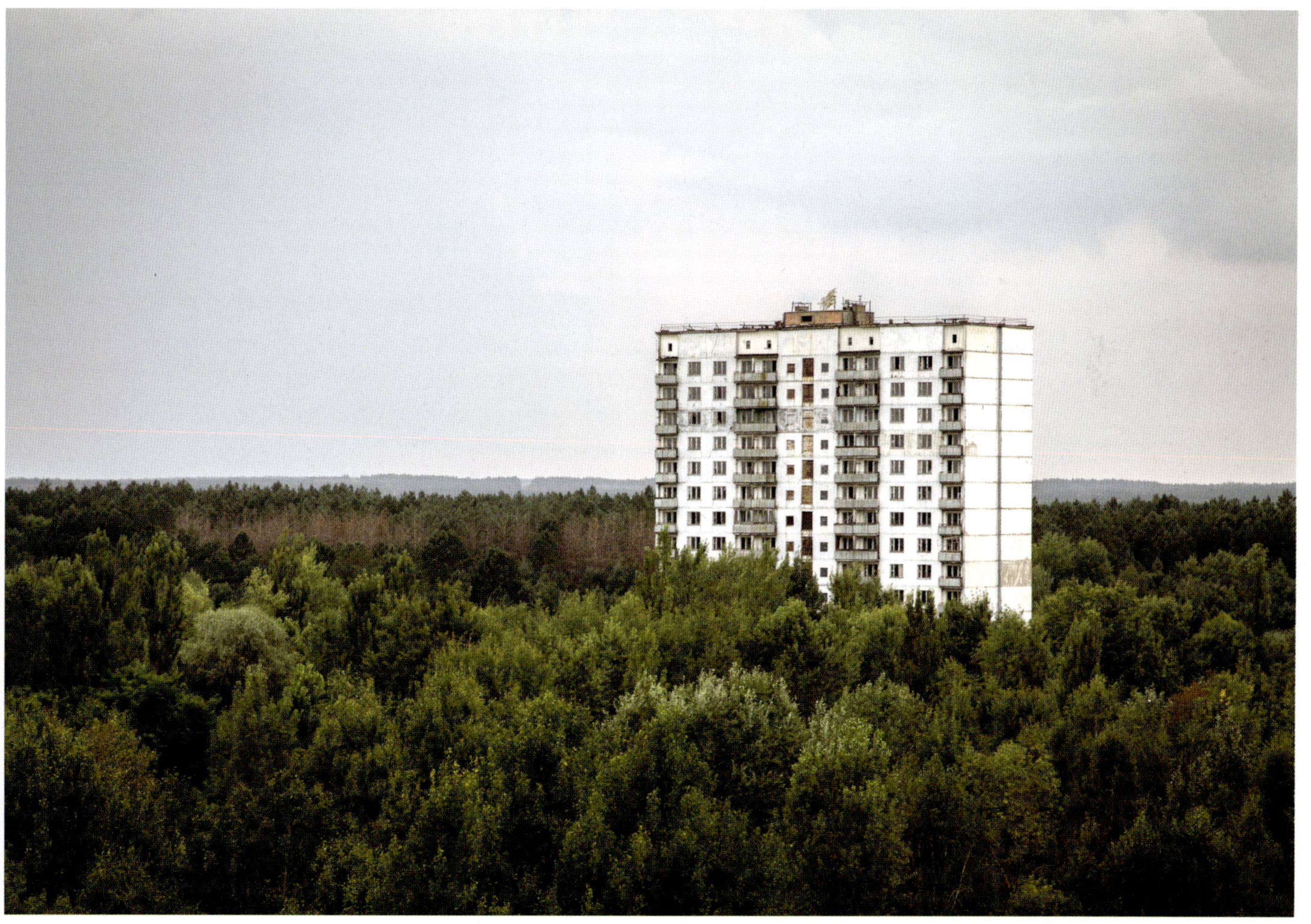

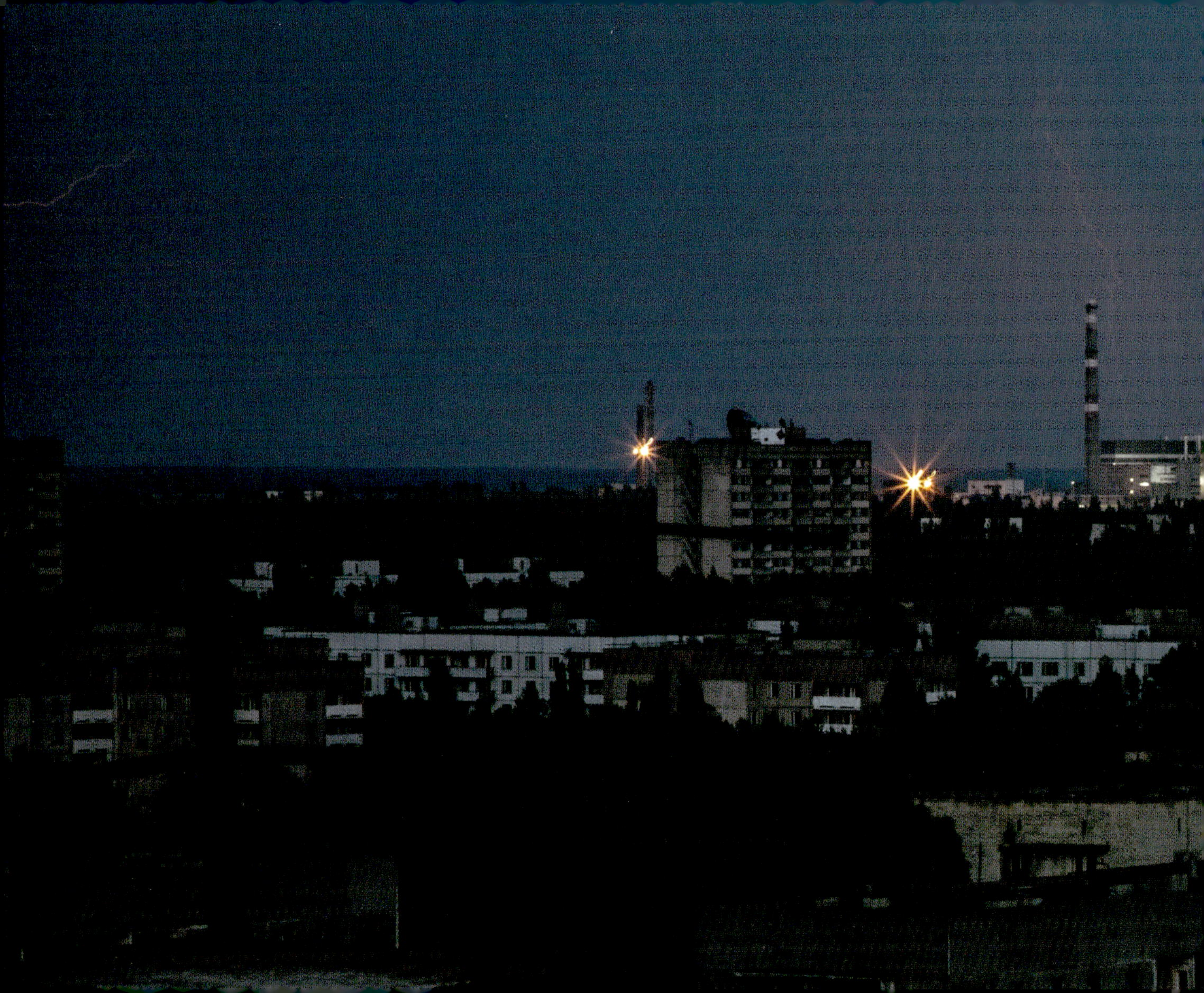

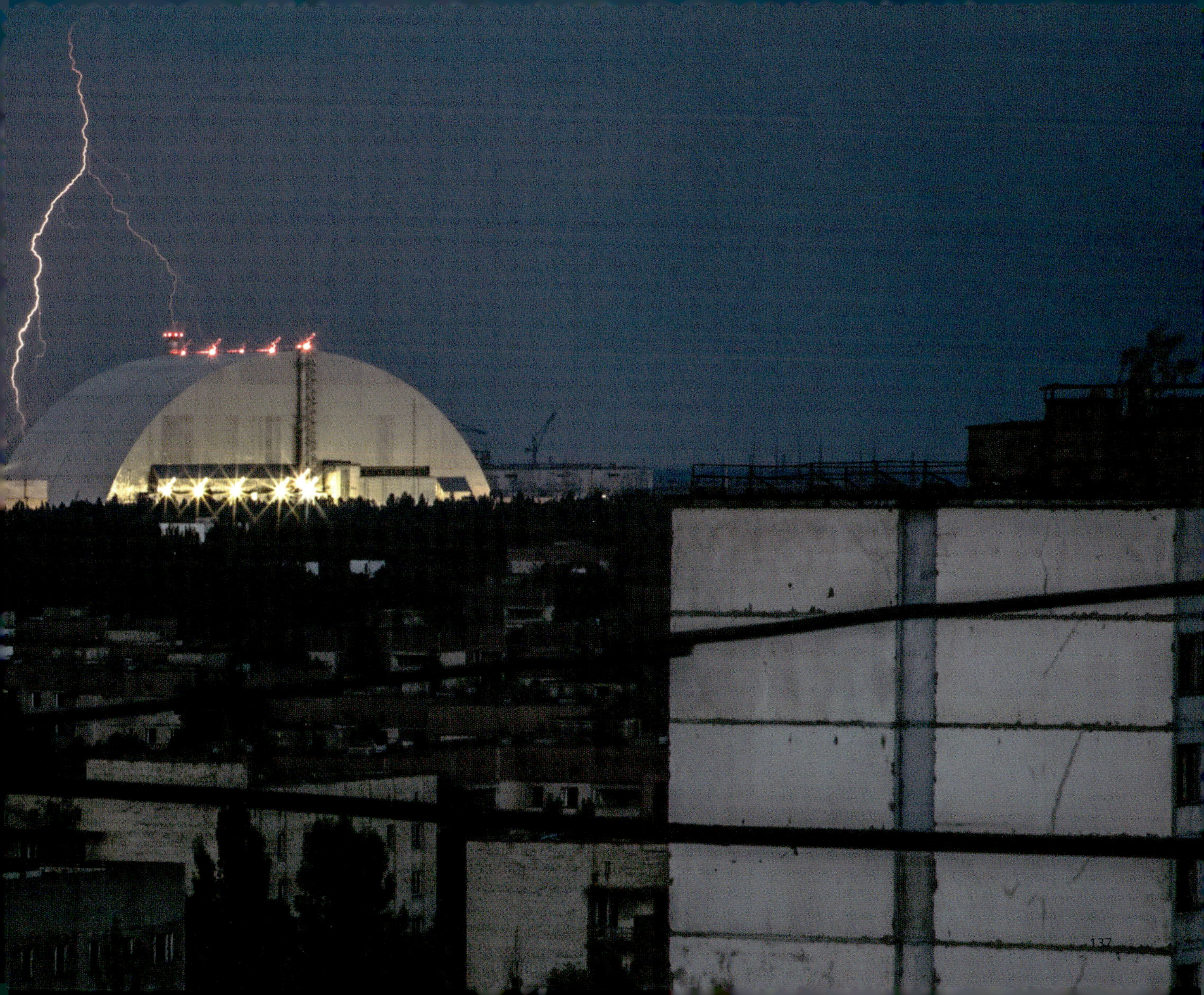

the distance, dominating the horizon and framed in tongues of blue-white electricity. The lightning is drawn to the metal arch, which crackles and glows while the city beneath sleeps in pools of deep blue shadow. We've got the beers with us and even teetotal Kirill grabs one for the performance.

The architects of the Atomic Era compared themselves to gods and Titans as they sought to submit nature to their will. However at Chernobyl, nature would not be tamed for long and atomic chaos was unleashed. The silver vault before us was humankind's last-ditch effort to put the atom back in its shackles and lock it down. As I watch the storm rage around it as if attempting to liberate the imprisoned power within, I feel I'm witnessing a spectacle never meant for human eyes.

EXTRACTION

At 7am we leave our apartment and walk to the Jupiter Factory – the same commute made daily by scores of workers before the accident. Skirting the bone-white blocks of the factory, we walk a further kilometre through fields then across train tracks. At an abandoned cargo-loading bay nearby, we meet our ride.

Leonid Demchenko is bald on top with a Homer Simpson comb-over. His beer gut pokes out from an unzipped camouflage jacket, and when he smiles, he shows a mouthful of sparkling gold teeth. He has spotted us long before we see him, and he lowers his binoculars to wave us over. 'Get in the truck,' he says. He's the first human outside our group that we've seen in three days.

Driving down the road in Demchenko's pick-up, with Kirill in the passenger seat, the rest of us crammed in the back probably look shellshocked, wincing and ducking whenever we pass another vehicle. The mood lifts when Demchenko begins singing *Yesterday* by The Beatles. He says he first heard it from a British liquidator, back in 1986. We all join in. Just before Leliv Checkpoint at the edge of the 10km Zone, Demchenko takes the turning towards the Duga, the same road we had sprinted across two days ago. He follows it for a while, then veers onto a logging track, the pick-up bouncing over ruts made by heavy timber-lorries, until we burst back onto the main road – only now we are on the other side of the security post. 'That's how it's done,' he chuckles.

Dytyatky Checkpoint is the final barrier between us and the world outside the Zone. Demchenko approaches slowly, coming close enough for us to get a clear view of the queue of tourists beside Chernobyl Tour's bright yellow 'Information Centres'. Abruptly, he turns down a side road. Demchenko himself will have no trouble passing through the checkpoint, but we stalkers must make a detour. Dropping us out of sight behind a cluster of derelict buildings, he wishes us luck.

An open meadow lies ahead of us: wild, yellowing grassland freckled with occasional bushes that grow gradually denser, until the grass and bushes give way to a dark line of

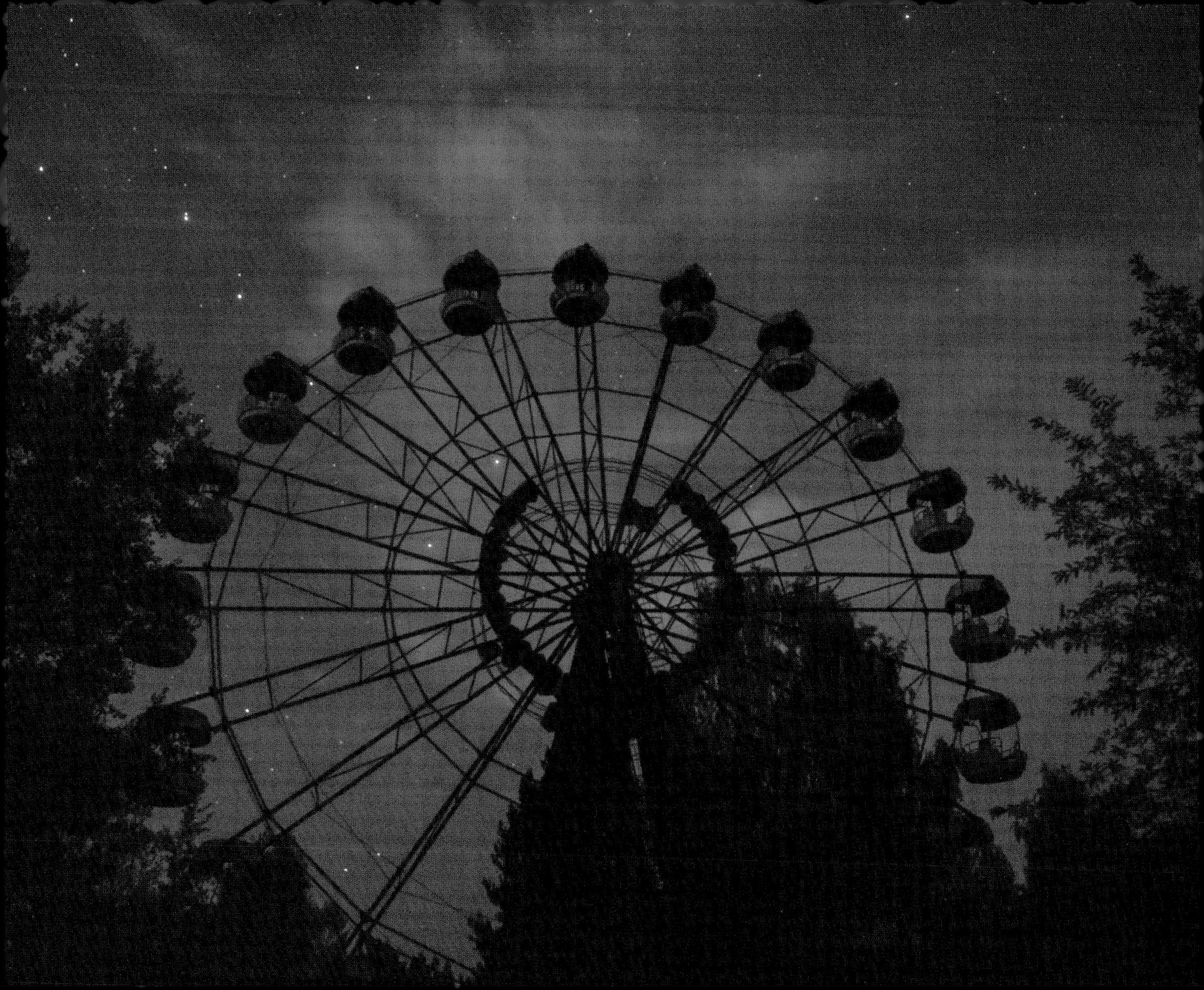

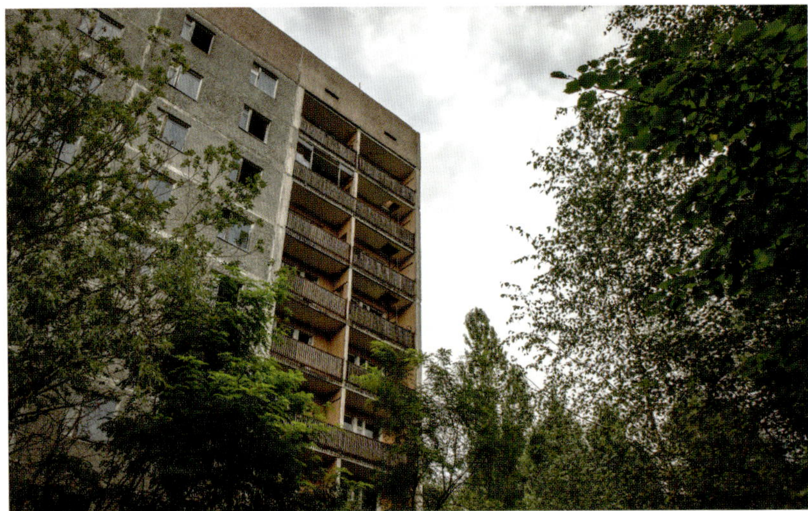

trees. Kirill tells us that somewhere among those trees is the fence that marks the perimeter of the Zone, but we're also only a stone's throw from Dytyatky Checkpoint, where guards patrol with Kalashnikovs. He warns us: 'Police can see us here. They are checking often.'

'Here we go then,' says Bradley. 'Our 200-metre dash to freedom.' Kirill nods, and we run.

I don't look back. I just run for all I'm worth. Keeping my head down, not even glancing towards the checkpoint, I dodge bushes and jump gullies, until I hit the finish line. Kirill and Wayne hold the strands of barbed wire apart as we tumble through one by one, then disappear into the forest beyond. A road cuts through the trees ahead, and we wait until Demchenko's pick-up pulls into view. He has a car behind him though, so he can't risk stopping. We wait for him to circle around again. This time he slows to a crawl beside the forest. We sprint from the trees, dive into the truck, slam the doors and we're off. Demchenko turns the corner onto the main road at Dytyatky, and suddenly we're face-to-face with the crowds waiting to enter the Zone; a queue of five or six buses wait while tourists shop for coffees and souvenirs. We drive right past them and away from the checkpoint. Demchenko breaks into another verse of *Yesterday* and we all burst into laughter, in a flood of relief, elation, and maddening exhaustion, as we head back to Kyiv.

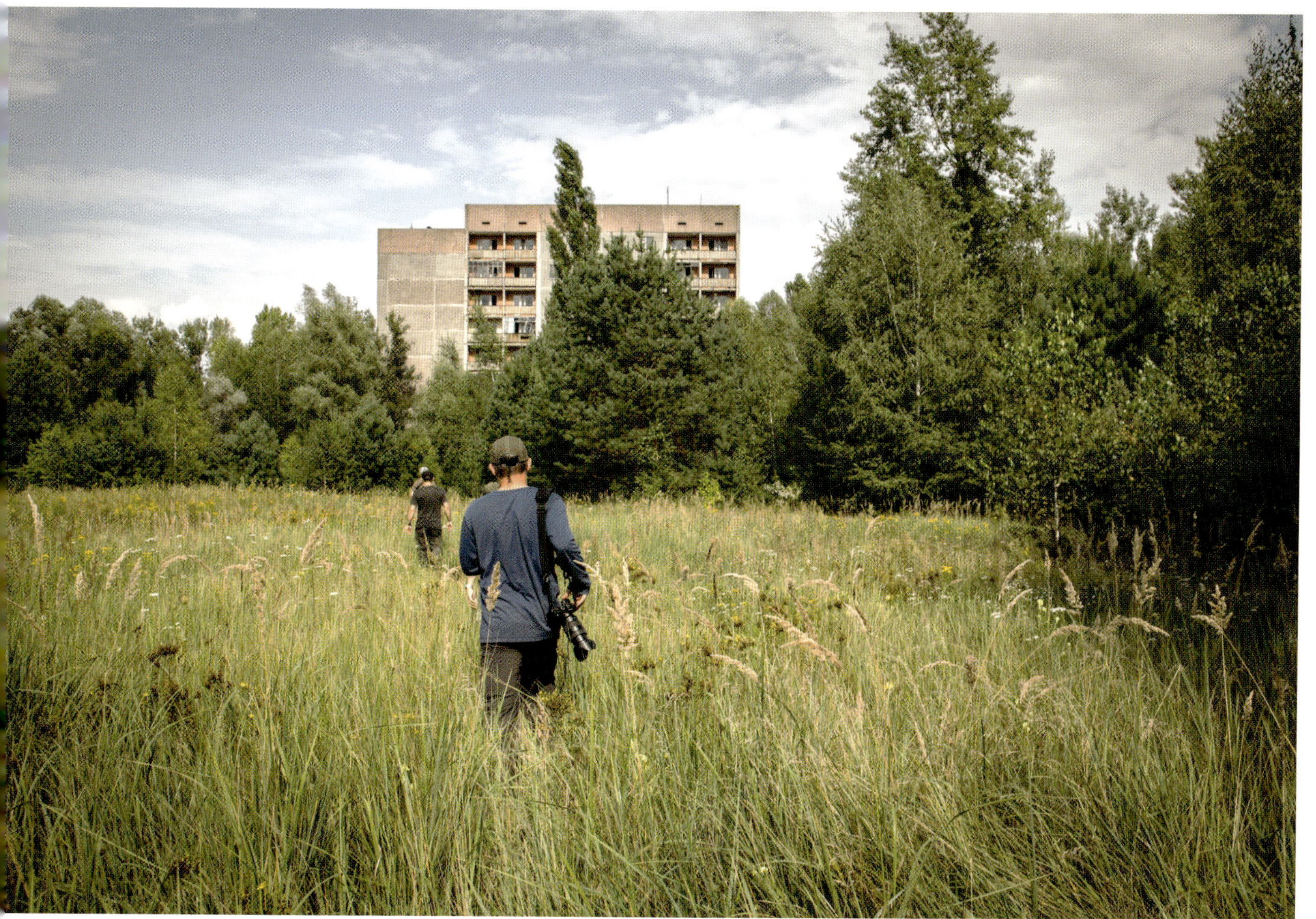

6. MONUMENTEERING

POST-ATOMIC COMMUNITY

Leonid Demchenko told me to take his number in case I ever needed his services again. I called later that summer, presenting him with the challenge of visiting every Soviet monument in the Zone. The subject appealed to me academically (I was studying for my doctorate on the ideological architecture of socialism), and it seemed like a good way to get to know the place better. This region had formed the front line between the Nazis and the Soviets during the later part of World War II (known as the 'Great Patriotic War' in the USSR). The monuments built here afterwards, commemorating battlefields and sites of victory or sacrifice, would act as orienteering points, giving us a reason to cross otherwise unmarked corners of the map and visit almost all of Chernobyl's abandoned villages in the process. I was also curious to see what life was like for this man who spent almost every day inside the Exclusion Zone. Demchenko and his wife, a radiologist, lived a couple of kilometres outside the Zone in a riverside village called Strakholissya. It was more convenient this way, he explained: he had a regular address for deliveries, and he could buy groceries and fuel in the village, while just a few minutes to the north lay his 2,600 square kilometres of playground. The best of both worlds.

We could do this the easy way or the stalker way, Demchenko told me. The stalker way would be cheaper, using back roads, but occasionally I'd have to duck down in my seat or hide under blankets in the back of the car. The easy way meant applying for my tourist permit and entering and exiting the Zone through Dytyatky Checkpoint as normal. I'd had my fill of Chernobyl infiltration, so I opted for the easy way.

Driving towards the checkpoint, we stop at a village shop where Demchenko fills the boot with bread, sugar, milk, eggs, and meat. At Dytyatky, I show the guards my passport. If Demchenko has official paperwork, I never see it – he just gives them a wink and a smile and drives on through. I don't see a dosimeter in the car either, and I ask Demchenko if he has one. He slaps the glove compartment, and sounds defensive when he answers: 'It's here… but I've been doing this thirty fucking years now. Don't you think I'd know where all the dirty places are?'

In Demchenko's company, the Zone takes on a different character altogether. We skip the usual tourist hotspots. Keeping mostly to back roads, we drive through forests and fresh green wilderness, pastures where deer skip between ruined farm buildings, and around marshes where storks circle looking for frogs. All the while, the large, aggressive, and insatiable mosquitoes follow us in swarms, hungry for blood.

It will take five days to see every monument in the Zone. We spend the first day in the south-east corner, where Demchenko seems to have a lot of friends. In almost every village, he stops to deliver food packages to the locals. Apart from a regular food truck that comes every two weeks,

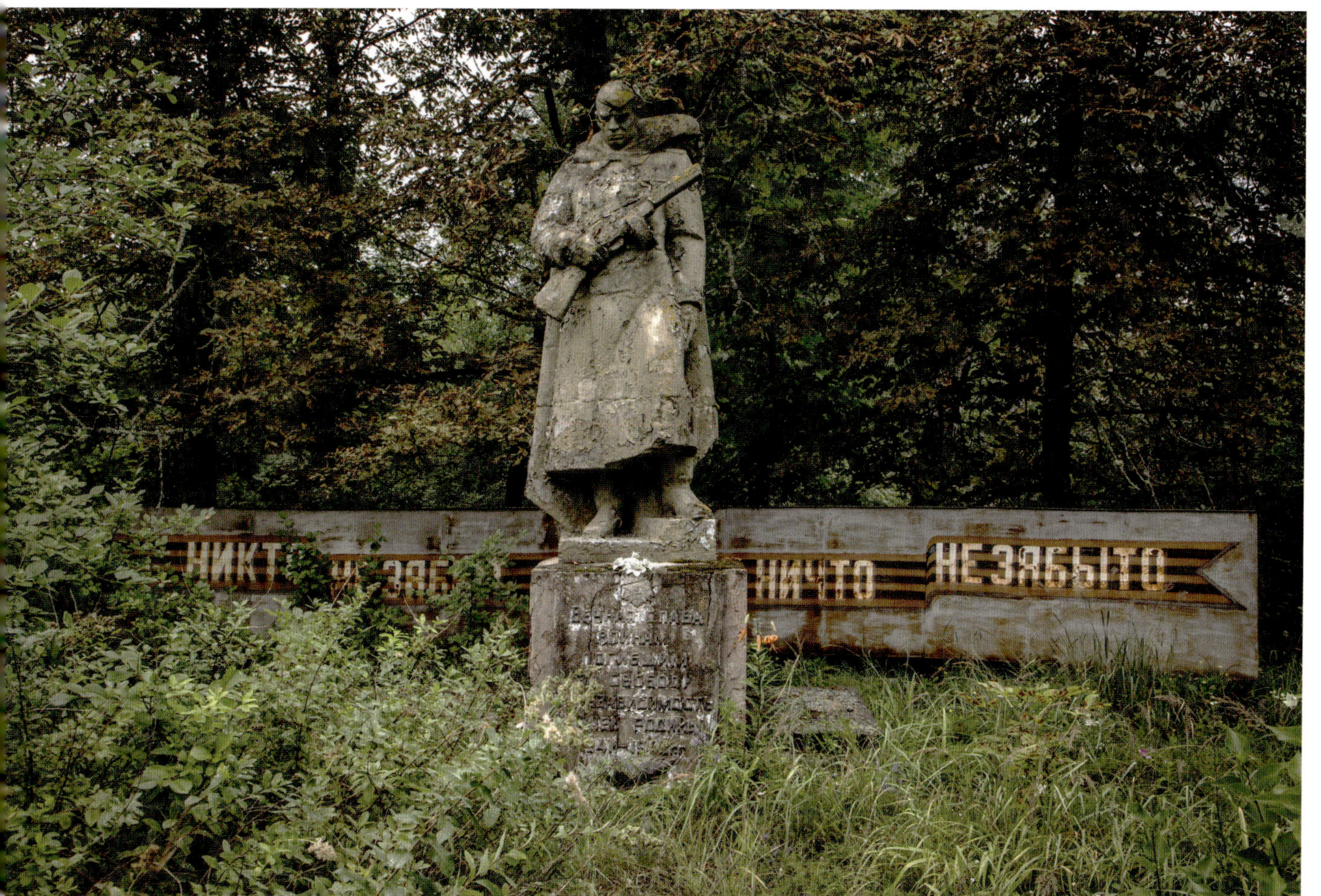
НИКТО   НЕ ЗАБ   НИЧТО   НЕ ЗАБЫТО

traffic is rare, and any that passes through a village like Gorodishche doesn't do so by accident. Baba Ganya hears us arrive, and immediately comes shuffling out to investigate, her eyes popping with excitement from under her blood-red shawl. 'Lyonya, Lyonya!' she cries. Her small hand closes like a talon around my wrist, and suddenly I'm being dragged into the house, where a pan full of fox mushrooms is sizzling on the stove. She insists that we eat, and we wash the mushrooms down with shots of bitter walnut vodka.

We see the village monument and another in Opachychi too, before stopping for lunch with Baba Sofia in Kupovate. Sofia's home is only 9 kilometres from Demchenko's. Both remember a time when they were neighbours, before the arbitrary line of the Exclusion Zone was drawn between them. Kupovate was evacuated, and overnight the official route from village to village became a 50-kilometre detour via Dytyatky. Sofia has cooked us lunch – chicken wings and grilled fish, pickles, bread, and soup with sour cream. Many of the ingredients came from her own garden and while Sofia pours shots from an unlabelled plastic bottle, Demchenko explains how soil, crops, and produce from occupied parts of the Zone are sent to a lab for testing every three months. He assures me that Kupovate has never shown anything above normal background levels.

Stopping that afternoon in Chornobyl town, Demchenko buys ice cream, beer, and water in the market. We then deliver these treats to the police at various checkpoints.

'This way, they always owe me a favour,' he says, flashing his gold teeth.

Demchenko's wife cooks rabbit stew that night, while he insists I sample four varieties of his homemade vodka. After a few drinks, I ask him how he got involved with the Zone. 'It's my home,' he answers plainly. 'I was never not involved.' Demchenko worked in a factory, making cheese and other dairy products. When they evacuated the Zone he lost his job. After a spell as a liquidator, he began looking for other income. Initially, he looted scrap metal, selling it to a buyer in Kyiv. 'They caught me in the end,' he grins. 'It was big trouble. But then the stalkers and tourists started coming… And that was even better money.' He sees me scribbling notes, and adds: 'You'd better not put this in your book!'

'What if I give you a fake name?' I ask. I glance to the newspaper on the table and read the first name I see.

'Demchenko?'

'That'll work. And make my first name Leonid… like Brezhnev!' he laughs.

I am still groggy the next morning, when we go looking for monuments in the north-east of the Zone. We have barely passed the power plant before a sudden boom rings out – something between a trumpet and synthetic thunder, so loud it seems to tear the heavens asunder. I nearly jump out of my skin, but Demchenko simply shrugs, explaining it's just the power plant's cooling system kicking in. We see monuments in Starosillya, Zymovysche, Krasne, and Masheve.

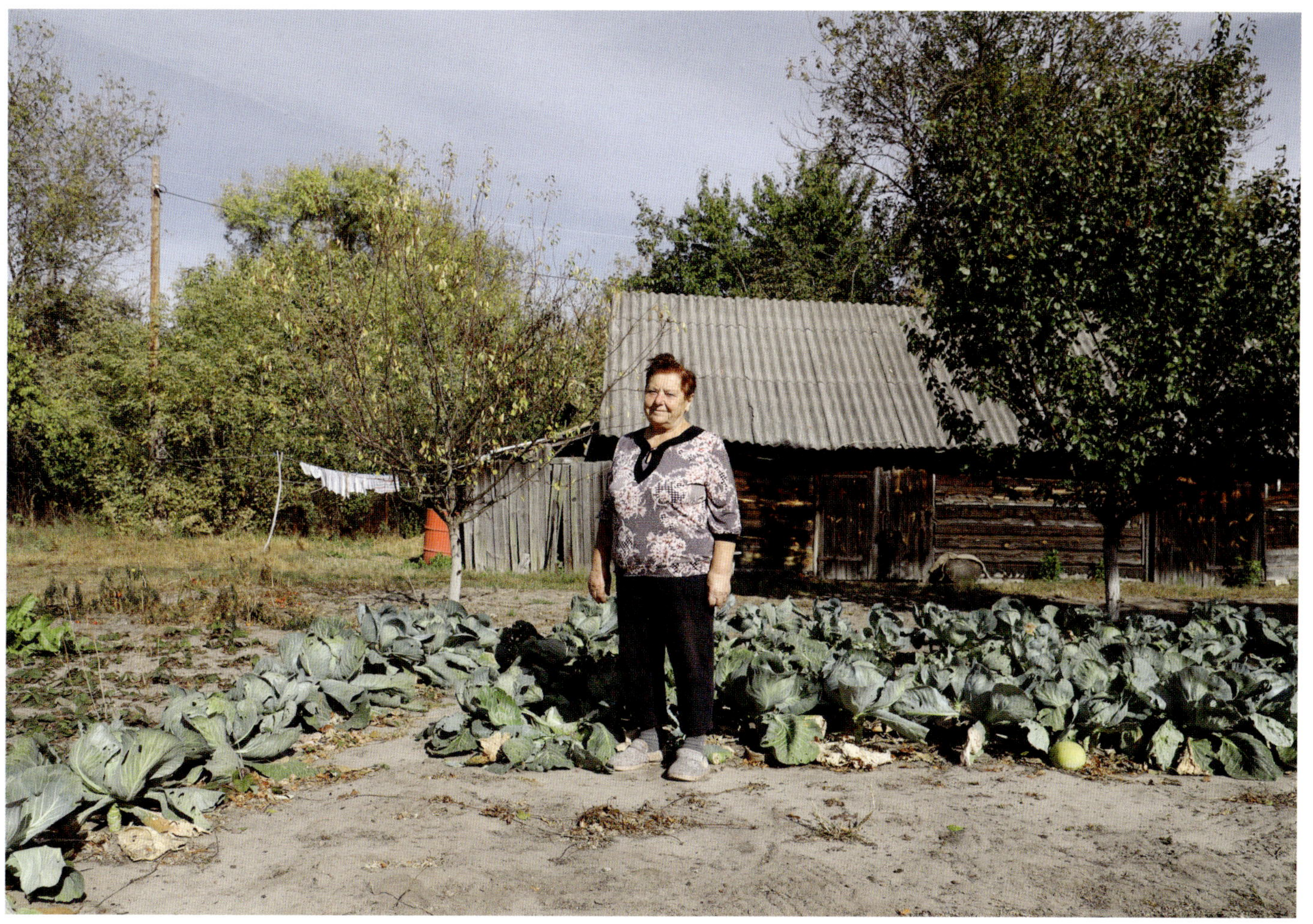

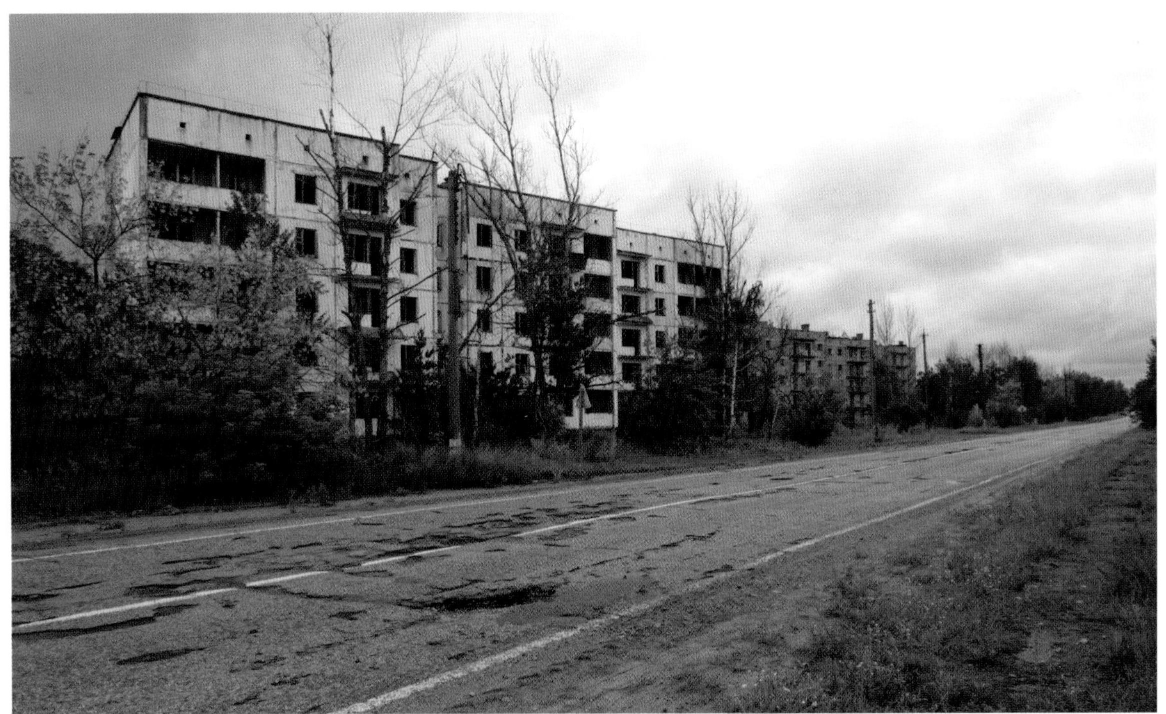

Passing a railway crossing, I stop to take a photo down the tracks. Suddenly the metal begins to ping with distant power, and moments later a train rattles past at high speed. I see the faces of hundreds of power-plant workers staring out of the windows at me. I guess it's not every day they see somebody out here in the overgrown wilds. 'Most of the tracks were replaced after '86,' says Demchenko. 'It still gets a lot of use. Not just the workers' train – clean-up crews too. They use trains to move dirty stuff to storage.' He tells me how a new track, still under construction, will be used to take the worst waste from the highly contaminated vehicle graveyard at Buryakivka, to the Zone's newest disposal site. 'Good luck to the buggers doing that job.'

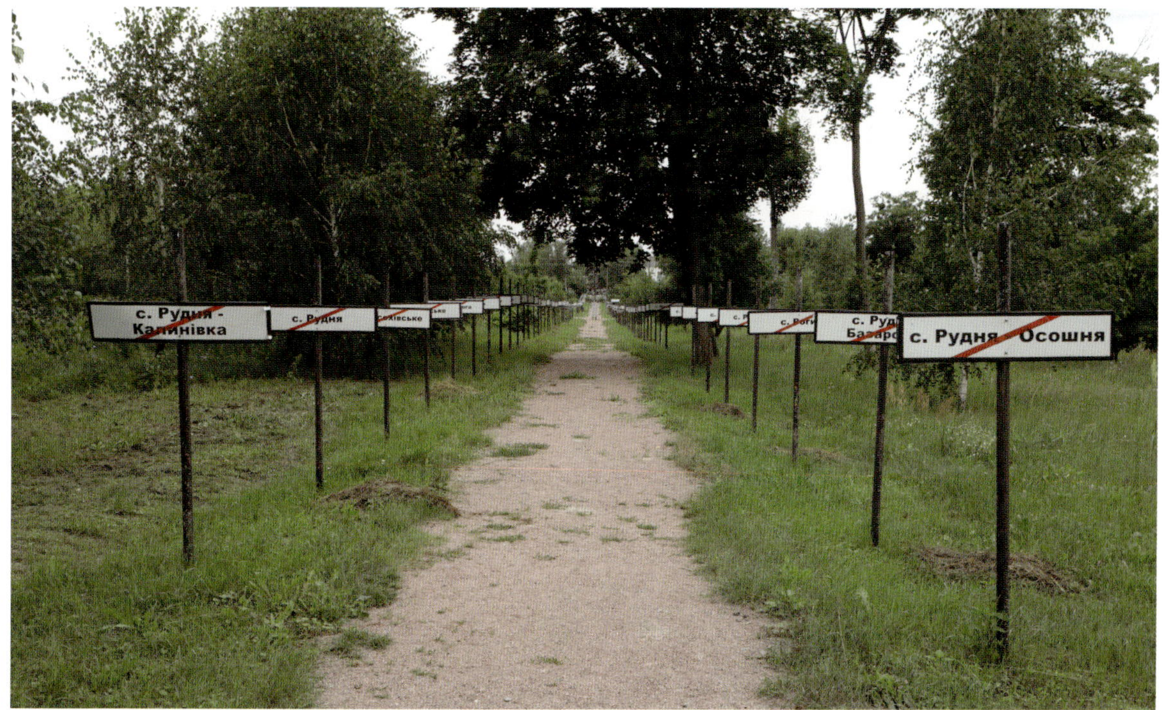

At Chapayivka we reach the northernmost part of the Ukrainian Zone. Here the road is bordered to the north by a fence, made from a single strand of barbed wire hanging from worn-out wooden posts. 'Past that is Belarus,' says Demchenko. I ask if I can cross, and he shrugs. 'Don't go too far or their patrols will get you.' Guided by a map on my phone, I traverse the field to the north and step into Belarus.

If I expected it to feel any different, I am disappointed – the Zone seems to recognise no borders but its own, and it's only the device in my palm that, against the judgement of all my senses, insists that this grass here is any different from that patch of grass back there. I don't stay long before heading back to the car.

We visit a man named Grisha who lives alone in a cottage

in Teremtsi. Beyond the iron gate, fecund apricot trees spill their fruit in sticky heaps across his yard. Grisha comes out to greet us with a wide, sad smile, and immediately begins pouring shots of walnut vodka for us at a garden table. His wife died the previous January and he seems glad of the company. Located at the confluence of the Pripyat and Dnieper Rivers, Teremtsi once had 500 citizens and a busy fishing industry. The water is strictly off-limits now, but Grisha remembers how the passenger boat used to stop here on its way from Pripyat to Kyiv. However, Teremtsi had always had it hard. In Soviet times, even when the catch was good, there might be no food in the shops. 'Everything was sent back to Russia,' he says, while Belarus, a couple of kilometres away, would always have food in stock. 'We made better money selling our stock over there.' Grisha laughs wistfully as he recalls how they would row pigs across the river to sell at Belarusian markets. We finish our drinks and leave him to his memories.

The war memorial in Teremtsi has a rough-spun, awkward quality to it, with its various elements struggling to come together into a coherent unit. The style of its central panel is reminiscent of a Modernist wood- or linocut, with semi-abstract human figures surrounded by a kind of oppressive heat-haze. They suggest a sense of affliction, a common theme for Soviet memorials to wartime sacrifice, only here the rendition feels far more Expressionistic than most Soviet Socialist-realism.

As I admire it, two women come out of their houses nearby. Baba Sonya and Baba Vanya have been neighbours here all their lives, staying put through both war and evacuation. 'There were partisans hiding here,' says Vanya, remembering the events that inspired the monument. 'But two boys from Teremtsi joined the Nazi police force. They gave up the partisans and the fascists came and shot them.'

'Right here,' agrees Sonya, standing on the patch of scrub where once a house had briefly served as a political prison. The old women continue to scold the wartime fascists as if these events occurred a week ago. Once again, I get the distinct impression that time works differently inside the Zone.

THE OTHER GHOST CITY

On our second evening Demchenko has some business in the village. Later, over dinner, I ask him about it. 'Polish stalkers. They come to Strakholissya, and I help them into the Zone.' Demchenko explains that they post his phone number in online forums. 'I'm their Chernobyl guy. I get them in, and I can get them out too – you know about that. These two have a long walk tonight, but we'll meet them for lunch tomorrow.'

We spend the next two days exploring the western end of the Zone. Pripyat wasn't the only large settlement evacuated on the Ukrainian side. We drive through thick

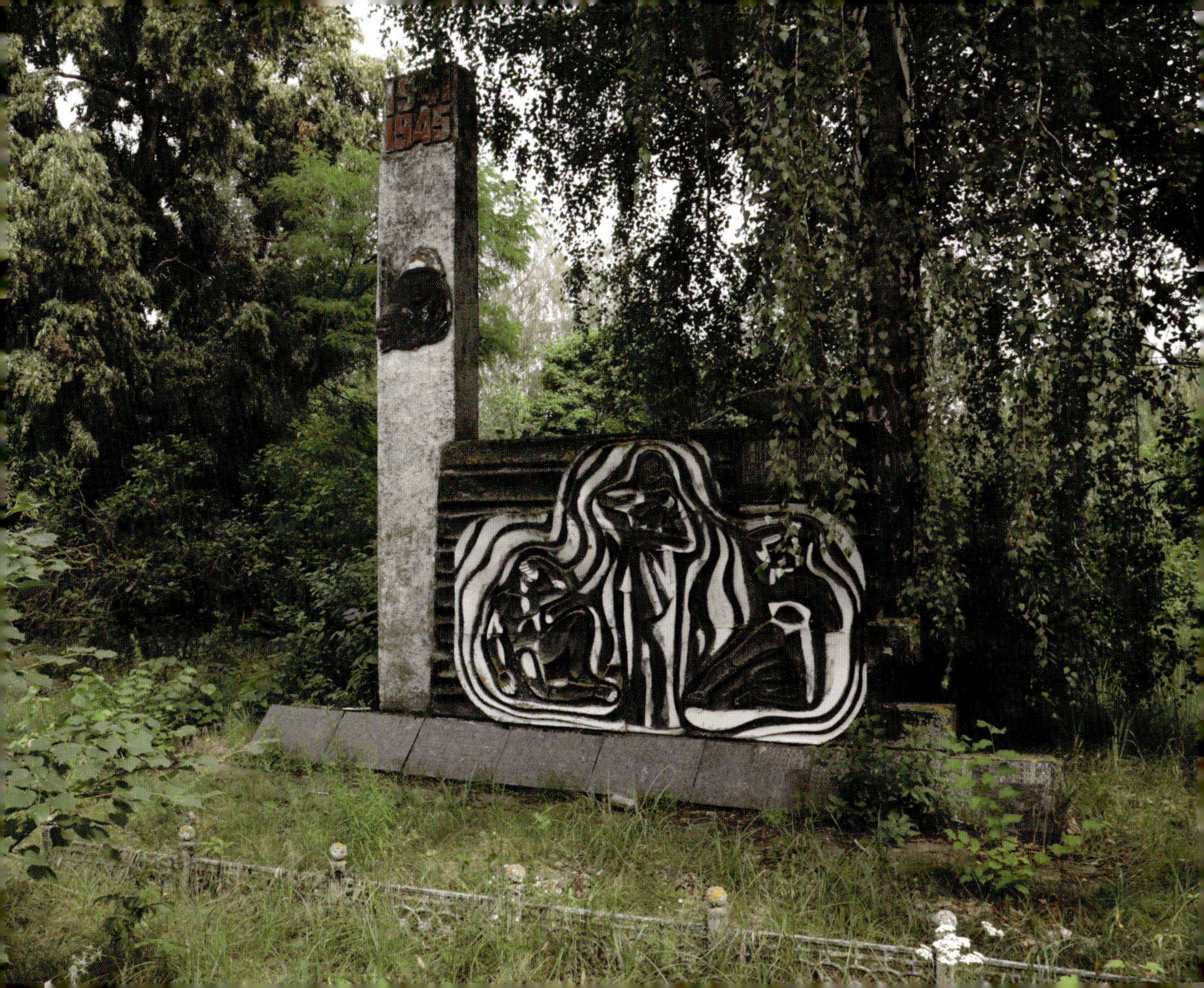
1941
1945

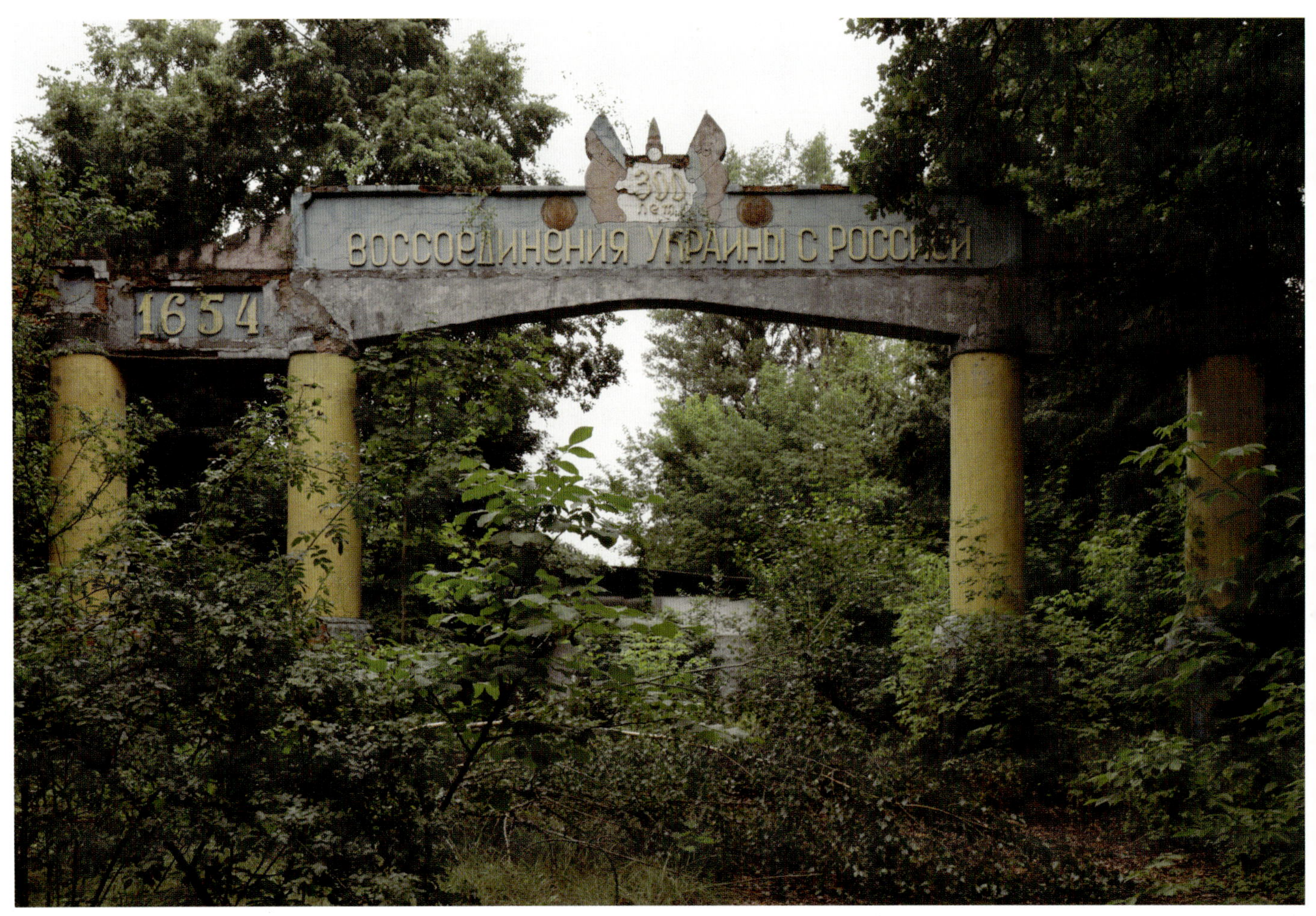
300
лет
ВОССОЕДИНЕНИЯ УКРАИНЫ С РОССИЕЙ
1654

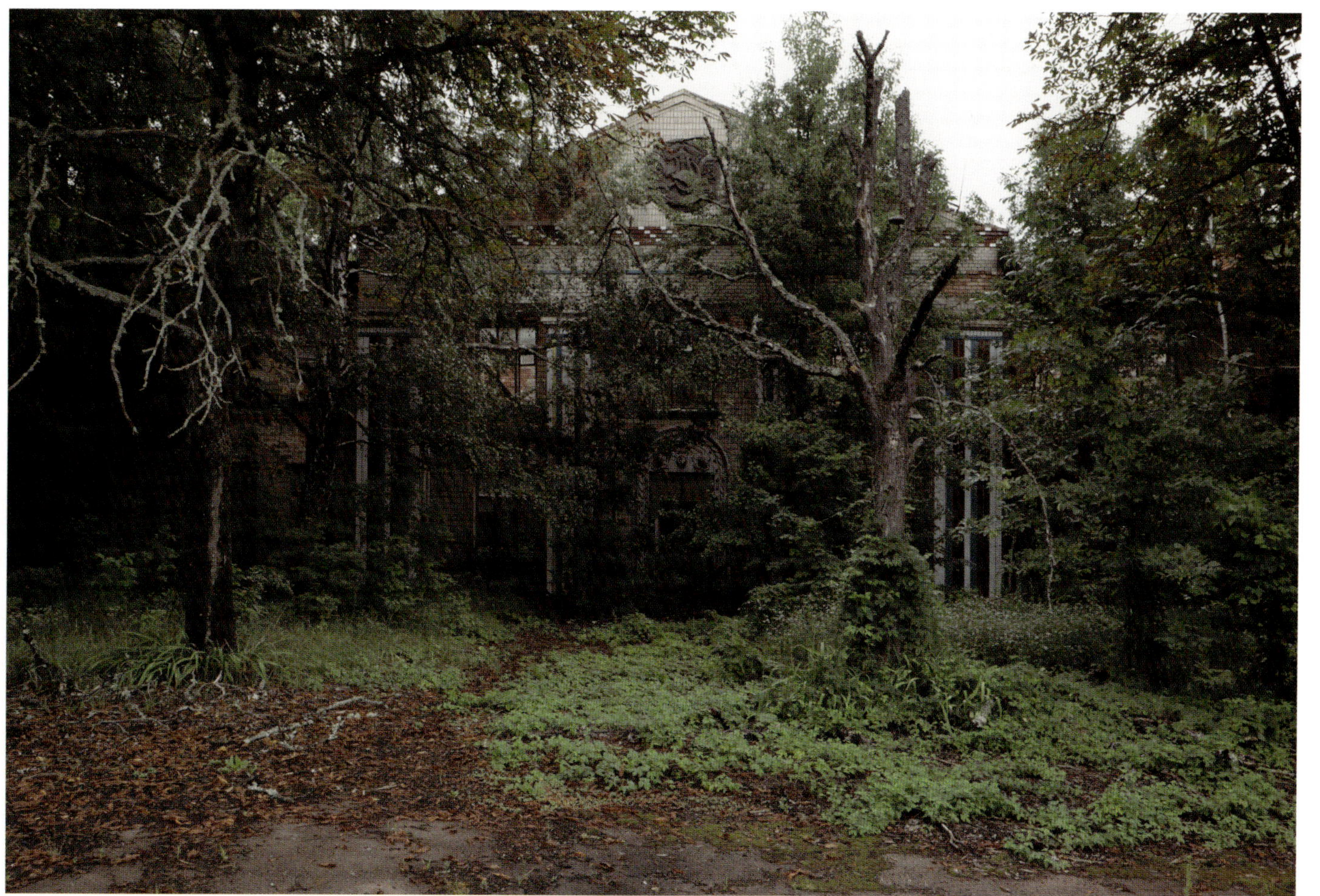

morning mist to reach Poliske, once a town of 13,000 people that sat outside the original 30 km Zone. But the contamination spread, and in 1993 its citizens were ordered to evacuate. 'Ordinary people knew more about radiation by then. Nobody argued this time.'

Chernobyl's western border is more fluid, and an entire stretch of the highway passes unhindered through the corner of the Zone near Ovruch, as building a replacement road outside it proved too expensive. Poliske feels like a smaller Pripyat, but empty of tourists. It is made up of the same essential structures – the central plaza, the apartment blocks – though here the architecture is older, Stalinist-classical replacing Socialist-modernism. We explore the red-brick carcass of the town's abandoned bread factory, and the decaying Palace of Culture, a cast-iron Soviet crest just visible between the trees that frame its entrance. The town's memorial complex is a ruin. An obelisk still stands in the centre, but across the road a concrete arch has been robbed of its bell. 'Solid metal,' says Demchenko. 'That's good scrap.'

After Poliske was evacuated Ukraine's National Guard commandeered the empty fire station. Now they use it for training, and we see uniformed soldiers hovering near the entrance. They acknowledge us with a nod. One soldier smiles and says, 'Don't worry if you hear us shooting today – we're not shooting at *you*.'

Tucked behind the fire station, a triumphal arch covered in faded yellow paint celebrates '300 Years of Ukrainian-Russian Friendship'. From somewhere in the distance comes a clattering, growling noise. 'A tank training in the Zone,' Demchenko says, 'ready for deployment against Russia.'

We take a wrong turn out of Poliske and find ourselves in a quaint backwater hamlet. Hedges are neatly manicured, and new satellite dishes adorn red-tiled rooftops. Demchenko asks directions from two old men who sit on a bench by the road, deep in conversation. This could be one of any number of villages anywhere in the world. Nearby, we enter the village where Demchenko's Polish friends have spent the night. He taps the horn twice and two pale young men wearing camouflage gear skulk cautiously out of a ruin. They are brothers from Krakow. Szymon, the more experienced of the two, became obsessed with the Zone after taking an official tour here. He started hiking in illegally, either with some Polish friends or on his own, and after a few early run-ins with police he gradually got better at evading capture. He smirks as he tells me how he celebrated New Year's Eve one year, by setting off fireworks from a rooftop in Pripyat. We eat lunch together, then leave them with a bag full of bottled water, beer, and sandwiches made by Demchenko's wife.

'Stalkers were here before tourists,' Demchenko tells me as we drive away. 'At first nobody paid them much attention. The administration kept changing anyway. Even now, it's just a small fine if they're caught.' I ask how many enter the Zone each year. 'Six or seven hundred. Mostly Ukrainians, Poles, Czechs… Then there's Russian and Belarusian stalkers, who come down over the border. Some come back every month. These Polish fuckers,' he stabs a thumb back towards the village, 'they come twice a month.' He explains that the best time to be here is in spring and autumn, when it's cooler and there are fewer mosquitoes. 'Summer's too hot… and winter's no good, the police see your tracks in the snow. Stalkers mostly keep out of Pripyat in winter. Better to stay in the villages, find an old house with a fireplace and keep warm.'

We pass a team of workmen in overalls at the roadside, tossing scrap into the back of a truck. It's the third such crew we've seen today. I ask Demchenko if this is all part of the same clean-up operation. He nods, but his mind is still on the previous conversation. 'More stalkers now,' he says, 'but more first-timers too. And some of them are fucking amateurs. Last week I saw four of them at the checkpoint, surrounded by police filling out paperwork. Apparently they went crying to the police, saying: "We can't go any further! Take us home!"' It seems to be a painful matter of principle for Demchenko, who is unusually emotive when he declares: 'A good stalker *never* gets caught. They don't give themselves up because they're too lazy to go back. And a real stalker earns money. They take a small group, charge a proper price, and they don't get caught.'

He sounds like he's describing himself, and I feel obliged to ask if he's *sure* he's not a stalker. His face softens. 'No, no, no, I just help them out,' he insists, laughing. 'For money.'

THE RED FOREST

Having seen the farthest corners of the Zone, we spend our last day in the villages closest to Pripyat and the power plant. In Zamoshnya we stop at the ruined Church of Our Lady of Kazan, built in 1898 by local Old Believers – a splinter sect of Orthodox Christians who were chased into exile by the Tsar. The red-brick church is little more than a husk now, its walls still scarred with shell damage from the Great Patriotic War. In Rud'ki, the war memorial has disappeared; instead we find rusted sports cars abandoned in a collapsed garage. In Richytsya, someone has graffitied a cartoon penis onto the monument, while Tovstyy Lis is missing its Lenin. 'There used to be a great big head here,' mutters Demchenko, poking around in the bushes outside the village club. 'This is how it happens. One by one, they go.'

Back on the road towards the power plant, I glance in the rearview mirror and see the Duga shimmering above the trees like some space-age apparition. I have still never been to the top of it, and half-joking, I ask Demchenko if he'd mind me climbing it today. 'Sure, you can climb it… but if you fall off I'm burying your body in the forest.' I laugh, but he's not smiling. 'If you die on my watch I could lose all my privileges! I could lose everything. Better you disappeared. I'll say the wolves got you.'

On the industrial island near ChNPP, we stop at a former fish farm that was briefly used post-disaster for radio-ecological testing. In a room that had been turned into a

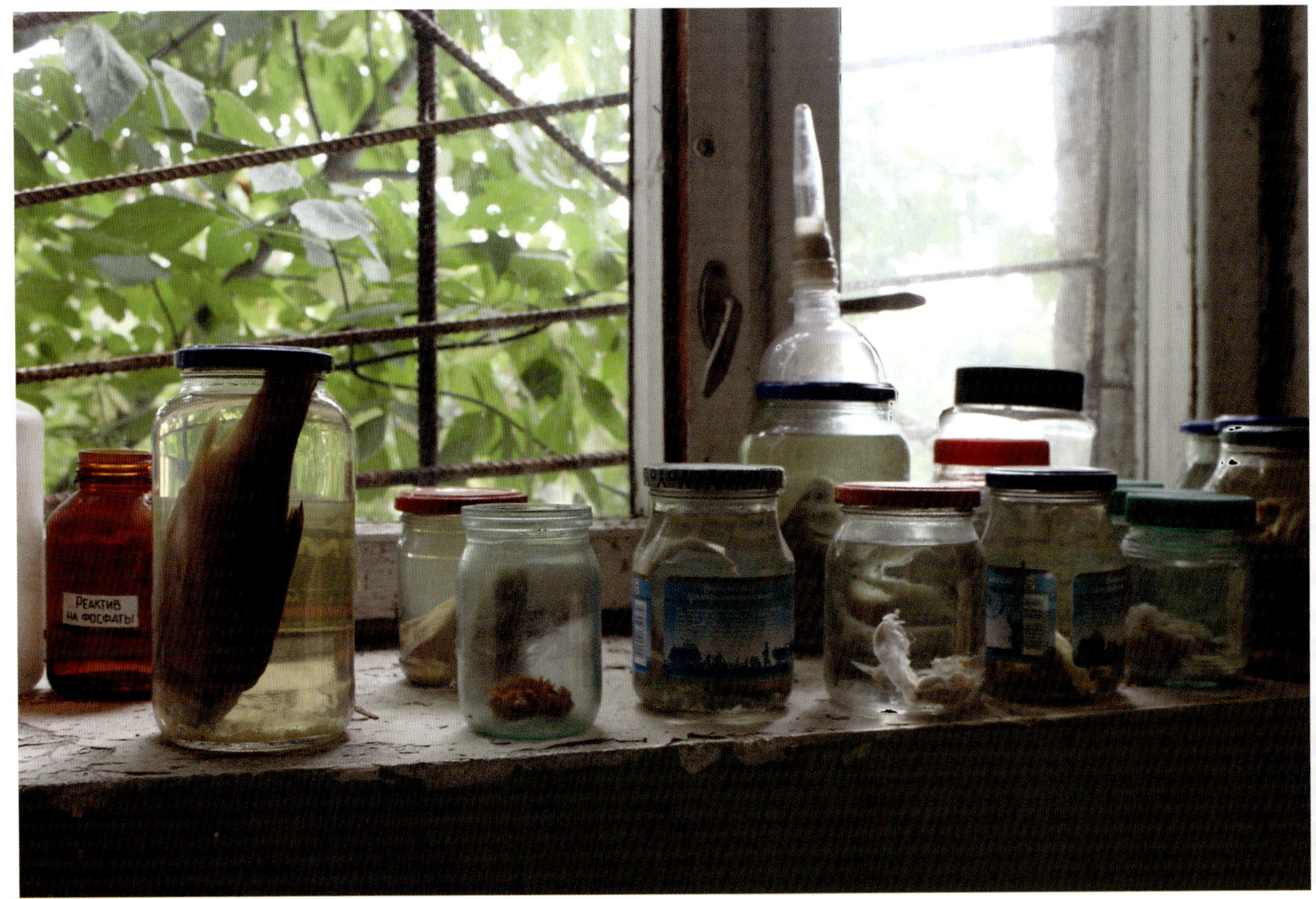

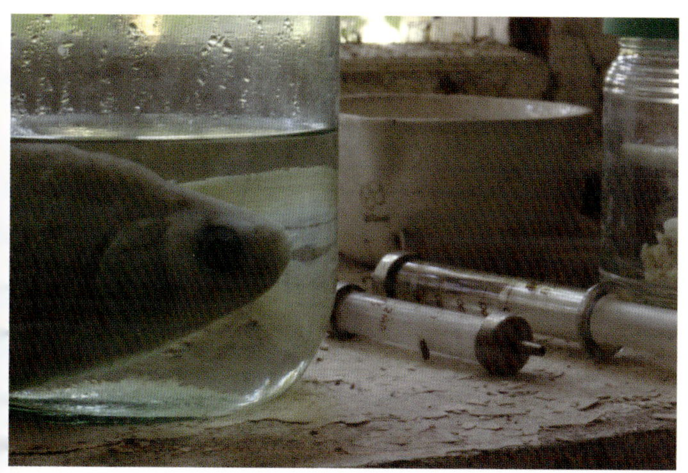
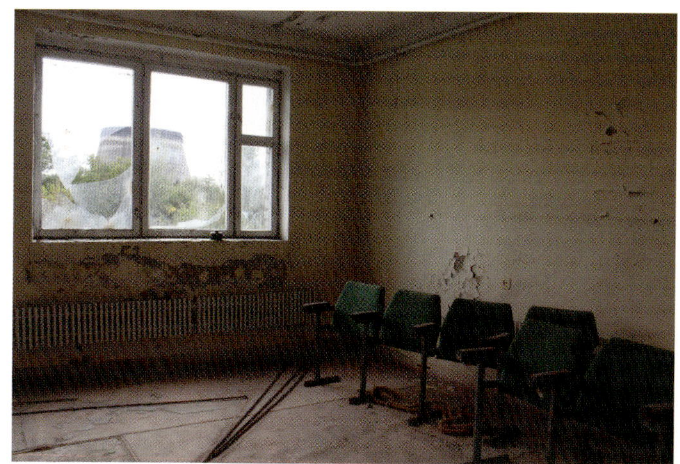
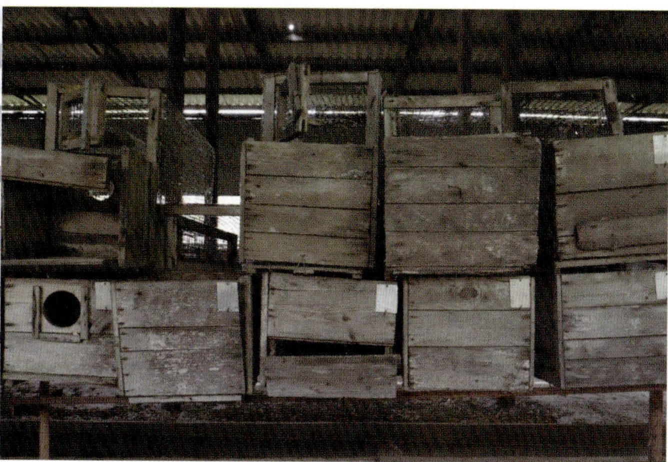
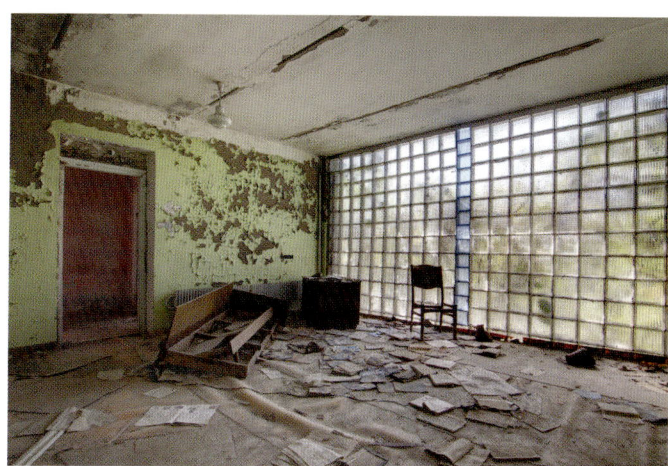

makeshift laboratory, the windowsill is stacked with fish heads in jars; floating in clear chemical preservatives, they're the only items in the building not showing their age. Around the back of the farmhouse, where the land falls away to the cooling ponds below, a simple, rectangular war memorial is just visible among the trees. The village here, called Nahortsi, was bulldozed to make way for the plant, but the Soviets retained the memorial to Nahortsi's wartime heroes.

We circle around the silver arch of the power plant in the direction of Pripyat. Just as we pass out of sight from the complex, Demchenko takes a turning into the woods. We stop in a small clearing. It isn't much to look at: an obelisk like many we've already seen, surrounded by a cluster of graves inside a knee-high metal fence. At the edge of the clearing, radiation signs warn against entering the forest. I walk between the graves and take a look at the obelisk. It has a plaque on it, decorated with the image of a tree with two horizontal boughs growing from either side of its trunk. I look to Demchenko and he nods. This is indeed the place where Chernobyl's cruciform tree once grew, and these graves belong to the partisans hanged from it. The tree itself didn't survive beyond the 1990s. Apparently it wasn't killed by radiation, but when the rest of the poisoned forest was buried, the soil changed and the old tree was exposed to winds. 'It died of loneliness,' Demchenko says.

We only have one place left to visit before we've seen every monument in the Ukrainian Zone. 'The problem is,'

says Demchenko, 'it's the worst place on earth.' We drive a few more kilometres, passing the Pripyat sign. Demchenko slows down, waits for a bus to pass then idles until it's completely out of sight. Suddenly he veers off the road to the west, and drives straight for the heart of the Red Forest. The turning is little more than a track, its crumbling tarmac giving way to grass and rocks, and as soon as we're hidden from the road Demchenko pulls over and switches off the engine. Outside of the sarcophagus itself, this is considered to be the most radioactive place in the Zone, and entry is absolutely forbidden to anyone. This is by far the strictest rule I've seen Demchenko break and I can tell he's out of his comfort zone, because for the first time on our trip he fires up his dosimeter. Immediately it goes berserk, and we watch the figure rising on the screen: 400 μSv/h… 850… 1,350… it settles just shy of 2,000 μSv/h. He punches a button to silence it. 'Better be quick,' he says, 'I don't want to fuck about in there.'

As we step into the forest, I catch my breath. It is beautiful. Thick, basil-green moss is spread over the ground, between noble pines and peeling white birch. A dusting of yellowed leaves breaks the strict geometry of the trees, while here and there, the crowns of speckled toadstools poke up through the carpet. We walk fast: Demchenko's sense of direction is faultless, and we reach the monument in moments. It is a simple affair, another rectangular slab of concrete propped up on its end with the dates 1941-1945 engraved on its side.

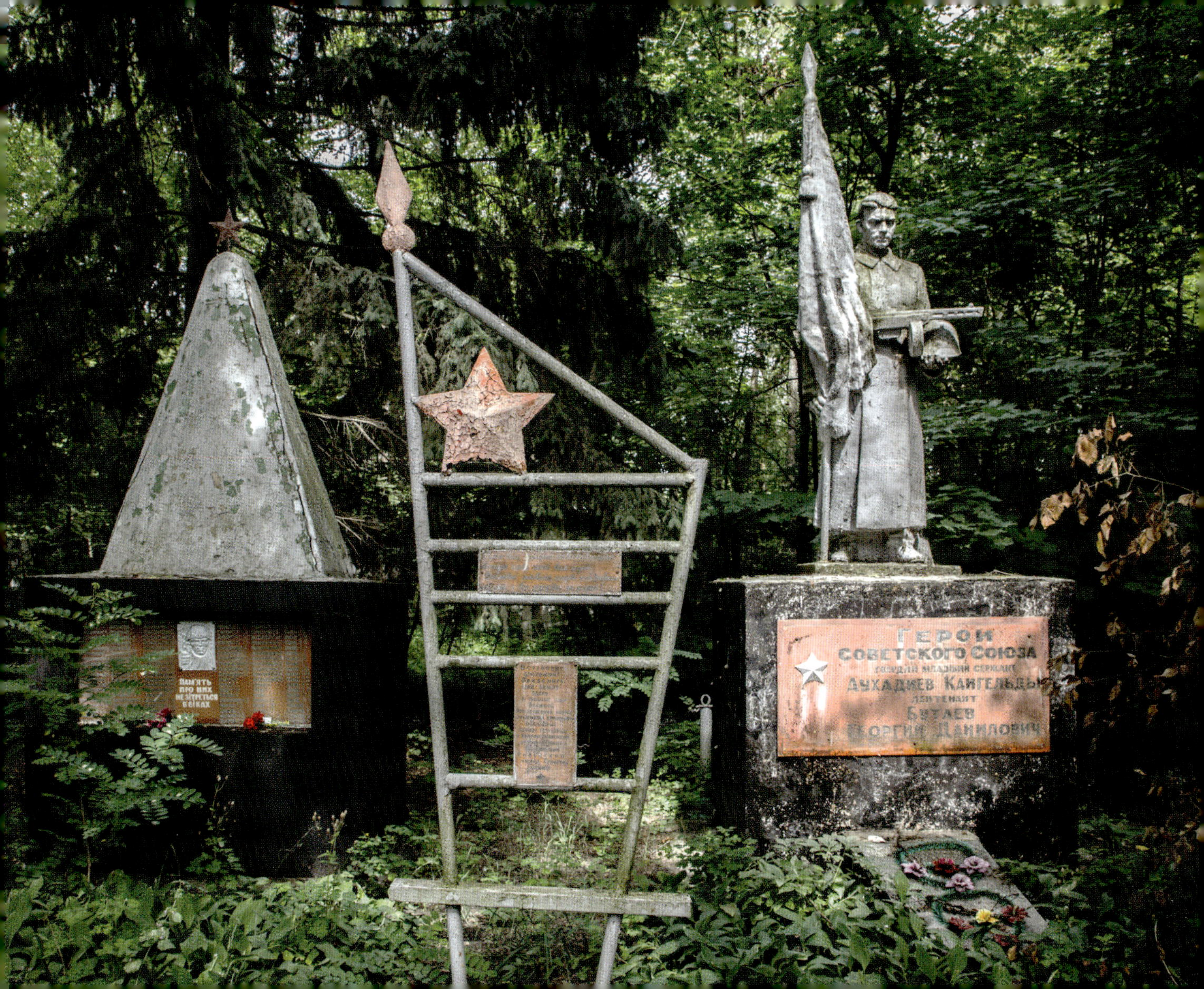

ПАМ'ЯТЬ
ПРО НИХ
НЕ ЗГАСНЕ
В ВІКАХ
ГЕРОИ
СОВЕТСКОГО СОЮЗА
гвардии младший сержант
ДУХАДИЕВ КАИГЕЛЬДЫ
лейтенант
БИТАЕВ
ГЕОРГИЙ ДАНИЛОВИЧ

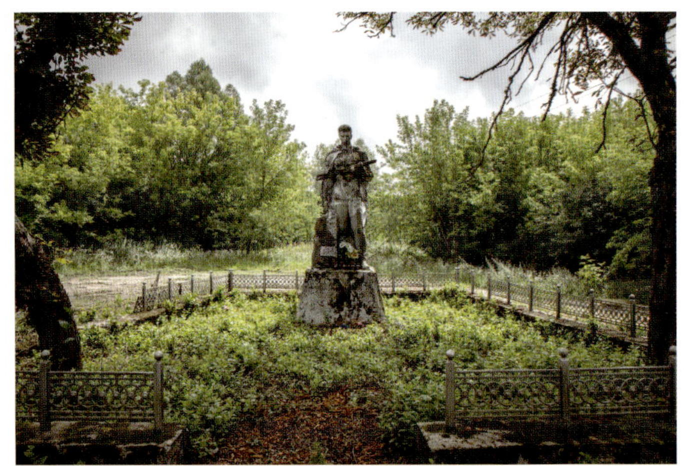
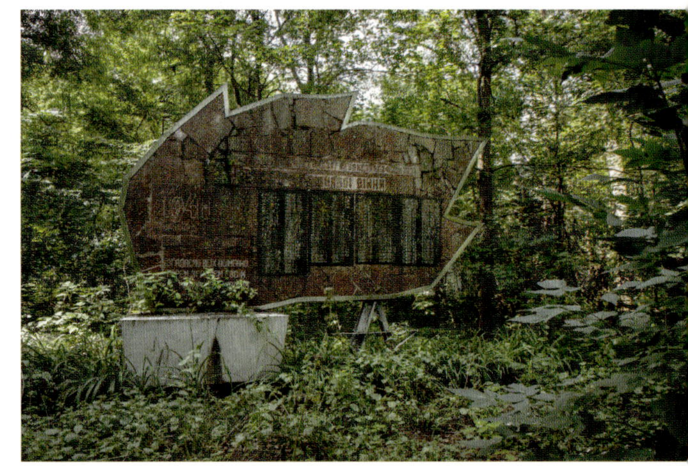
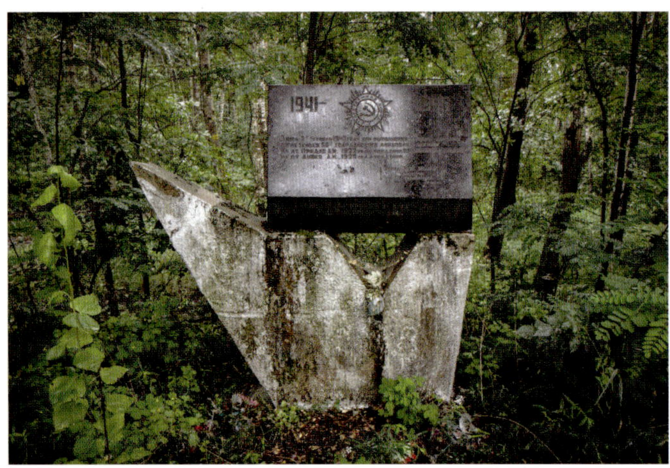
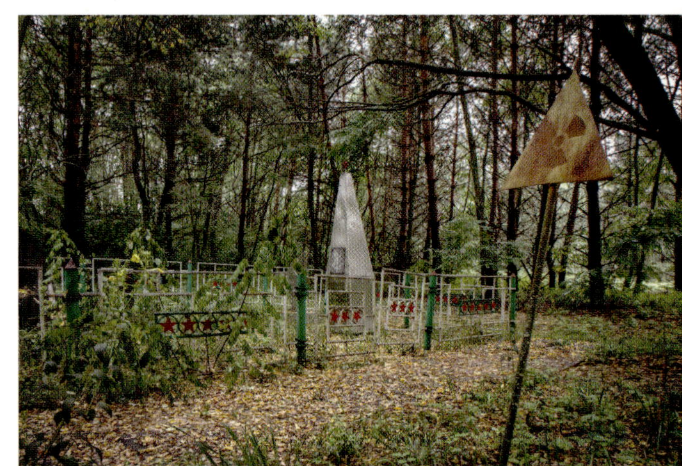

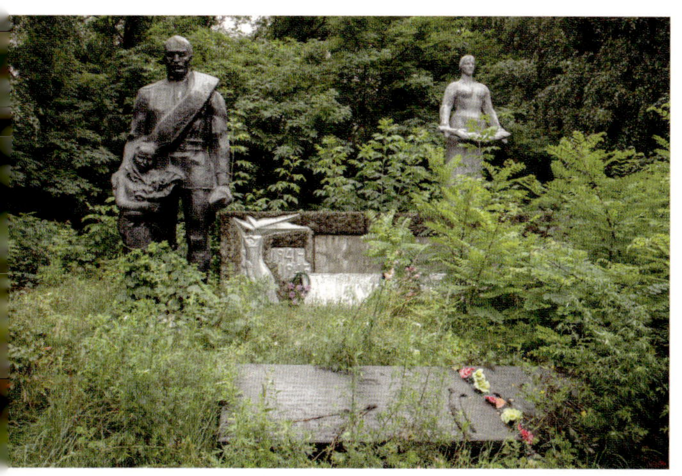
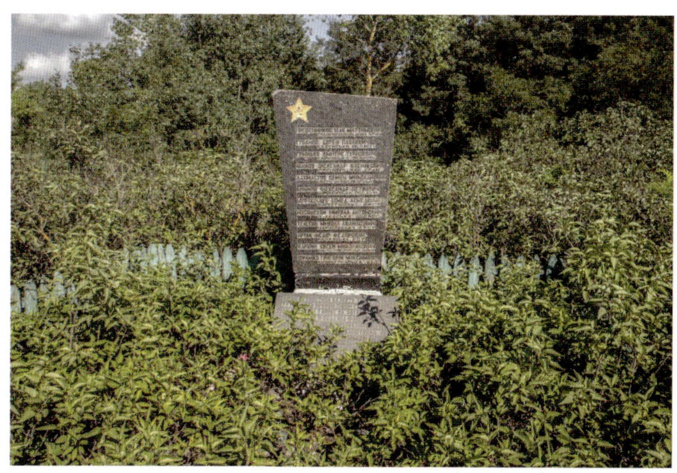
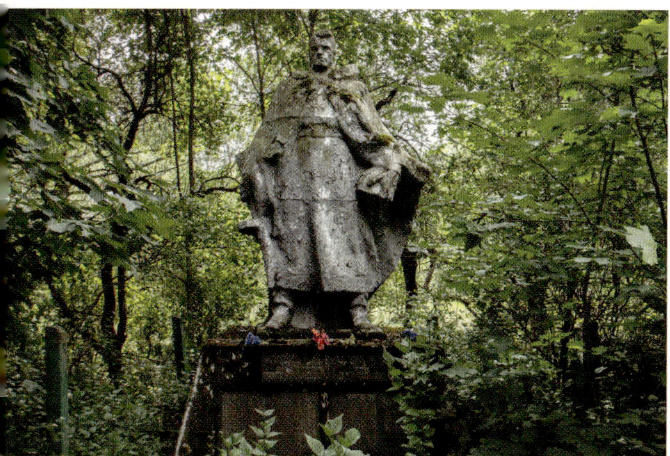
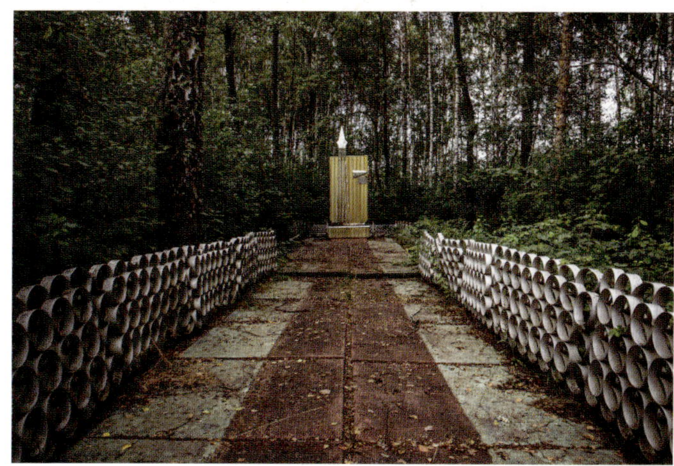

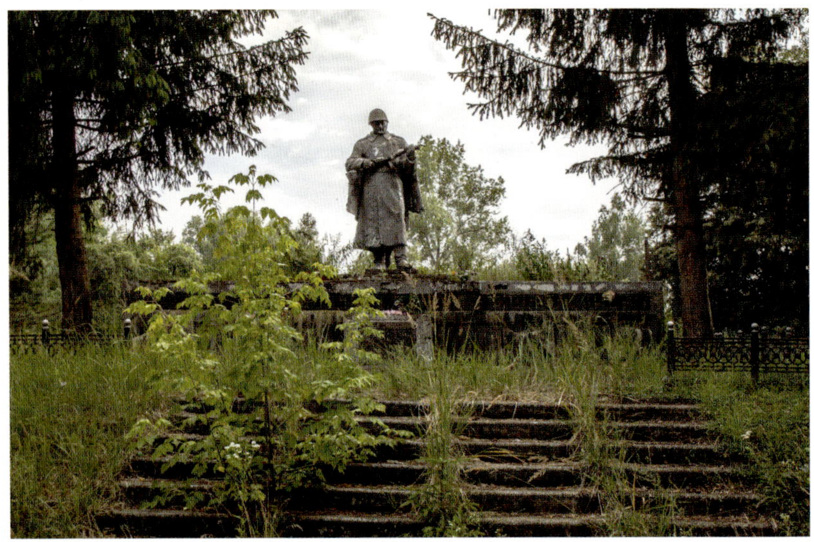

Nearby lies the circular metal plate that also used to adorn it – a factory-stamped Soviet crest, now bent and forgotten. The dosimeter starts beeping again, and Demchenko hits the silence button. I look over his shoulder: the reading at this monument is the highest I've ever seen – roughly 10,000 µSv/h. A chest X-ray delivers a single dose of approximately 100 µSv, so standing here we could almost be receiving the equivalent of two chest X-rays every minute.

As I turn from the meter to gaze into the forest, I remember the stalker proverb – *no dosimeter, no radiation* – and I catch myself wanting to believe it. We might be the first people to visit this place since the disaster. I look at the perfect, unspoiled moss beneath my feet, as clean and soft as a freshly made bed, and feel a powerful desire to lie down on it and sink into the forest.

A nudge. 'Let's go,' Demchenko says quietly. By now we've probably had ten X-rays each, so we start retracing our steps towards the car. Halfway, I pause when I glimpse something that makes me gasp out loud: the vast silver arch, glinting in the sun, framed between the natural hues of pine needles, bark, and moss: cause and effect in a single picture. I admire the view for a moment longer – one more X-ray – and then we're gone, rushing through the trees, out of the forest to the car, both of us swearing we'll never set foot in that beautiful, terrible place again.

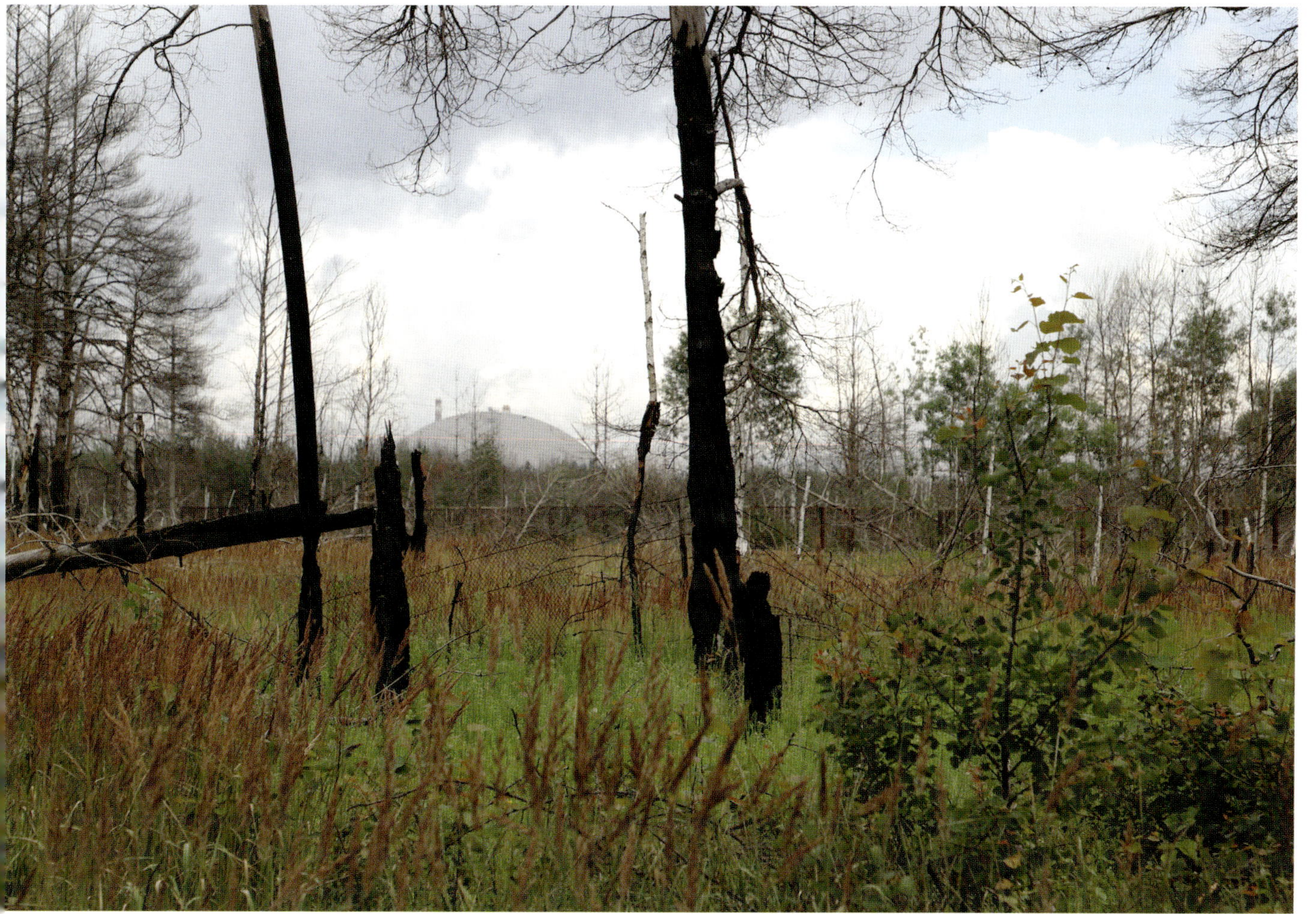

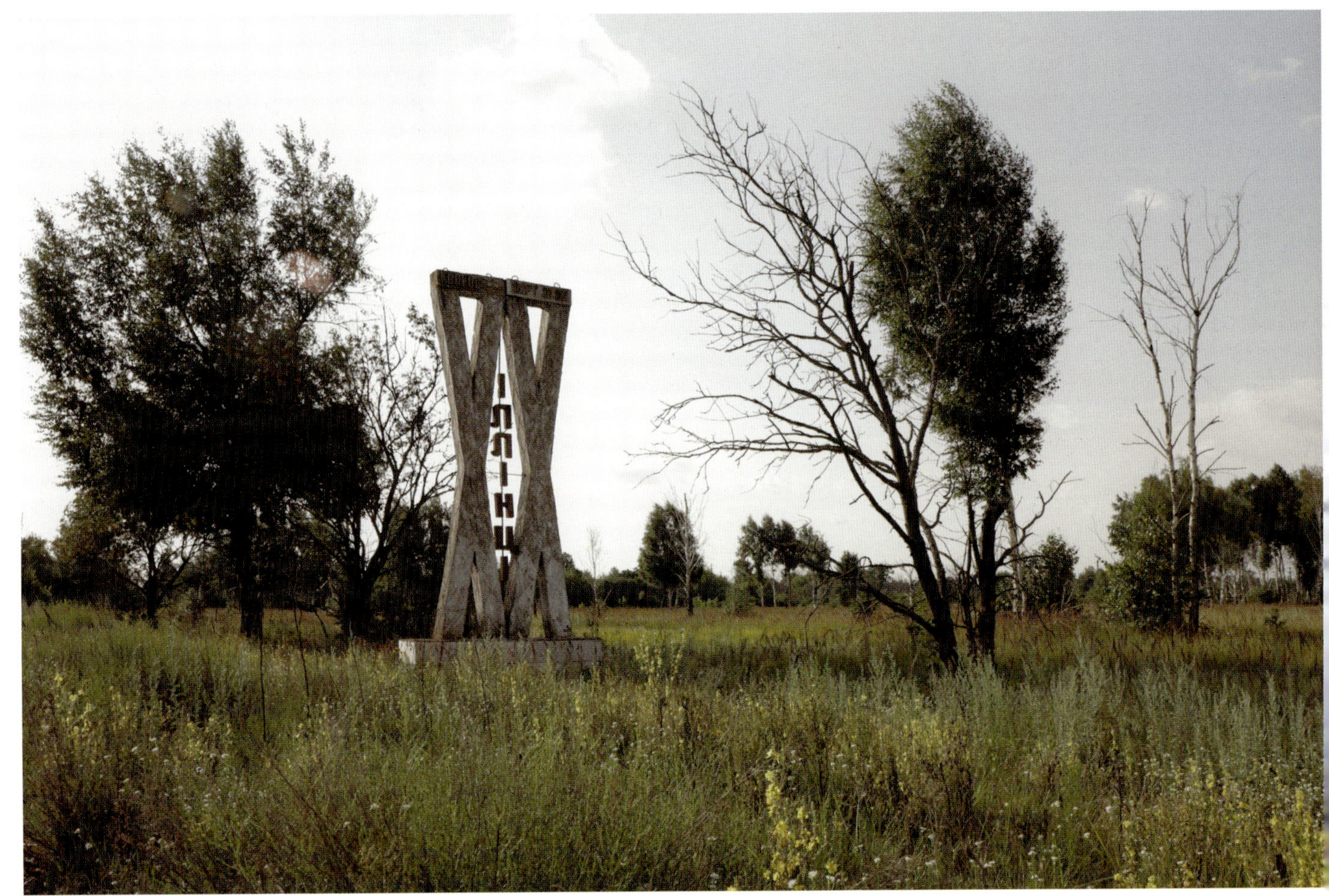

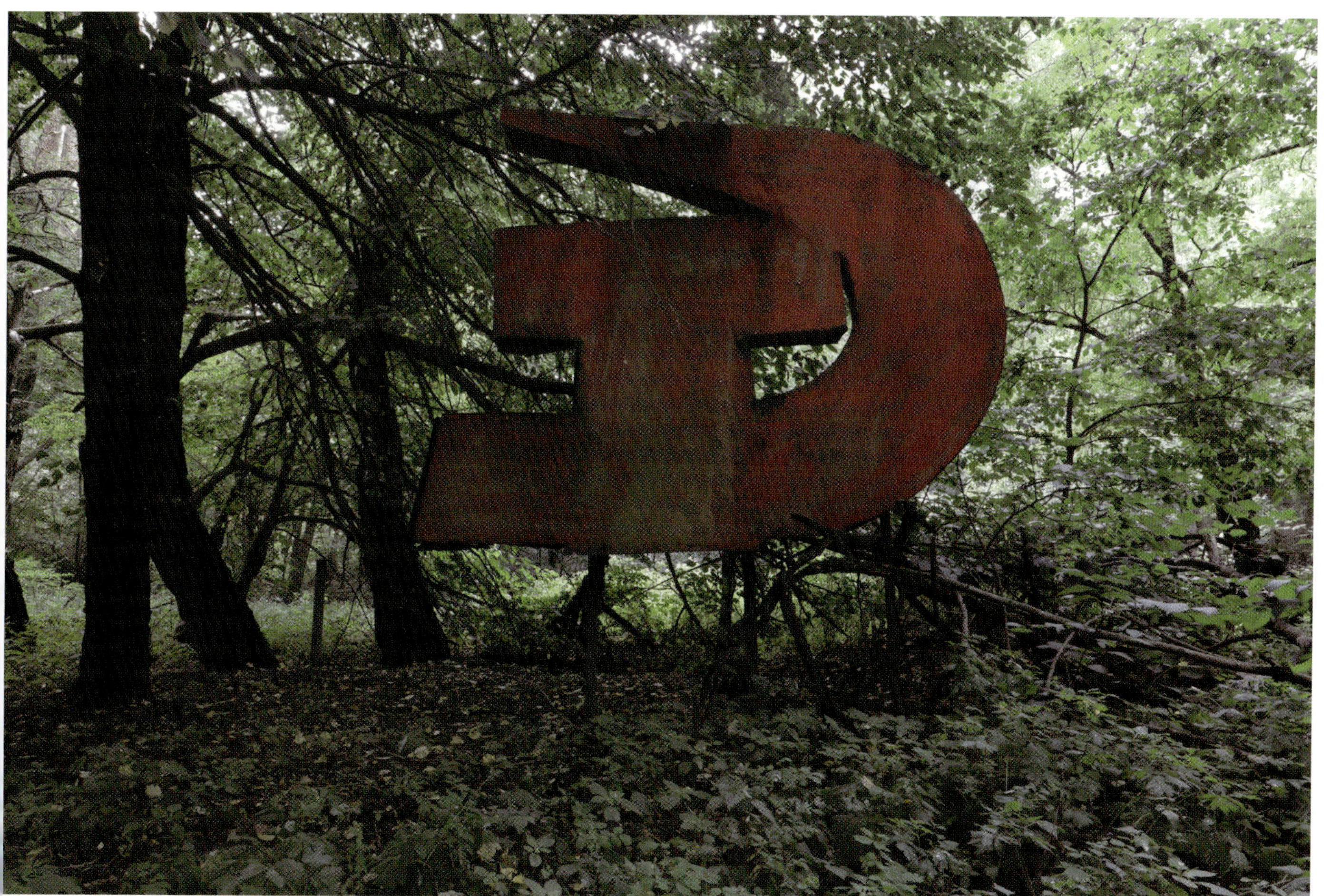

7. BELARUS

THE RADIO-ECOLOGICAL RESERVE

Following the Chernobyl disaster, roughly two-thirds of the territory of Belarus suffered significant radioactive contamination. The Belarusian government designated the most densely toxic area, along the Ukrainian border and closest to the plant, the 'Polesie State Radio-ecological Reserve', and this restricted zone was used exclusively for scientific monitoring and research. In November 2018, authorities tentatively began offering tour routes through the Reserve and the following summer I decided to pay it a visit. The prescribed tours usually took the form of highly structured one-day itineraries visiting selected locations; but I asked if it might be possible to explore further afield, on a two-day 'monumenteering' trip, and the Reserve's administration approved my request.

I invite a few colleagues along, and we meet our guide, Karina, outside Minsk's central train station – a pristine work of post-modernist design, all futuristic glass and steel, facing 1950s Stalinist towers still adorned with hammers and sickles. The city feels almost unnaturally clean. Even at this late hour, a team of staff is polishing the station's glass façade to a perfect finish. On the pavement out front, skater kids are wearing freshly ironed T-shirts.

Karina has only been to the Reserve ten times herself. She is bright and energetic, a sharp contrast to many of the jaded veteran Ukrainian guides I know, whose Zone visits number in the hundreds or even thousands. Her independent tour company, Walk to Folk, specialise in adventure trips. For three years they have offered kayaking, hiking, camping and cultural tours around Belarus. In December, a month after the Reserve was opened for tourism, Karina was invited on a promotional trip there, and soon after her company made it a regular tour offering.

We take the overnight train – seven hours in a sleeper carriage – to Rechitsa in Gomel Province. As stipulated by Belarusian law, our group will be accompanied throughout by scientists from the Reserve. Our scientist guides are waiting for us at the station, both of them dressed in military-style camouflage gear. Dmitry is a botanist, around fifty years old, with a kind face, eyes the colour of Arctic glaciers, black hair, and a perfectly trimmed Freddie Mercury moustache. Leonid, our driver, is larger, with short fair hair. He appears almost intimidating at first, until he smiles, and suddenly looks more like a teddy bear. Karina doesn't know either of them – she is assigned different scientists every time, she says.

Our tour is conducted in a classic UAZ-452 van, owned by the Polesie State Radio-ecological Reserve. The Reserve's own vehicles are the only ones ordinarily allowed into the restricted area – these Soviet-built machines are not just best suited to the terrain, but are also the easiest to maintain and repair. Phone coverage is non-existent in much of the Reserve, so each vehicle is fitted with a radio. Our small group huddles in the back, sitting on benches facing one another, as Leonid drives us across a vast, flat stretch of

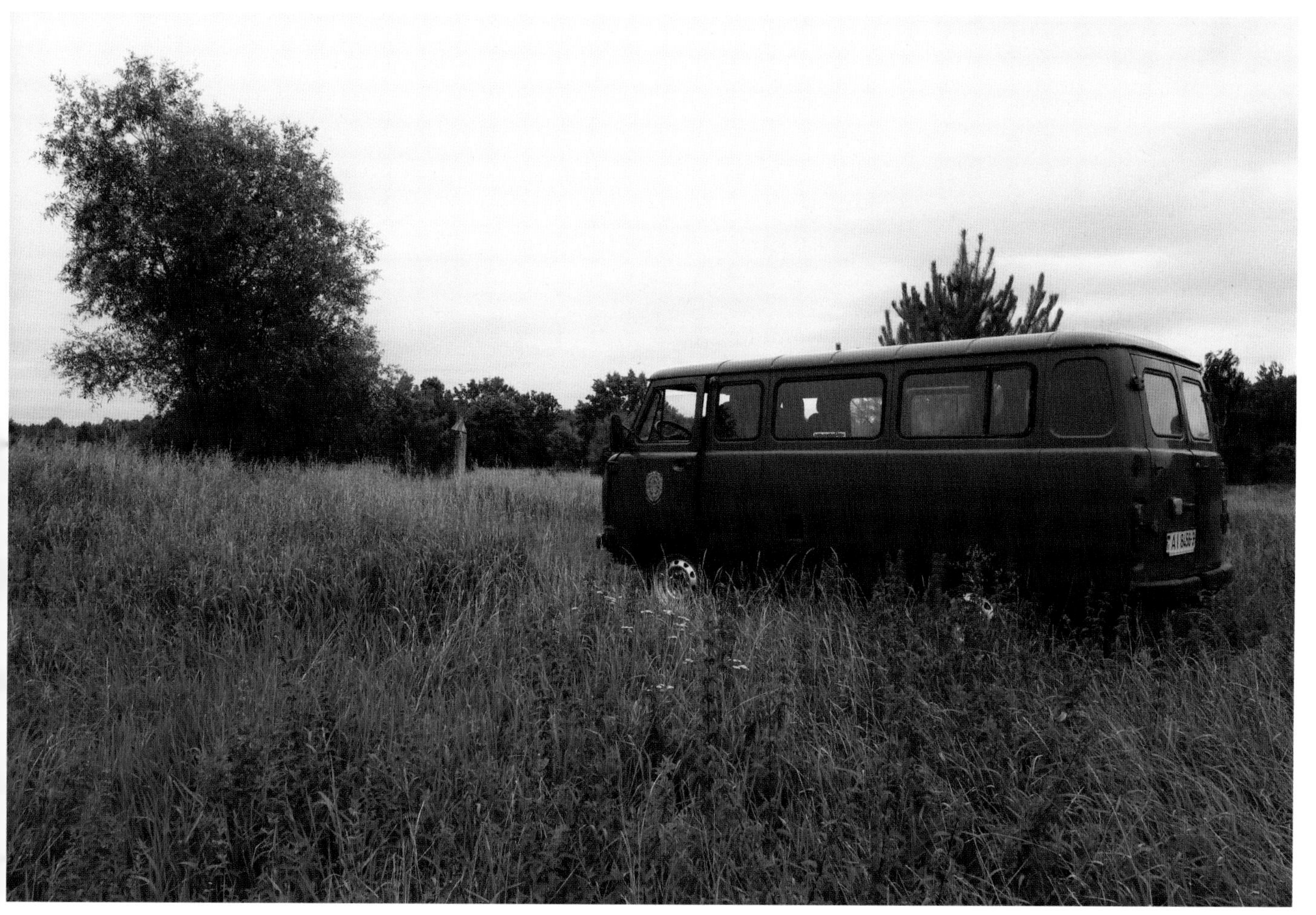

cornfield that was once given over to collectivised farming. Any houses we see are built to a uniform design, as though they were all produced during the same burst of construction. We pass a new solar farm, and Dmitry shouts something back that Karina translates: 'Are you interested in monuments generally, or just monuments in the Reserve?'

'Generally,' I answer, keen also to avoid giving the impression that we are 'disaster tourists', interested in local culture only after it has been abandoned. Abruptly the van pulls over in the village of Malodusha, and Dmitry begins explaining a monument dedicated to local children who were killed in 1959 by a mine left over from WWII. 'The echo of war', reads a small sign marking this as a national historic site, and Dmitry explains how even inside the Reserve, the government still maintains every memorial.

The entrance to the Polesie State Radio-ecological Reserve looks similar to one of Ukraine's smaller 10 km Zone checkpoints: no modern buildings, no soldiers with guns, and certainly no souvenir van. While a sleepy-looking guard pushes open the gate, Karina reads us the rules for the Reserve, which essentially are the same as those of the Ukrainian Zone. Today is a busy day, with two tour groups inside the Reserve at once. As we listen to the rules, the other group pulls up in their own Soviet-era van, and their guide comes over to talk briefly with ours. He grins as he vigorously shakes hands with each of us. After he leaves, Karina says: 'We call that guy Stalker Peter.' His group are

Belarusian ruin enthusiasts on a day-trip. 'Some of them have gone to the Ukrainian side as many as ten times. They're real fans,' says Karina, though she explains that visitors to the Reserve are more often Polish and Czech. 'For most Belarusians, the Zone is not so interesting. Many of us know someone who died or suffered from the disaster, so we already know as much as we want to. Besides, the place is hardly unique for us – there are plenty of villages in north Belarus where you can see abandoned buildings that look exactly the same as the ones here.'

The Polesie Reserve, established in 1988, now covers an area of more than 2,000 square kilometres and is divided into three regions: Brahin, Khoiniki, and Naroulia. Before the disaster, this largely agrarian region was home to more than 22,000 people spread across ninety-five villages, including numerous settlements of Old Believers. Now it's home to moose, deer, lynx, and bison, as well as forty-eight of Belarus's 189 species of endangered plants. No one officially lives in the Reserve, though 746 people work here, including forty-two scientists divided into departments for, among other things, zoology, biology, and ornithology. Other Reserve employees work as border security, in forestry, or for fire-prevention teams.

After heading through the gate, we stop at monuments in the first few villages, most of them sites of wartime atrocities. The contrast with Ukraine is striking. Whereas Ukraine's Soviet-era monuments have suffered greatly under

page 165: Polesie State Radio-ecological Reserve, Belarus. State-owned UAZ-452 vehicles are the standard mode of transportation within the Reserve.

right: Great Patriotic War Memorial, Babchin. Erected in 1970, this monument honours the 294 locals who died fighting the Nazis, and a further 21 who were executed by them in a single day.

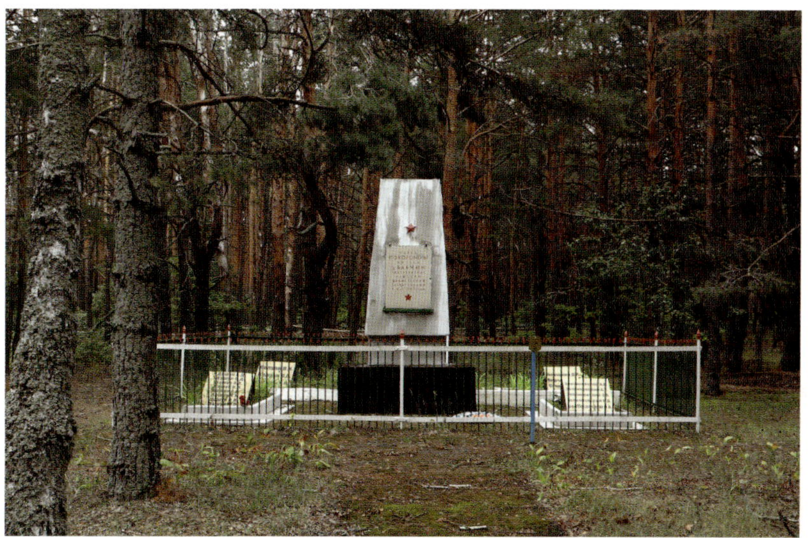

the country's decommunisation law – either being removed altogether, or (particularly within the Zone) allowed to fall into states of severe disrepair – here the monuments remain cherished focal points of local and national history. Even within the Reserve, surrounded by collapsing and ruined buildings, tumble-down pig sties and overgrown roads, each village memorial we see is freshly painted. Many are also accompanied by a laminated sign bearing a title, some historical context, and a number relating to Belarus's official list of heritage sites.

Dmitry, our quiet scientist guide, is quite willing to tell us about every monument – but his real passion is for plants. On the outskirts of Babchin, beside a memorial to a massacre,

he draws our attention to a succulent. 'Russian houseleek – it's extremely rare,' he says, lowering his voice as if to avoid disturbing the vegetation. 'It only grows here, inside the Reserve.' Dmitry is from Brest, in western Belarus, on the border with Poland. He trained in forestry there, before taking a work placement at the Radio-ecological Reserve. After an initial apprenticeship, he decided to stay on. While he has no personal connection to the disaster, or the lands most directly affected by it, this is an excellent opportunity for a career scientist, he explains. Dmitry enjoys his work in the Reserve. He loves the plants and seems to have a healthy respect for radiation: 'This is the average in the Reserve,' he says, holding up the dosimeter for us to see the reading

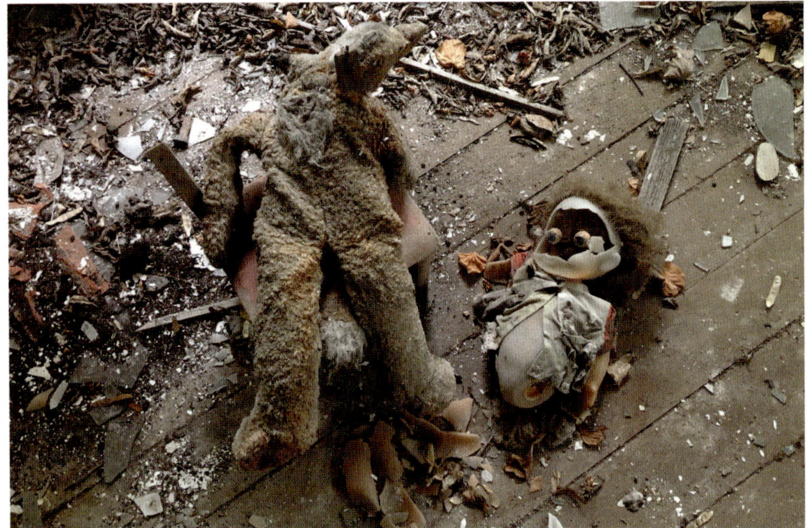

left: Vygribnaya Sloboda village school. Previous visitors have arranged the children's toys for dramatic effect.

right: Pogonnoe village council office. A poster of Lenin is propped up in this otherwise completely stripped building.

of 0.5 μSv/h. 'But later, I will show you some dirtier places.'

For the most part, the Reserve's buildings are bare: tables, chairs, occasionally an abandoned boot or book, but none of the ghoulish decorations that characterise tourism in the Ukrainian Zone. However, in Vygribnaya Sloboda we enter a deserted school to find dolls propped upright on shelves, a scattering of gas masks, and books of fairy tales that have been left open beside maps and globes. I ask Karina who arranged them. She sighs: 'One of the guides did it, the way they do in Ukraine. Many of the visitors have a code: they don't want to touch things or move them around themselves, but they also want those photos – so this makes it possible. And when they share their photos online, more

come.' She adds without enthusiasm: 'It's good marketing.' Ukraine's Chernobyl tourism industry is already committed to this type of sensationalism, but a conflict of approaches exists in Belarus: they want to use the Reserve for research and the sharing of knowledge, to preserve and respect its authenticity; but they recognise that dolls and gas masks are where the money is.

I ask Karina if the authorities want more tourists to visit. 'Yes – but it seems we can't agree on how to do this.' She explains how Reserve officials have stated that they don't want more than ten groups in any month. The approach of using their own vehicles and scientist guides means they're limited by the size of their staff and fleet. More than that,

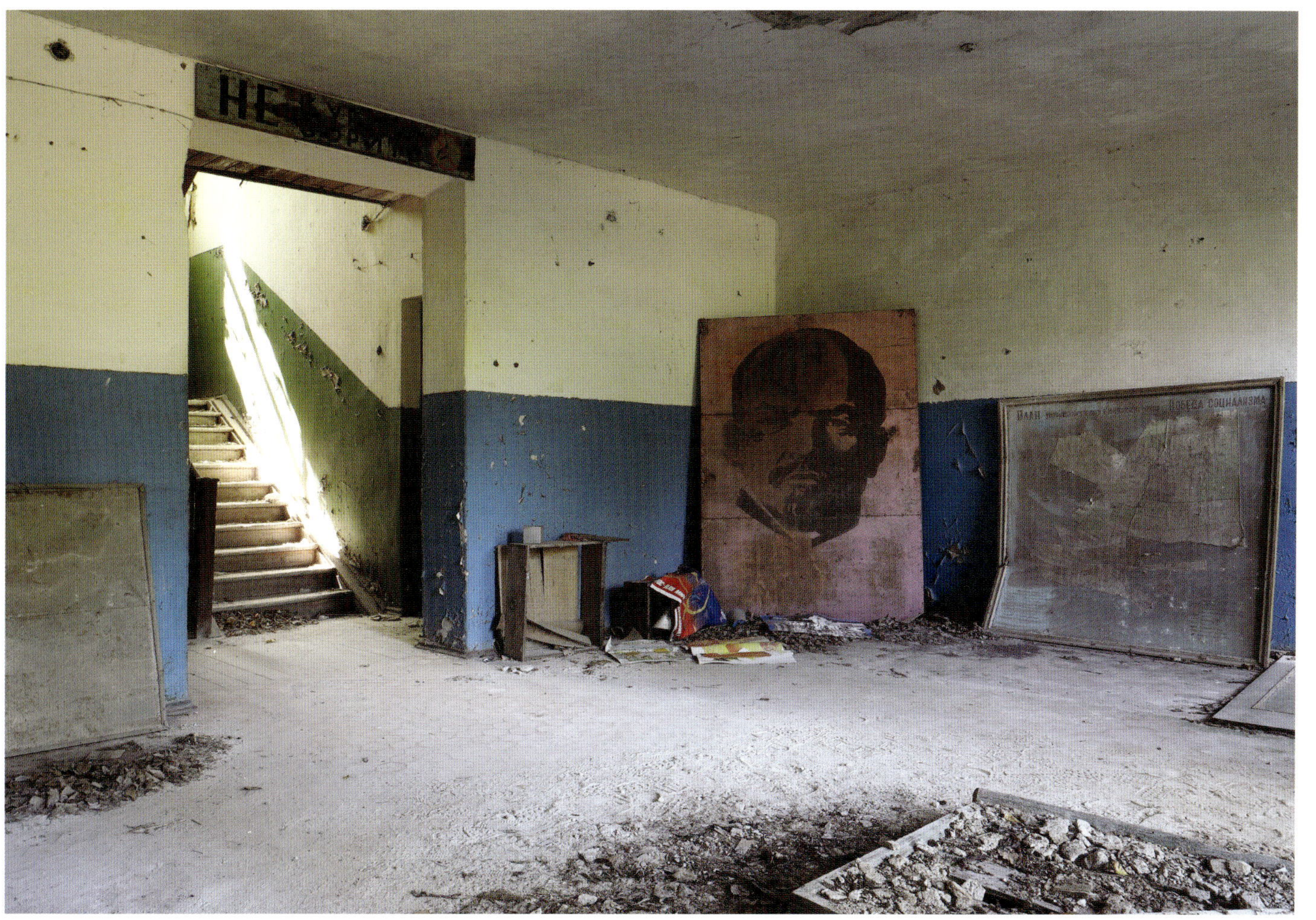

they don't like the idea of the Reserve being 'sullied' by over-tourism. As we leave the school, Dmitry draws our attention to a tree growing beside the building, with a modern plaque that details its genus and estimated age. 'That's a special one: Karelian birch,' says Karina. 'Dmitry found it in April last year, and put up the sign in August.' Back on the road a little later, Leonid pulls over to marvel at a mushroom the size of a watermelon.

We eat a lunch of pickles, sandwiches, cured meat, and boiled eggs, on a fold-out table that only just fits inside the back of the van. Karina talks about the evacuation in 1986: 'They made a mistake evacuating villagers to the city,' she says. 'These people had lived their whole life in the village, working at the collective farm, and then they were relocated to flats. They were called "Chernobyl houses" – around Malinauka district on the east of Minsk. A lot of those people died young. Many became depressed and started to drink. They couldn't find work and just couldn't deal with the city. So the second wave of people who were resettled, from the edges of the Reserve where it wasn't so urgent, were given houses in other villages instead. The government learned from their mistake.'

After lunch we visit Zherdnoye, one long village street lined on either side with decrepit wooden houses. Hidden among the foliage, beams carry hand-carved details, loving touches of individual artistry now lost to the forest. All around the village are fields of corn. 'Are they growing food?' I ask.

'For the cows,' says Karina. *But who eats the cows?* I wonder.

I discover that much of the Radio-ecological Reserve has been converted back into farmland. Aside from corn and cattle, we drive past fields of freshly mown grass used to make hay for the horses that are bred here, which are then sold for riding and farm work. 'We have Przewalski's horses too,' says Dmitry proudly. 'They were originally released in Ukraine, but they've started crossing the border, to come and live in our Reserve.' I cannot bring myself to tell him that his neighbours are turning them into sausages, but I do wonder if perhaps the horses feel safer on this side of the border. By the roadside, we pass huge quantities of massive logs stacked ready for collection. Much of this goes to Lithuania, a country with a booming manufacturing industry – including the large-scale production of IKEA furniture.

On the drive back out we pass a village sign that reads 'Prosmychi'. Nearby an old man leans on his rake to watch us. The beautifully maintained village houses are painted in a striking palette of purples, oranges, and navy blues. Tidy stacks of black plastic-wrapped silage bales stud the field behind the houses. In the distance, smoke rises dirty-yellow from a crop fire. Planted in the bushes at the road's edge is a solitary radiation-warning sign – the only acknowledgement that this village is in any way unusual. We haven't passed radiation control yet and there has been no indication that we've even left the Reserve. I ask if we're still inside the

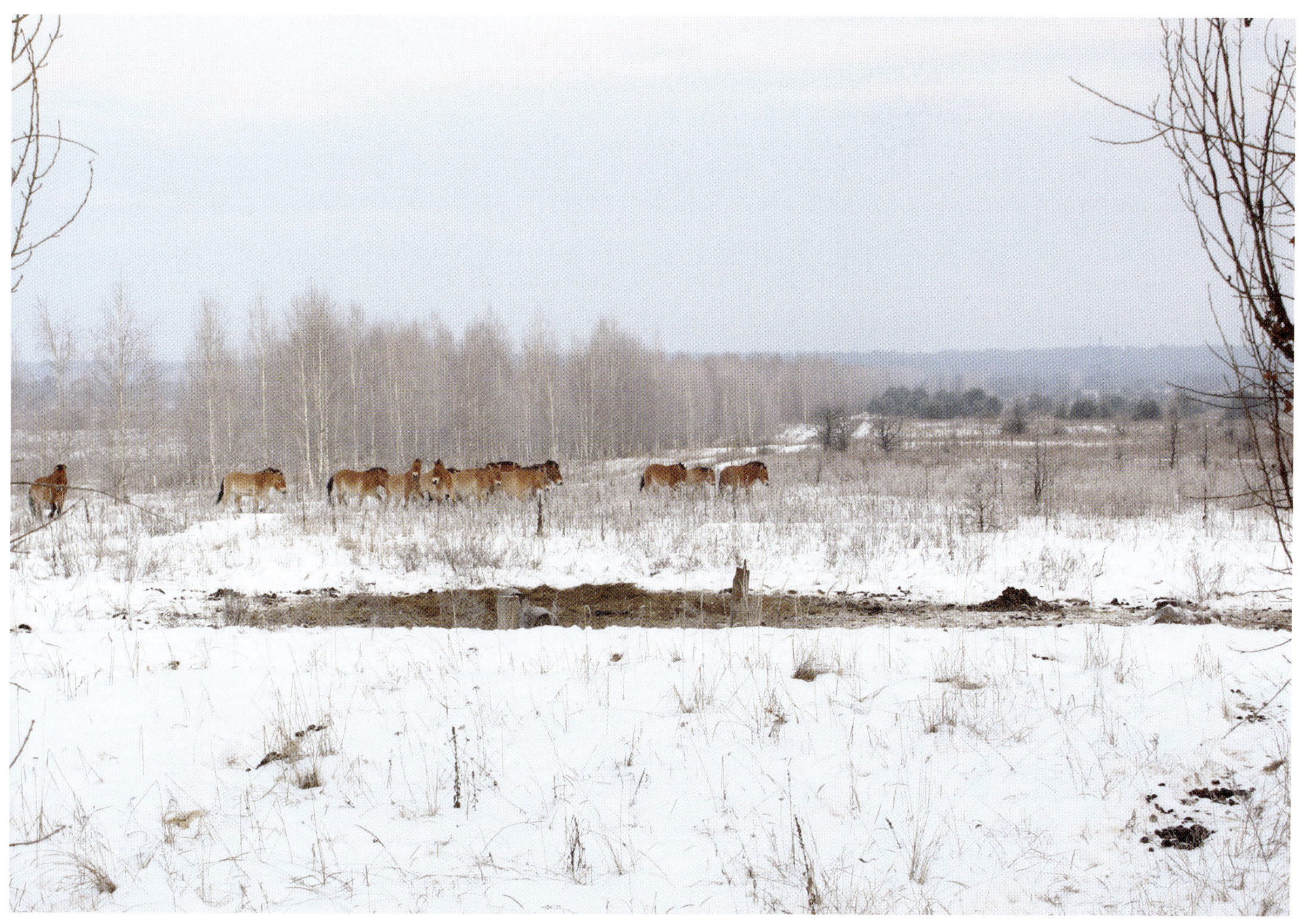

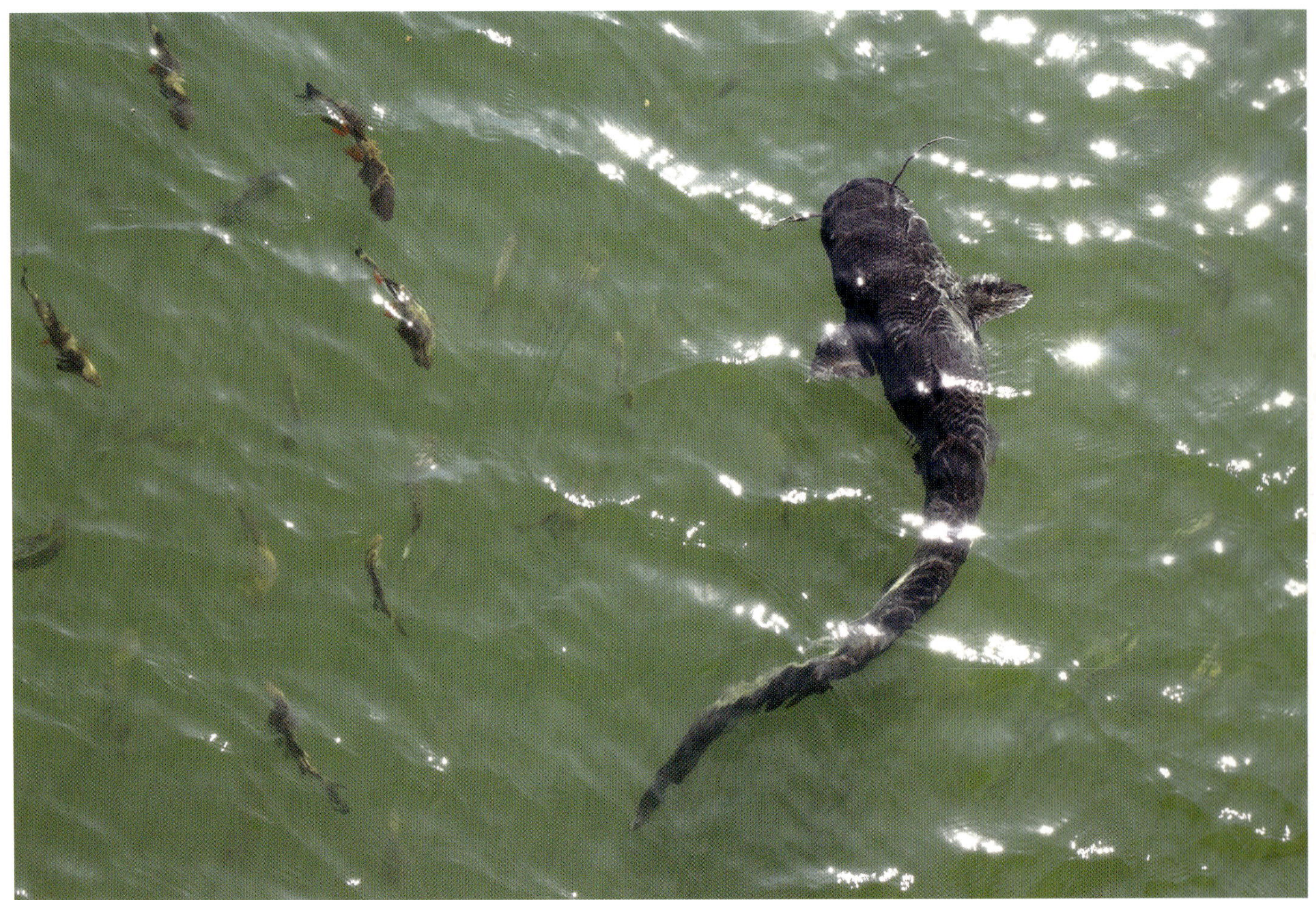

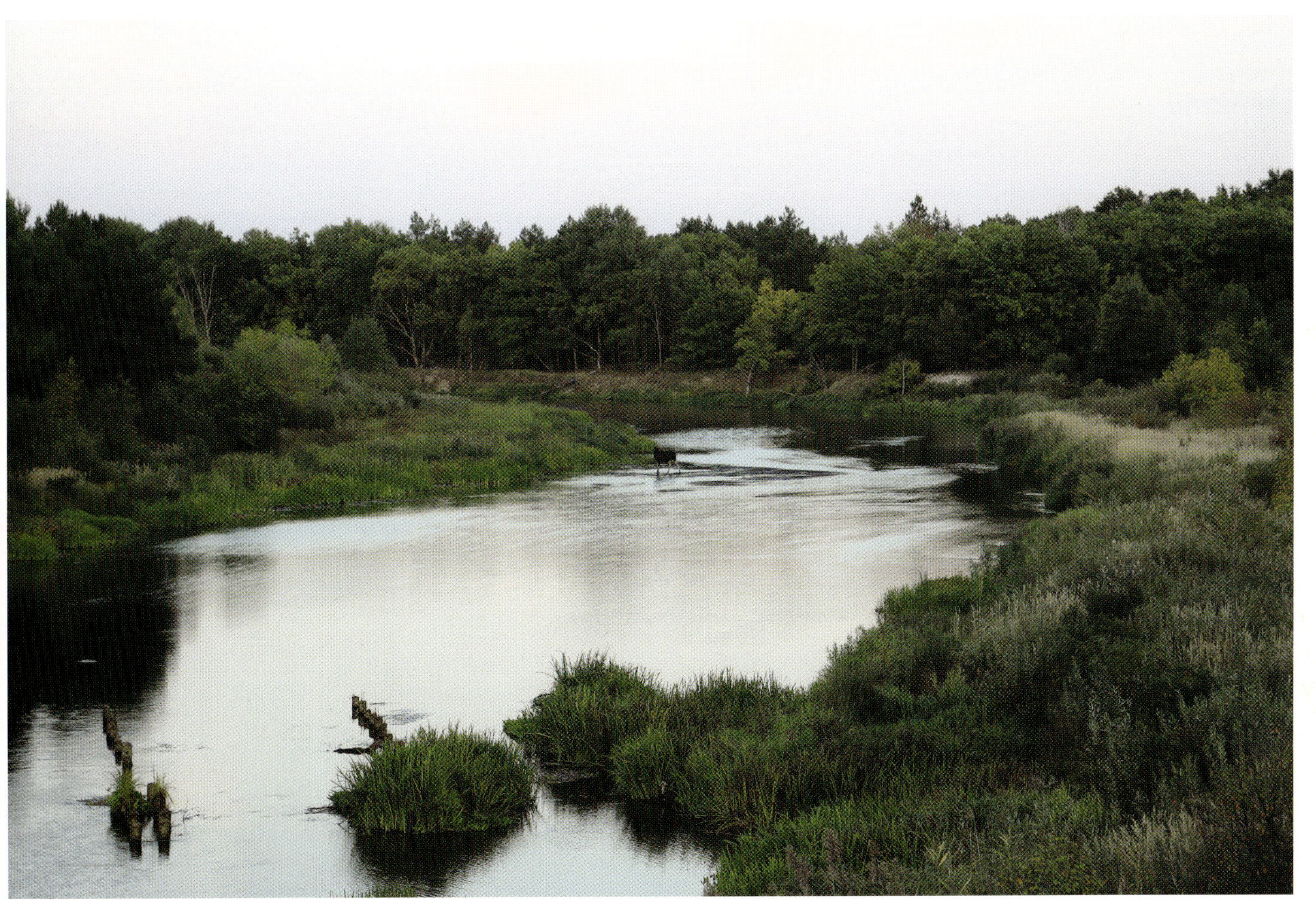

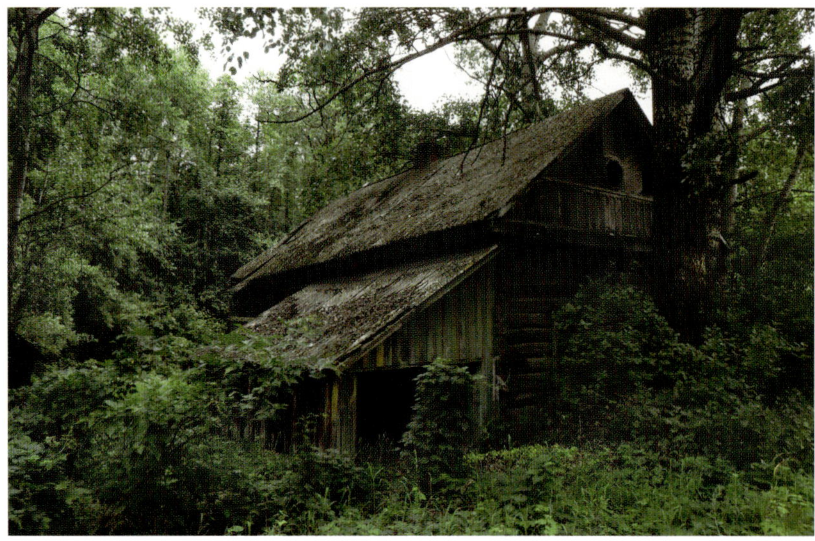

30 km Zone. 'No, we left a while ago,' says Karina, 'but now we need to drive back to the entrance for a radiation check.'

The Belarusian Radio-ecological Reserve's lack of a solid border marks a striking difference from the situation in the Ukrainian Exclusion Zone. It would be easy for anyone to ignore the warning signs and just walk straight in. 'So why don't they?' I ask. Karina explains that the penalties are severe for anyone caught trespassing in the Reserve. However, once a year, on the weekend after Easter, the citizens of Belarus are given free rein to drive their own vehicles into the Reserve and visit their former homes and the graves of loved ones. Children can go too, and while all visitors are expected to carry ID, they are not required to pass through radiation control. 'Ukraine has the same thing,' says Karina. I ask what stops these people from stealing metal, or entering the 10 km Zone – which, even on this occasion, remains strictly off-limits. 'Because they know it's bad to be caught.' Then as if reading my mind, she adds: 'The penalty is even worse for foreigners.'

Looping through the town of Bragin, back towards the entrance to the Reserve, by 4.30pm we're pulling up beside the checkpoint we passed through this morning. Leonid toots his horn and a grey-haired man in camouflage makes his way slowly over from the security hut. He carries a full-size radiation detector, and one by one he waves the wand across our boots. We're all clean and Dmitry, grinning, tells

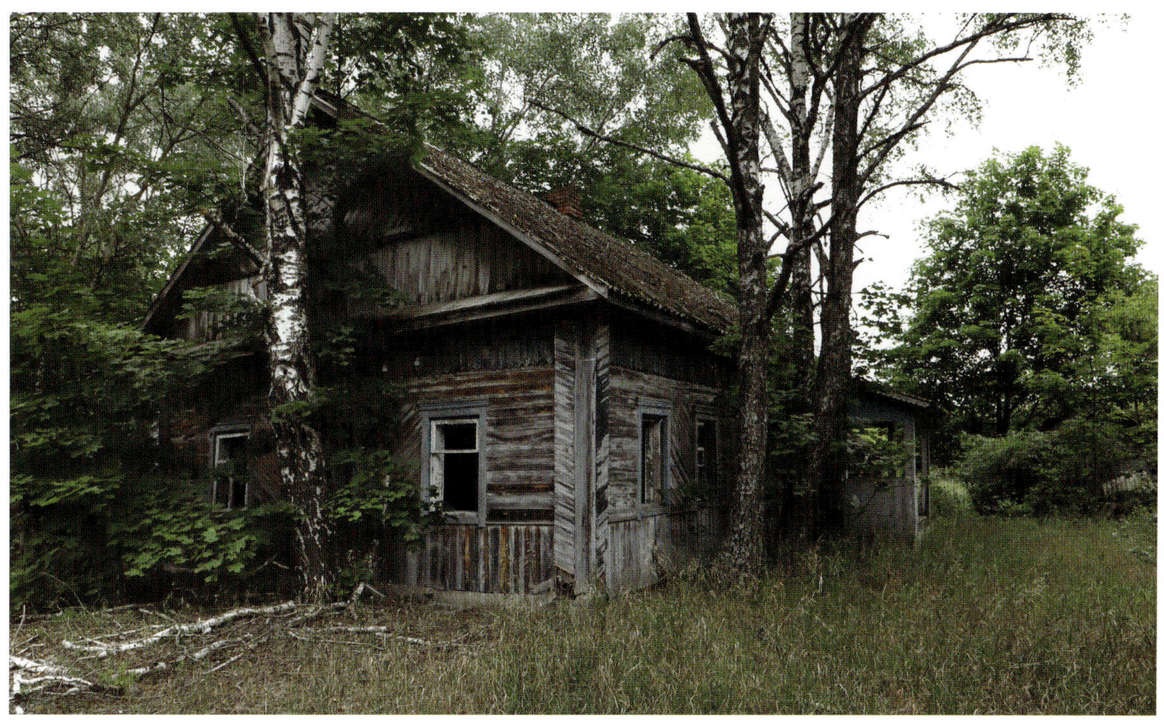

us we've likely received a total dose of around 1.5 μSv. 'One day in the Reserve, the equivalent of half an hour in a plane,' he says.

We spend the night in Khoiniki, one of the closest inhabited cities to the Reserve. Before 1986 it had a population of 17,000, and its own university – but after the disaster and the dissolution of the USSR, many left, including large numbers of young people, and the population of Khoiniki rapidly decreased in size. Karina says, 'This area became very depressed after the disaster. There are some initiatives to turn things around, but these take time and we're not seeing any results yet.' We sleep in simple, comfortable rooms at a former students' dormitory. In the morning, we eat breakfast at a little restaurant in town. The staff have seen our type before: 'Around three tour groups come through here each week,' says the waiter, delivering coffees to our table. 'Mostly foreigners, mainly German.'

Having explored the Bragin region of the Reserve yesterday, today we're in the Khoiniki region, and one of our first stops is at a radiological laboratory in Babchin. This village is best described as the Belarusian version of Chornobyl – a town within the evacuated area, which has now largely been cleaned and repurposed as a base for administrative and scientific work. Beside the war memorial in the main square, the Palace of Culture is abandoned; but across the road, parked outside the lab and the small museum beside it, is a row of up-to-date cars.

Inside the laboratory, the scientists seem genuinely pleased to see us and we're given a tour through the various departments. The place has a lived-in feel, its 1970s-style décor and faded blinds complemented by an incongruous array of shiny new machines. 'People send us samples, and we process them,' says our scientist guide, a balding man in a lab coat and spectacles, who looks very much the part. The laboratory is equipped with technology from around the world – state-of-the-art equipment, he boasts, pointing out his favourite machines: 'This one is Soviet… and this is a new scanner, best in the world, made in Canberra, Australia.'

In one device, a tray of wood chips waits for analysis. We're informed that different levels of radiation are considered acceptable depending on the wood's destination:

the tolerance for wood for burning in stoves, for instance, is much lower than for wood for outdoor furniture. In Belarus, the state harvests the wood, then it's the responsibility of the buyer to have it checked. The scientist explains that most of the samples here come from wood that is due to be sold; but other samples come from trees that were cut down to create firebreaks, and these are tested purely for research purposes. After a forest fire in 2015, the team decided to create a mobile lab, which, once complete, could run these tests on location in the Reserve. I ask if they check the corn too, along with other produce grown in the Zone. 'When the client requests it, yes,' he replies. The wood, the corn, the cattle… while the lab seems thorough in analysing whatever samples are provided, I do wonder about the potential for blind spots in such a system.

The tray of chips in the machine right now shows a reading twenty times higher than would be acceptable for firewood. 'Shall we show them the 200-times sample?' asks one of the other lab researchers.

'Perhaps not,' our guide answers. Before we leave he motions us to a metal storage cylinder and challenges any of us to lift off the lid. One of my friends tries, nearly bursting a blood vessel in the process. 'That's one ton of solid lead,' smirks the scientist, as his colleagues laugh.

Afterwards, we briefly tour the adjacent museum, which features a collection of stuffed animals from around the Reserve in addition to an exhibition of traditional tools and

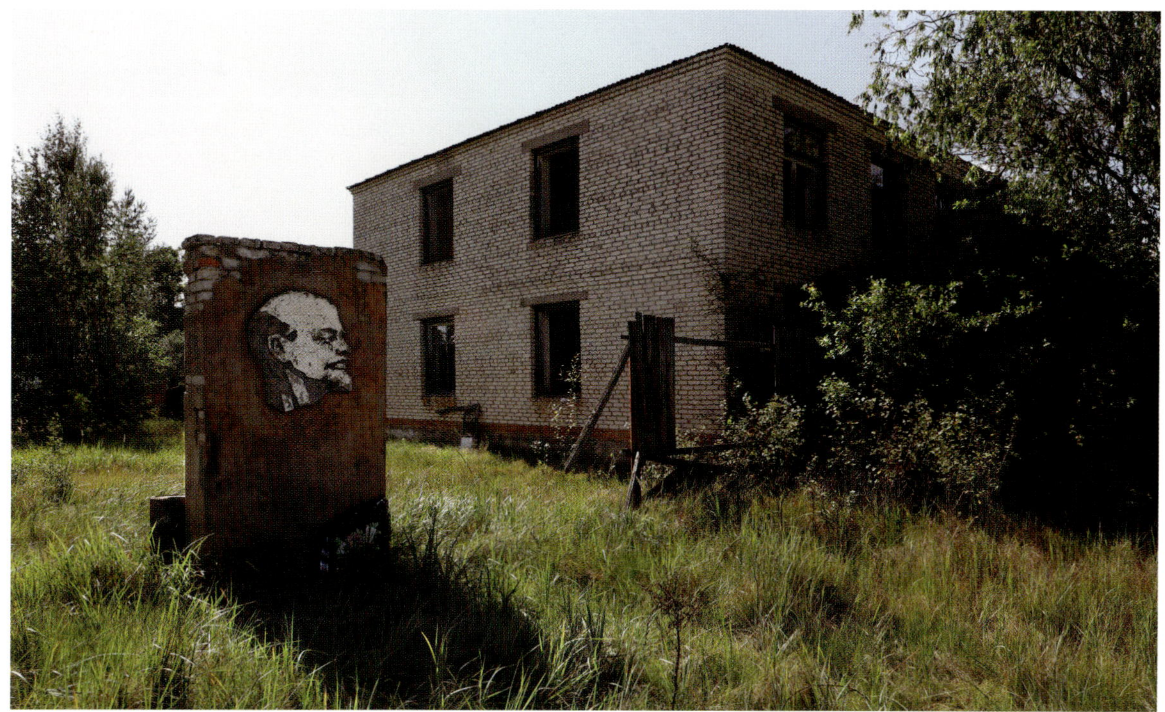

folksy homeware from the region. On the road out of Babchin, we stop to inspect a honey farm where bees swarm around colourful wooden hives. In among them is a pine cabin that serves as a miniature guesthouse. 'Have you ever slept on a bee bed?' Dmitry asks. An artificial hive has been built inside the cabin's wooden bed. 'It vibrates. You can feel them making honey beneath you while you sleep. It's very relaxing.'

He shows me the vent in the outer wall where the bees can fly in and out as they please. The farm has already produced two tons of honey this year. 'It's excellent!' he says, reassuring us that the dirtiest batch measured just 5 per cent above normal radiation levels. The honey is sold locally, but has to be pre-ordered because of its popularity. President Lukashenko, we're told, has sampled it himself.

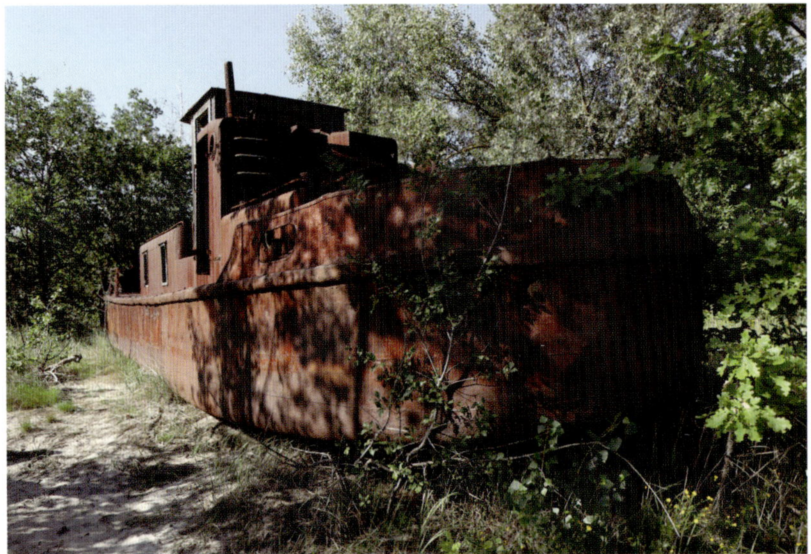

Boat graveyard, River Pripyat. Evacuated villages nearby, such as Krasnoselye and Dovlyady, once fished this river, which flows from Mazyr in Belarus, eventually joining the Dnieper and passing through Kyiv.

We drive through more villages concealed within the lush forest, with only the houses bordering the roadside still visible. Stopping at a former collective farm, all run-down cowsheds and a chemical store that stinks of iodine, I find a mantis in the grass. Dmitry, waving his meter, informs us: 'This place is quite dirty… 0.8 microsieverts per hour.' A small fleet of combine harvesters is scattered haphazardly across an overgrown meadow, rusting slowly into dust. 'They were still new,' he laments, 'only used for one year!'

Along the riverbank near Dovlyady we see abandoned boats sinking into the mud. Nearby in Pogonnoe we visit the Palace of Culture, its walls dense with words scratched into the plaster. 'Greetings to our people – from Vova Chumenok,' reads one from 6 May 2008. I notice the narrow range of dates and realise that for years former residents have been returning to this village in the week after Easter, and leaving messages for each other in this way.

Later that day we pull up by a cluster of abandoned buildings, some of them four storeys high. Dmitry calls this the 'Belarusian Pripyat'. Before the disaster, this residential microdistrict had housed people working at a nearby animal-feed factory; one of the largest in the USSR, it produced pig food for export. Dmitry takes us into the main factory hall. The rusting machinery inside gives few clues as to its

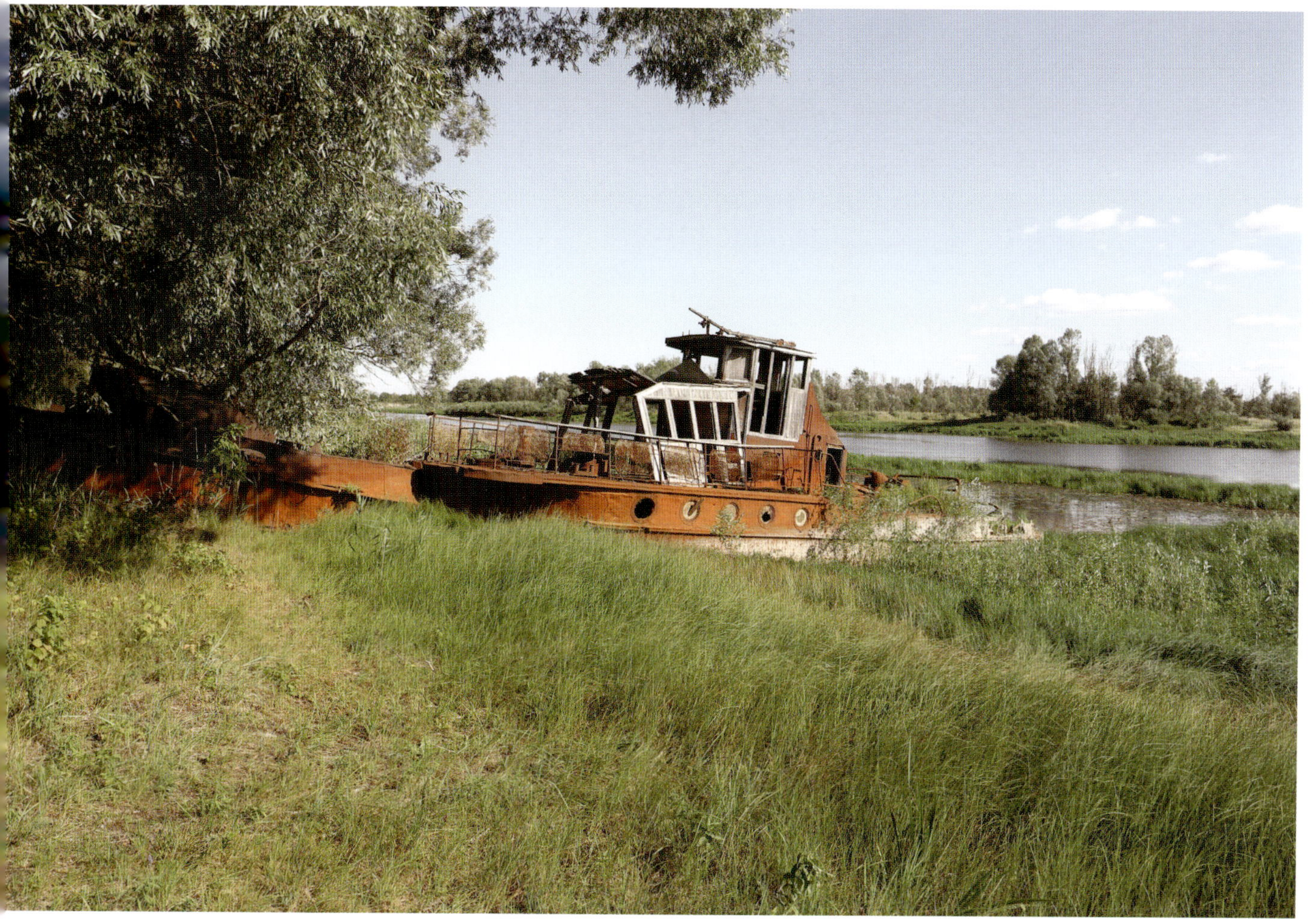

former use, but our guide explains: 'This was a highly advanced process. Workers came by bus from nearby towns, and it created great employment.'

Exploring these devastated factories and humble villages, it occurs to me that for many tourists the Belarusian Reserve might not be very interesting. It feels like one final injustice: Belarus lay directly in the path of the fallout from the Ukrainian nuclear reactor, and received a higher level of contamination as a result. Yet it was Ukraine that collected on all the big-ticket tourist attractions afterwards: the power plant, the cooling tower, the Duga, and Pripyat.

The last thing Dmitry shows us is a fire watchtower near the former village of Krasnoselye. Unlike the Ukrainian guides, who are (officially) far too safety conscious to let tourists climb anything, Dmitry invites us to admire the view from the top. Ladders zigzag, top to toe, up inside the narrow steel trunk of the tower. As I climb, I try to ignore how it sways in the wind, instead looking upwards, until I reach a hatch. Flipping it open, I scramble from the metal frame into a hexagonal wooden booth. The space smells musty: it's mostly empty, with just some cushions, a couple of empty bottles, and a faded magazine. But the view is what we climbed up here for, and the fire watchtower's 360-degree windows open onto a breathtaking sea of green, a wild panorama of largely unspoilt nature. The few villages, with their collapsing red-tile roofs, have been almost swallowed up by the encroaching forest that spreads out in all directions towards the horizon. One object dominates the skyline, a modern structure that rises in sharp contrast to its rural surroundings: the silver arch over the distant Chernobyl Nuclear Power Plant, sparkling in the sunlight, and looking as alien as if it had just landed from space. How sadly ironic, I think to myself, that even on a tour of the Belarusian Reserve, the dramatic final highlight involves looking into the distance at an object situated on the Ukranian side of the border.

'The factories are our monuments,' says Dmitry, as much to himself as to any of us, as we drive back towards the radiation control checkpoint.

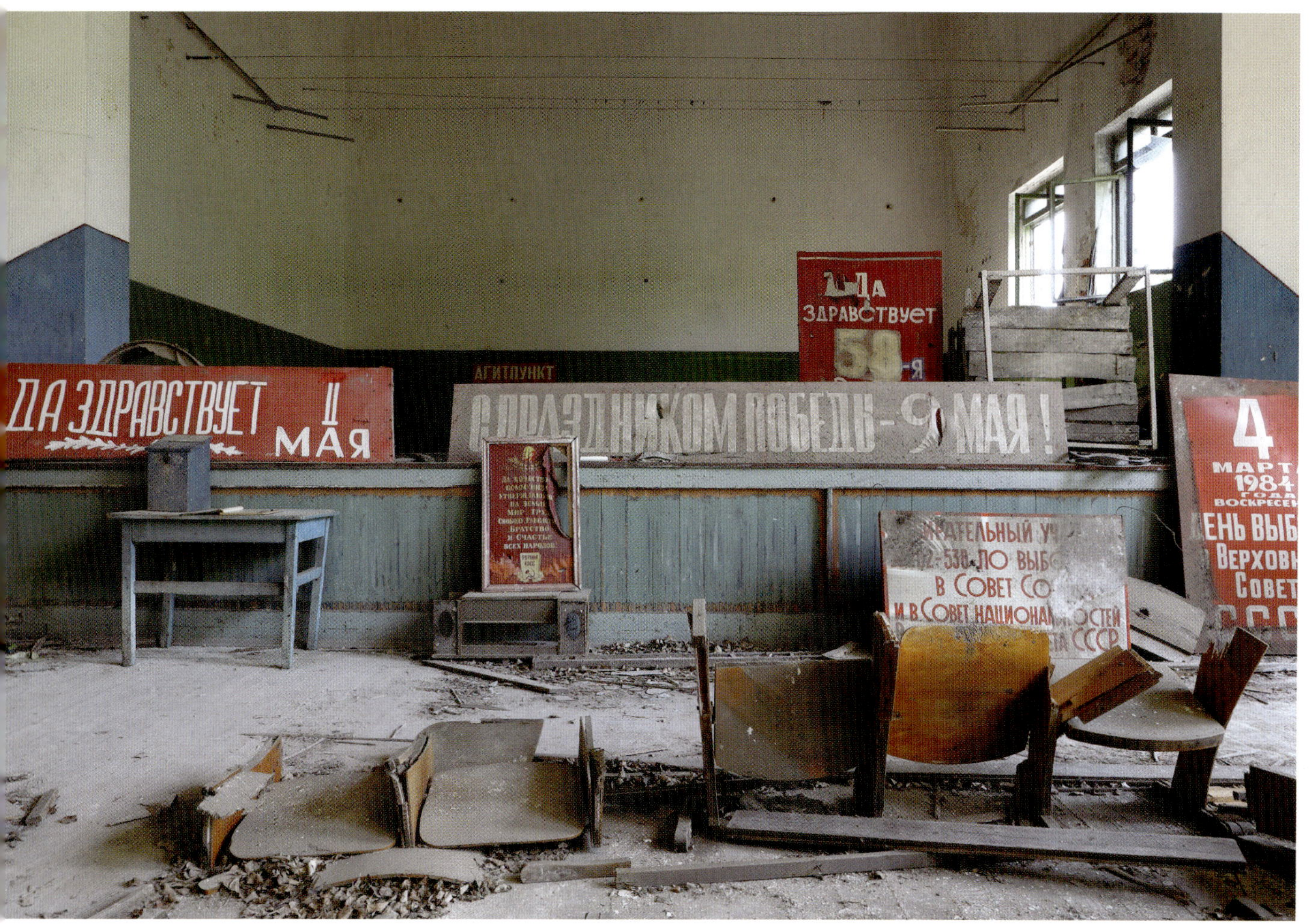
ДА ЗДРАВСТВУЕТ 1 МАЯ
АГИТПУНКТ
С ПРАЗДНИКОМ ПОБЕДЫ - 9 МАЯ !
ДА ЗДРАВСТВУЕТ 58-Я
4 МАРТА 1984 ГОДА ВОСКРЕСЕНЬЕ
ДЕНЬ ВЫБОРОВ В ВЕРХОВНЫЙ СОВЕТ СССР
ИЗБИРАТЕЛЬНЫЙ УЧАСТОК
№ 62-538 ПО ВЫБОРАМ
В СОВЕТ СОЮЗА
И В СОВЕТ НАЦИОНАЛЬНОСТЕЙ
ВЕРХОВНОГО СОВЕТА СССР

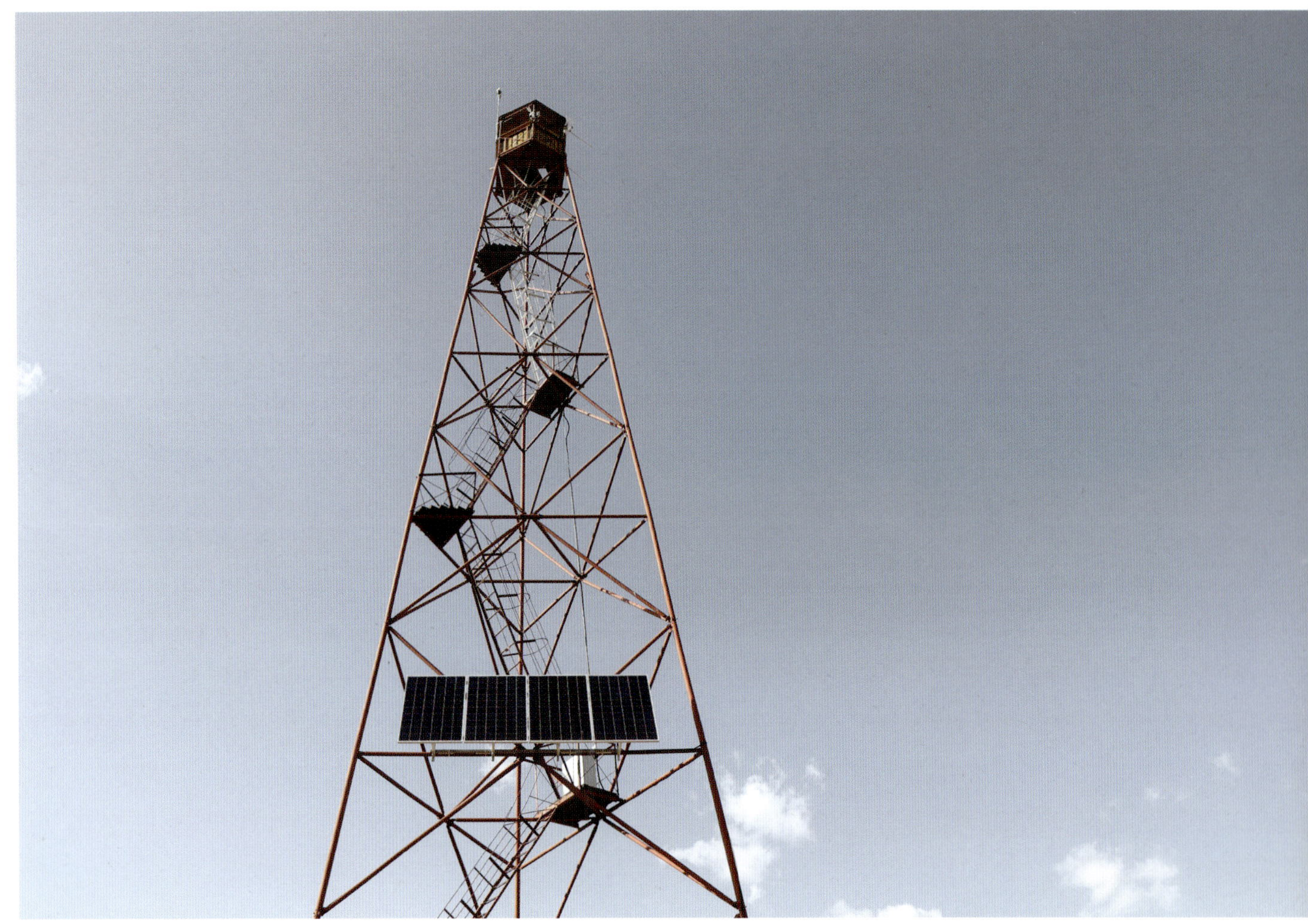

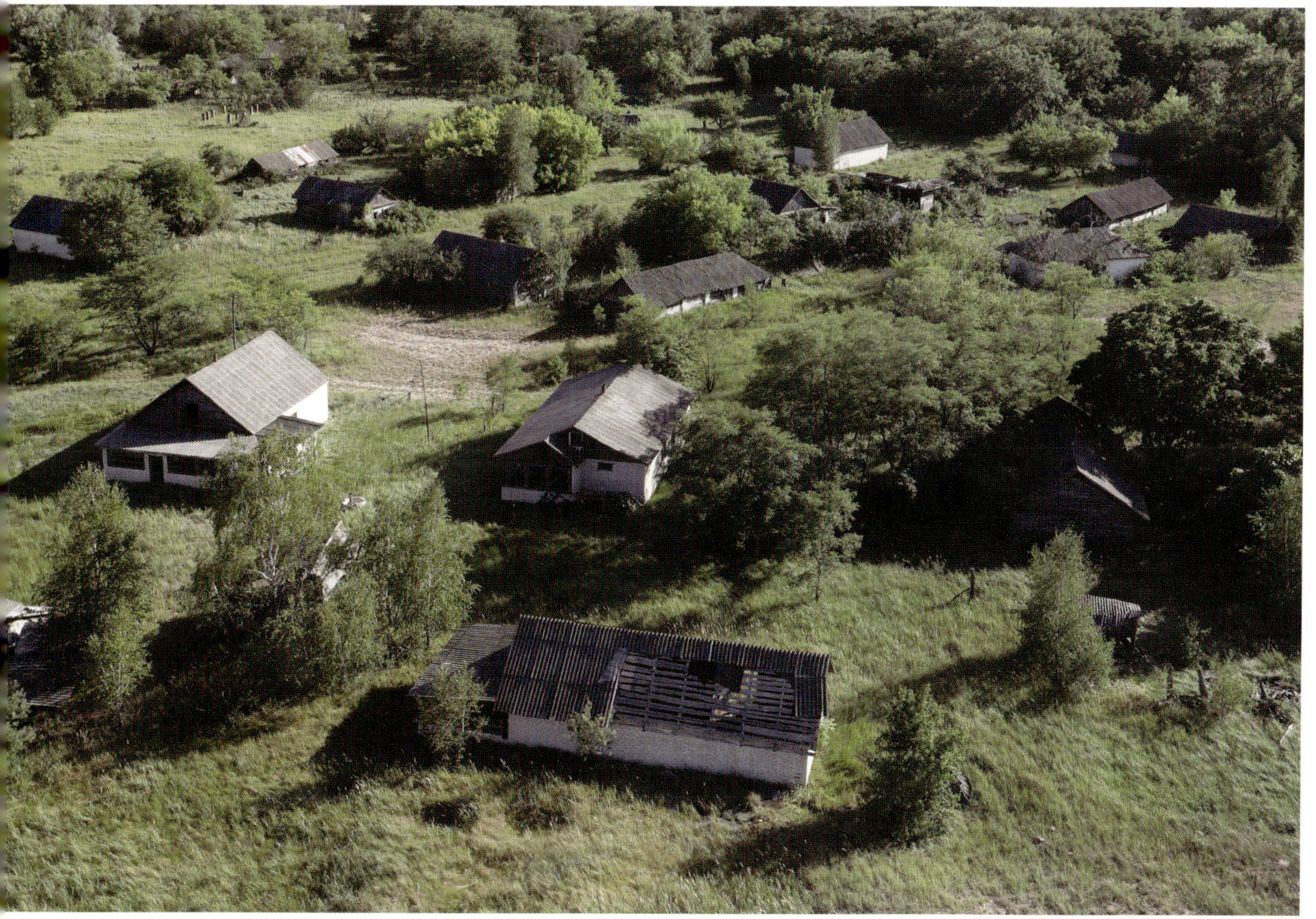

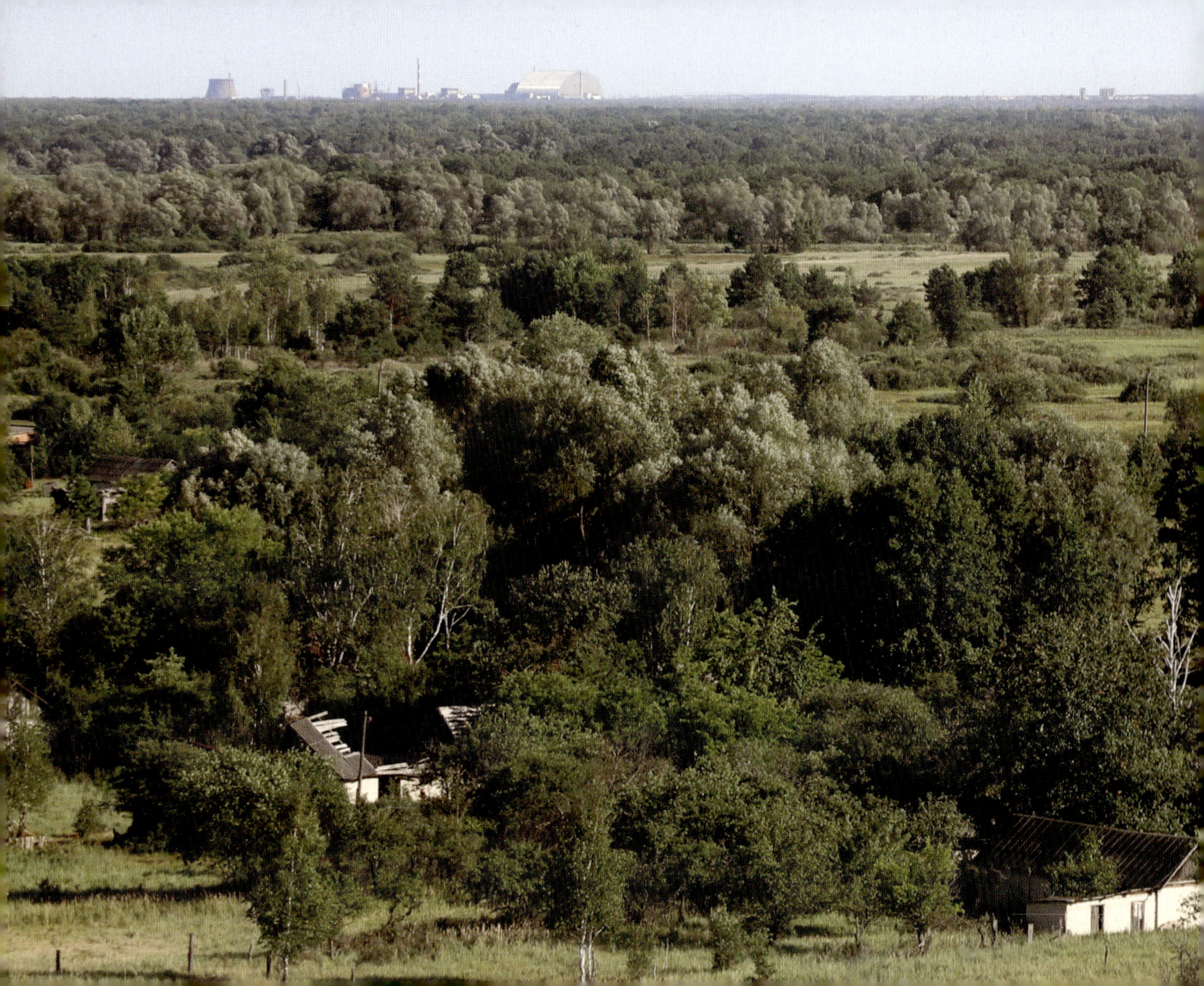

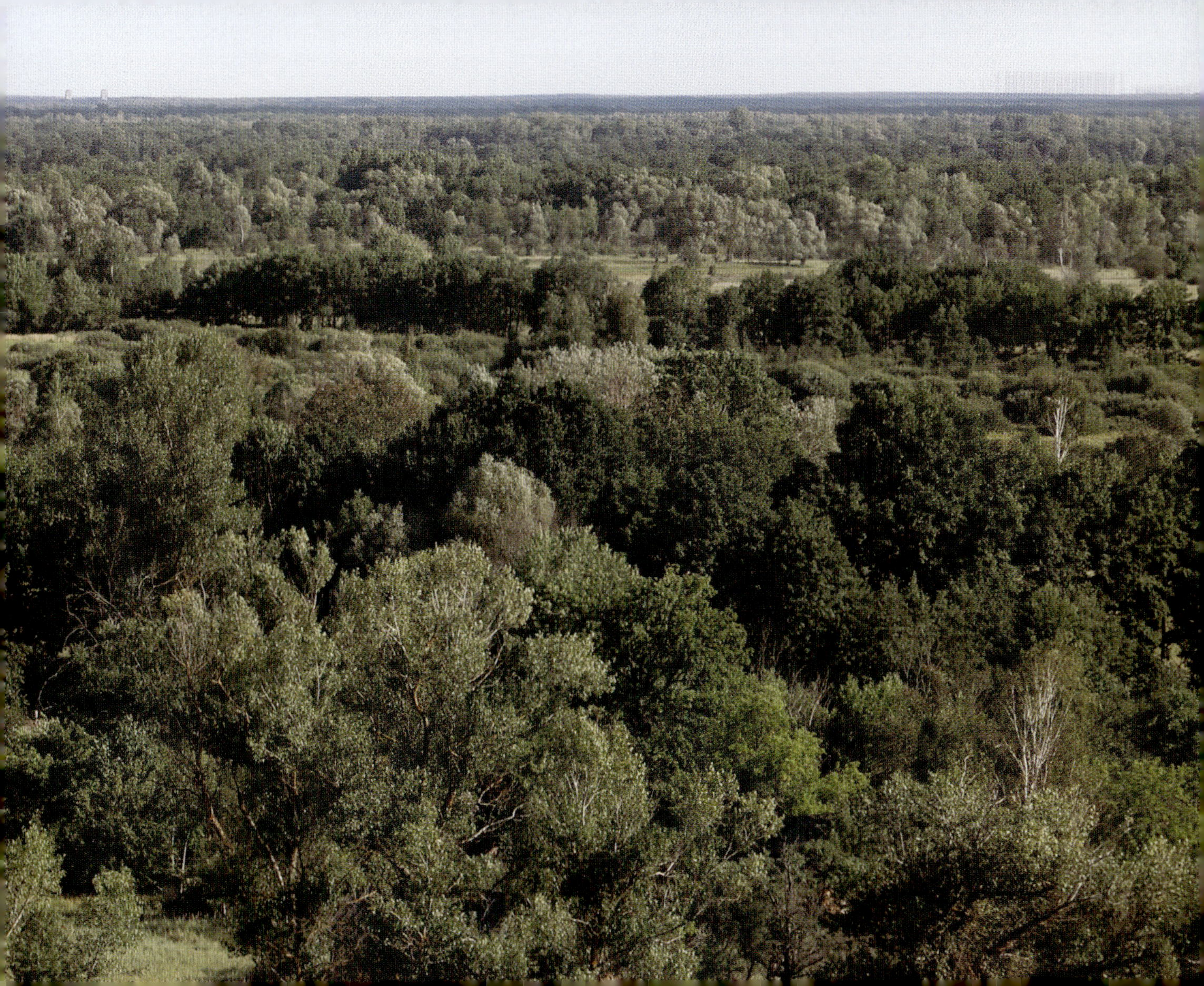

8. THE ROOM

'I am Oz, the Great and Terrible,' spoke the Beast, in a voice that was one great roar.
'Who are you, and why do you seek me?'
L. Frank Baum, *The Wonderful Wizard of Oz*

THE WORKERS' TRAIN

Summer mist lies thick over the station, as passengers shamble up the steps to the platform. Dressed in skirts or shorts, sandals or high-heels, with Gucci handbags or faded T-shirts bearing the names and tour dates of their favourite bands, they stare into their coffees or at their mobile phones. While it may look like any regular commuter station, these nuclear engineers and plant workers are about to travel to one of the most contaminated places on earth.

The workers' trains depart from Slavutych at 6.30am, 7.20am and 7.40am. There's a late train too at 10am – the 'drunk train' – for anyone who missed the first three. We board the 7.20am train. The regular passengers have already marked their territory with jackets, lighters, and cigarette packets, and I have to walk through several carriages before finding a vacant seat. With a hiss, the old Soviet engine pulls out of Slavutych to begin the forty-minute journey to Chernobyl.

We enter the Exclusion Zone with a roar: ten minutes out of Slavutych the route cuts through the corner of Belarus, crossing a steel bridge over the Dnieper River before bursting into the abandoned lands beyond. Light strobes between the bridge supports as the train rattles and shakes across, and then we're inside. The next half hour is like a wetland safari seen through dirty glass stencilled with *Ne Prytulyatysya* ('No Leaning') signs. We pass forests, lakes, and wild meadows. Deer watch from the waterside, while hawks circle above, but the commuters seem to barely register this scenery –

many will have made this trip a thousand times already.

Semikhody Station sits adjacent to the power-plant complex, its building sealed against the Exclusion Zone around it. The platform is an island of normality: workers disembark dressed in civilian clothes, and I follow the current of commuters through dimly lit corridors past locker rooms, showers, and walk-through radiation scanners. Street clothes are replaced with branded plant overalls, and then from out of this warren of pipes, steam, and flickering neon lights, an army of uniformed workers emerges blinking into the sunlight. Buses wait outside to transfer the arrivals to their workplaces, while just beyond the station looms a colossal silver arch that dwarfs every other building in the complex.

ChNPP

Even after the 1986 meltdown in Reactor 4, the plant continued producing electricity for another fourteen years: safety standards were improved, and more than ever the USSR needed a return on its investment in the plant, to help fund the clean-up project. (My friend Demchenko, though, figures it must be safer to let the fuel rods in Reactors 1-3 burn out, rather than forcibly removing them. 'Say you leave your cigarettes in your back pocket, and sit on them,' he says by way of analogy, 'then try yanking them out when they might be bent and broken, you'll end up getting loose

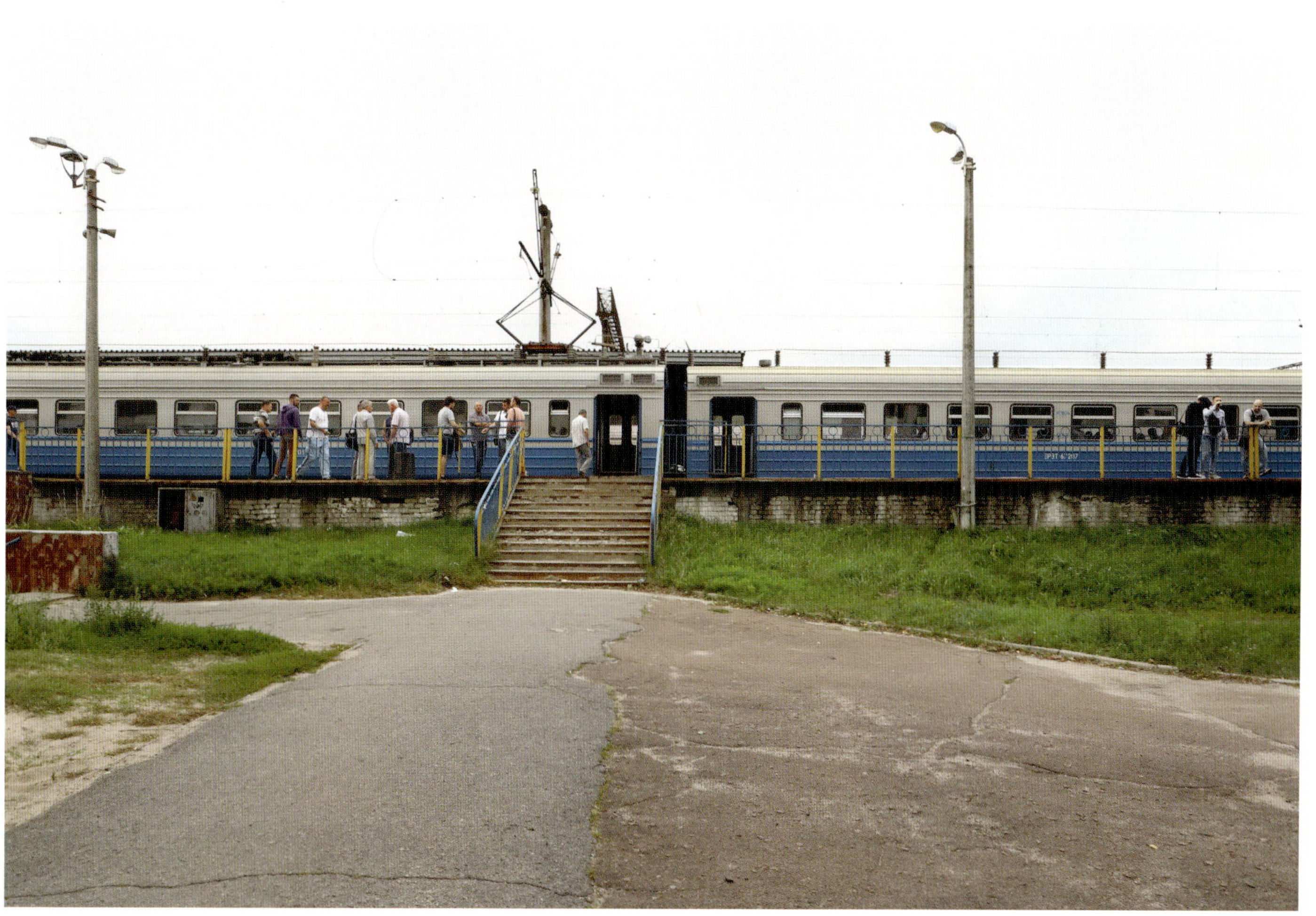

tobacco everywhere.') Reactor 2 was closed after a fire in 1991. Reactor 1 stopped in 1996, and Reactor 3 followed in 2000.[1] Now all three face a lengthy – though fairly typical – decommissioning process. This is happening in tandem with the extraordinary clean-up operation at Reactor 4. Back in 1986, the devastated Block 4 was encased in a simple sarcophagus, officially called the 'Shelter Object'. Then in 2016, the Shelter Object itself was entombed within the New Safe Confinement, or 'New Arch'.

Reactors 1, 2, 3 and 4 are all reached through the same building network, and its administrative core is where most plant employees work today. The power-plant complex also includes a number of other key locations. Alongside the main building, the distribution substation and switchyard appears as a forest of pylons peeking over a security fence. The original Interim Storage Facility for spent nuclear fuel – ISF-1 – was built alongside Block 4 and currently contains the used (though potentially recyclable) fuel from Reactors 1, 2 and 3; but in 2001 construction began on a replacement facility nearby. ISF-2 was designed to store 21,900 used fuel assemblies from Chernobyl, more than 90 per cent of which contains radioactive materials such as partially burned plutonium and uranium.[2] (The Russian name for these facilities gives the acronym 'ХОЯТ', which my tour guide friend Orest would jokingly pronounce as 'Hyatt', like the hotel chain.) Across the cooling canal, meanwhile, on an industrial island, stand the unfinished Blocks 5 and 6, along with their

incomplete cooling towers; and the nearby canteen is now used by both plant workers (who eat lunch from 12-1pm) and tourists (from 1-2pm).

Today, the Chernobyl Nuclear Power Plant employs roughly 2,500 people (though it used to have twice that number when the plant was generating power). Time spent on site is strictly regulated by dosimetric control – workers are permitted to receive up to 20 mSv (20,000 µSv) on average per year, for any five-year period, or an absolute maximum of 50 mSv in a single year, a typical maximum for radiological workers anywhere in the world. (By comparison, the National Commission for Radiation Safety of the Ministry of Health of the USSR had set the acceptable limit for liquidators working in the Zone immediately post-disaster at 250 mSv per year – a figure that was still often exceeded.)[3]

The plant's Block 4 is an international celebrity, and the project to dismantle it has attracted substantial investments from overseas; but by contrast, Ukraine is largely alone in its project to decommission Blocks 1, 2 and 3. In recent years, ChNPP has begun embracing tourism as a potential new stream of funding.

Through ChNPP's official website, it costs $100 to add a tour of the plant to a pre-booked tour of the Chernobyl Zone. We took our groups inside on a number of occasions. The bus parks near the Prometheus monument, and a guide from the plant leads visitors through full-body metal detectors into the administrative building. In a changing room upstairs,

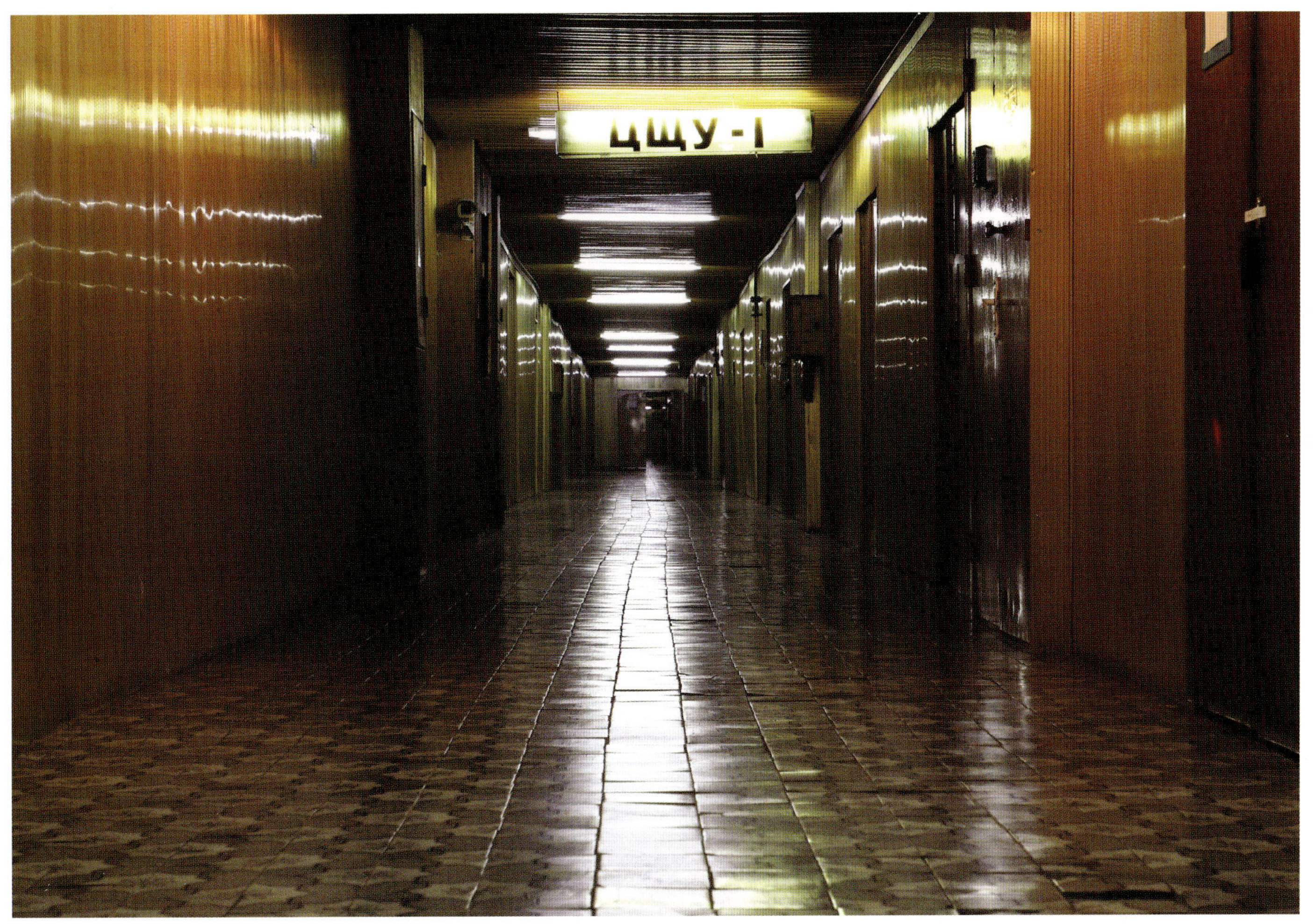
ЦЩУ-1

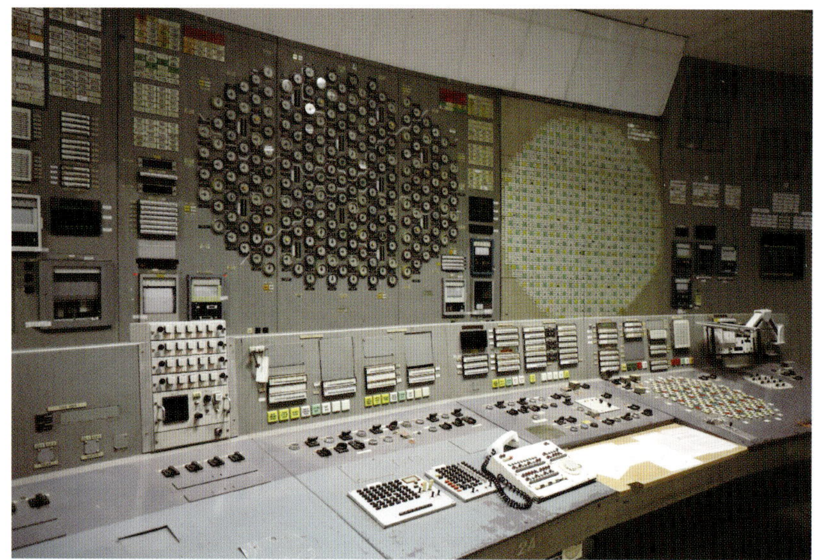

left: Control Room 3, ChNPP. This room and the associated Reactor 3 were put out of service following an agreement with the EU in 1995. Now, along with Reactors 1 and 2, it is undergoing a decommissioning process.

right: Switchyard Control Room, ChNPP. The site's electrical substations survived the disaster largely intact. Today the switchyard is used to direct power into, no longer out of, the plant, partly to ensure the safe cooling of spent fuel assemblies in storage.

overleaf: Reactor Hall 3, ChNPP. Visitors walk across the top of the fuel-channel caps, which form a layer called 'Scheme G' positioned above the cover plate of the reactor.

regular clothes are replaced with starchy, white cotton pyjamas, a protective hat, a facemask, slippers, and gloves. Visitors are taken down the so-called 'Golden Corridor', its 1970s industrial décor (black and white floor tiles, walls of dusty-yellow corrugated metal) like a set from a Kubrick film. This passageway connects the administrative block to the two pairs of similarly designed reactor units: first Blocks 1 and 2, with their identical control rooms and reactor halls, then the control room in Block 3, a twin of the room where the disaster happened. Deep inside these corridors of the plant, visitors are also shown the monument to Valery Khodemchuk, a night-shift pump operator who was trapped in the collapsing structure, becoming the first victim of Chernobyl. Beyond that, at the far end of the Golden Corridor, the highly contaminated Block 4 is subject to a much tighter security regime.

On one January tour of the plant the temperature was -12°C outside, and snow lay thick over the pipes, cranes, and switchyards. Even inside, it was close to freezing, and our group shivered as we stripped in the changing room, donning thin cotton suits that exacerbated the problem. 'It's too cold in here,' complained our plant guide, Anton Povar, as he led us down the Golden Corridor. 'We don't have enough radiators. We don't even have enough winter coats

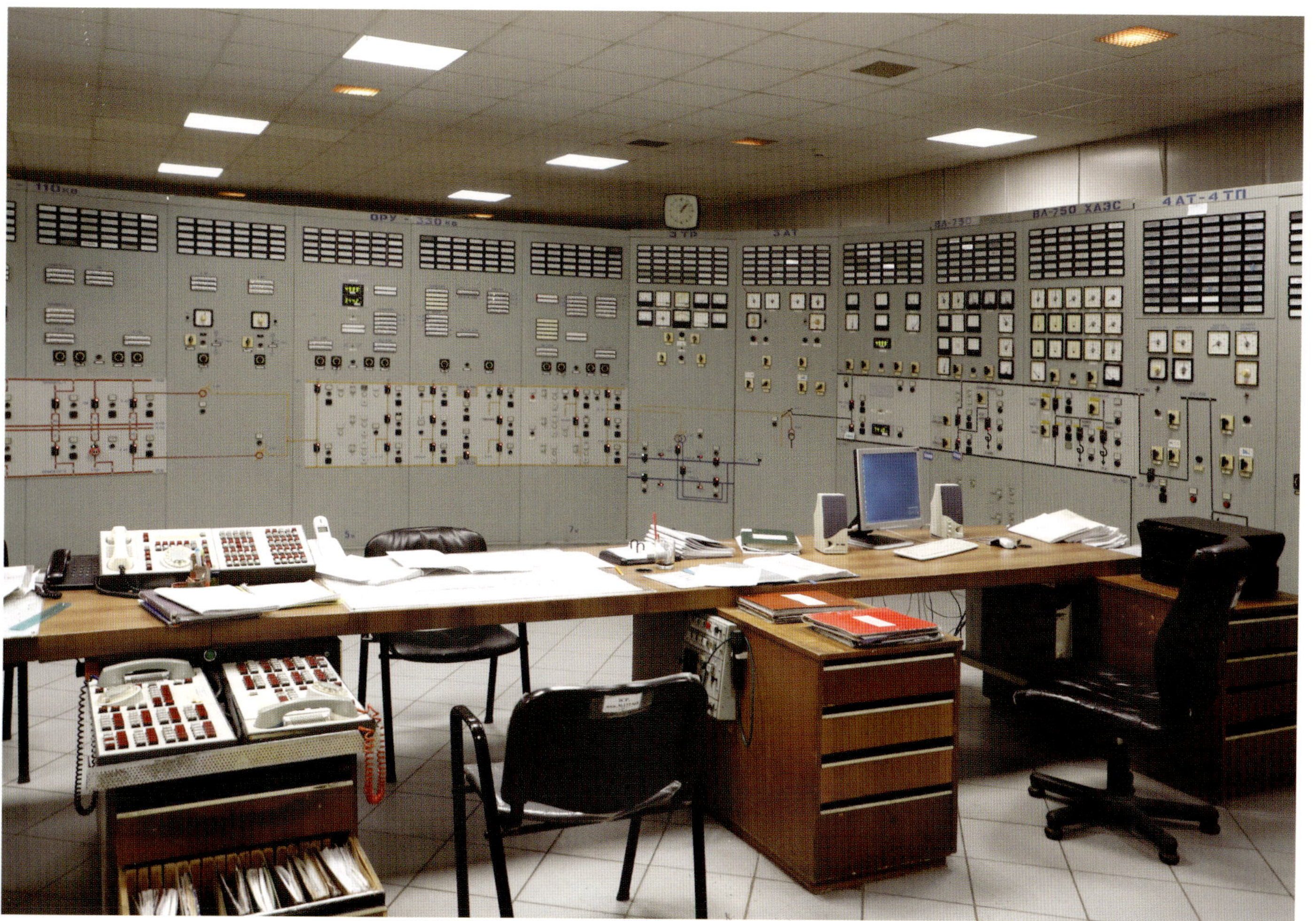

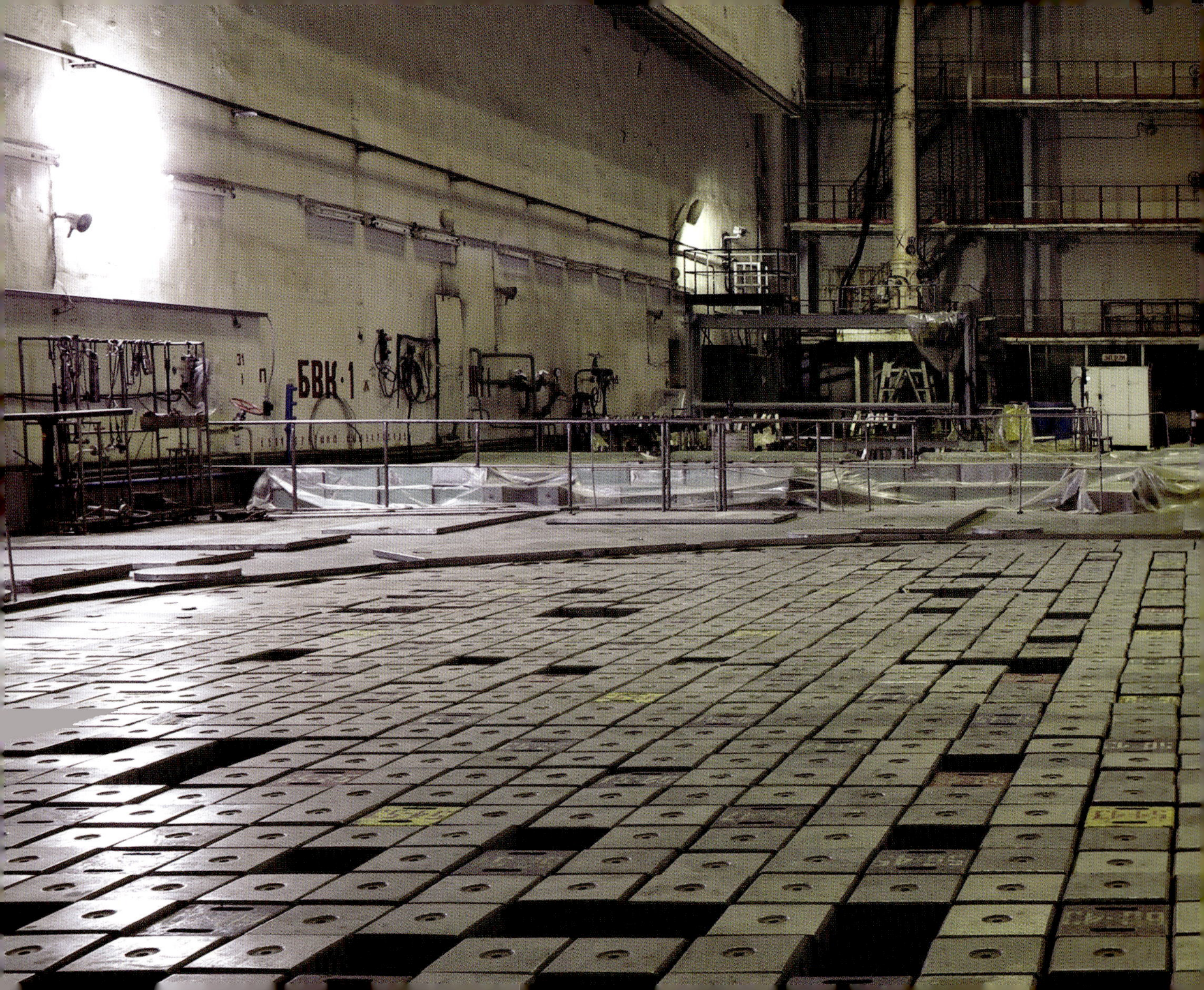
БВК-1

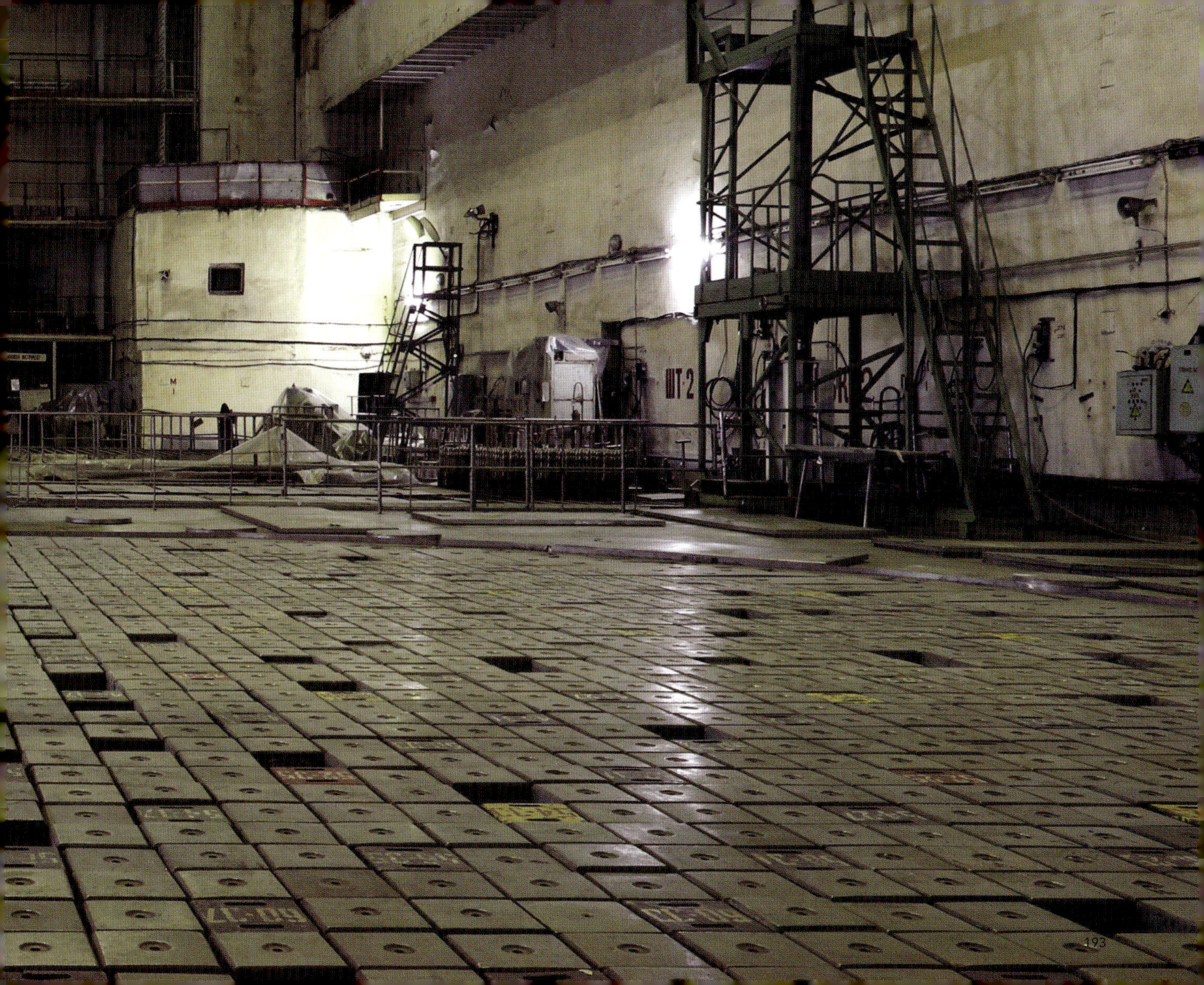
ШТ 2

for everyone.' A few of the workers we passed on the corridor wore thick blue jackets stencilled with the plant's initials: ЧАЕС. Others, like us, were shivering in pyjamas. Povar leads regular tours around the plant for foreign tourists and journalists. 'In 2016 the power plant had 6,000 visitors,' he told us. By 2017 that number had decreased to 4,500, and while foreign money continued to be pumped into the high-profile international project at Reactor 4 next door, the Ukrainian-led decommissioning process at Reactors 1-3 felt vastly underfunded.

After showing us Control Room 3, Povar led us up an unlit stairwell, its steps covered in protective plastic, to the enormous hangar-like reactor hall itself. Located in the centre of the floor, the circular reactor cover measures 15 metres in diameter, and consists of approximately 2,000 individual cubes marking the position of each of the fuel channels. To one side rises the crane arm that was used to lift and insert fuel rods into the reactor. I stood on top of the hefty cover plate and tried to imagine the force it would take to blast this 1,000-ton object into the air, as had happened in the identical reactor hall next door. We didn't linger there for long, but it was the freezing cold, rather than any particular fear of radiation, that made us feel most uncomfortable.

Aside from tourism, ChNPP found another source of revenue by leasing land at the plant to other companies. One such company is the Ukrainian-German project Solar Chernobyl, which established a 1-megawatt solar farm alongside the old reactors in 2018. It was the fourth solar farm in Ukraine (the country lost its largest two in 2014, following Russia's annexation of Crimea). Because of the laws that prohibit digging inside the Zone, the whole installation was constructed on top of a concrete platform. The designers took advantage of the fact that Chernobyl's electrical transformer substations were still largely intact, and connected to the national grid. Consisting of 3,800 photovoltaic panels, the project generates enough power for up to 2,000 homes, and has the capacity to add a further 99 megawatts. Nevertheless, a single 100-megawatt solar farm can hardly fill the gap left by four nuclear reactors producing 1,000 megawatts each.

right: Reactor Hall 3, ChNPP. In recent years, the plant employees have begun leading small groups on officially sanctioned educational tours of the complex.

page 196: Control Room 2, ChNPP. The operators' map of the fuel channels in Reactor 2, similar to those of Reactor 3 shown on pages 192-195.

page 197: Control Room 2, ChNPP. A tourist studies the consoles, decommissioned after a fire in 1991. The controls are no longer operational and occasionally plant employees will allow visitors to push buttons and switches.

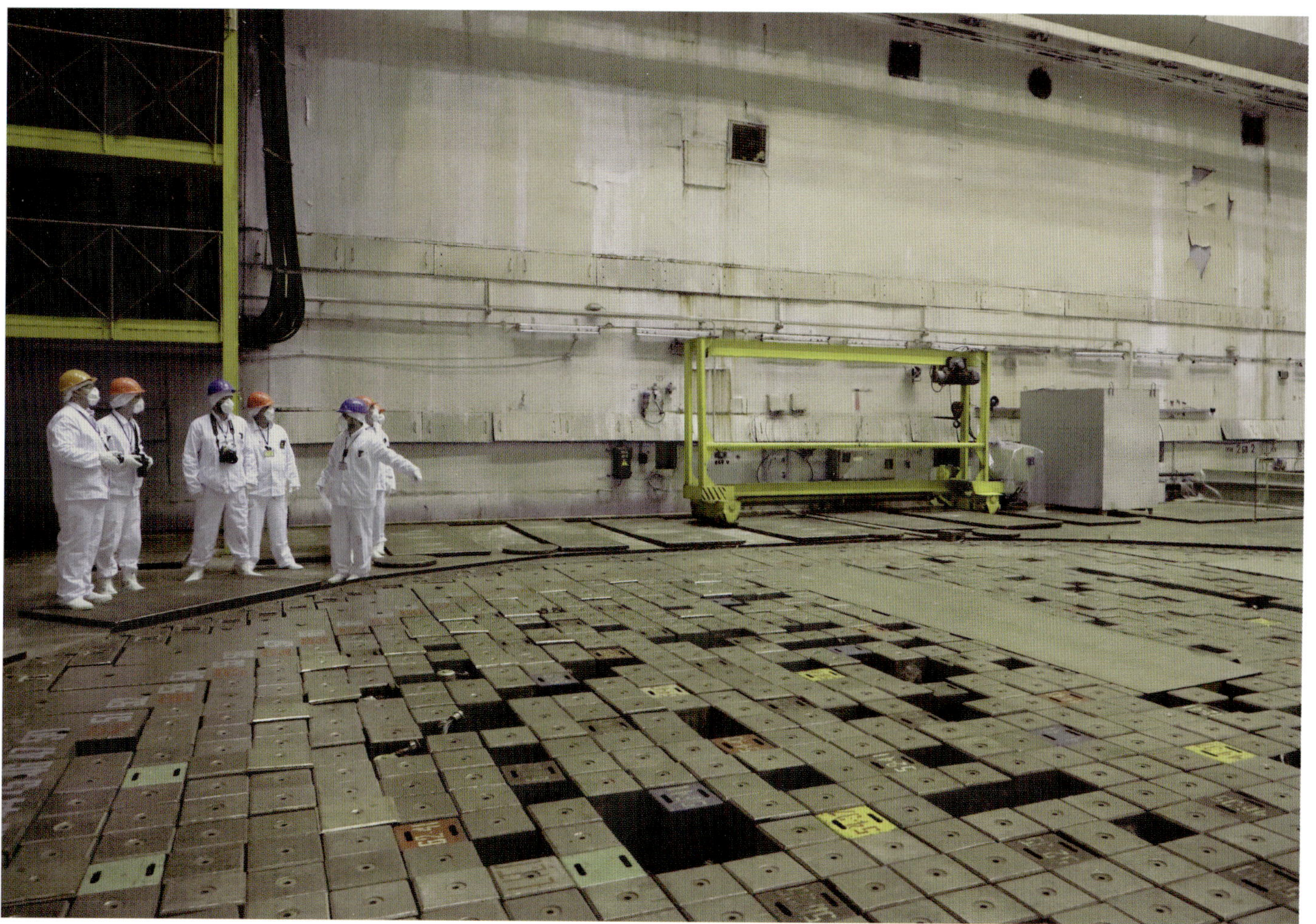

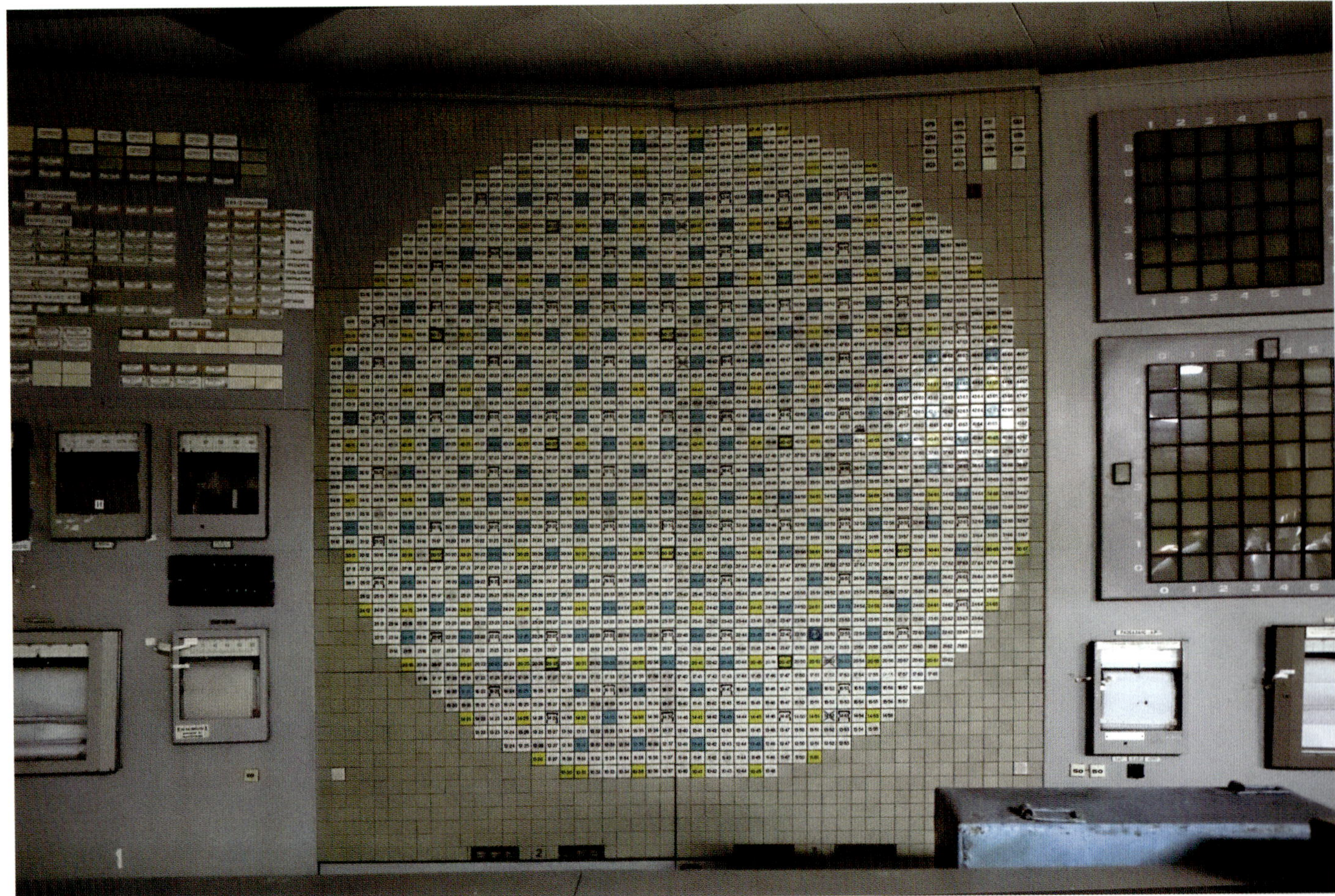

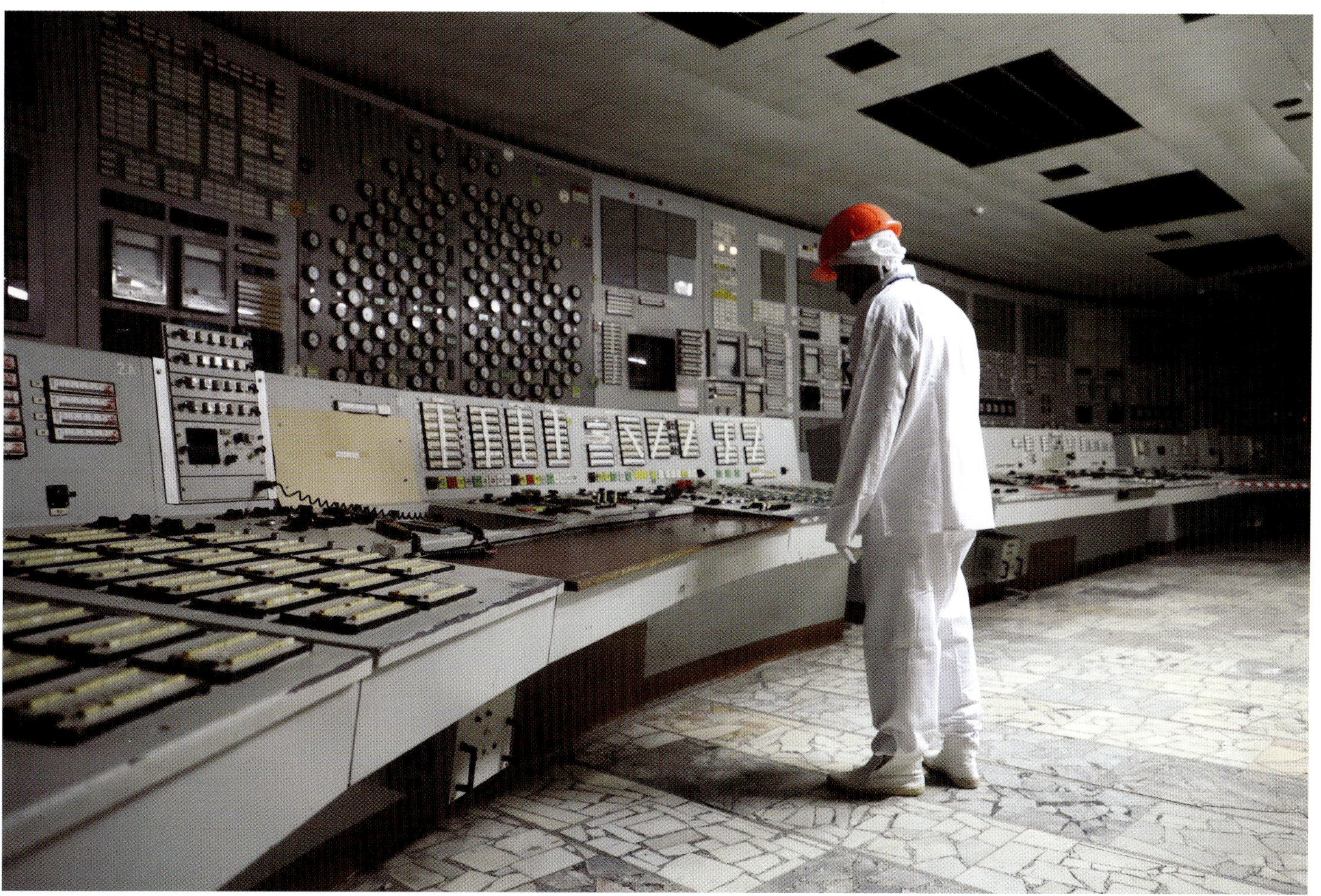

CONTROL ROOM 4

On a clear spring morning in 2018, I am back in the Ukrainian Zone with Demchenko, photographing the unfinished Block 5 building. From the outer villages, to this broken concrete colossus that remains officially off-limits to tourists, I am beginning to feel that I've seen most of what the Zone has to offer me – but there is still one notable omission on my map. For all the time I've spent exploring the regions affected, I am yet to see the place where the disaster actually happened: inside Reactor Block 4 of the Chernobyl Nuclear Power Plant, the heart of the Zone. Entry is not impossible – a handful of international journalists have already been permitted inside (it won't be until autumn 2019 that ChNPP begins to offer public tours of Control Room 4) – though my own chances don't strike me as particularly good. I am surprised, therefore, when Demchenko says, 'Why not? I think it's possible.' He says he has a contact – the friend of a cousin of a colleague, or some such – who holds a powerful position in the Zone administration. 'I can make some calls, but this won't be cheap.'

Demchenko calls a week later to tell me that for $1,000, I can have complete, unlimited access to the ChNPP complex: 'All doors will be open to you.' This will be a one-time cash deal, with payment made after the tour. I will not be told the name of the fixer; I am simply to present myself to security staff, who will receive me as an important visiting scientist and escort me around the plant. It seems like a lot of money, but Demchenko explains how the people we're dealing with already earn premium salaries. 'These guys won't get out of bed for less than $1,000. We have to make it worth their time.'

I had been told that in 1986 a huge Lenin head was built for display in Pripyat but was never put in place. After the disaster it ended up buried deep in a warehouse somewhere inside the plant. 'Can I see the Lenin?' I ask.

'All doors,' he repeats.

'Under the New Arch too?'

'Everywhere,' he insists, and that settles it for me. Because once the Shelter Object is penetrated, and robotic crane arms begin to gather spilt uranium fuel out of the ruins, no visitor will set foot beneath the New Arch again, at least not in my lifetime. It's now or never. I agree to the terms, and a date is set.

The arrangements are handled swiftly and soon I am back in Demchenko's car, parked outside the entrance to the ISF-2 facility. Behind the chainlink fence, men in overalls and hardhats are busy at work; but we're watching the road, waiting for a car from the main plant complex. This designated meeting place feels deeply suspect, like a venue for a drug deal – and I'm nervous. Demchenko looks nervous too. The wild Zone is his home, but here making cash deals in carparks with top security officials, he seems decidedly uncomfortable. 'You know they used convicts to work on the reactor?' he says, breaking the silence. 'They had to

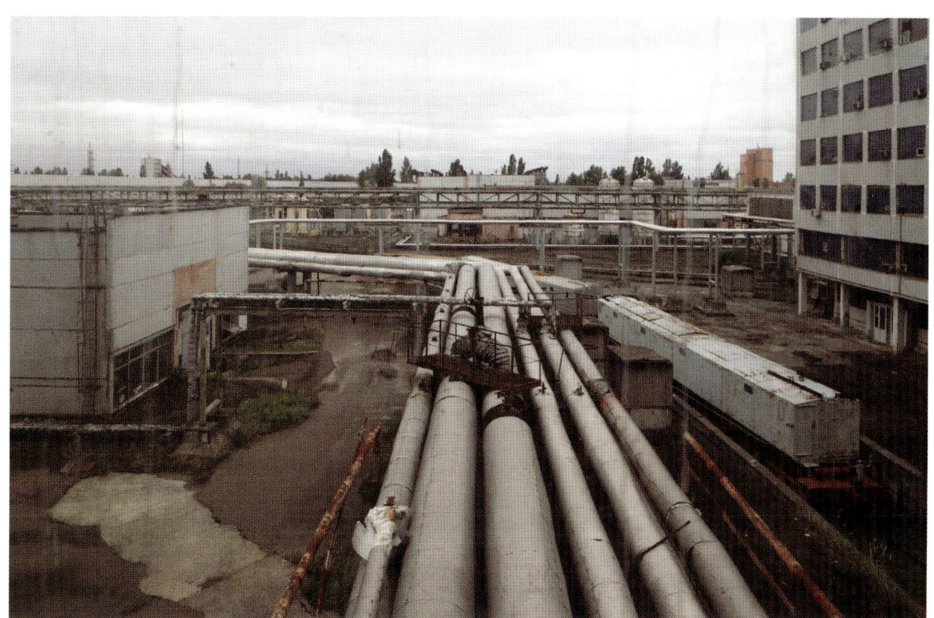

cut the old ventilation pipes so the New Arch would fit. It was dirty, dangerous work, so they gave it to prisoners on life sentences.'

Eventually a car pulls in alongside ours. I get out to meet a short, stocky man wearing the navy-blue ChNPP uniform. He squeezes my hand and introduces himself: 'Anatoly.' I wave goodbye to Demchenko as we turn around and head towards the plant.

Anatoly came to Chernobyl in 1987, but he wasn't assigned to the clean-up – he worked on the reactors that were still producing power. He met his wife soon afterwards, a woman from Pripyat who had stood on the so-called 'Bridge of Death' to watch the ionising light-show above the plant on the night of the disaster. The friends who were with her that night died not long afterwards, but she survived. When cancer took her in 2014, it was impossible to determine if Chernobyl had been the cause. Anatoly had steadily advanced through the ranks of the ChNPP to become a senior security officer. For all his privileges though, and despite the cloak-and-dagger nature of our meeting, the tour he gives me is thoroughly pedestrian.

'This is exclusive,' Anatoly insists. 'Visitors never see this stuff,' he adds as he walks me down the Golden Corridor, stopping at the same rooms I'd seen on the $100 tour. When I ask about Control Room 4, he says it's impossible: 'Far too dangerous… nobody goes in there.' As for the New Arch, Anatoly tells me the deconstruction work began a week ago. I ask about the Lenin head. 'Gone,' he says, 'moved to Slavutych. It's not here anymore.'

Putting my disappointment aside, I quiz Anatoly about the New Arch project. 'There is roughly 200 tons of melted uranium fuel somewhere inside there,' he says, gesturing in the vague direction of Reactor 4. 'And we don't even know what state it's all in – solid, molten, or mixed up with lead and sand. Our job is to safely dismantle that mess and replace it with a pretty, green lawn.' There's a satirical tone to his voice, as if he is acknowledging that no one alive today will be around to see the project completed. 'All this too,' he says, slapping the metal wall of the Golden Corridor. 'This whole thing is contaminated now. We'll have to bury it all some day.' I ask how long that will take, and he shakes his head. 'There's no precedent for something like this. We already have young people coming here and beginning to take over the deconstruction work. After them, *their* children will come, and so on.'

As we walk, the HBO *Chernobyl* series comes up in our conversation. 'At first they wanted to film it here inside the plant. Can you believe that?' When it was decided that filming on site would be too dangerous, the crew moved production to a twin plant in Lithuania instead. I ask what the plant workers thought of the series, and Anatoly replies: 'It's fine, in theory. Respectful and… *mostly* accurate. They even hired some of our people as consultants.'

The tour finishes and Anatoly walks me back out through security, to the carpark and the Prometheus monument. I nod towards the Titan and ask why they moved it here from Pripyat. 'It's a symbol of life,' he says. 'Wouldn't have been right to leave it in a dead city.'

Demchenko is waiting in his car outside. 'How was it?' he asks, and I tell him I saw nothing I hadn't already seen for a tenth of the price. He sighs, swears, then says, 'Okay… Let me fix this.' He makes a call, says a lot of things in angry, loud Russian, then abruptly hangs up. 'We come back tomorrow,' he announces.

The next day we meet at the main entrance. This time, Demchenko will join me inside to make certain I get what has been promised. Anatoly greets us with artificial warmth; we are here to do things that yesterday he declared were impossible. I assume his words had more to do with convenience than truth, but neither of us comments on my return as we head back to the changing room, suit up, then make our way straight for the control room of Reactor 4.

At the end of the Golden Corridor, Anatoly stops at an office window to file paperwork for our visit. 'Wait here,' he says, 'or take photos if you want. You remember the way to the Khodemchuk memorial, right?' I don't exactly, but I nod anyway then wander off with Demchenko down a corridor into the bowels of the power plant. We don't find the monument but end up instead in a large chamber full of water tanks, where giant pipes form an industrial obstacle course. The extraordinary realisation hits me that we are exploring the halls of Chernobyl Nuclear Power Plant, completely unsupervised, and I guess the same thought occurs to Anatoly too – because a minute later I hear him anxiously calling us back to the Golden Corridor.

Another guide is waiting for us. Gleb is a senior technician and he will accompany us inside Control Room 4. He instructs us to follow closely, warning that while most of the dangerous dust has been long since blasted away, some parts of this block, particularly around the graphite and fuel assemblies, still emit up to 3 Sv/h. That's roughly 10 million times the background level in London, and the same dose that Police Chief Inspector Moskalenko received from his front-row view of the disaster. Gleb leads us through a series of doors that look more like airlocks, then through a floor-to-ceiling turnstile whose dozens of rotating bars can only be unlocked using security cards and codes. We enter a small antechamber where flickering strip lights are reflected in wet floors, and old industrial debris lies piled against bare concrete walls. The only point of colour in this monochrome scene is a bright red fire extinguisher stencilled with instructions in bold Cyrillic. Gleb's industrial-size dosimeter starts beeping

a warning – thankfully, just 40 µSv/h (which means an hour spent here gives the same dose as one whole week in London; unusual, but not scary). Then, finally, we enter the Room itself.

In *Stalker*, Tarkovsky never allows us inside the Room (or 'Bunker 4', as Professor calls it). After the long, mystical journey that his protagonists undergo to reach the heart of this sentient landscape, it is hard to picture any tangible physical space that wouldn't be an anti-climax; instead, we are left to imagine it. Stepping across the threshold into the control room of Chernobyl's Reactor 4, I feel closer to Dr. David Bowman in Kubrick's *2001: A Space Odyssey* – reaching the end of a vortex of colour and light to find myself not in a temple, a palace, or any other place of suitably alien grandeur, but rather in a surprisingly mundane non-place, where there are no cosmic answers, only an uncanny reflection of the world I left outside.

The Room is small, grey, and dimly lit. Its surfaces are dulled by decades of corrosion. The control panels are arranged as a semi-circle of metal desks that look smaller and flimsier than I had imagined. Half of the buttons are missing now: some were stripped because of contamination, and Gleb says others were taken as souvenirs by the liquidators. I get the impression I'm standing in a low-budget film set – a shoddy, three-quarter scale imitation of the control room featured in the HBO miniseries. The Room doesn't even feel much like a room. A new wall was installed

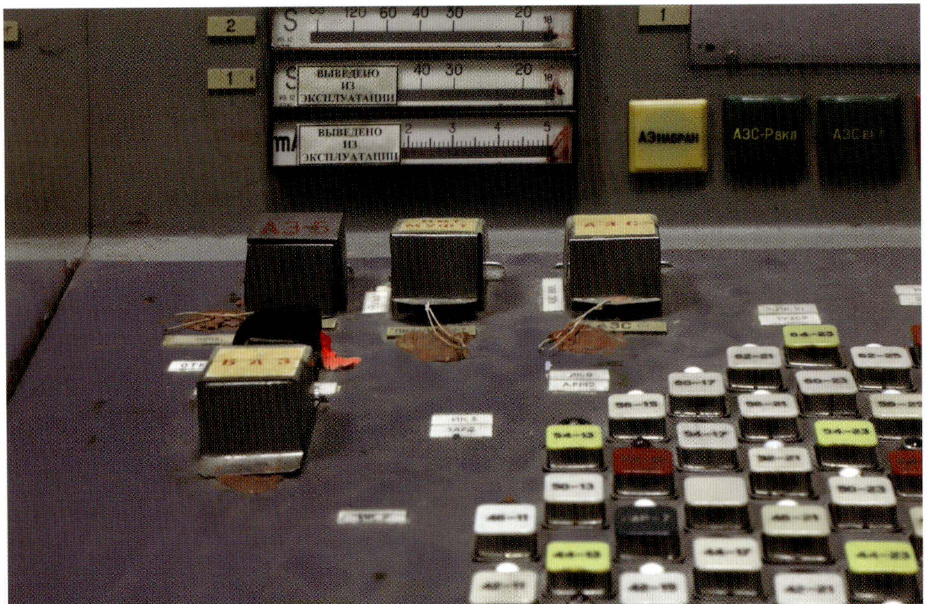

during the clean-up operation, cutting the consoles off from the open floor space behind the operators, where the supervisor's desk had been. Now, the semi-circle is pinched at either end to form unnatural corners against the partition, giving an appearance not of design, but rather of accidental space, like the leftover gaps between two misaligned buildings. The control room feels unwelcoming, but this isn't a hostile sentience so much as bad Feng shui.

There seems to be a palpable heaviness in the air, coupled with a dead silence that feels ominously deceptive – like standing in the eye of a storm. When Anatoly says, 'just five minutes more,' he's almost drowned out by the hush. I try to picture this place in operation: technicians sitting at every desk and wall displays illuminated. I run my gloved fingers along a bank of buttons and think how a particular sequence of actions, initiated with these very controls, had been responsible for thousands of deaths. Hard to imagine that this crusty, tin-can room with its junkyard consoles had been the drafting table for humankind's greatest nuclear catastrophe.

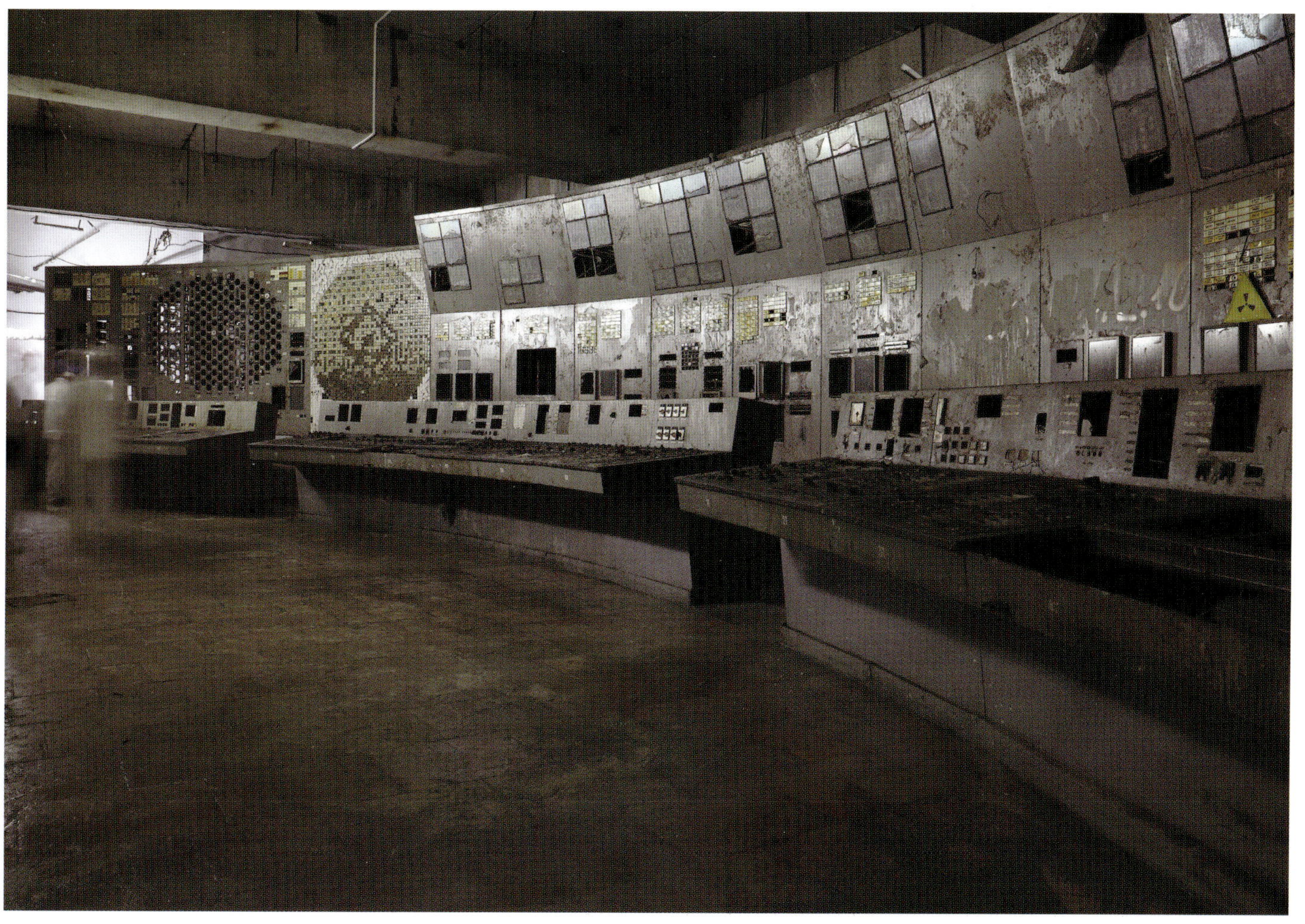

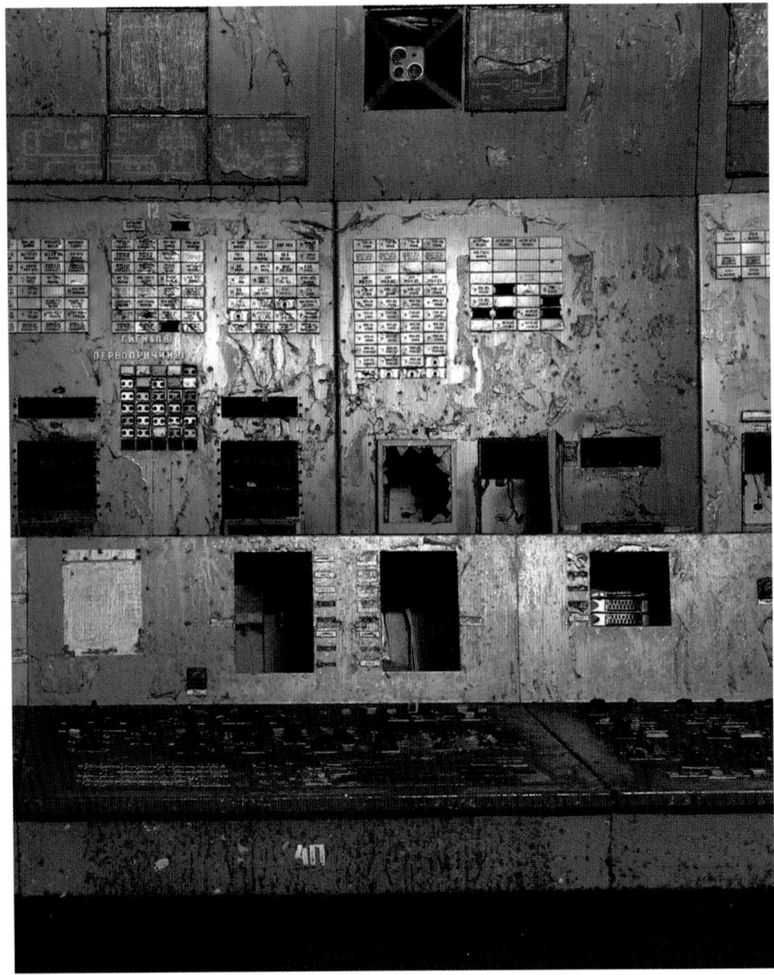

page 202: Control Room 3. The top left of these cube-shaped shielded buttons marked *A3-5* – or 'AZ-5' – was the 'scram' kill switch. This manually operated control would immediately terminate the fission reaction by inserting all the control rods at once. In neighbouring Control Room 4, on 26 April 1986 at 1.23.40am, this switch was flicked and a malfunction occurred, causing the meltdown.

page 203 and left: Control Room 4, the room where the 1986 disaster originated. Now stripped of many of its fittings and cleaned of dust, it has been declared safe for visitors. Since autumn 2019, the power plant authorities have included it on official tours.

right: Operator panels in the Control Room of Chernobyl Reactor Block 3. This room was a twin of Control Room 4, where the accident occurred.

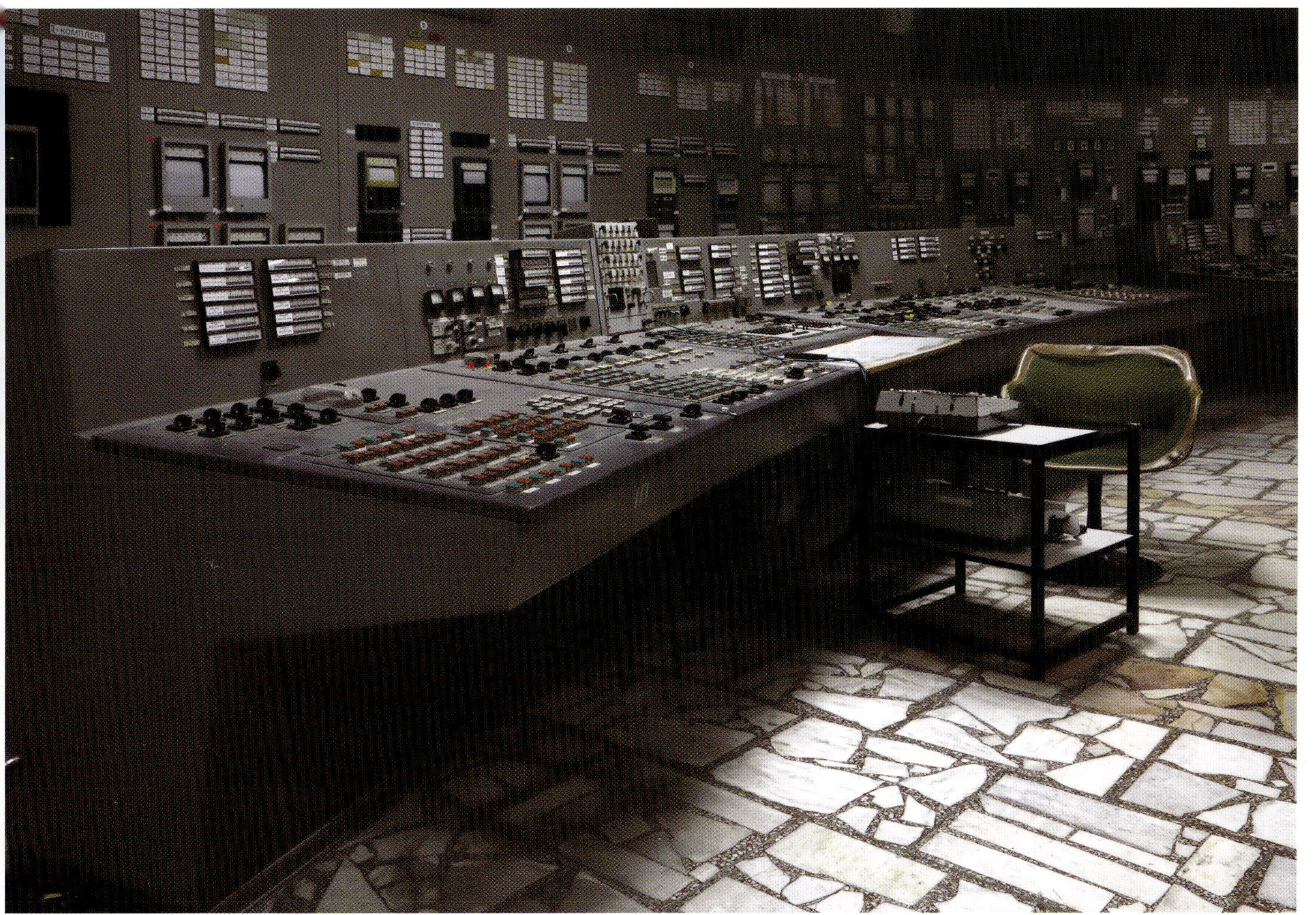

Anatoly takes a control room selfie before we leave – it's his first time too – then back in the changing room, he tells us to wash our hands using only cold water. He explains that hot water opens the pores, which could make it easier for radioactive particles to get in. 'You feel tired? Jet-lagged?' Anatoly says it's radiation that causes jet-lag after being in a plane, and we've just had the equivalent of a seven-hour flight in fifteen minutes. 'Drink some red wine tonight,' he adds. 'It helps. Now, are you ready to see inside the arch?'

THE NEW ARCH

After the disaster, Chernobyl's Reactor 4 was encased in a concrete sarcophagus known as the 'Shelter Object'. However, that protective seal only offered a short-term solution, so in November 2016 – after twenty years of planning and seven years of construction – the New Safe Confinement, or 'New Arch', was installed over the Shelter Object. The New Arch is essentially a colossal bread bin, consisting of an inner and outer casing that trap a cushion of air between them, the total shell measuring 10 metres in thickness. The installation cost a total of €2.15 billion (€1.5 billion of which was spent on the arch itself), and was overseen by the French consortium Novarka, whose name is derived from the Ukranian for 'New Arch'. At 108 metres high, the Statue of Liberty could fit inside. The structure was assembled on tracks 180 metres away from the reactor, in order to minimise radiation risk for the construction crews (according to Demchenko, convicts were made to complete the dirtier close-up work). The first time I visited Chernobyl, in 2013, the structure was still being built and the crusty grey-blue concrete box of the older sarcophagus remained on full display, exposed to the elements. In 2016, the New Arch – the largest ever man-made moveable object – was slowly inched along its tracks and into place over Reactor Block 4. Once it was in position, the 150-centimetre gaps between it and the buildings within (both ChNPP's Main Building and the NSC's new Technological Building) were hermetically sealed. Inside, plasma cutters, diamond saws, and remotely operated bridge cranes will be used to dismantle the old structure, before the pieces are decontaminated using processes of vacuuming, grit-blasting, and hydro-demolition. The waste will be securely sealed in long-term storage containers. The New Arch project is nothing short of a technological marvel.

We drive from ChNPP administration around the silver arch to the rear of the complex, where a tour group is busy taking photographs in front of the memorial to the liquidators. A few of them watch as I pass by with my escort alongside the barbed-wire fence and through the security checkpoint. Despite being located at either end of the same building complex, ChNPP and Novarka feel like very different organisations. ChNPP is staffed by what seems like a close-knit clique of long-term veterans, behind a front line of new

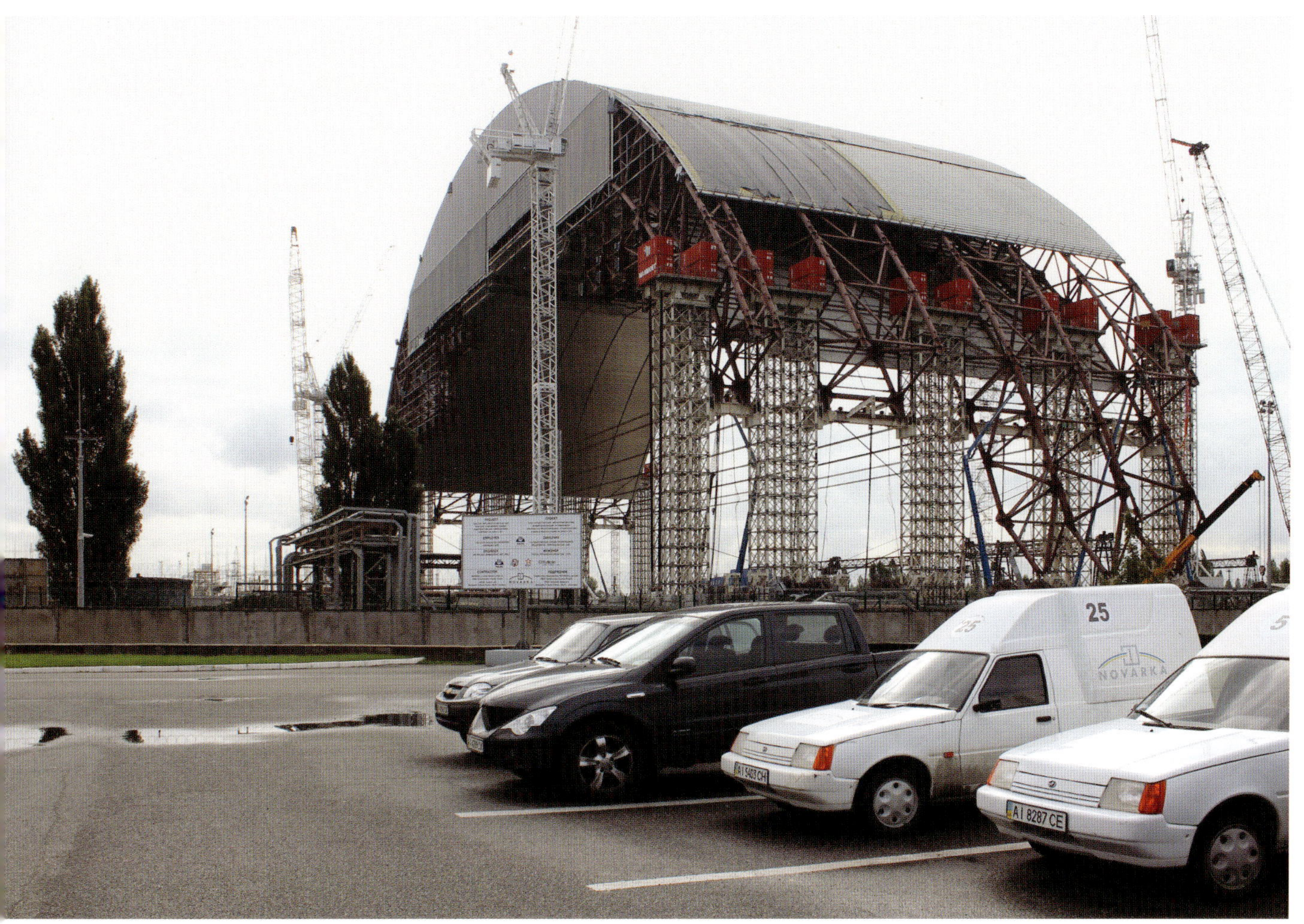

recruits, their building a gritty warren of faded 1970s décor. It feels far more Soviet than the Novarka side, where an international team works in a brand-new state-of-the-art facility. Security feels more severe here too: Novarka has the same full-body metal detectors, but its guards are less chatty and brandish their weapons more openly.

A Novarka representative named Sasha meets us at the barrier. As we change into protective suits – by now a familiar procedure – Sasha says that in addition to many Ukrainian staff, 10,000 foreign specialists were involved in the construction of the New Arch. Some stayed in Slavutych, but others were accommodated in Chornobyl: the new 'Polissya' Hotel and its 'Fairy Tale' Canteen (just recently made available to tour groups) were built originally for these workers. In April 2020, with the construction finished, responsibilities for the New Arch were transferred to ChNPP and the Ukrainian Project Management Unit, and Novarka employees began leaving the site.

Beyond the security building, we enter a yard at the rear of the sarcophagus. I have seen this structure several dozen times before, but never at such close quarters; it's larger than I remember. Sasha leads us across the broad, open space where the arch was built, and in the shadow of the silver vault we pass a group of three young female workers, all with blond hair cascading from their red safety helmets. Sasha sighs. 'We used to have a lot of beautiful Ukrainian girls working here, but then they started marrying these

visiting French specialists, and now it seems they're all leaving Chernobyl for Paris.' He explains that the construction of the New Safe Confinement had been a prestigious job. It broke records, earned massive acclaim in the media and scientific communities, and many international firms had wanted to attach their names to its success. However, now that the glamorous work is over and the rock-star scientists have all gone home, it's left to Ukraine alone to fund the less newsworthy job of actually putting the technology to use.

We reach a door set into the flat end wall of the arch. It seems comically small compared to the sheer cliff of the building that rises above us. Inside, we pass a series of bright, sterile halls smelling of bleach and new plastic. 'Here's where the waste will be packaged, ready for storage,' says Sasha, his voice muffled through his facemask. An unused, shiny yellow bridge crane hangs overhead, custom-designed in the US. Parked to one side of the clinically clean hall is a factory-fresh forklift.

'Here we go,' says Sasha, shepherding us through a final security door. Nothing could have prepared me for what lies beyond. The feeling is profoundly surreal: I am inside the biggest building I've ever seen, a horizon-breaking landmark, yet inside it stands an apparently even bigger building. The old blue-grey sarcophagus that once dominated this flat landscape towers above me – only now it looks like it has been mothballed in a storage warehouse. Around and

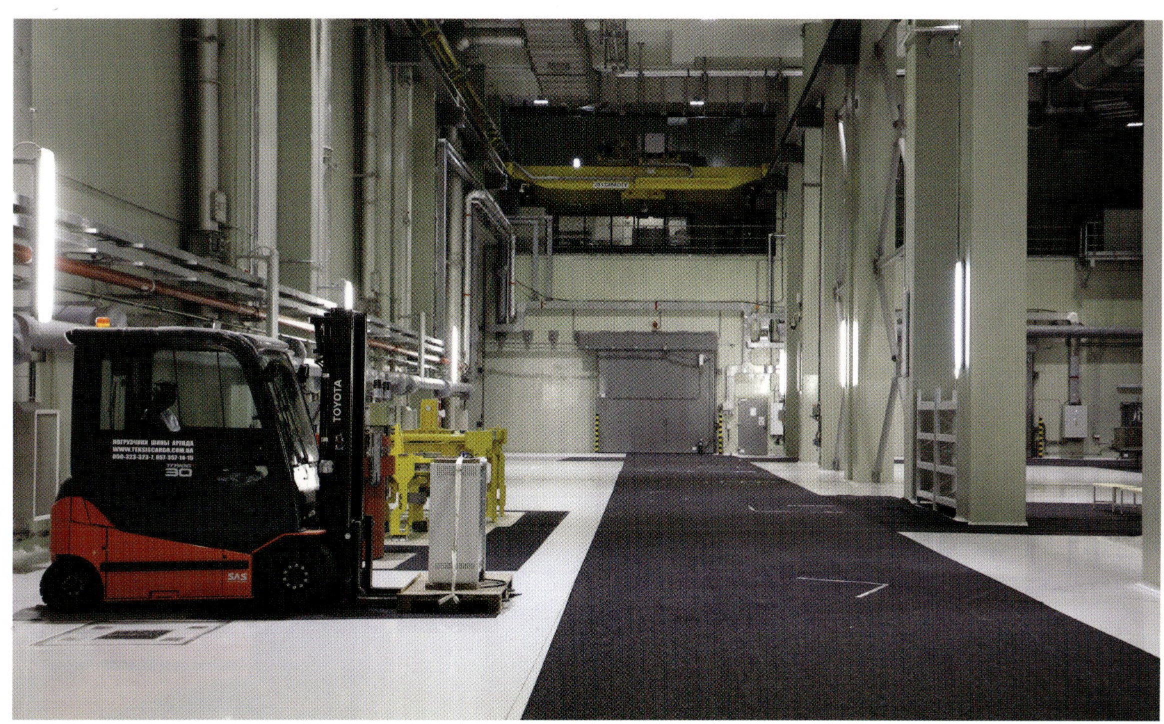

above it, the silver interior of the New Arch curves away into the far distance, and my brain struggles to make sense of this new perspective – as if the world has been turned inside out.

'Five minutes,' says Anatoly again, and as I float wide-eyed towards the behemoth, he hangs back to chat quietly with Sasha, like two mothers on a playground bench.

Meanwhile, I am struggling to comprehend the view. Stretched above simple supporting steel ribs, the metallic skin of the arch seems almost featureless, like baking foil, with no obvious indication of scale. My brain tells me it's smaller and closer than it really is, but then I turn my attention to the concrete bulk beneath, count the seventeen flights of steps lacing up the scaffold around the bulwark and

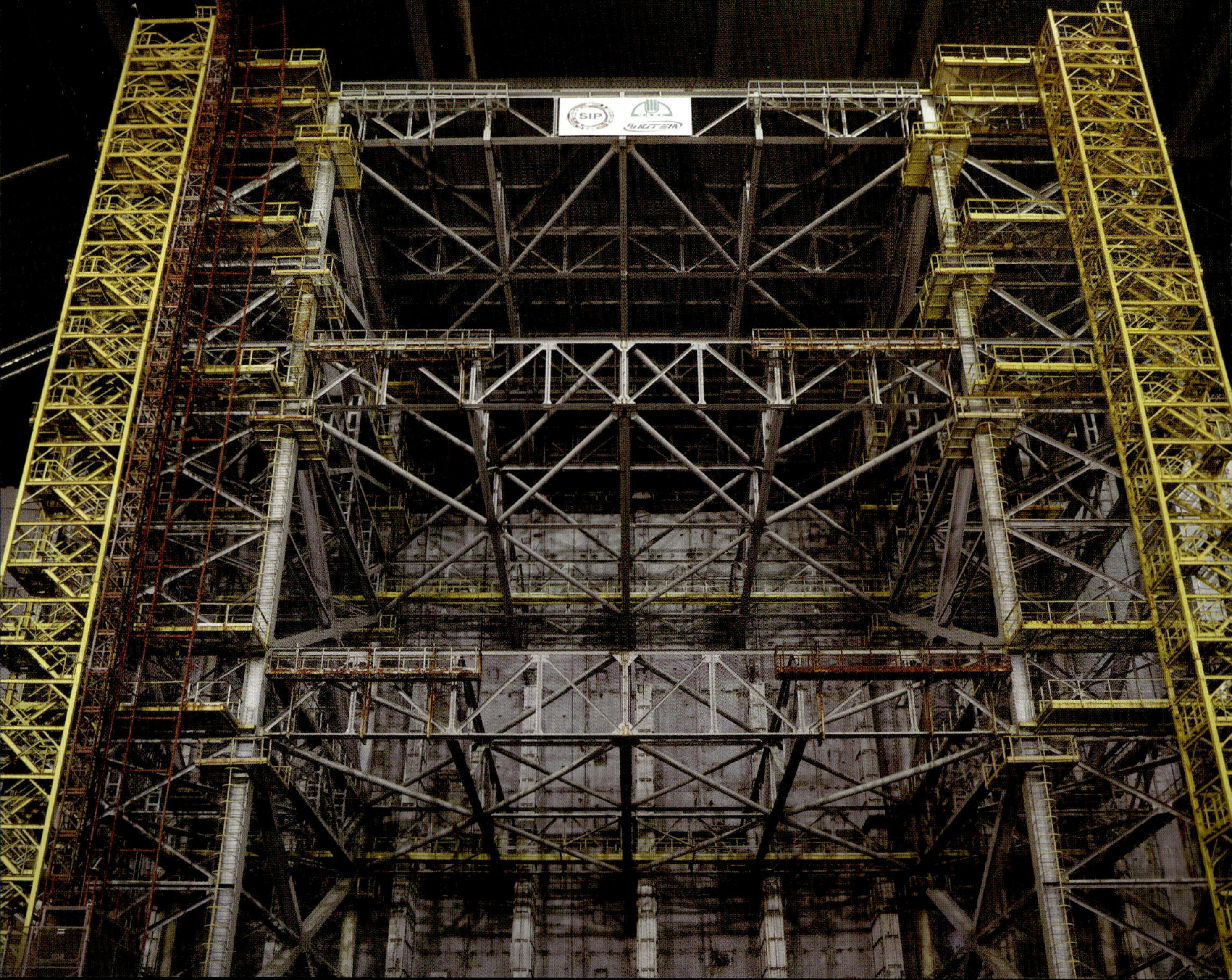
SIP

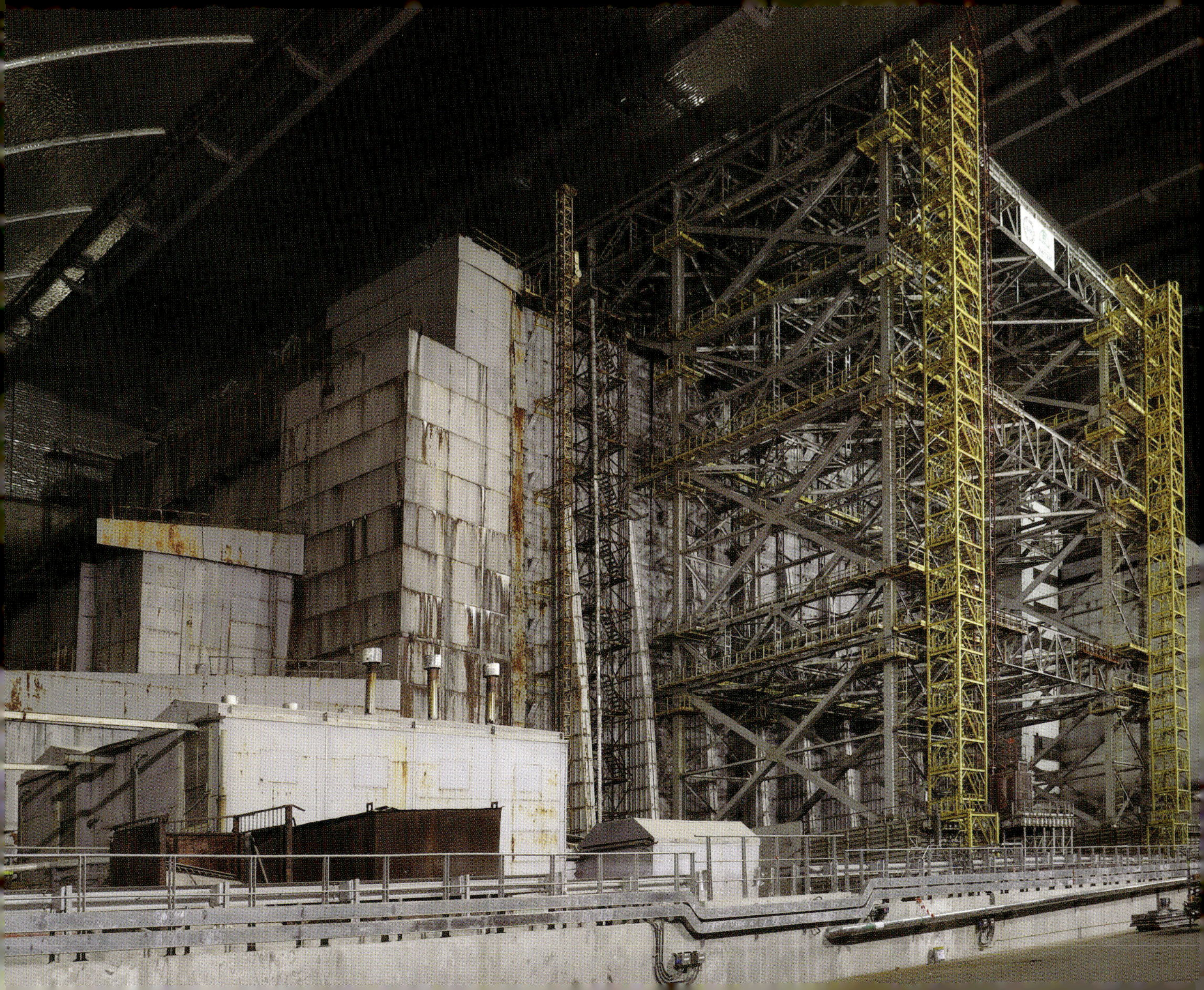

suddenly I begin to feel dizzy. This shouldn't fit. The spectacle is almost incomprehensible, as if someone let M.C. Escher design a far-future factory biodome.

The tarmac access road that circles the industrial tomb is unnaturally clean: no dust or dirt, no oil stains or debris. I wonder what type of vehicles use it. The only image that seems to fit is a moon buggy, as if outside the silver vault lie the barren deserts and unfamiliar constellations of an extra-terrestrial landscape. I follow the road around the reactor block, and at the far end of the building I spot workers dressed, like us, in white suits, hats, and masks. They seem to be making an inspection of some kind, but before I can figure it out, Anatoly calls me and I turn to see him tapping his watch emphatically. I walk over and he shows me the dosimeter – it's dirtier here than in the Block 4 Control Room, with a reading of around 60-70 µSv/h. Only guaranteed to last around thirty years, this crumbling old sarcophagus has passed its expiry date – as the reading indicates. Studies have revealed cracks in the shelter structure that are releasing radiation from within. In addition, before the New Arch was installed, it was shown that rain water was getting inside the shell, becoming contaminated, then constantly having to be drained out to the Liquid Radioactive Waste Treatment Plant.

I remember an article I wrote some years ago, which listed folkloric sites reputed to have been entrances to the Underworld. Iceland's Mount Hekla and the Japanese Mount Osore are volcanoes said to be gateways to Hell, but just as often such places took the form of barrows, or other uncanny rises in the landscape. According to Welsh mythology, Glastonbury Tor (an ancient conical hill in Somerset, England) contained the entrance to the Otherworld called Annwn. Now here I stand inside a great metal barrow, before a sarcophagus that is struggling to contain an invisible force of unspeakable destruction; and I wonder, if future civilisations should ever lose our practical knowledge of nuclear technology, what stories they would tell about a place like this, and what sense they would make of the poisonous atomic legacy we are leaving for them.

pages 210-211: Chernobyl Reactor Block 4. The heart of the Zone, viewed from between its inner and outer protective shelters – the 1986 Shelter Object within the 2016 New Arch. The Shelter Object will be deconstructed using remote-controlled technology. Once this process begins, it will no longer be safe to enter this area.

right: Gantry cranes, Chernobyl Reactor Block 4. These irradiated machines are left over from the construction of the sarcophagus in 1986.

overleaf: New Arch over Reactor Block 4. Designed to safely secure its contents for a period of no less than 100 years, at 108 metres high, it is considered the largest movable structure ever built.

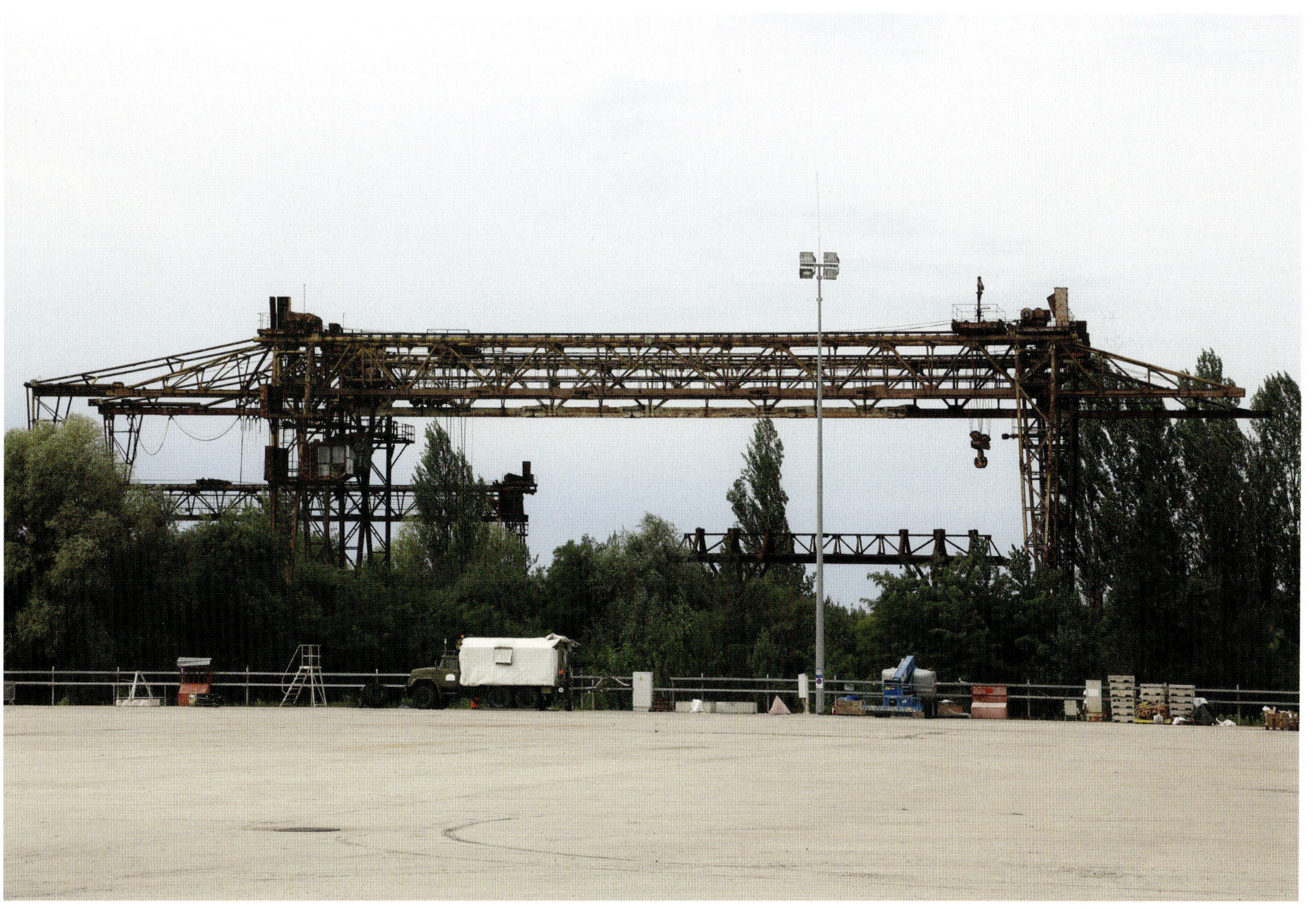

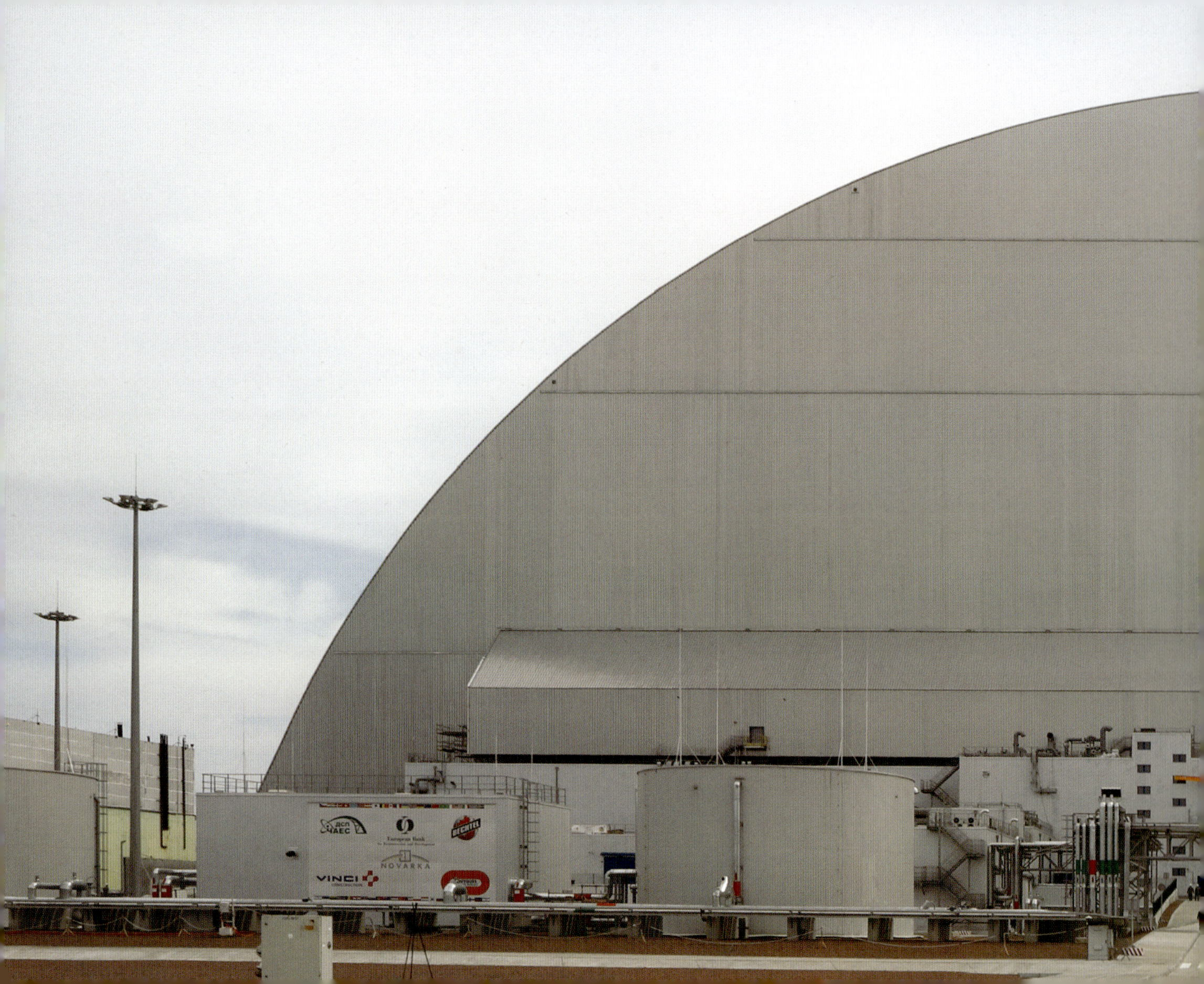
ДСП
ЧАЕС
European Bank
for Reconstruction and Development
BECHTEL
NOVARKA
VINCI
CONSTRUCTION

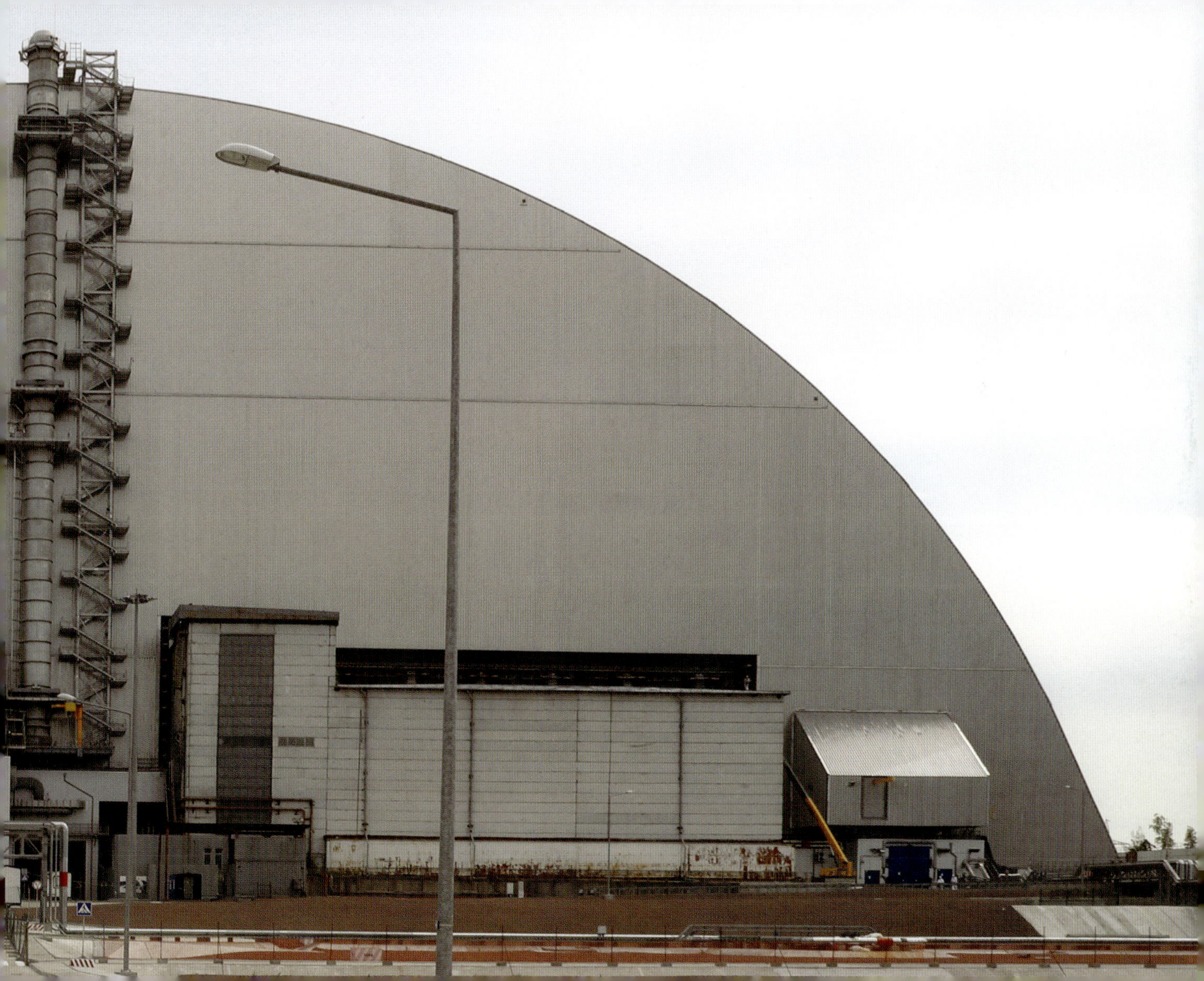

9. HALF-LIFE

Inscription on the tomb of Khentika Ikhekhi
(Vizier to the Egyptian Pharaohs Teti and Pepi of the 6th Dynasty)

NUCLEAR SEMIOTICS

Chernobyl today is a territory defined by extremes. Visitors gaze at outdated Soviet megastructures – the Duga, the power plant, the cooling tower – in a landscape forever changed by events that occurred at an atomic scale. In one day, they'll learn about issues that will impact on this planet for longer than our own civilisation has existed.

The explosion at ChNPP on 26 April 1986 released a cloud of radioactive isotopes into the environment. Two of the most dangerous contaminants were strontium-90 and caesium-137, each of which has a half-life (the time it takes for the level of radiation emitted to decrease by half) of roughly thirty years. While human bodies reject caesium, strontium has a similar molecular structure to calcium, which means the body can mistakenly use ingested strontium in the production of new bone matter. Plutonium-239, another of the contaminants released, is the primary isotope used in the creation of nuclear weapons, with a half-life of more than 24,000 years. It is generally considered safe only after a period of ten half-lifes, or a quarter of a million years, has expired. If we're living in what some geologists are calling the 'Anthropocene' – the period in which human activities begin to have profound and significant impact on the earth's ecosystems – then there cannot be a better illustration of it than the infamous Chernobyl disaster.[1]

Beneath the New Arch lie yet more problems. The fuel used by Chernobyl's RBMK reactors contained three isotopes of uranium: U-234 has a half-life of 246,000 years, U-235's half-life is over 700 million years, while the half-life of U-238 is around 4.5 billion years. Experts believe around 200 tons of melted uranium fuel remains somewhere inside the ruins of Block 4. But Dmytrii Korchak, a communications specialist with ChNPP, tells me that no one really knows for sure what's going on within the Shelter Object. 'We can see that the temperature is changing,' he says. 'There's a self-contained reaction inside. Something is still there, but I don't know if anyone can say for sure how much material there is, or what type it is.'

All things considered, the Chernobyl liquidators did an extraordinary job of cleaning the region after the disaster. But their work still represents just the tip of the iceberg. A significant quantity of nuclear by-products remains unchecked in the environment, while the project to dismantle, clean, and secure the contaminated remains of Reactor 4 is ambitious to say the least. The New Arch over it has been guaranteed for a lifespan of 100 years, but no one can say for sure if that will be enough time to finish the work inside. Even after that, the arch itself – tainted by its contents – will also need to be disassembled and stored as radioactive waste. There is still much work to be done.

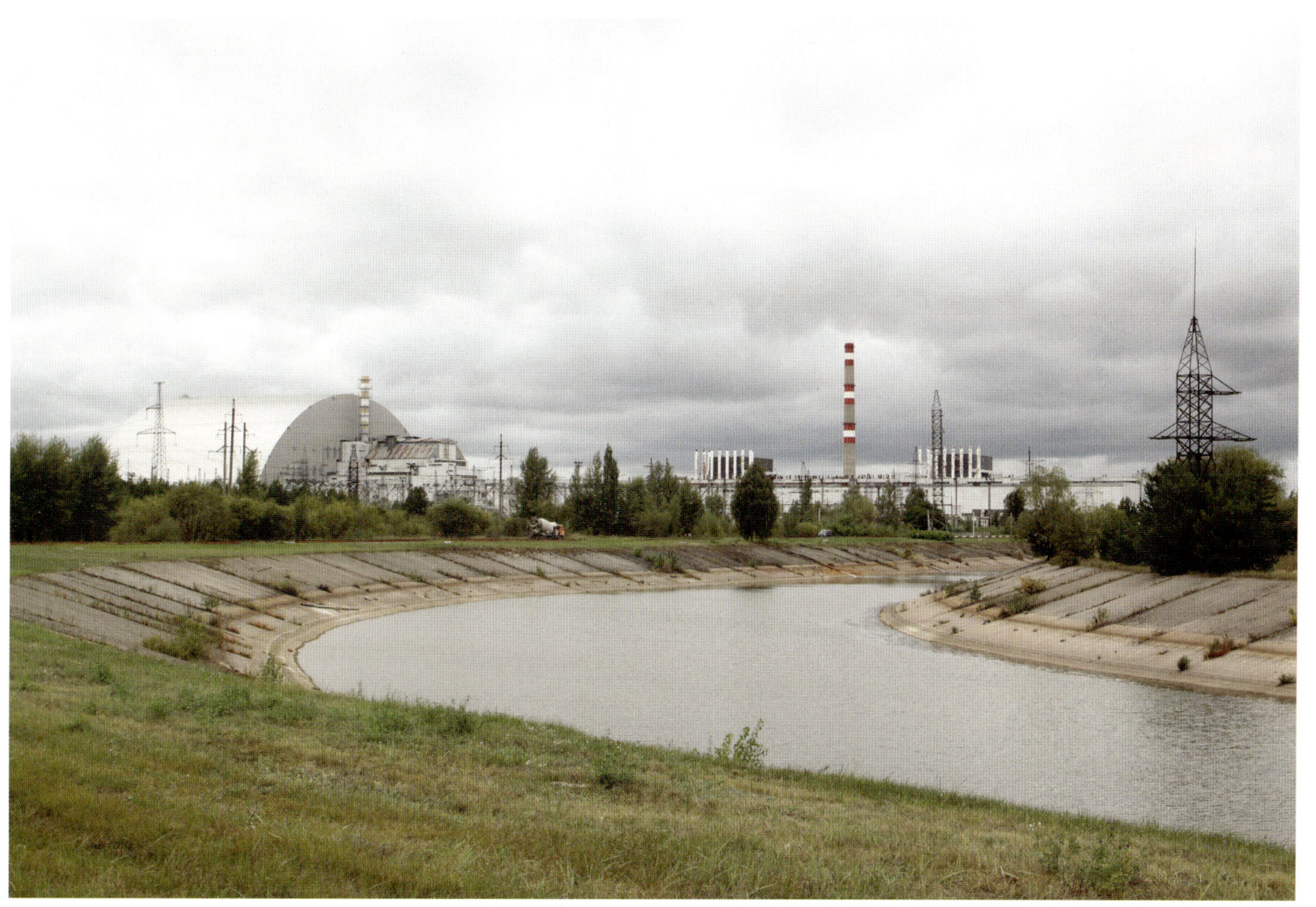

The safe, long-term storage of nuclear waste is one of the greatest challenges faced by the societies of the Anthropocene. No nuclear storage facility in use today offers a permanent solution. Even the new ISF-2 facility at ChNPP, with its capacity for 75,000 cubic metres of nuclear waste stored in secure double-walled canisters, will inevitably be deemed unsafe after it passes its 100-year expiry date. For now we are simply postponing the problem in the hope that future generations might be able to solve it. In France and Sweden, efforts are underway to construct 'deep time' burial sites, while Finland's Onkalo spent nuclear fuel repository is already on track to begin disposal – but the structure itself is still only half the answer. The future security of this deadly material will also depend on any containment being able to withstand human curiosity – and as a species, we're not very good at listening to the warnings of our ancestors. The citizens of Feudal Japan, for instance, marked the coastline with 'tsunami stones' that warned future inhabitants against building below the danger line. The inscription on one such stone in Aneyoshi, Iwate Prefecture, reads: 'High dwellings ensure the peace and happiness of our descendants.' Hundreds of these stones exist today, some of them having been in place for six centuries, and yet many people have been killed by tsunamis after ignoring their warnings.

This problem gave birth to a new field of study, named 'nuclear semiotics'. Since the 1980s, deep-burial projects such as the Waste Isolation Pilot Plant (WIPP) in New Mexico have been welcoming multi-disciplinary attempts to solve the problem of devising warnings that will last for many millennia, and will continue to be understood by all future generations across potentially unimaginable changes in culture, technology and language. One proposal came from the Polish science-fiction author Stanisław Lem (a colleague of the Strugatskys, whose novel *Solaris* was also adapted for cinema by Tarkovsky). He suggested a mathematically coded warning could be bio-engineered into the DNA of 'atomic flowers', to create a whole crop of warning signs that could perpetuate themselves, generation after generation.[2] Emil Kowalski, a Swiss physicist, envisaged storage structures so advanced they could only be opened by cultures with at least an equal level of technology to ours.[3] Françoise Bastide and Paolo Fabbri – a French author and an Italian semiotician – imagined a species of genetically engineered cat that changed colour in the presence of radiation, thus warning its human companions of nearby danger.[4]

Other approaches involved altering the landscape itself. In 1992, the architectural theorist Michael Brill designed his 'Spike Field', or 'Landscape of Thorns', an installation so unwelcoming as to deter future human incursion into the territory.[5] (Although as British writer Robert Macfarlane points out, 'such aggressive structures might act as enticements rather than cautions… Prince Charming hacked his way through the briars and thorns to wake Sleeping Beauty.')[6]

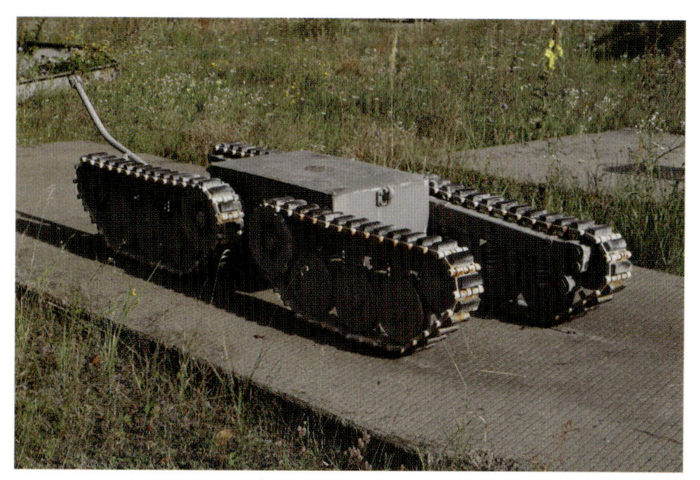

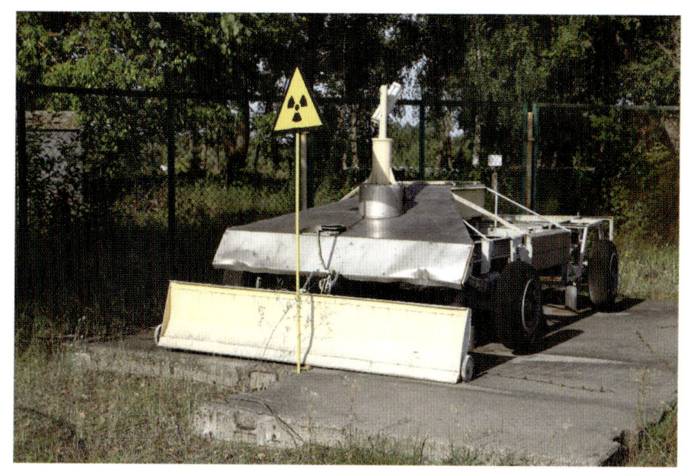

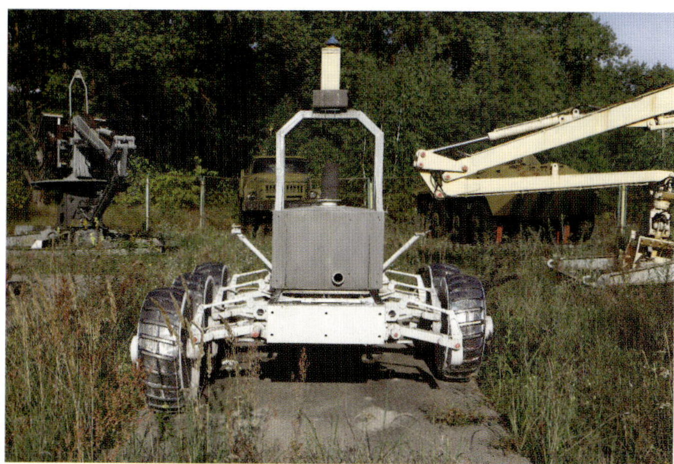

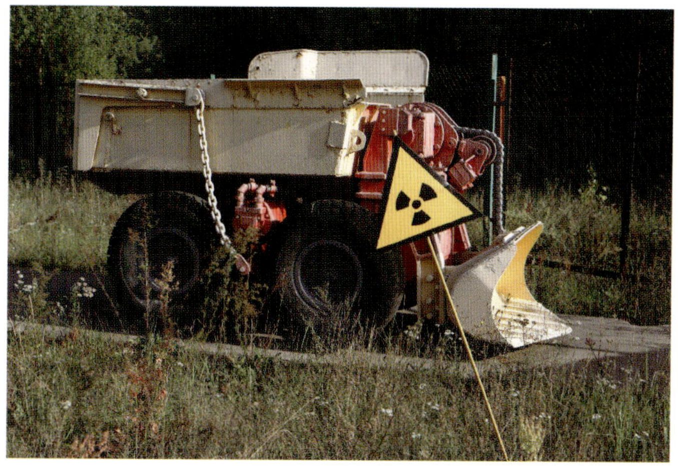

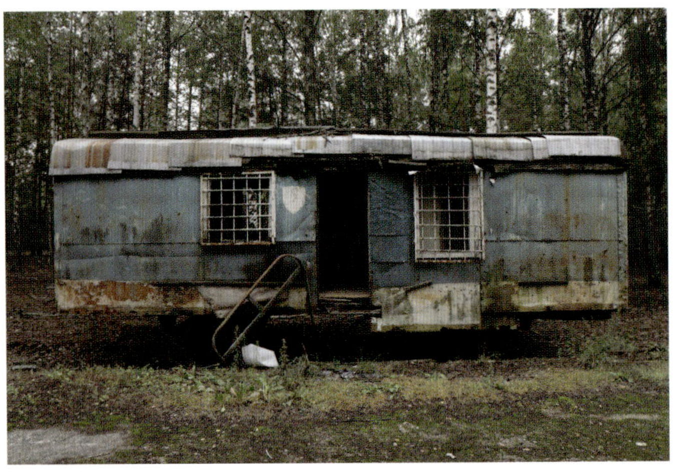

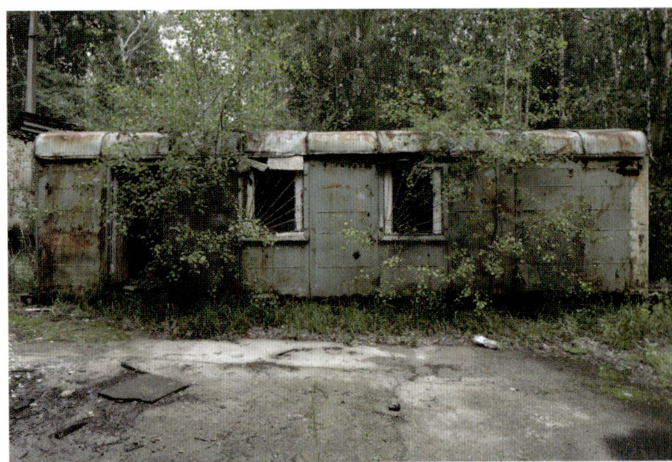

Rozsokha village. For many years after the disaster this place housed a huge collection of abandoned machines and vehicles, including helicopters, all of which had been highly irradiated during the clean-up process. Most have now been buried, with only a few elements of machinery and caravans remaining.

right: Power-plant complex outskirts. This Soviet-era ISU-152 tank is a relic of WWII. Nicknamed 'Zveroboy' (the 'Beast Killer'), its 152mm-calibre cannon was capable of firing powerful anti-tank or anti-masonry rounds. Several tanks of this type were brought to Chernobyl during the clean-up, with the intention of piercing a hole in Reactor 4's bubbler pool to alleviate the risk of a secondary steam explosion. However, the pool was drained manually by Alexey Ananenko and his team (page 96) and the ISU-152s were instead used to demolish buildings in contaminated villages.

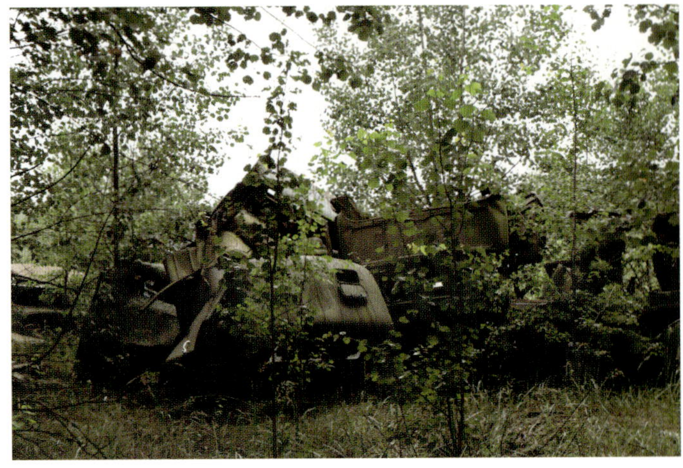

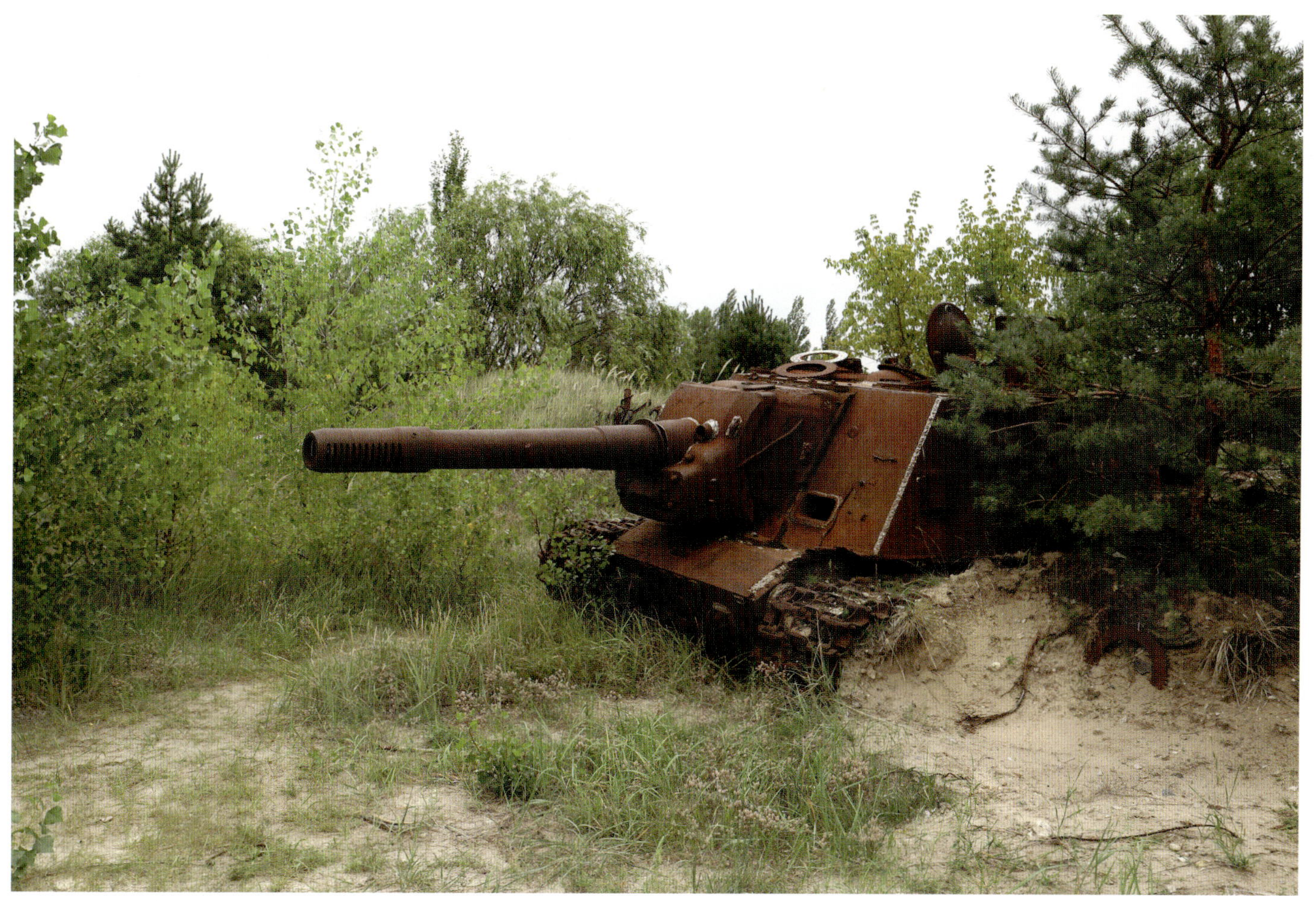

In 2015, artist Alexis Pandellé proposed that a scar-like mark be drawn on the earth above the 100,000-year storage site being built at Bure, France; he called it 'Prométheé oublié' ('Prometheus forgotten.')[7]

However, the possibility remains that the earth itself may take an active part in the decontamination process.

RADIOSYNTHESIS

The curious relationship between radiation and fungi has been observed and theorised for almost as long as humans have worked with nuclear power. More recently, research in this area has accelerated with the growing availability of field laboratories at Chernobyl and other sites of nuclear testing, storage, or disaster.

In 1998, the Biochemical Society published a study investigating 'Fungi as potential bioremediation agents in soil contaminated with heavy or radioactive metals'. The paper explains that, whereas cleaning contaminated water is relatively straightforward, the decontamination of soil is a more complex process – and so the discovery that radioactive caesium, released during the Chernobyl disaster, had since been absorbed and contained in plants and fungi, was a noteworthy new development. It was shown that at Chernobyl, caesium-137 in particular was being absorbed by fungi 270 times faster than plants could absorb it.[8]

In 2004, a group of Ukrainian scientists demonstrated that soil fungi was attracted to sources of ionising radiation.[9] In a span of fifteen years prior to the publication of their results, the team discovered around 2,000 strains of 200 species of fungi at ChNPP. Many of these were capable of growing among the 'hot particles' – such as contaminated graphite from the reactor – and decomposing them. The implication was that this directional growth was not random, but that beta and gamma radiation were promoting it: the fungi appeared to be trying to reach the source of the radiation.

This work caught the attention of Ekaterina Dadachova and her colleagues at the Albert Einstein College of Medicine in New York, who had previously been studying ways to treat fungal diseases in immunosuppressed patients. One of the options was radioimmunotherapy – the treatment of fungal diseases using radioactive isotopes. During research, they discovered that many fungi were extremely resistant to radiation, the doses of radiation needed to kill them being several thousand times higher than the dose fatal for humans.[10] The New York team also discovered that certain types of fungi selected for their tests grew faster in the presence of ionising radiation.[11]

Inside the ruins of Chernobyl's Reactor 4, there are varieties of 'black fungi' – such as the melanin-rich *Cryptococcus neoformans* – that have been shown to adapt and even thrive in the presence of radiation, their resilient melanin molecules breaking down the radioactive isotopes into a form of weakened energy which they can then use for growth.

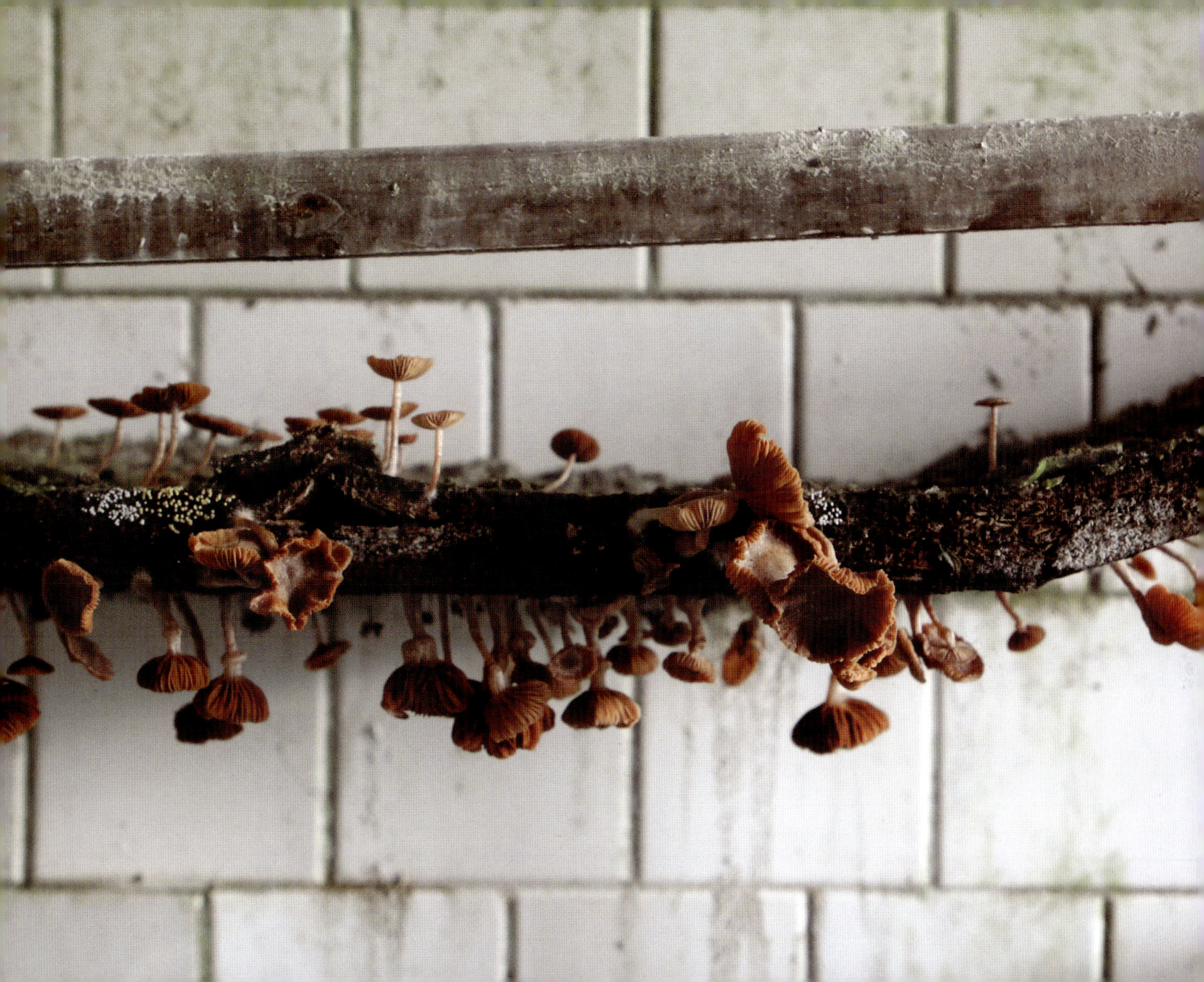

Essentially, they seem to be feeding on radiation, a process some researchers have referred to as 'radiosynthesis'.

Where nuclear semioticians have largely proposed one-off interventions to guard the distant future against the dangers of radioactive waste, perhaps ultimately, more organic, evolutionary approaches are more likely to succeed. In human cultures too, ideas are most effectively transferred across vast periods of time when encoded into organic, flexible systems of cultural practice – such as religions – as opposed to fragile, time-sensitive messages carved in stone.

In pre-colonial Igboland, a region of south-eastern Nigeria that is home to the Igbo people, advanced local iron-working traditions were interwoven with religious practice. Smiths became ritual workers, priests guarded the shrines of iron deities, and in this way complex metalworking techniques were preserved through many generations in the form of an inherited sacred tradition.[12] Perhaps this was the kind of thing the linguist Thomas Sebeok had in mind, when in 1984 he proposed the creation of an 'atomic priesthood'.[13]

Sebeok hypothesised a system in which 'information be launched and artificially passed on into the short-term and long-term future with the supplementary aid of folkloristic devices, in particular a combination of an artificially created and nurtured ritual-and-legend.' Initiates would pass down warnings about nuclear burial sites and by adapting these warnings into narrative myths, they might survive across changes in culture, technology, and language. Rather than appealing to our descendants' scientific caution, he wrote, 'accumulated superstition [would be the reason] to shun a certain area permanently.'

Against the backdrop of a collapsing Soviet Union, however, one group of scientific minds would propose an approach to the question of nuclear power and its by-products that was more radical still: in order to work effectively with an energy source whose half-life is measured in millennia, humans themselves would need to attain immortality.

GAVDOS

On the southernmost tip of Europe, goats pick precarious paths between leathery blooms of cacti, as waves crash relentlessly into rocks below. Gavdos is not the easiest place to reach: there's an overnight ferry from Athens to Crete; then a drive across the island, to board a smaller boat that skirts the shoreline, beneath soaring mountains that loom over a series of isolated villages accessible only by sea. Finally turning south, this boat makes the choppy crossing to the farthest of Greece's islands. It is August, and Gavdos' port is busy with islanders collecting deliveries of food, water, and fuel for cars and generators. To the north, the mountains of Crete are still visible, their sharp peaks appearing to float above the sea mist. Geographically, we're closer now to Africa than Athens.

I came to Gavdos to meet the members of a commune

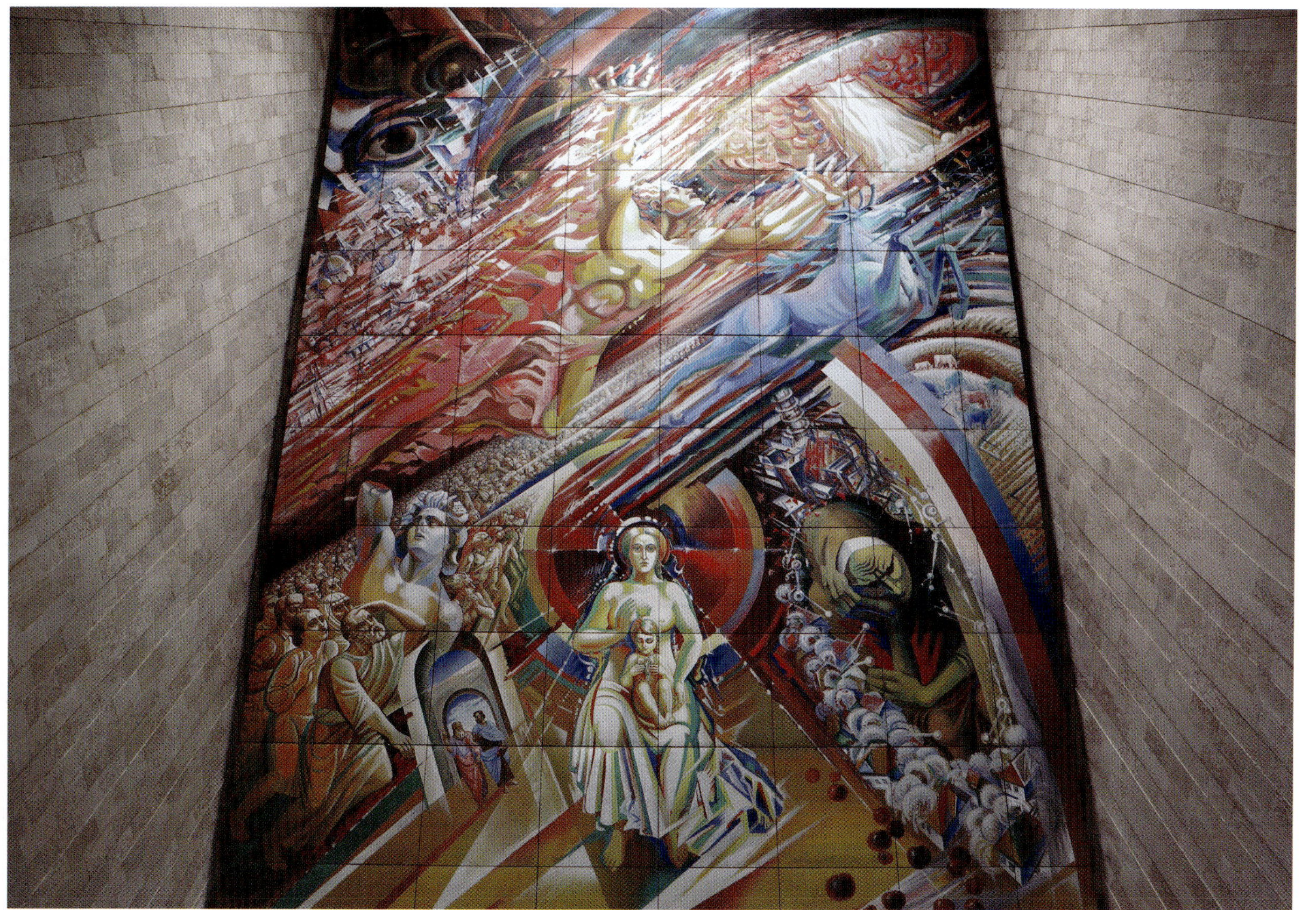

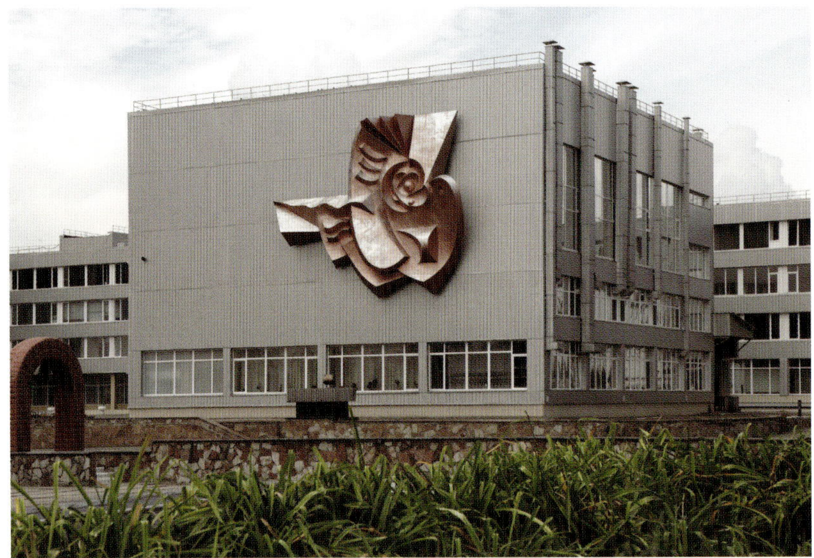

which the media has dubbed 'the Immortals': ex-Soviet scientists who settled here after the break-up of the USSR, to establish the Pythagorean Institute of Philosophical Studies for the Immortality of Man. Today the group is spread between bases in Venezuela, Russia, and Georgia, but they still communicate regularly online. Currently just two members remain on Gavdos full-time: Alla, a Ukrainian, and Aleksey, a Russian. Their home perches on a remote, rocky outcrop on the south of the island, looking out across the Libyan Sea.

We discuss mythology, and the philosophies that tie the institute's research to Greece and the ancient world. I mention the Prometheus-Chernobyl connection, and Aleksey says,

'We have our own interpretation of this myth: Prometheus stole the knowledge to make alcohol. Because there is fire in the water. When you drink fire, you change your consciousness… you find inspiration, achieve a godlike state. But you will pay for it with your liver.'

Aleksey, a former physicist, describes his position on religion not as poly-, or mono-, but ligo-theism: 'Just a few gods.' He indicates a small measure with thumb and index finger. 'The twentieth century had two main events,' he explains. 'The first was the discovery of nuclear energy, an inner source of energy. Before that we knew only one god, one outer source of energy – the sun. All life exists between

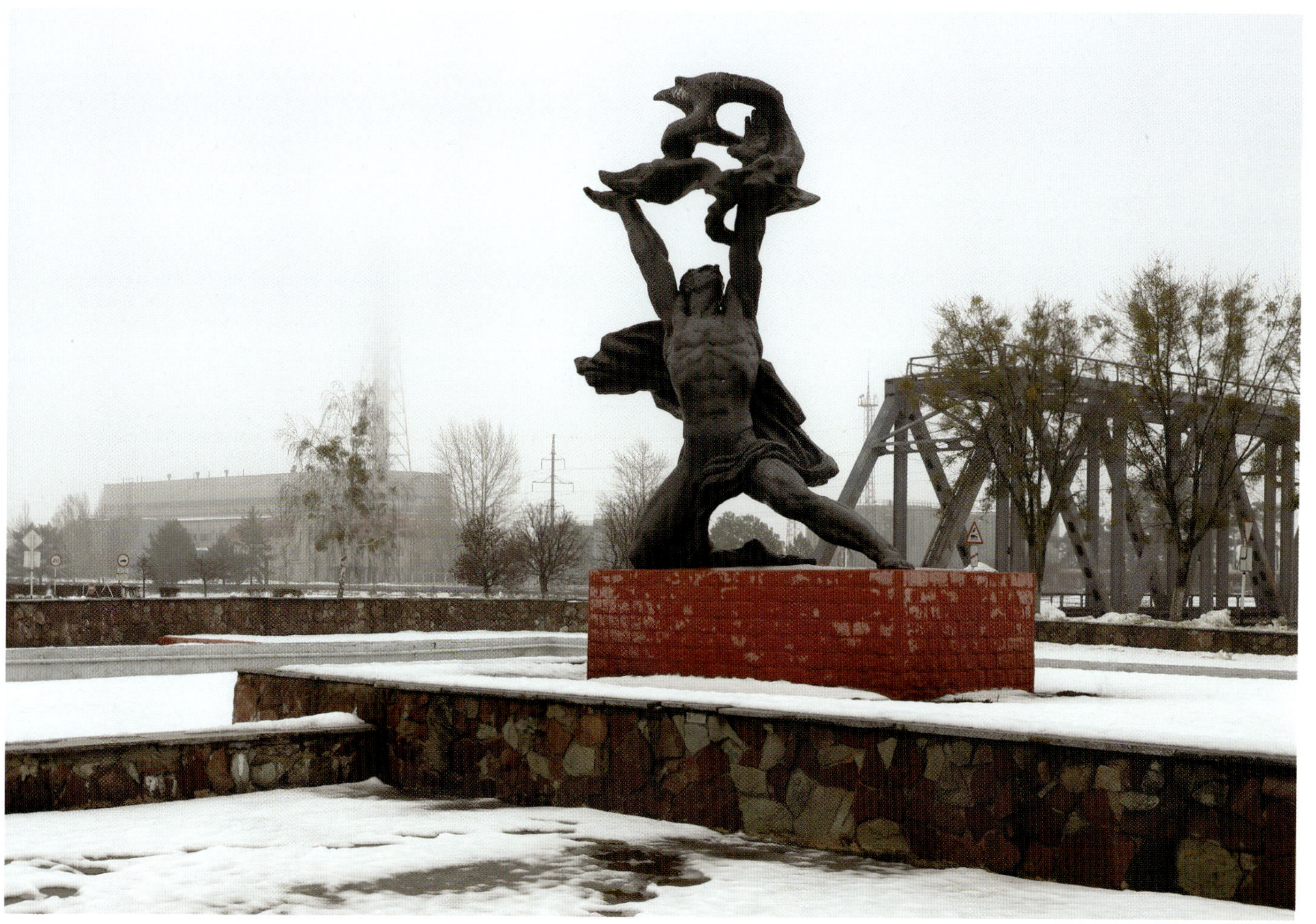

these two energetic sources, the inner and the outer.' He refills our vodka glasses, adding, 'The second main event was man's exit into space. Human power reached a planetary scale, and now our mistakes and misunderstandings have not only local, but planetary consequences.'

One of the group's founding members, Andrey Drozdov, worked at the Kurchatov Institute at the time of the Chernobyl disaster, and was part of a research team that visited the site soon afterwards. He toured nearby towns and villages, post-evacuation, and noted in his memoirs: 'In all things you could feel the breath of irreversibility.'

Another member of the Gavdos Institute, Oleg Kalyaskin, had been part of a team that used helicopters to drop sensors inside the destroyed Reactor Block 4, and had workers drill a hole through the side of the reactor so they could insert a periscope and see the damage for themselves. 'It was empty, just like a drum!' Oleg later wrote, proposing that temperatures in excess of 3,500°C during the disaster had converted the fuel to plasma, dispersing it immediately into the atmosphere. He theorised that the radiation measurements taken at the time had related only to the fuel assemblies and other irradiated wreckage. 'Nowhere have we or any other liquidators detected any noticeable fuel concentrations. It makes it clear how much unnecessary work has been done… dropping lead, boron and sand from helicopters.'

In the course of his research, Andrey suffered extreme exposure to radiation. After a series of health scares he retreated to the countryside, deciding to pursue a simpler life of honest, physical labour while studying the great works of philosophy. This period saw the collapse of the Soviet Union and in the uncertain times that followed, Andrey was joined by other intellectuals – ranging from physicists to psychoanalysts – who shared his interest in re-evaluating the aims and objectives of human life on earth.

Before joining the group, Alla worked at a university institute investigating solid-state physics, laser technology and the properties of crystals. 'When the Soviet Union broke up,' she says, 'we lost not only a political system, but a way of life and a way of thinking too.' She explains how the transition offered new freedoms such as that of travel, but alongside new philosophical choices: 'To understand what I would like to do, it is necessary to understand what exists.' It was around that time that she met the rest of the group. 'We were in love with the energetic world,' she remembers, 'with energetic systems. Nuclear energy was a part of that.'

'Of course [our group] was influenced by communist ideals,' adds Aleksey: 'that nuclear energy can provide for all human abundance, satisfy all our needs, while eliminating the reasons for theft, or wars waged over resources. That may seem idealistic, but many of the earliest physicists working in atomic energy research – Curie, Hahn, Meitner, Fermi, Heisenberg – shared this same idea. The condition of scarcity is a sickness on our consciousness.'

The Chernobyl disaster did little to dampen the group's

enthusiasm for nuclear energy. Alla explains that a kilogram of fossil fuel releases around 10 kWh of energy, of which as much as 90 per cent can be lost through shipping, processing, and production waste. In comparison, one kilogram of nuclear fuel gives 100 million kWh. Abolishing nuclear technology would represent a significant step backwards, the group explained in an open letter to Angela Merkel in 2014, urging the German chancellor to consider reopening the country's nuclear power plants. What was needed instead, they reasoned, was a new global energy strategy that focused on three criteria: 'safety, efficiency and safe recycling of waste.'

'The Chernobyl reactor, this kind of reactor, was created to produce plutonium for weapons,' Alla tells me. 'Energy was a second priority, a by-product. It was not a holistic approach to the energetic system, and this situation is the result. It's no surprise.' There are other types of reactor that come with fewer risks. Lead coolant is one safer option, where in the event of a meltdown the metal itself melts around the reactor to seal the contamination. 'It was known thirty years ago,' says Aleksey. 'The principle is known everywhere. The Japanese are even trying a new system of molten salt reactor.'

'The amount of waste is terrible,' Alla laments. 'These older reactors use only a fraction of their fuel. The rest of it – as much as 96 per cent – is polluted by the reaction, making it unusable. Can you imagine? Mankind needs to grow up,' she says, explaining that if we can figure out a way to minimise wastage and use nuclear fuel to its full potential, 'We won't even need to dig for new ores. We have ample fuel on this planet to supply all human energy needs… but only if it is organised in the right way.'

'We have calculated that 2 or 3 per cent of the world's population is capable of providing for the other 97 per cent,' adds Aleksey. 'But then the question arises – what will they do with their freedom? Many people live just to survive. They work, earn money to provide for themselves. They still don't know what to do with their lives, and they're afraid of this. If we have an abundance of everything, what will they do? This is a very interesting problem to consider.'

Alla and Aleksey were interviewed a number of times for Greek television in the wake of the *Chernobyl* miniseries. 'It was well researched,' says Alla. 'From the scientific and engineering point of view, it was good work. Of course, there was some bullshit too. The Americans made it look so bleak, but it was not like this. It was impossible to achieve these things if you didn't have some humour.' We are interrupted when a bus pulls up on the dusty road outside.

This recent wave of publicity has spread word of the Gavdos philosophical commune, and tourists visiting from the mainland now often call in to see them. 'In summer, we sometimes get groups every day,' says Aleksey. The tourists want to photograph the views as well as the curiosities in their clifftop garden: Aleksey's sculptures, and various inventions, including a rudimentary light-beam projector, built from mirror-panels arranged in a bowl around a single lightbulb, and a pyramid of green glass bottles that channels solar energy into a stone-walled outhouse.

When the tourists have left, Alla leads me to an underground bunker constructed by the group. Sprigs of dried lavender lie piled across the doorstep to deter scorpions. After descending a flight of steep steps, we enter the pentagonal hall used for group meetings. A shaft above allows the sun to illuminate the space, and it's refreshingly cool underground. 'Sometimes we sleep down here in the middle of the day,' she says. 'The sun's radiation is more energy than we need!'

Unlike on mainland Greece, there are no cicadas to be heard on Gavdos. The sun sets to the sound of goat bells, clanging above the relentless churning of the waves. We eat dinner beneath the radiant glow of the Milky Way. The stars here are incredible, a million pinpoints of light in a rich purple aura that fills the sky. The last time I saw them as bright was back in Chernobyl. After a while, the conversation turns to immortality.

'It takes 24,000 years for the intensity of these radionuclides to halve,' says Alla, referring to Chernobyl's plutonium problem. 'To work with these kinds of materials, with this kind of energy, it is necessary to be another level of human being – to be immortal. You need the ability to think not in years, or even hundreds of years, but in hundreds of thousands of years. Immortality is necessary to understand how the world – how different *worlds* – can be organised. One life is not long enough.'

Aleksey believes that human beings already have the capacity to evolve beyond the present inevitability of death. 'One philosopher claimed that this is our unique and only destiny,' he says, 'unlike animals, for whom there is no question – the moment of their conception is also the beginning of their death.'

Alla explains: 'There are already medical, scientific ways to extend our lifespans. But it's not enough, just to have an immortal body – what do you do with it then?'

'What to do? The same bullshit!' laughs Aleksey.

'To reject what we have is stupidity,' says Alla, meaning technology in general but nuclear power in particular. 'We need to move forwards, and this technology demands that we advance to the next level of consciousness. The problem is, with human beings behaving like they do now, perhaps we have no right to immortality.'

right: *Third Angel* (2010), by Anatoly Gaydamaka. Standing in the centre of Chornobyl, this sculpture was installed on the 25th anniversary of the disaster.

overleaf: 'Skazochniy' ('Fairy Tale') Pioneer Camp. This woodland camp consisted of dormitory buildings, a theatre, outside activity areas, and decorative mosaic sculptures such as the three-headed dragon Zmiy Horynych, a creature from Slavic folklore.

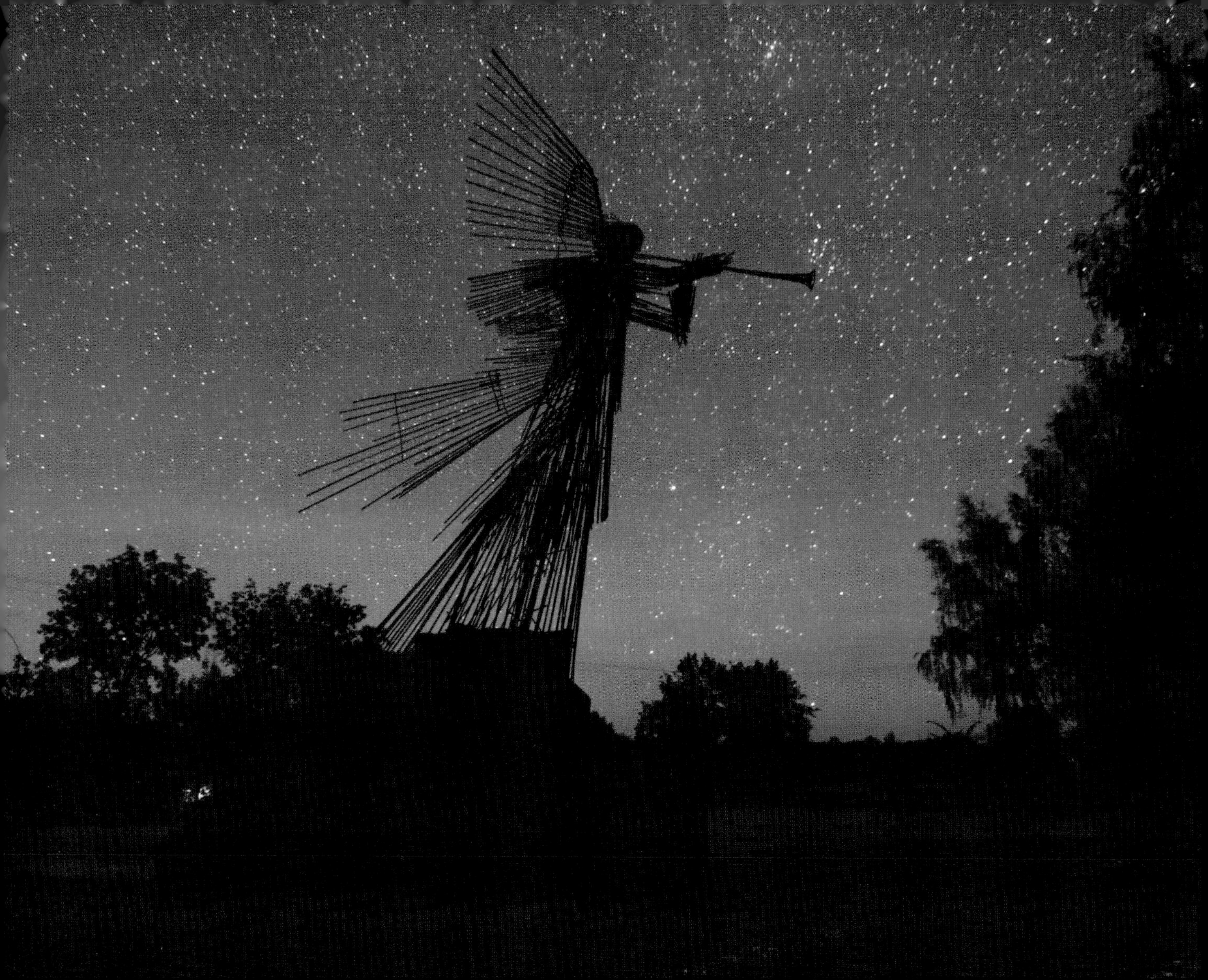

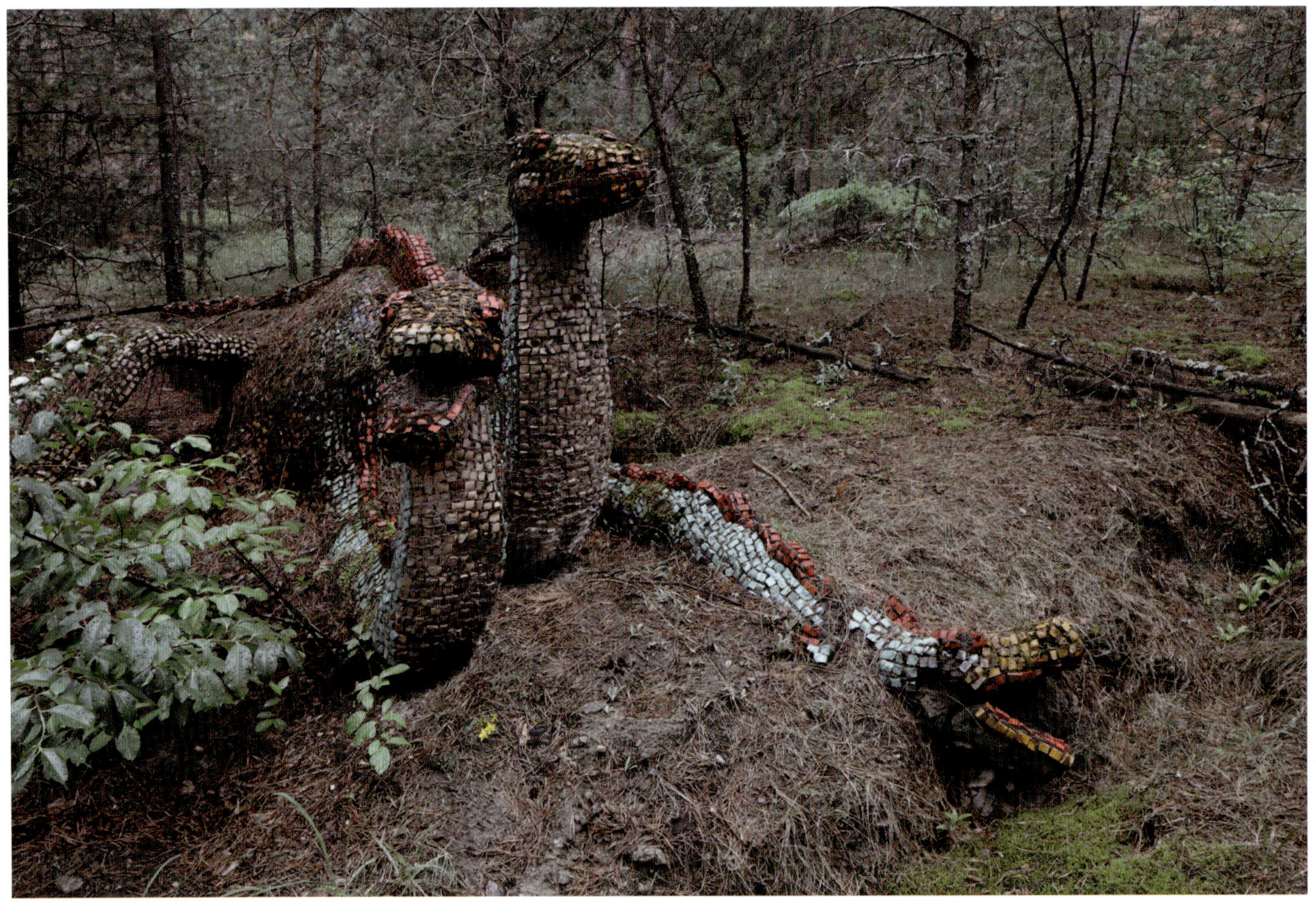

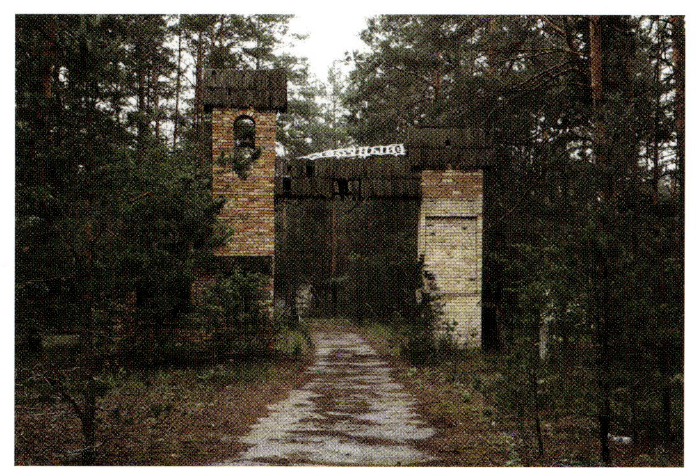
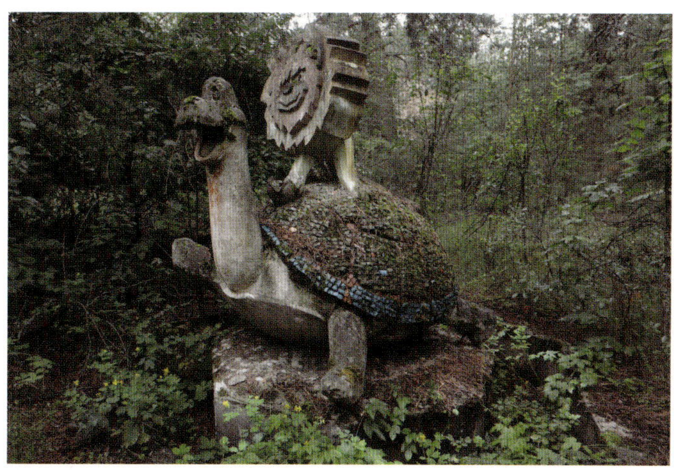
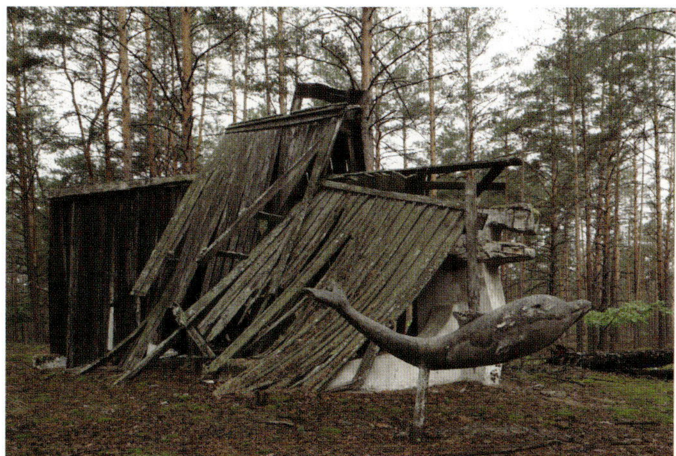
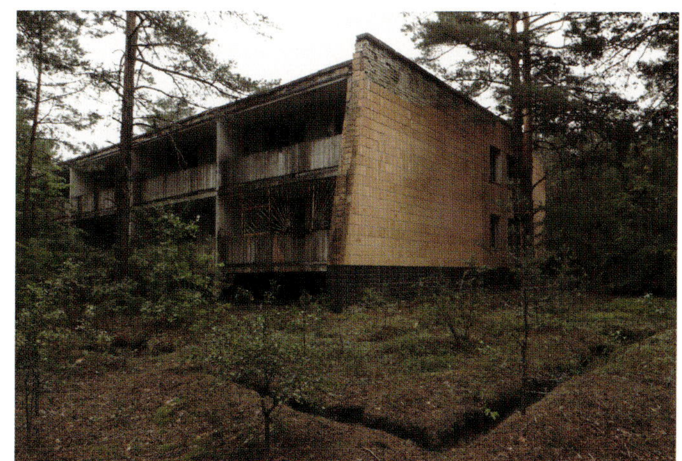

EPILOGUE: THE CHERNOBYL RAVE SCENE

The village of Hubyn was never officially evacuated – but over the last thirty years so many people have left that the effect is the same. Of a few dozen houses, most stand empty. A single multipurpose shop caters to an ageing population. Plastic flowers adorn a Soviet war memorial engraved with symbols no longer tolerated in Kyiv. The road that once connected Hubyn to its local municipal town – Chornobyl – was blocked three decades ago, when the border of the Exclusion Zone was drawn along the village's northern edge. We drive into Hubyn in the middle of the afternoon. Two old men sit on a bench, and a handful of women wearing shawls plod along the main street, their footsteps synchronised with the rhythm of the pounding industrial techno. Outside the long-abandoned village club, young Ukrainians in dreadlocks and neon rave gear drink beers and share a joint as they wait for the party to begin.

The rave in Hubyn is the brainchild of Igor Oprya. For several weeks he and a team of volunteers have been sweeping debris into piles inside the old club building to make space for dance floors and a bar. The promotion of the event was controversial: an online video clip showed a masked man daubing paint in rainbow colours over the town sign in Pripyat's Microdistrict 4, with a caption that read: 'I Invite Everyone to Chernobyl Future Rave.'

Some stalkers were outraged at what they considered to be a desecration of the Zone. I spoke to Stepan, one of a number of stalkers who smuggled in pots of grey paint to return the sign to its original condition. 'These people call themselves AVO,' he told me. 'Anarkho-Vandalskyy Otryad ['Anarcho-Vandal Squad']. I hate them. They are mostly drug addicts, who want to destroy the main attractions in Pripyat, to stop tourism.' Stepan showed me photographs from a few months earlier of another site, the well-known white, 3-D Pripyat sign near ChNPP, also painted in rainbow colours. In that instance, it was the Zone administration that restored it.

AVO's social-media feed describes the project as 'performance art theatre', and calls for the decommunisation of Pripyat. A previous rave they held in the Zone was named 'Tripyat', and their next event, 'Chillnobyl', was only a week away. I was curious to know how AVO justified their interventions in the Zone and it seemed the best way of finding out would be to go along to the rave and ask them.

By dusk the village club is crowded and notch by notch the music gets louder. A local woman in her mid-fifties approaches the hall. I assume she's come to complain, but instead she begins introducing herself to the partygoers. We talk. Her name is Valya and she lived in Donetsk, but came to stay with her family in Hubyn when conflict broke out in east Ukraine. She's reluctant to talk about the war, so instead I ask her what she thinks of the rave. 'Wonderful,' she says. 'Hubyn is mostly abandoned. It's a sad place. When they closed the Zone it became a dead end. It's good to see young people here!' Before the party kicks off, a film is projected onto a wall once hung with noticeboards and

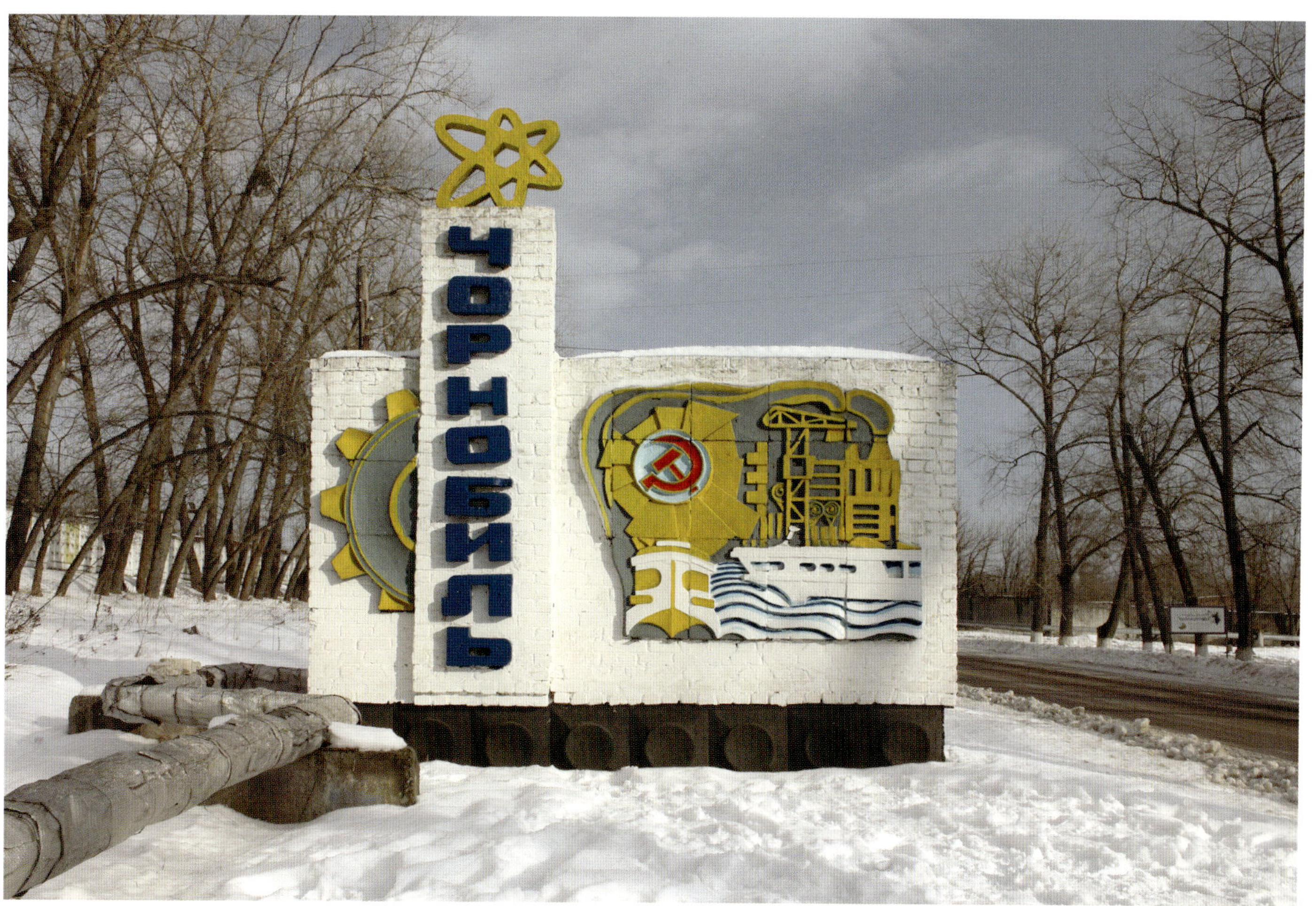

Чорнобиль

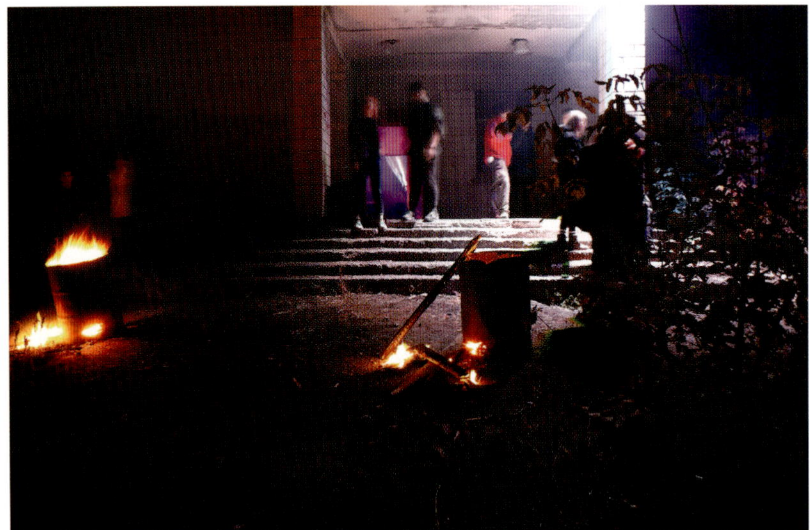

decorated with portraits of Soviet leaders. Valya fetches two elderly female neighbours from the village and together we watch the documentary *The Babushkas of Chernobyl* (2015).

By nightfall the dance floor is manic. Pumped-up ravers in neon costumes swing glow sticks and blow whistles. By 10pm one partygoer has already passed out on a sofa, and after his friends help him outside, he promptly staggers back in and collapses again in the same place. People gather around fires on the lawn outside; stray sparks and cannabis smoke hang in the air as local babushkas drift in and out of the crowds. I buy a 'Black Stalker' (whiskey and cola) at the surprisingly well-stocked bar and take it outside, where I get chatting to a techno DJ waiting for his early-morning slot.

'Techno is pure emotion,' he says, between swigs of an energy drink. 'The most honest of all musical genres.' I ask him who these partygoers are – stalkers, or ravers? He gazes at the crowd for a moment. 'Some stalkers, I think, but a lot of these people I know. It's like the Kyiv rave scene, taking over the Zone. I thought it was strange at first, when they asked me to play here. But then I thought, why not? Chernobyl is ours, it's our history. I think it's good to bring life back here, to express new emotions in this place.'

Stalker tour operator Vladyslav Suvorow arrives around midnight. He's fresh from an illegal hike – and apparently it was a total disaster. It had rained heavily all day, soaking their party of eight to the skin and turning the soil into

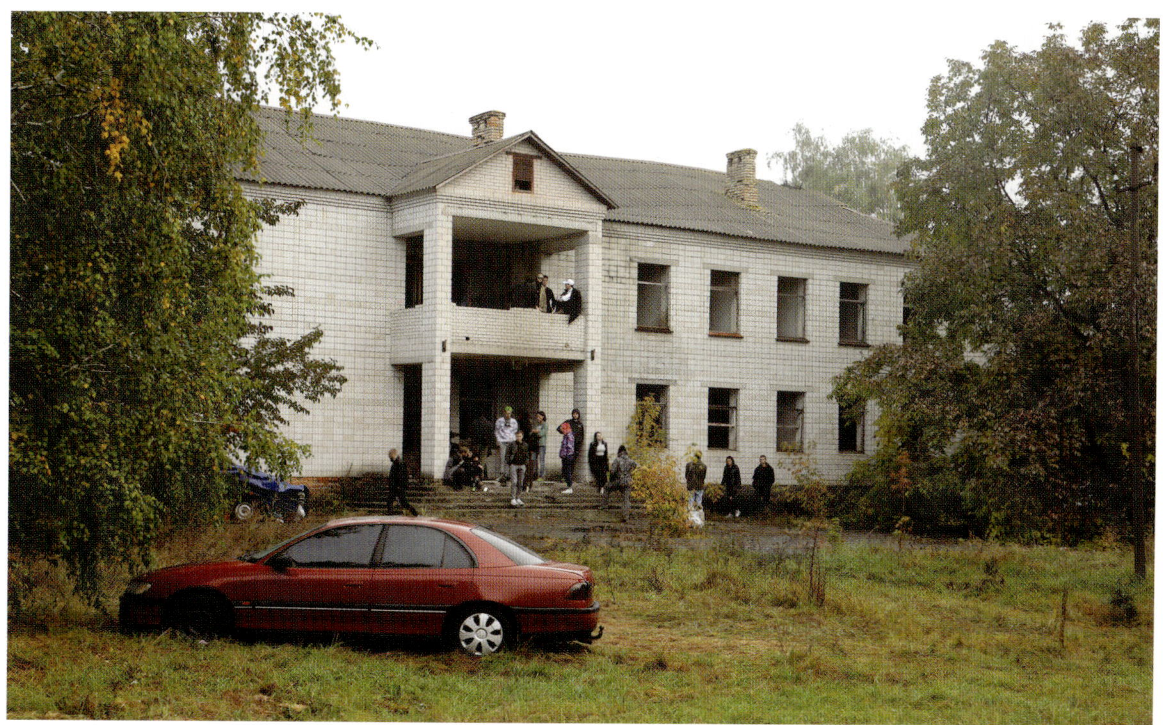

slippery mud. After 10 kilometres they gave up, deciding to surrender themselves to the police for an easy lift back to the checkpoint. But one of the tourists had no passport, which would have meant lengthy questioning by the border guards. So Vladyslav stayed with him, and the two of them walked for another nine hours through the rain to get safely out of the Zone. My own stalker guide, Kirill, arrives a little later, though I almost don't recognise him. Last year he had been a teetotal, contemplative sort, who seemed more at ease in the Red Forest than around other humans. But tonight Kirill is a celebrity – everyone at the rave seems to know him, and he shouts, swaggers, dances, and drinks his way through the crowds. When I say hello, he greets me warmly – but he isn't in any state for a conversation.

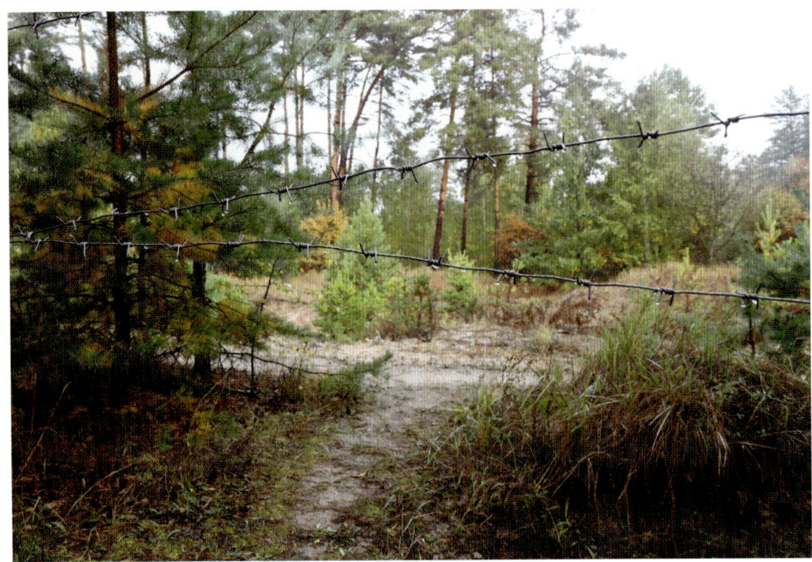

left: Perimeter fence, Chernobyl Exclusion Zone. Behind the village of Hubyn, rusted barbed wire hangs across a footpath leading into the Zone. From this location, a trespasser would have to walk for a full day before encountering significant levels of radiation.

right: Crane claw, Yaniv (Pripyat outskirts). This piece of equipment was used to clean debris from Reactor Block 4 during the 1986 clean-up. Today it gives a potentially dangerous dosimeter reading of up to 600 μSv/h. In late 2019, it became the target of purported 'performance art' and was painted bright pink. This began an ongoing battle between graffiti artists and the purist stalkers who would attempt to restore its original colours.

The only sober person in the hall seems to be the rave's organiser, Igor. He's constantly on the move. Now he's rushing from an electrical failure in the second sound system, to tend to a passed-out drunk in the garden. It isn't until some time in the early hours that I manage to pin him down for a chat.

'A lot of people here have never been to Chernobyl before. We are trying to draw attention with our performances in the Zone – even if it's negative attention.' Igor, whose interest in the Zone was partly inspired by the *S.T.A.L.K.E.R.* games, says he has made more than thirty illegal visits since 2012. He worked briefly as a waiter at one of the hotels in Chornobyl, and it was while talking to tourists there that he became concerned about the nature of the industry. 'I am not against tourism – I'm pro-tourism. But official tourism in the Zone today is vicious and corrupt. All the tour companies pay into a criminal kickback scheme, when really the money should be going to the national budget.'

Igor says his group, AVO, provides a protest movement. 'It's a virtual counter-subculture,' he says. 'It started in 2010 as a joke. Our mission today is to transform Pripyat – not destroy it as some are saying, but to use performance to bring attention to it. Okay, so we painted a sign… so what? No one got hurt, and already it has been painted back to

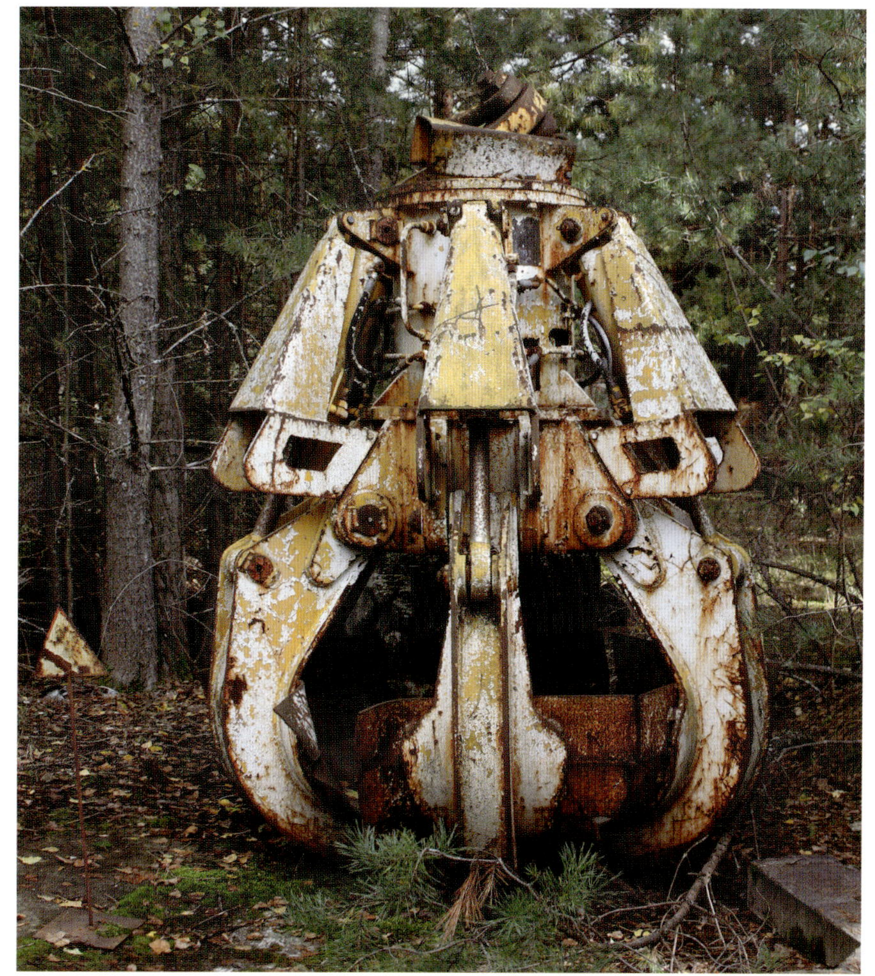

its original colour. There's a Soviet crest on top of a building... by law it must now be removed. So how about instead we paint it pretty pink? Ukraine's decommunisation law is absurd, and this is how we answer it – with absurdity, with post-irony.'

A few weeks later, AVO's next stunt is to paint Chernobyl's famous abandoned crane claw bright pink. A highly irradiated object, it isn't as easy to restore as previous targets were. Online, Igor writes: 'On the outskirts of the city of Tripyat there is a crane claw that was used to scoop up the Chernobyl reactor debris... Now tourists will be less likely to endanger their health, because they will no longer photograph themselves in front of this beauty.'

I sleep in a friend's car, waking at dawn to the ceaseless drumbeats. A handful of zombies are still dancing in the hall. Some huddle in corners or sleep in tents pitched in storerooms, while others sit outside, smoking cigarettes and staring blank-faced into the embers of last night's fires. Behind the village club, the old road, its tarmac edges overgrown with grass, leads north towards the forest. I follow it past the graveyard with its war memorial, until it stops abruptly where the earth has been bulldozed into a ridge marking the outer border of the Exclusion Zone.

A few rusted strands of wire swing lazily between the trees. Distant electronic beats pound through the forest, shaking dewdrops from the pines. High above, a woodpecker responds with its own staccato counter-rhythm as I step into the Zone. Inhaling deeply, I feel a tremendous sense of freedom – a vast and complex terrain stretches before me, where nature thrives untamed, and those who remain submit themselves to its mercy. Strange utopian art from the old regime lies waiting to be discovered beneath the trees and steel giants – towering technological wonders of the Cold War era – rise up like rusted guardians over this timeless no-man's land. As I walk into the sentient forests of Chernobyl, I hear the words of Tarkovsky's Stalker:

'Everything is already taken from me, there, on the other side of the barbed wire. All I have is here. Can you understand?! Here! In the Zone! My happiness, my freedom, my dignity – everything's here!'

right: Mural on a residential building, Heroes of Stalingrad Street, Pripyat. This Socialist-realist mural depicts virtuous citizens (a farmer, a construction worker, a police officer, and a Young Pioneer) under a radiant Soviet crest.

overleaf: The 'Bridge of Death,' on the road between Pripyat and the power plant. It is claimed that on the night of the disaster a number of Pripyat residents stood here to get a better view of the burning plant. The bridge derived its nickname from the widespread – but incorrect – belief that all the spectators died soon afterwards from radiation exposure.

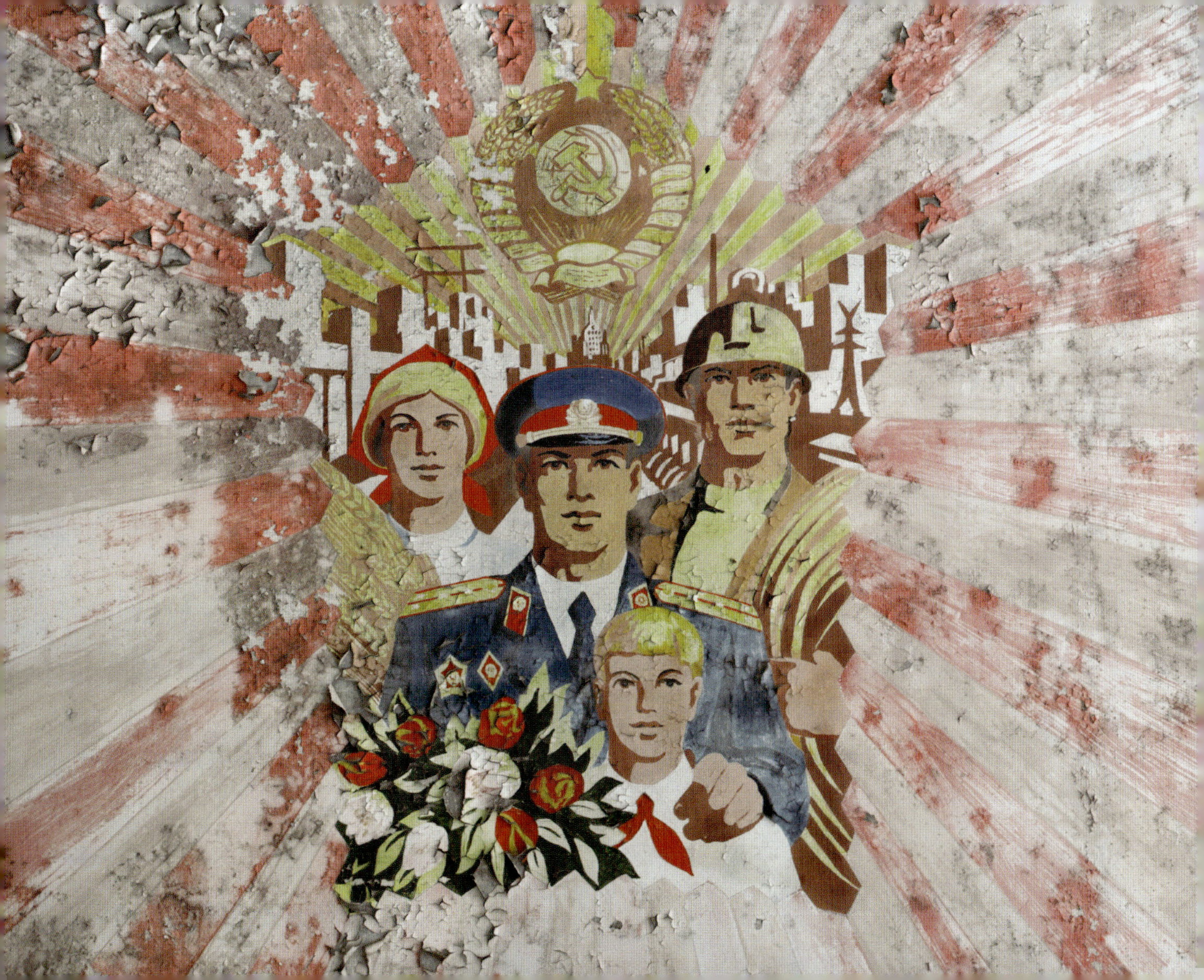

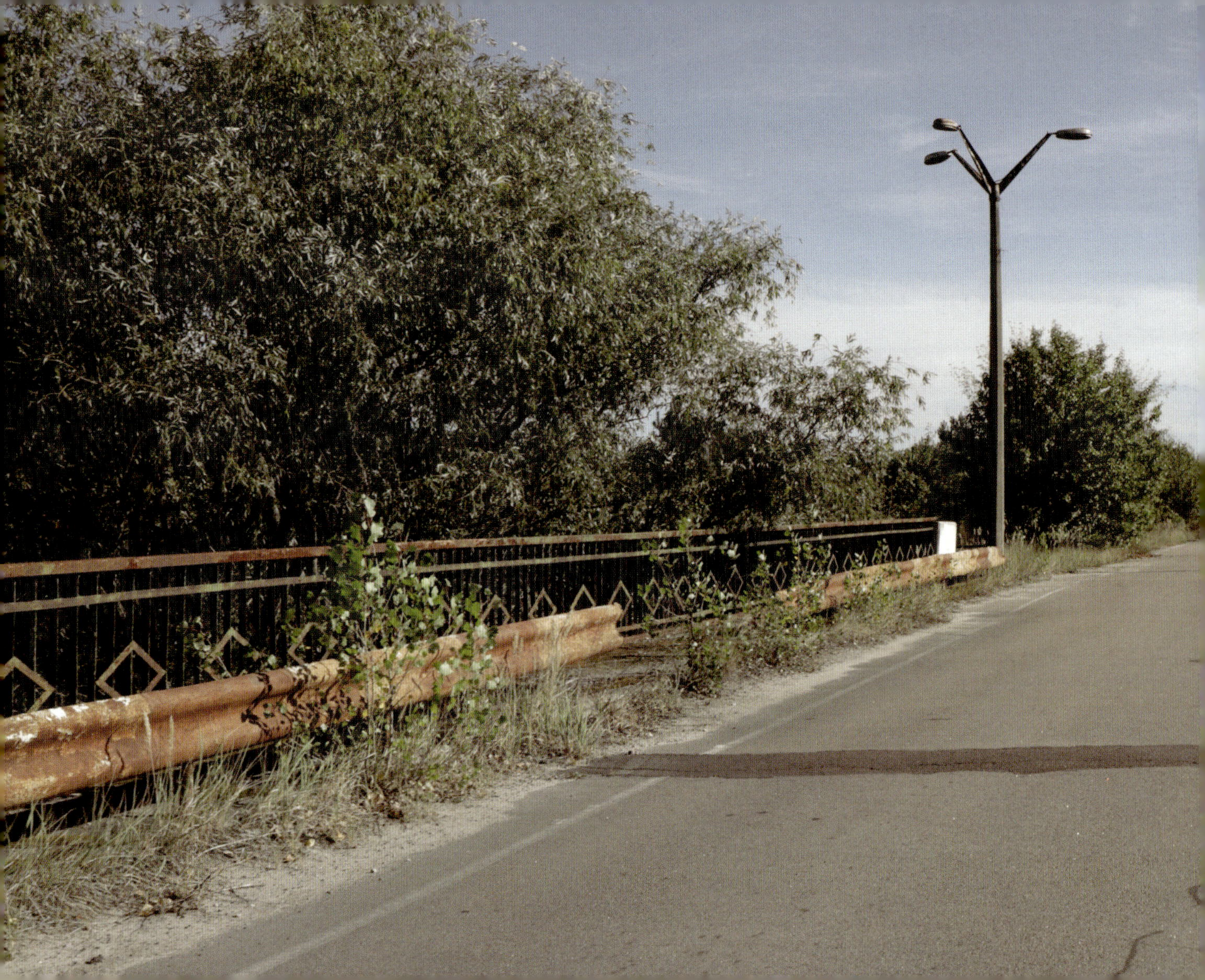

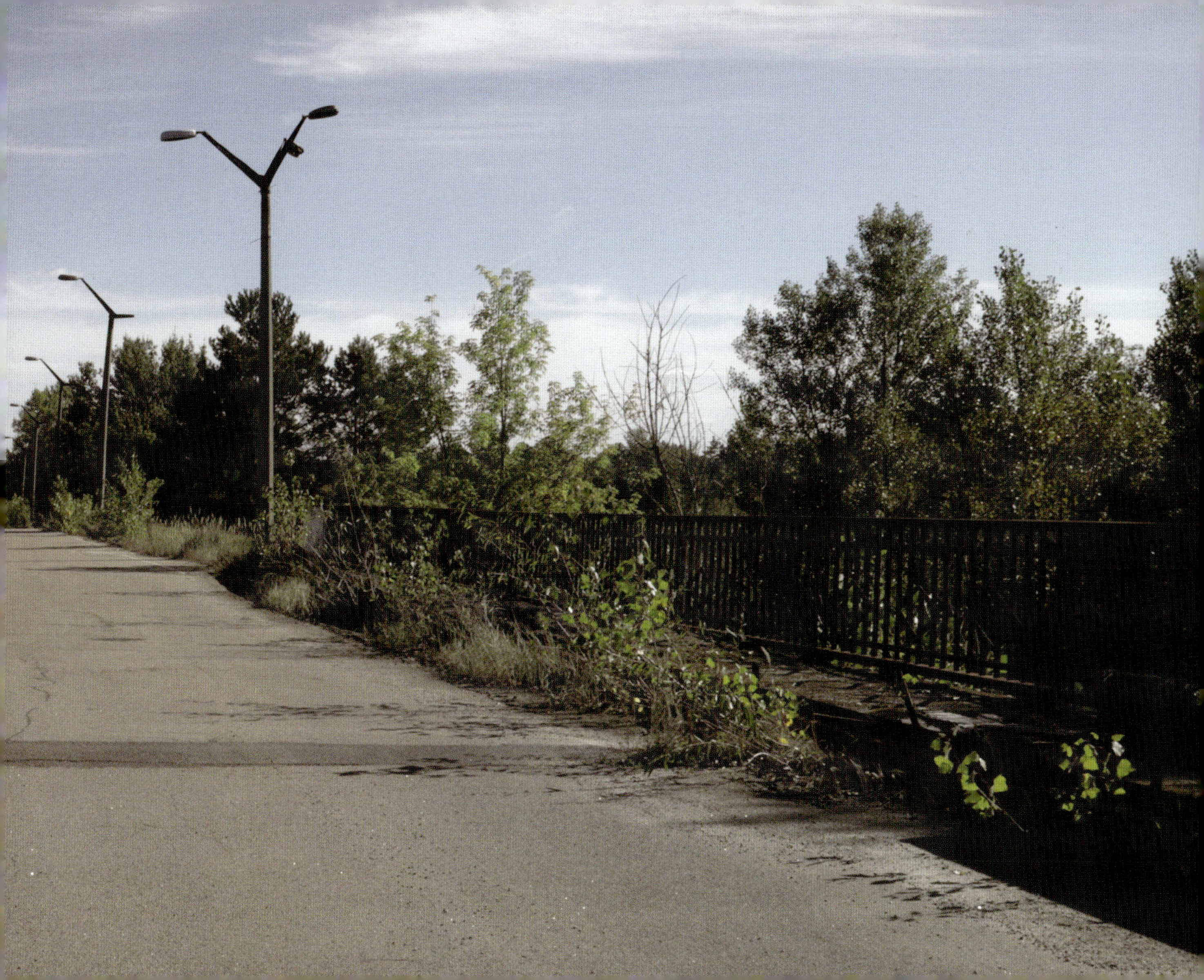

RADIATION DOSES IN MILLISIEVERTS (mSv)

1,000 µSv = 1 mSv; 1,000 mSv = 1 Sv

6,000 mSv / 6 Sv A typical dose received by those Chernobyl workers who died within a month

5,000 mSv / 5 Sv A potentially fatal dose with a 50 per cent chance of survival

1,000 mSv / 1 Sv Causes nausea and radiation sickness, but not necessarily fatal

350 mSv A typical exposure level for those evacuated from contaminated areas of Chernobyl

10 mSv Equivalent to a full-body medical CT scan

10 mSv (in one hour) Author's own measurement in the Red Forest

6.5 mSv (in one hour) Maximum level measured in Pripyat in the days after the disaster

2 mSv (in one year) One year's worth of normal background radiation

0.1 mSv / 100 µSv A single chest X-ray

0.06-0.07 mSv / 60-70 µSv (per hour) Author's own measurement inside the New Arch structure

0.04 mSv / 40 µSv (per hour) Author's own measurement inside the Reactor 4 Control Room

0.0003 mSv / 0.3 µSv (per hour) The typical background radiation level of a city like London

0.0001 mSv / 0.1 µSv (per hour) The typical background level in most areas of Chernobyl

NOTES

1. NIGHTMARES AND PREMONITIONS

1. 'Text of Hirohito's Radio Rescript', *The New York Times*, 15 August 1945.

2. Susan Sontag, 'The Imagination of Disaster' (1965), *Against Interpretation and Other Essays* (New York: Dell, 1979).

3. James Chapman, 'The BBC and the Censorship of The War Game (1965)', *Journal of Contemporary History*, 1 January 2006, Vol.41(1), pp.75-94.

4. Erik Simon, 'The Strugatskys in Political Context', *Science Fiction Studies*, November 2004, Vol.31(3), pp.378–406.

5. Ursula K. Le Guin, 'Foreword' in Boris & Arkady Strugatsky, *Roadside Picnic* (Chicago: Chicago Review Press, 2012).

6. V. A. Kostyuchenko & L.Yu Krestinina, 'Long-term irradiation effects in the population evacuated from the East-Urals radioactive trace area', *Science of the Total Environment*, 1994, Vol.142(1-2), pp.119-125.

7. Boris Komarov, *Destruction of Nature in the Soviet Union* (London: Pluto Press, 1978), p103.

8. Jim Hoberman, '*Andrei Rublev*: An Icon Emerges', *The Criterion Collection*. Retrieved 18 April 2019. [www.criterion.com]

9. Andrei Tarkovsky, *Sculpting in Time* (University of Texas Press, 1986).

10. Sigmund Freud, *The Interpretation of Dreams*, 3rd edition, translated by A. A. Brill (New York: The Macmillan Company, 1913).

11. Sophie Fiennes, James Wilson, Martin Rosenbaum, Katie Holly, Slavoj Žižek & Magnus Fiennes, *The Pervert's Guide to Ideology* [film], 2014.

12. Walter Goodman, 'Andrei Tarkovsky, director and Soviet émigré, dies at 54', *The New York Times*, 30 December 1986.

13. Stas Tyrkin, 'In *Stalker* Tarkovsky foretold Chernobyl', *Komsomolskaya Pravda*, 23 March 2001. [www.nostalghia.com]

2. ATOMGRAD

1. Brian Wang, 'Background radiation levels', *Next Big Future*, 19 July 2012. [www.nextbigfuture.com]

2. Timothy J. Jorgensen, 'Air Travel Exposes You to Radiation – How Much Health Risk Comes with It?', *Scientific American*, 8 June 2017. [www.scientificamerican.com]

3. 'Transforming Chernobyl brochure', EBRD, 11 March 2015. [www.ebrd.com]

4. Adam Higginbotham, *Midnight in Chernobyl: The Untold Story of the World's Greatest Nuclear Disaster* (New York: Simon & Schuster, 2019), p.340.

5. Zhores A. Medvedev, 'Collapse of atomgrads', *The Moscow Times*, 3 March 1993. [www.themoscowtimes.com]

6. 'Припять в цифрах' ('Pripyat in numbers'). [www.pripyat.com]

7. Paul Brown, 'The football team destroyed by the Chernobyl disaster: FC Pripyat', *Four Four Two*, 23 September 2019. [www.fourfourtwo.com]

8. Karl Marx, *The Difference Between the Democritean and Epicurean Philosophy of Nature*, 1841, Pub. 1902 in *Marx-Engels Collected Works* (Moscow: Progress Publishers).

9. Victoria E. Bonnell, 'The Iconography of the Worker in Soviet Political Art', in Lewis H. Siegelbaum & Ronald Grigor Suny (eds), *Making Workers Soviet: Power, Class, and Identity* (Cornell University Press, 1994), pp.341-375.

10. Andrew Osborn, 'Chernobyl's "illegal" tours stopped,' *The Telegraph*, 20 September 2011. [www.telegraph.co.uk]

11. Svetlana Alexievich & Keith Gessen, *Voices from Chernobyl: the oral history of a nuclear disaster* (New York: Picador, 2006).

12. Neil Schlager, *When Technology Fails* (Detroit: Gale Research, 1994).

13. Boris Komarov, *Destruction of Nature in the Soviet Union, op. cit.*

14. '5N32 Duga [Arc] Steel Yard OTH', Global Security. [www.globalsecurity.org]

15. 'Чернобыль-2, он же ЗГРЛС "Дуга"' ('Chernobyl-2 and ZGRLS "Duga"'). [http://www.adsl.kirov.ru]

16. Pavel Kotlyar, 'Чернобыльский дятел Страны Советов' ('Chernobyl woodpecker of the USSR'), *Gazeta*, 26 April 2016. [www.gazeta.ru]

17. Brian Rogers, 'Mystery Soviet Over-The-Horizon-Tests', *Mystery Signals of the Short Wave*, February 1977. [www.mysterysignals. signalshed.com]

18. David L. Wilson, 'The Russian Woodpecker... a Closer Look', *Monitoring Times*, Summer 1985. [www.mysterysignals.signalshed.com]

19. Adam Higginbotham, *Midnight in Chernobyl, op. cit.*

3. WORMWOOD STAR
1. Robert W. Davies & Stephen G. Wheatcroft, *The Years of Hunger: Soviet Agriculture 1931–1933* (Basingstoke: Palgrave Macmillan, 2010).
2. R. F. Mould, *Chernobyl Record: The Definitive History of the Chernobyl Catastrophe* (Bristol, UK: Institute of Physics Publishing, 2000).
3. Saint Demetrios Greek Orthodox Church, 'The Story of the Precious Wood that was used to construct the Holy Cross'. [www.saintdemetrios.org.uk]
4. Archimandrite Sergius (recorded by Valentina Serikova), 'Чернобыльские чудеса', ('Chernobyl wonders'), *Pravoslavie*, 26 April 2016. [www.pravoslavie.ru]
5. Flavius Josephus, *The Wars of the Jews or History of the Destruction of Jerusalem*, translated by William Whiston, Book VI, Chapter 5, c. 75CE. [via www.gutenberg.org]
6. M. Sahota (dir), A. Smith (nar), G. Lanning (prod) & C. Joyce (ed), 'Meltdown in Chernobyl', *Seconds From Disaster*, S01E07, *National Geographic*, 17 August 2004.
7. Zhores A. Medvedev, *The Legacy of Chernobyl* (New York: W.W. Norton & Company, 1990).
8. Burton Bennett, Michael Repacholi & Zhanat Carr, 'Health Effects of the Chernobyl Accident and Special Health Care Programs', W.H.O., 2006. [www.who.int]
9. Adam Higginbotham, *Midnight in Chernobyl, op. cit.*
10. Ievgeniia Gubkina, *Slavutych: Architectural Guide* (Berlin: DOM Publishers, 2015).
11. Igor Osipchuk, 'Всевидящее око сверхсекретного объекта «чернобыль-2» фиксировало учебные запуски американских ракет, старты «шаттлов» и даже метеориты' ('The all-seeing eye of the top-secret Chernobyl-2 object recorded training launches of American missiles, shuttle launches and even meteorites'), *Fakty*, 12 June 2001. [www.fakty.ua]
12. 'Чернобыль-2, он же ЗГРЛС "Дуга"' ('Chernobyl-2 and ZGRLS "Duga"'). [http://www.adsl.kirov.ru]

4. NUCLEAR TOURISM
1. 'Зону відчуження цьогоріч відвідали понад 100 000 людей' ('The Exclusion Zone was visited by over 100,000 people this year'), *State Agency of Ukraine for the Management of the Exclusion Zone*, 1 November 2019. [www.dazv.gov.ua]
2. 'The Chernobyl Nuclear Disaster', *Wise International*. [www.wiseinternational.org]
3. Mike Eckel, 'The Politics Of Memory: A Struggle For An Institute And What It Means For Ukrainian Identity', *Radio Free Europe*, 20 October 2019. [www.rferl.org]
4. Kate Brown, *Manual for Survival: A Chernobyl Guide to the Future* (New York: W.W. Norton & Company, 2019).
5. Max Hunder, 'HBO show success drives Chernobyl tourism boom', *Reuters*, 4 June 2019. [www.reuters.com]
6. Vitaliy Petruk, 'Розвитку туризму в зоні відчуження' ('Tourism Development in the Exclusion Zone'), *State Agency of Ukraine for the Management of the Exclusion Zone*, 1 June 2016. [www.dazv.gov.ua]
7. 'Зону відчуження Чорнобильської АЕС цього року відвідали понад 63 тисячі людей' ('This year the Exclusion Zone of Chernobyl NPP was visited by more than 63,000 people'), *Radio Svoboda*, 18 December 2018. [www.radiosvoboda.org]
8. 'У Чорнобилі відзвітували про рекордну кількість туристів' ('Chornobyl reported a record number of tourists'), *Glavcom*, 26 January 2020. [www.glavcom.ua]
9. Tiffany Lo, 'Scientists made Chernobyl's first homebrew vodka – and it's radioactive-free', *The Mirror*, 8 August 2019. [www.mirror.co.uk]
10. Megan Nolan, 'Chernobyl welcomes the tourists – "a messy and morally queasy experience"', *The Guardian*, 4 June 2019. [www.theguardian.com]
11. Ruchira Sharma, 'The dubious tale of influencers taking inappropriate selfies at Chernobyl is now an abuse-ridden mess', *iNews*, 13 June 2019. [www.inews.co.uk]
12. Mykola Berdnyk, 'Ukraine troops hold target practice in Chernobyl Exclusion Zone', *Deutsche Welle*, 1 August 2019. [www.dw.com]

5. JOURNEY TO THE CENTRE OF THE ZONE
1. Tatjana L. Zharkikh & Nataliya I. Yasynetska, 'Ten years of development of the Przewalski horse population in the Chernobyl Exclusive Zone', January 2019. [via www.researchgate.net]

8. THE ROOM
1. 'Decommissioning at Chernobyl', *World Nuclear News*, 26 April 2007. [www.world-nuclear-news.org]
2. 'Interim Spent Nuclear Fuel Dry Storage Facility (ISF-2)', *Chornobyl NPP*, 26 March 2013. [www.chnpp.gov.ua]
3. Gryshmanovskiy & Beskrestnov, '**Временные санитарные требования безопасности при выполнении работ по ликвидации последствий аварии на Чернобыльской АЭС, Гришмановский, Бескрестнов**' ('Temporary sanitary safety requirements during the liquidation of the accident at Chernobyl Nuclear Power Plant'), *Ministry of Medium Machine Building*, 8 July 1986. [via www.feerc.ru]

9. HALF-LIFE
1. Ashley Dawson, *Extinction: A radical history*. (New York: OR Books, 2016).
2. Mikael Böggild Jensen, 'Radiation protection principles and development of standards for geological repository systems', in Michael J. Apted & Joonhong Ahn (eds), *Geological Repository Systems for Safe Disposal of Spent Nuclear Fuels and Radioactive Waste* (Duxford: Woodhead Publishing, 2017), p.618.
3. Scott Beauchamp, 'How to Send a Message 1,000 Years to the Future', *The Atlantic*, 24 February 2015. [www.theatlantic.com]
4. Ariel Schwartz, 'Color-changing cats were once part of a US government plan to protect humankind', *Tech Insider*, 16 August 2015. [www.businessinsider.com]
5. Michael Brill, *Site Design to Mark the Dangers of Nuclear Waste for 10,000 Years* (Buffalo: The Buffalo Organization for Social and Technological Innovation, 1991).

6. Robert Macfarlane, *Underland: A Deep Time Journey* (London: Penguin Books, 2020).
7. 'Andra 2015 Call for Artistic Projects: memory of waste storage sites radioactive for future generations', *Andra*, 2015. [www.andra.fr]
8. S.N. Gray, 'Fungi as potential bioremediation agents in soil contaminated with heavy or radioactive metals', *Biochemical Society Transactions*, 1998, Vol.26(4), pp.666-670. [via www.portlandpress.com]
9. N.N. Zhdanova, T. Tugay, J. Dighton, V. Zheltonozhsky & P. McDermott, 'Ionizing radiation attracts soil fungi', *Mycological Research*, September 2004, Vol.108(9), pp.1089-1096. [www.ncbi.nlm.nih.gov]
10. Ekaterina Dadachova, Roger W. Howell, Ruth A. Bryan, Annie Frenkel, Joshua D. Nosanchuk & Arturo Casadevall, 'Susceptibility of the Human Pathogenic Fungi *Cryptococcus neoformans* and *Histoplasma capsulatum* to γ-Radiation Versus Radioimmunotherapy with α- and β-Emitting Radioisotopes', *The Journal of Nuclear Medicine*, 1 February 2004, Vol.45(2), pp.313-320. [via www.jnm.snmjournals.org]
11. Albert Einstein College of Medicine, '"Radiation-eating" fungi finding could trigger recalculation of earth's energy balance and help feed astronauts', *ScienceDaily*, 23 May 2007. [www.sciencedaily.com]
12. Onwuka N. Njoku, 'Magic, Religion and Iron Technology in Precolonial North-Western Igboland', *Journal of Religion in Africa*, August 1991, Vol.21(3), pp.194-215. [via www.jstor.org]
13. Thomas A. Sebeok, *Communication Measures to Bridge Ten Millennia* (Columbus, OH: Office for Nuclear Waste Isolation, 1984). [www.osti.gov]

ACKNOWLEDGEMENTS

A debt of gratitude is owed to every person who agreed to be interviewed for this book. I thank my guides in the Zone (Orest, Demchenko, Kirill, Dmitry) and my travel companions (Nate and Phillipa, Lisa, Aram, Wayne and others). I thank Andrew and Iryna for arranging my first Chernobyl trip, and all those who later joined my own tours, allowing me to see the place through fresh eyes every time. Crucially, this project would have been impossible without Anton Lebedev: the invisible translator in many of these scenes, plus an invaluable co-researcher and fact-checker.

I have been greatly aided by the contributions of Alexey and Valya Ananenko, Myroslava Hartmond, Vladyslav Suvorow, Tatiana Retivov, Niels Ackermann, Max Deputatov, Karina Sitnik and the team at the Reserve, and on Gavdos, Alla and Aleksey. I thank my proofreaders: Hans Krauch, Evan Panagopoulos (who also facilitated my Greek expedition) and Jesse Nagel (who spent many hours helping to research the Zone's monuments).

For their invaluable scientific guidance: Dmytrii Korchak, Tim Shaw, Dan and Rachel; and for mystical inspirations: Frank Albo, Chris Rutkowski, and Jim and Jake at Tonkiri. Additional support and sound advice has come from Gergana Dyakova, Bradley Garrett, Tao Tao Holmes, Larissa Hayden, Mihail Kondov, Donald Niebyl, Philip Stone, Allison C. Meier, Fergal Stapleton, Damon Murray and Stephen Sorrell at FUEL Publishing.

First published in 2020, reprinted in 2021

FUEL Design & Publishing
33 Fournier Street
London E1 6QE

fuel-design.com

Text and photographs © Darmon Richter

Design and edit by Murray & Sorrell FUEL
Copy edited by FUEL and Fergal Stapleton

Distribution by Thames & Hudson / D. A. P.
ISBN: 978-1-9162184-2-0
Printed in China

DISCLAIMER
In the course of making this book, some people have been good enough to share very personal stories with me. Where those stories might cause problems, details such as names, precise locations, or dates have been altered slightly to protect them or others. In one instance, a composite character has been created from a merging of three different people whose words and actions would otherwise have been simply impossible to share. I have named them 'Demchenko'.

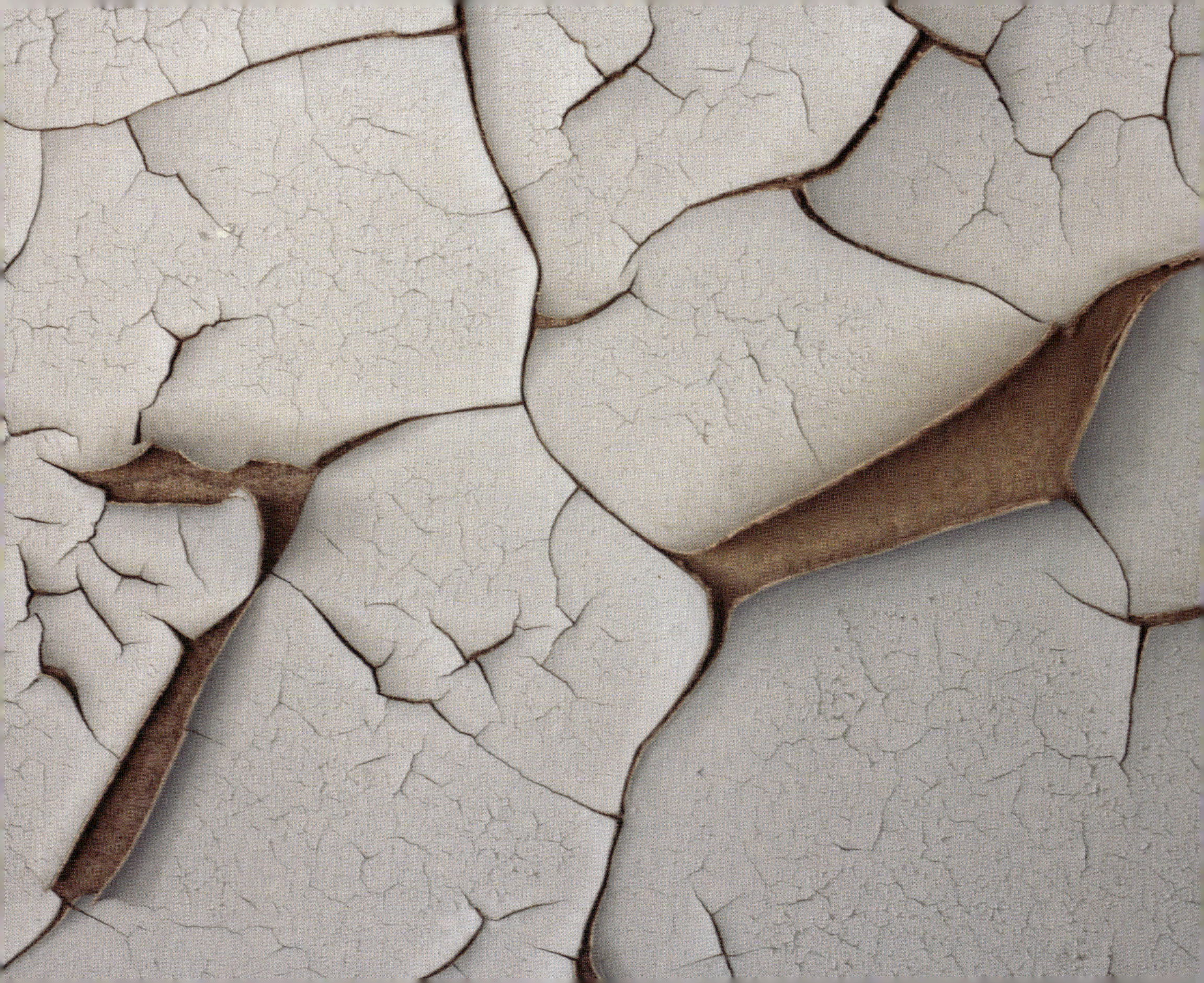

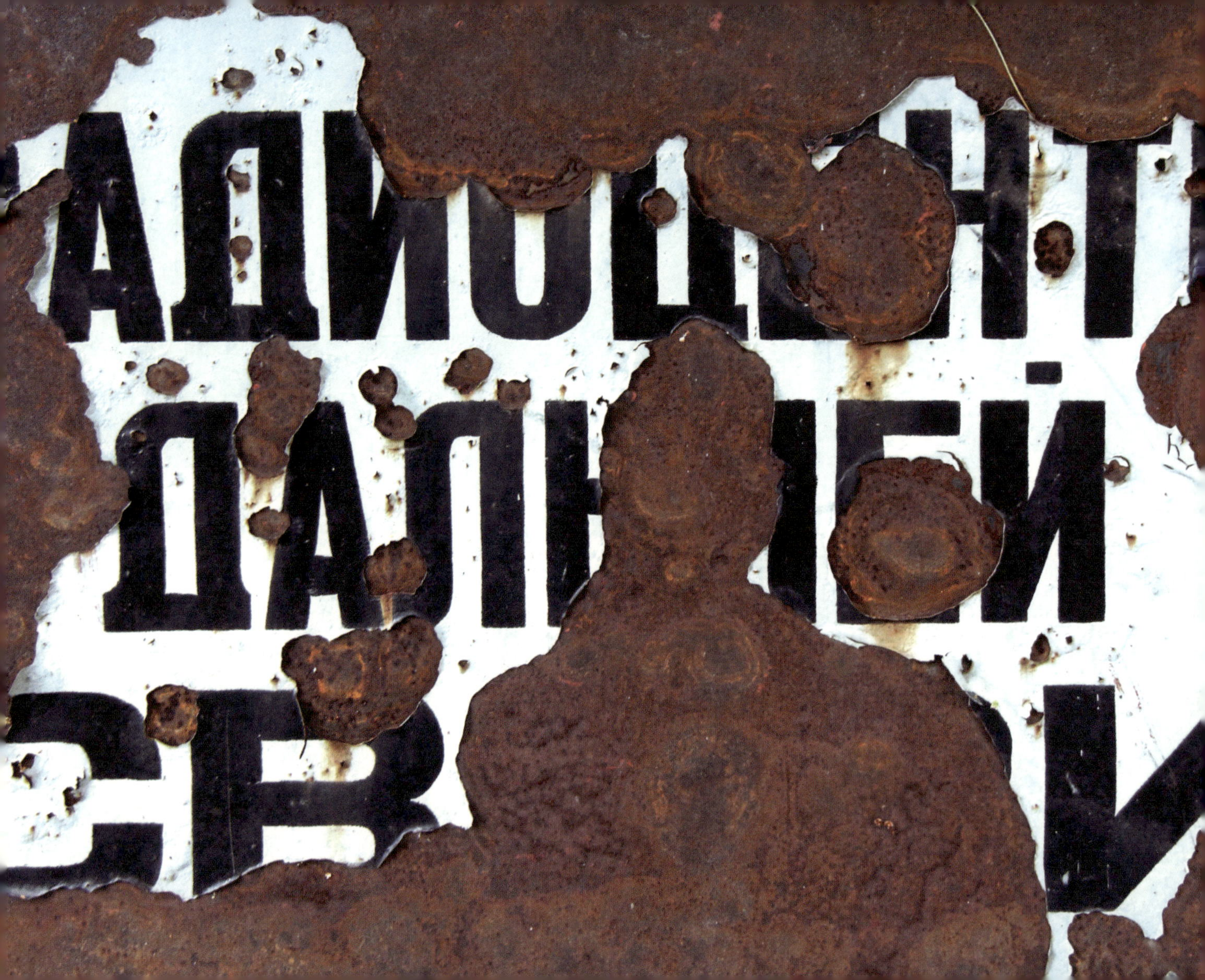